MODERN HUMANITIES RESEARCH ASSOCIATION

TEXTS AND DISSERTATIONS

(formerly Dissertation Series)

VOLUME 24

Editor

A. J. HOLDEN

(French: Medieval)

THE SECOND CONTINUATION OF THE OLD FRENCH PERCEVAL

A Critical and Lexicographical Study

THE SECOND CONTINUATION OF THE OLD FRENCH PERCEVAL

A Critical and Lexicographical Study

by

CORIN F. V. CORLEY

LONDON

THE MODERN HUMANITIES RESEARCH ASSOCIATION

1987

Published by

The Modern Humanities Research Association

Honorary Treasurer, MHRA

KING'S COLLEGE, STRAND
LONDON WC2R 2LS
ENGLAND

ISBN 0 947623 11 6

324801

Printed in England by
W. S. MANEY & SON LIMITED
HUDSON ROAD LEEDS

CONTENTS

ACKNOWLEDGEMENTS

This work is a revision of my doctoral thesis, Edinburgh 1983. Some of the material used in Chapter 2 has appeared, in a slightly different form, in *Romania* 103 (1982), 235–58, while Chapter 5 appears, virtually as it stands, in *Romania* 105 (1984), 351–59.

My heartfelt thanks are due to W. Roach, G. Runnalls, and I. Short, whose criticisms and counsels contributed to the work of revision, and most of all to A. J. Holden, whose hand on the tiller has steered this work past many shoals and reefs.

Also special thanks, for a variety of reasons, to Philip Bennett, the staff of the Taylorian Library, Oxford, and Shian.

INTRODUCTION

Aims of this study

The main aim of this study of the second continuation of the *Perceval* of Chrétien de Troyes is not to undertake a literary examination of the text, but rather to provide a solid base for such work. That is to say, to establish exactly what the Second Continuation consists of, where it begins and ends, whether it is a single unit — and if not to what extent it is not — and, having examined the question of which manuscripts appear best to represent the primitive text, to resolve any textual problems, firstly through this examination of the manuscript tradition, and secondly with the help of a glossary. The disputed attribution of the text to Wauchier de Denain will be briefly examined, as will some other questions of a more literary nature, such as literary influence.

The Continuations

Chrétien de Troyes left his fifth romance, the *Conte du Graal* (*Perceval*), incomplete, apparently because he died before he could finish it. This prompted the composition of several additions to the text, known as the Continuations. Of these additions, which are four in number (see below), three merit their title of continuation, at least broadly. They are the Second Continuation, or Perceval-Continuation (= C2), by Wauchier de Denain; the Continuation of Gerbert de Montreuil (= CG); and the Continuation of Manessier (= CM). The other, the First Continuation, or Gauvain-Continuation (= C1), which is anonymous, is rather a collection of disparate adventures, almost entirely unconnected to the major theme of Perceval's quest for the Grail. Indeed, with the exception of the first Branch, C1 has no real links with the *Perceval*. C1, C2, and CM (together with extracts from CG) were edited in the last century by Ch. Potvin.[1] Potvin's edition, based almost exclusively on MS P, see below, has been entirely superseded by the excellent edition of W. Roach, for C1, C2, and CM, and for CG by the edition of M. Williams and M. Oswald. All references in this study are to the editions of Hilka (*Perceval*), Roach, and Williams/Oswald.

Redactions and Manuscripts

Roach published three versions of C1: the Mixed (vol. I), Long (vol. II), and Short (vol. III/1)[2] Redactions. He divided the text into six Branches, and subdivided these into episodes. In addition, the texts of MSS L and A are printed separately, on facing pages, in vol. III/1. The Second Continuation (vol. IV) and the Continuation of Manessier (vol. V) are simply divided into episodes, but the former is given in two redactions (Short and Long), on facing pages, up to l. A 10268 (= E 20530).

The Continuations are found in the following manuscripts;[3] for full details, see Roach, I pp. xvi–xxxiii.

A	Paris, Bibliothèque Nationale f.fr. 794	C1, part of C2.
E	Edinburgh, National Library of Scotland 19.1.5	C1, C2, CM (incomplete).
K	Bern, Stadtbibliothek 113	C2.
L	London, British Library Add. 36614	C1, C2.
M	Montpellier, Bibliothèque de l'Ecole de Médecine H. 249	C1, C2, CM.
P	Mons, Bibliothèque publique 331/206	C1, C2, CM.
Q	Paris, Bibliothèque Nationale f.fr. 1429	C1, C2, CM.
R	Paris, Bibliothèque Nationale f.fr. 1450	part of C1.
S	Paris, Bibliothèque Nationale f.fr. 1453	C1, C2, CM.
T	Paris, Bibliothèque Nationale f.fr. 12576	C1, C2, CG, CM.
U	Paris, Bibliothèque Nationale f.fr. 12577	C1, C2, CM.
V	Paris, Bibliothèque Nationale n.a. 6614	C1, C2, CG (incomplete), CM (fragments).

There is also a fragment of C1, see Bibliography, under Brayer and Lecoy.

This gives the following distribution: C1 AELMPQ(R)STUV. C2 AEKL-MPQSTUV. CG TV. CM EMPQSTU(V).

There is also a prose version dating from 1530 (= G), and a Middle High German translation (= D). The 1530 prose contains the equivalent of the *Perceval*, C1, C2, and CM, and is closely related to MS E.

Authorship and division of the corpus

It is now generally accepted that, of the whole vast compilation known as the *Perceval* and its continuations, the part due to Chrétien de Troyes himself does not extend beyond about 9234 (Hilka). From this point on, scholars have distinguished four continuations, of which the first, C1 comes to an end at A 9456 of the Roach edition, and the second, C2 stops at 32594. Of the three redactions into which Roach divides C1, the Long (LRed.) is some 10150 lines longer than the Short (SRed.), which is now universally regarded as primitive; the Mixed (MRed.) seems to be later than both SRed. and LRed., and is generally thought to be of lesser importance. Roach also distinguishes two redactions for C2, SRed. and LRed., at least up to 10268 of the SRed.; at that point, the SRed. seems to disappear, and all the MSS which contained it, except for A which breaks off, continue with the same text as the LRed. MSS.

After C2 comes CM (32595–42668). Between them, in two MSS, T and V, is CG, whose author, Gerbert, was identified by M. Wilmotte[4] as Gerbert de Montreuil, author of the *Roman de la Violette*; this identification has been convincingly demonstrated by Ch. François.[5]

Thus the corpus of some 59000 lines, or even 69000, if we count the LRed. of C1, rather than the SRed., has been divided into five parts: the work of Chrétien; C1, which is anonymous; C2, whose attribution to Wauchier de Denain has been disputed; and the continuations of Gerbert and Manessier. In addition, there are two prologues, neither one primitive, the *Elucidation* (484 lines, of which 6 are borrowed from Chrétien),[6] and the *Bliocadran* (800 lines).[7]

The orthodox view

In general, these divisions are now accepted by most scholars. To my knowledge, no one has questioned the authenticity of Gerbert's work, nor that of Manessier. On the other hand, there has been discussion as to how much of the corpus is the work of Chrétien, and notably Wilmotte[8] seemed to attribute to him at least all of the text up to (A) 7130, that is, *Perceval*[9] and most of C1.[10] He did allow that this text had doubtless been subject to later reworking and interpolation. Wilmotte's principal arguments were firstly the anonymity of C1 (and of C2, since he rejected the attribution to Wauchier de Denain)[11] and secondly the evidence of Gerbert[12] and Manessier, who do not mention any continuator, and speak only of Chrétien himself.[13] Wilmotte's arguments were mainly demolished by F. Lot,[14] and it is unlikely that anyone would now subscribe to the idea that Chrétien wrote C1 or C2. However, Lot broadly accepted Wilmotte's rejection of the attribution of C2 to Wauchier. In general, scholars have adopted the opinion of Lot and Wilmotte, that is, that Wauchier is simply invoked as an authority. G. Vial's recent article, in which he re-establishes this attribution,[15] seems to have convinced Roach, at least, see Chapter 5, *infra*.

In addition to these broad divisions of the corpus: Chrétien (= 1–9234), C1 (= 1–9456), C2 (= 9457–32594), CM, CG continuing from there, there are certain sections of the text which it is generally accepted are interpolations. Chiefly, these are C1 Branch V episode 5, C1 (LRed.) Branch I episodes 6 and 8, and perhaps Branch III ep. 9,[16] and C2 episodes 2, 6, 7, and 8. There has been no real change in these opinions since the work of H. Wrede.[17]

Basis and validity of the orthodox view

We have seen that the corpus is divided into five sections: *Perceval le viel* (the work of Chrétien), C1, C2, CM, and CG. What is the basis for this repartition, and does it have any weaknesses?

The end of the *Perceval* and the beginning of C1 are indicated firstly by the fact that one MS, B stops after 9234, and at the same point MS A has the words

Explycyt Percevax le viel,[18] while MSS C and H stop shortly before, at 9228, and F stops at 8608. However, the other MSS, ten in all, continue directly with C1, without marking this break in any way. It is therefore largely because of the difference of style that scholars have accepted that 9234 definitely marks the end of Chrétien's work. A detailed stylistic study is not really necessary: it is obvious that the style of C1 is not that of Chrétien. Nevertheless, the break is to some extent disguised, as the author of Branch I of C1 (Roach (A) 1–1172) who, as we shall see, is probably not the author of Branches II to VI, did his best to imitate the style of the Master. He was reasonably successful, at least as regards the versification, as he achieved a rich rhyme percentage of 31%, or 26.5% if we follow the text of MS L, which corresponds very closely to the percentage in the *Perceval*. The only difference is in the proportion of leonine to rich rhymes.[19] All in all, there is clearly a *Perceval*-C1 break, and it is doubtless right to situate it at 9234 (Hilka), rather than at A 1172.[20]

The third break, marking the end of C2 and the beginning of CM and CG, is the most clearly defined. The Continuation of Gerbert, only in MSS T and V, was probably inserted between C2 and CM by a remanieur, who would also appear to have amputated the end of it, replacing it by a short piece borrowed from C2. This break comes at l. 32594, and MS L breaks off at this point. MS K comes to a rapid, not to say abrupt, end after 32594.[21] Of the other MSS containing C2, EMPQSU continue with CM, while in TV, CG follows C2, and is in turn followed by CM. A little over 6000 lines of CG are missing from V, which contains only a few fragments of CM. It is important that the two texts CM and CG begin at the same point, and the break is definitely established, to within a few lines, by Manessier himself, who says he: 'conmença au soudement De l'espee sanz contredit'.[22] He is referring to the incident at the end of C2 episode 35, where Perceval joins the two halves of a broken sword. If necessary, the versification — more than 50% of rich rhymes in CM, as against some 15% in C2 — would show clearly that he cannot mean another incident, where the smith Tribuet repairs a broken sword for Perceval (CM 38923–39026). A similar, but greater, difference applies to CG in relation to C2; CG has over 65% of rich rhymes.

I have left until last the second break, the division between C1 and C2, as it is the least clear-cut. The suggestion that the division comes at l. 9456,[23] first put forward by G. Paris,[24] reposes in no small measure on the change in the manuscript relations which occurs there. Certainly, there appears to be a major shift at this point, which may be summarized thus: ASP, L (SRed.); TV (MRed.); EMQU (LRed.) becomes AKLMQSU (SRed.); EPT (LRed.). In reality, however, we shall see when we examine the manuscript tradition that this substantial change is in no small degree an illusion, for which the presentation of the Roach edition of C1 is mainly responsible. There are, nevertheless, two other facts which prompted the idea of a break at 9456.

Firstly, and most obviously, the hero is no longer Gauvain or at least his brother, Guerrehés, but Perceval. Secondly, it is at this point that MS K begins. In fact, of the whole vast compilation, K contains only C2. Lot said that this division was 'conjecturale, mais . . . sensée'.[25] As he said, there had been no word of Perceval for some 14000 lines. However, a change of hero does not, *a priori*, mean a change of author;[26] Chrétien alternates between Perceval and Gauvain in the *Perceval*; the latter reappears in C2, whose main hero is Perceval; and C1 changes from Gauvain to Guerrehés, leaving aside Branch III, probably added *en bloc*, whose hero is Caradoc. We may add that the C2 in MS K hardly appears to have been an independent poem, or independent of C1, despite its individual conclusion. Here are the opening lines of this MS:

> Do roi artu lairai atant
> Et si orés dor en avant
> Le bon conte de percheval
> Et le haut livre do greal (Roach var. 9457–58)

These lines seem less like an introduction than a transition, as in the other MSS, compare the first couplet of C2 in E. They suggest that the MS was copied from an incomplete model, or else with the intention simply to provide the sequel to Perceval's adventures, although K does not contain the *Perceval*. All things considered, the reasons for believing that there is a break at 9456 do not seem to be cogent. Lot, in concluding his article, said: 'La pause au v. 21917 (= 9456), si elle n'est pas décisive, reste provisoirement, si l'on veut, la plus satisfaisante'.[27] Now that the Roach edition has made available the evidence of all the MSS, I hope to demonstrate that this conjectural break is no longer the most satisfying.

This brings us to the accepted interpolations in the corpus. First of all we have C1 Branch V, episode 5, in which the Fisher King tells Gauvain the story of the Grail (*Gralvorgeschichte*), and how Joseph of Arimathea brought it to Britain; the essence of the account is similar to that in Robert de Boron's *Joseph*, though there are important differences.[28] There are several reasons why this episode is almost universally considered to be interpolated. Firstly, there is the manuscript tradition: the episode is found in A and L, and in MQU, but it is lacking in S, P, and TV. Importantly, though, we should not be misled by the lacuna in E in this part of the text into thinking that E, like MQU (EMQU = Roach's LRed.), contained V/5, for this was not the case. We might deduce this from the amount of text missing in E,[29] but it becomes a near-certainty when we see that this episode (V/5) is not found in the 1530 prose version. The correspondence between the 1530 edition and E is at all times so close that we can be sure that, had E contained V/5, it would be in the prose.

The manuscript evidence, which will be gone into more fully in Chapter 1, is inconclusive. What does seem clearly to support the interpolation theory is the fact that at no point, when relating his Grail adventure, does Gauvain ever mention that he learnt anything about the Grail. Indeed, he implies that he did not, since he '. . . perdi par son dormir Les grans mervelles a oïr' (L 8283–84; = A 8291–92, cf. L 7729–30 = A 7691–92, and L 7736–40 = A 7698–7702), which is what happens in those MSS without V/5. It could be argued that this simply means he missed hearing further wonders, after the story of the Grail, but these events are related four more times, twice in C2: 29115–48, 31228–42, and twice in CM: 35059–70, 35239–53, and at no point is there any suggestion that the Fisher King told Gauvain about the Grail. Note also that Gauvain says (L 7741–49) that he wishes to return to the Grail Castle, to learn 'La maniere et le bel service Et del Graal et de la biere' (7748–49). The same lines, approximately, occur in MQU (17814–15), and TV (13551–52).) Equally important is the fact that Gauvain is reproached by the inhabitants of the countryside, partially restored from its wasted state, 'Por çe qu'il ne te lut oïr Del Graal por quoi il servoit' (L 7778–79 = A 7750–51). This surely implies that Gauvain learnt nothing about the Grail, and while none of this is absolutely conclusive, there is certainly good reason to suppose that C1 V/5 is an interpolation.

C1 I/6 and I/8 need not trouble us for long. Found only in MSS E and U, as against MQ, TV, see the manuscript tradition, in Chapter 1, they show, as Wrede pointed out, a marked difference in style (extensive use of saints' names, high level of enjambement), when compared with the surrounding text. There is little doubt that they are interpolated.

C1 III/9 is inordinately long, and tedious, and missing from MS P, which in this section has the same text as EMQTUV, see Chapter 1. However, it is precisely this isolation of P, and the fact that in P (for P's text see Roach III/1, Appendix I) the three friends, Caradoc, Cador, and Aalardins, seem to set off for court, then leave without having arrived, which suggest that this episode is not interpolated in EMQTUV, but omitted by P. The versification would also accord with this view. The question is not one of great importance, given the banality of the episode, which is simply a long description of a tournament.

In C2, episodes 2, and 6, 7, and 8 present the same basic reasons for us to consider them interpolated. In each case, they are poorly represented in the MSS: 2 is in EPT, versus AKLMQSU, and 6, 7, and 8 are in EPS, versus KLMQTU, and in each case they furnish data which do not accord with preceding or subsequent events. In episode 2, as Wrede pointed out, King Arthur states his intention of setting out to look for Perceval, accompanied by many of his knights, but no such expedition ever takes place. In 6, 7, and 8, we are told things about Perceval's loss of the stag's head which do not fit with what we learn later,[30] and we would expect to learn the identity of the knight Perceval kills in episode 7, but we do not. In addition, the proportion of rich rhymes in episodes 6–8 is some 27%, while in the remainder of C2 (episodes 9–35) it is about 15%. Episode 2 is too short for such comparisons. All in all, there are no real grounds for doubting that these episodes are indeed interpolated.

To sum up, the only clear weakness in the accepted view of the *Perceval* corpus is the idea that we should divide C1 from C2 at l. 9456. I shall attempt to show that the real break occurs not at this point, but rather at A 10268 (= E 20530), i.e. the point at which MS A breaks off. First, however, it will be necessary to examine closely the structure and composition of C1, since it is impossible to dissociate the two texts, as we shall see. Before we examine either text in any detail, though, it will be convenient and useful to look at the manuscript tradition.

CHAPTER 1

THE MANUSCRIPT TRADITION

The aim of this necessarily brief examination of the manuscript tradition of the *Perceval* corpus is to establish where there are major shifts in the manuscript relations, and whether these generally appear to correspond to clearly defined sections of the text. Subsequently the manuscript tradition of C2 will be examined in more detail, with a view to establishing which MSS seem to represent the most primitive state of the text.

The method used is a comparison of the MSS, not on the basis of common errors, but of common additions, omissions and, to a lesser extent, inversions.[1] This has the advantage of yielding a large amount of evidence, and eliminates the need for deciding what does or does not constitute a common error. At the same time, a possible drawback of this method, the fact that two scribes might independently omit the same section of text, is largely offset by the quantity of evidence; it is generally clear when coincidence can be ruled out. Nevertheless, the evidence of common errors has not been entirely disregarded, in particular for C2.

No evidence will be provided for the manuscript groupings put forward. This is primarily so as not to overburden the reader, who may well be unfamiliar with the labyrinthine construction of C1 in particular. In addition, the method used is essentially non-controversial, in that a line either is, or is not, present, and the reader can if he wishes refer to Roach's edition for the relevant evidence, since this examination of the manuscripts is based, not on the manuscripts themselves, but on a reconstruction from that edition.

The bulk of the detail here will be devoted to C1, simply because the manuscript tradition of that text is so complex, and because C2 cannot be considered independently, isolated from the evidence of C1.

Roach, as we have seen, divides C1 into three redactions: Short (SRed.), represented here by L and A (principally); Long (LRed.), represented here by E (when present); Mixed (MRed.), represented by T. As the name Mixed Redaction suggests, this tripartite division essentially represents two redactions, with T(V) alternating between them, but the details of this will be given below.

It should be pointed out that one of the main reasons for this examination of the manuscript tradition is that, for C1, Roach's presentation of the three redactions gives an inexact, and even erroneous picture of the manuscript relations. C2 is divided into SRed. and LRed. until E 20530 (= A 10268).

THE CORPUS

Throughout, roman numerals represent C1 branches, arabic numerals represent episodes, both for C1 and C2. Thus I/3 = Branch I, ep. 3, etc. First of all let us resume the major manuscript groupings and changes of group throughout the corpus. These will then be looked at in more detail.[2] Note that I/3–4° = Branch I, ep. 3 and part of ep. 4; I/°4–6 = Branch I, part of ep. 4, and episodes 5 and 6, etc.

Perceval[3]   AL,U — MQ,E — PS —TV

C1
I/1–2   E 1–944   EU,MQ // ASP,LTV
I/3–5°   E 945–1756   EU,MQ // ASP // LTV

I/°5°   E 1757–1844   EU — MQ,TV // ASP // L
I/°5–10   E 1845–5508   EU // MQ,TV

-- A

II/1°   E 5509–5756   MQ — EU — L — TV / AS,P
II/°1–5°   E 5757–6172   MQ // EU,L — TV /AS,P
II/°5–8°   E 6173–6622   MQ // EU,L — TV,AS,P

II/°8   E 6623–6670   EU,MQ / L,TV,ASP
III/1–6°   E 6671–7536   EU,MQ // TV — L,ASP
III/°6–10°   E 7537–9786   EUx,MQP,TV // L,AS (P om. III/9)
III/°10–11°   E 9787–9922   EU(x),MQ,TV // L,ASP
III°11–14°   E 9923–11747   Ex,MQ,TV // L,ASPU
III/°14–15   E 11748–12270   E,MQ // TV — L,ASPU. -------------- B
III/16   E 12271–12506   E,MQ,TV / ASPU,L
IV/1–4   E 12507–13610   E,MQ,TV / ASPU,L -moving to:
                                    L / E,MQ,TV / ASPU

IV/5°   E 13611–14172   PU — E,MQTV // L,AS

IV/°5–16°   E 14173–16682   L / E / MQ,TV — PU,AS
IV/°16–V/1°   E 16683–16888   LU / MQ,TV — P,AS

V/°1–4	E 16889–17552	L,U,MQ — TV,P,AS (or — TV — P,AS)
V/5	E 17553–17778	(E)PSTV // LMQU,A
V/6–VI/4	E 17779–19006	L,U,MQ — TV — P,AS (or — TV — P — AS)
VI/5–8	E 19007–19606	L,U,MQ / E — T(V) — P,AS (or — T(V) / P,AS)
C2 Intro'–5°	E 19607–20530	E,T(V) — P — AS,KU,MQ — L[4]
		C
°5°	E 20531–20620	EPS — K,LT(V) // MQU
°5–30°	E 20621–30252	ES,P // KU,MQ — L,TV
°30–35	E 30253–32594	E,MS — P / U,Q — K,L,TV
Manessier		P — U / E,Q — MS — TV

Gerbert   We can safely leave aside CG, found only in TV.

The broken horizontal lines indicate major shifts, excluding the frequent to-ing and fro-ing of TV. The lines indicated by A, B, C, represent the points at which I consider the text divides naturally, although A should strictly come at the end of I/5. This will be discussed fully in the next chapter. Let us now look at the details of this picture.

Perceval

Micha[5] gives the following approximate *schéma* for the manuscript groupings in *Perceval*: A(B)L,RU — FMQ(E),CH — PS — TV. We can disregard B, C, F, and H, none of which contain any part of the Continuations. In addition, in this chapter I have disregarded R, which contains only Branch I, episodes 1–5 of C1, and whose text appears to be radically expanded.

Certain of Micha's remarks concerning individual manuscripts and their characteristics are worth bearing in mind, as they seem to apply, to a large extent, throughout the corpus. Notably, he says that Q is substantially reworked, and tends towards omission rather than addition; M contains no additions at all; S is the most reworked of all the MSS.

The First Continuation

Branch I

First of all, we see a clear EMQTUV // LASP opposition, in that the latter contain only episodes 1–5, and not 6–10. Secondly, this former group resolves itself into EU // MQTV, since the latter do not contain episodes I/6 and I/8.[6]

Looking at this Branch in more detail, we find that in episodes I/1–2, LTV and ASP give us one version, although A and TV show a certain amount of variation. The standard form of the text seems to be that represented by L. In I/3, a clear division appears between ASP and LTV — one might call it two separate redactions — and this continues into I/4–5. However, early in I/5, at around T 1048 (= E 1756, L 1016)[7] TV move to join EU,MQ, and the EU — MQ distinction, which has been visible throughout Branch I, now becomes EU — MQ,TV. This pattern, of course, is what we see in I/6–10. As to the question of which SRed. (i.e. L or A) the (EMQU) LRed. is based on in I/1–5, I would say that in I/1–2 we cannot say, and in I/3–5 the LRed. is nearer to ASP.

Branch II

Broadly speaking, EU follow the redaction of L throughout, except that II/1 shows major recasting, and EU has points of similarity both with L and with A. MQ have their own redaction here, for E 5757–6656, printed by Roach in an appendix (vol. II). The MQ version of this branch would appear to be a recasting, but this is not absolutely certain. Curiously, in II/1, where MQ mainly = EU, it seems to be largely the parts of EU which = L which are not found in MQ. TV start closer to EU — L than to AS,P, but move in II/5 (around T 2566 = E 6172, A 1576) to join the latter. MQ rejoin EU towards the end of II/8; from E 6622 onwards they give partially the same text.

Branch III

In this branch we can add the slender evidence of the fragments published by E. Brayer and F. Lecoy,[8] which I will call x, and which contain parts of episodes III/9 and III/14.

Up to around T 3634 (= E 7536) in III/6, nearly the end of that episode, the basic pattern is: EMQU // TV — L,ASP. We should note that EMQU is not a reworking of L or A here, but a totally new redaction of the same basic plot. This is the case throughout Branch III/1–15. At around E 7536, TV and P[9] shift to the LRed., thus: EMPQUx,TV // L,AS, where the details of the LRed., which alone contains III/7–9, are: EUx,MQP,TV. P omits nearly the whole of III/9 (E 8079–9568) and rejoins the SRed. at E 9787 (= L 2597), the end of III/10, giving us: EUx,MQ,TV // L,ASP. However, at E 9922 (= A 2638) U, which has been closest to Ex, joins the SRed. It is curious that this shift occurs only some 40 lines (in A) after P's return to the SRed. This represents some 130 lines in EU. We now have: Ex,MQ,TV // L,ASPU. Only the LRed. contains III/13. There is another shift to come, however. At around T 8179 (= E 11747, in III/14) TV shift back towards the SRed., and we have: EMQ // TV — L,ASPU. It is easy to see why Roach called TV the Mixed Redaction. This pattern continues to the end of III/15, approximately. It is in III/16 that the LRed. once again appears as a reworking of the SRed., rather than a completely new text, and TV seem to have retraced their steps once more: E,MQTV / ASPU,L. In places, L is closer to the LRed. than are ASPU.

Branch IV

In IV/1, we have the same pattern as in III/16, with L sometimes closer to EMQTV than are ASPU. This latter tendency is more pronounced in IV/2, where we might express the relationship thus: L / EMQTV / ASPU.[10] This applies equally to IV/3, although sometimes L — ASPU are opposed to EMQTV. In IV/4, there is a similar pattern, but towards the end of the episode there is a clear indication of the following: L — E — MQ,TV — PU,AS. IV/5 is a special case, in that briefly, roughly E 13611–14172, we have a pattern: PU — E,MQTV // L,AS, where L,AS give the version of the Pucelle de Lis incident[11] in which there is no hint of rape, while the other MSS give differing versions of the story in which Gauvain forces his attentions on the girl. In spite of the unreliability of P, I am inclined to think PU have here retained the most primitive version, as P. Gallais has suggested,[12] followed by EMQTV, while the LAS version is a recasting. I doubt, however, if this is demonstrable. From IV/6 onwards, we see approximately this pattern: L / E / MQ,TV — PU,AS, although there are still traces of L + ASPU. This pattern, which we saw emerging from IV/4 onwards, and which is only a variation of what we saw in IV/2–3, continues, with minor variations, to about A 6630 (= E 16682) in IV/16, where U joins L. However, E is missing from the picture from 16579 onwards, until 19006, owing to a lacuna.

Now, one of the features of this section of the text is that, in general, those passages in A which correspond to L are also found in E, so E has passages = L, passages = A, and passages = AL. A possible, though greatly over-simplified *stemma* for this part of the text might be:

A.

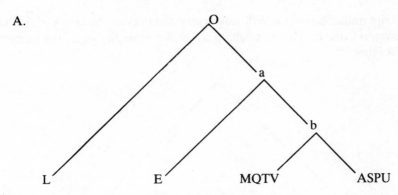

where *a* represents an expansion of O, and ASPU a reduction of *a*. The difficulty of drawing up an accurate *stemma* becomes apparent if we take an example of how this process might work. Looking at E 13528 ff. (from IV/4), we find:

> Kex a le premerain mes pris 13528
> Devant lou roi sans demorer.
> Une grant teste de sengler
> (Li a portee liemant;
> Et puis aprés delivremant) 13532
> A chascun la seue dona.
> Et dit que . . .

However, as the brackets indicate, 13531–32 have been introduced by the editor from Q, to correct the obviously defective reading of E:

> Kex a le premerain mes pris
> Devant lou roi sans demorer
> Une grant teste de sengler 13530
> A chascun la seue dona 13533
> Et dit que . . .[13]

Let us now look at the reading of L for the corresponding passage:

> Quex a le promerain mes mis, 4134
> Devant le roi fist aporter
> Une grant teste de sengler. 4136
> A cascun la soie douna,
> Puis leur dist: . . . 4138

It is easy to see how a slip by the model of E, carelessly writing *sans demorer* instead of *fist aporter*, would leave a faulty reading, corrected in MQTV by the addition of two lines, as we have seen. In theory, this process could have occurred in the reverse order, MQTV ◊ E ◊ L, but I think it unlikely in this instance. The reading of AS, which differs from E 13529–30: 'Devant le roi an tailloër [14] Mist une teste de sengler' could be either a correction of E, or a variation of L, and the fact that here PU = L illustrates the complexity of the manuscript tradition, and the difficulty in ascertaining the exact place of ASPU in relation to L and E. This particular passage, for example, suggests a *stemma* more like this:

B.

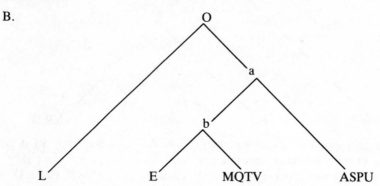

Of course, there are other possibilities, such as contamination in E of both L and A, which I think we can discount, or the reverse *stemma*:

C.

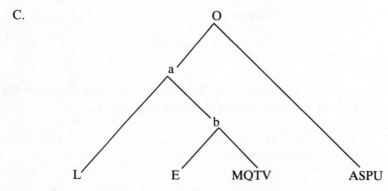

Nevertheless, my feeling is that one of the first two *stemmata* is more probable, and I believe that, in this section of text at least, L offers the best representative of the primitive text.[15]

Branch V

E is missing throughout. For the position of E, particularly in V/5, we can consult the 1530 prose, see *supra*, Introduction, p. 5 V/1 starts with this pattern: LU / MQ,TV — P,AS, but at 16889, the point where, according to Roach, U moves from ASP to MQ (the SRed. to the LRed.), we see another shift, this time to approximately this: LMQU,AS,PTV. Given that MQ were closer to ASP than to LU, we would assume that they have moved, rather than that LU have joined MQ, and TV moved away to ASP. There is a LMQU — ASPTV distinction, but it is not very pronounced, and one might justifiably call this a single redaction. Thus the apparent shift of U to the LRed. is actually a shift of the main LRed. MSS MQ, to join LU, leaving TV as the best representatives, indeed the only ones, of the so-called LRed.[16] This pattern continues in V/2, with clear MQ, MQU, TV, and AS (P) sub-groups, but in V/3 and V/4 the pattern is rather: L,U,MQ — TV — P,AS; however, this is a minor distinction. V/5, like IV/5, is a special case, in that it presents a different manuscript grouping to the sections of text which precede and follow it: (E)PSTV // LMQU,A. Here, of course, it is simply the case that the latter MSS contain the episode, the former do not.[17]

At first sight, if L does give the most primitive version of the text, this would imply that this episode, the *Gralvorgeschichte*, is primitive. However, the isolation of A from PS, and particularly from S, generally closest of all to A, means we can draw no real conclusions from that sub-group, and we are left with a straight LMQU — (E) TV choice. We have seen[18] that there is other evidence to suggest the episode may not be primitive, and it may be that here, as in IV/5, P (= (E)STV) has preserved the more authentic text.

The pattern in V/6–8 is the same as before V/5.

Branch VI

For the first four episodes of this branch, the same pattern is visible as in most of Branch V, although sometimes P is almost closer to TV than to AS, so we might express this as: L,U,MQ — TV — P — AS. From the beginning of VI/5 (E 19007) to the end of C1 we again have the text of E, and the pattern is approximately: L,U,MQ / E — TV / P — AS (or P,AS). Sometimes AS are closer to E than to LMQU, TV or P, and sometimes TV have sections of text corresponding to LMQU, against E or ASP, which show that our projected *stemmata* were, almost inevitably, over-simplified.[19]

The Second Continuation

Introduction — episode 5.[20]

First of all, we have a clear distinction in this section: EPT(V) // AKL-MQSU[21] as can be seen from ep. 2, which is present in the former group, absent from the latter. As we have seen,[22] there is little doubt that the A group have the more primitive text. Within this broad framework, KMQU form a definite sub-group, and MQ a pair within that, as they have throughout the corpus. L shows a substantial amount of individual variation, so we have: L — AS,KU,MQ.[23]

In the Introduction, we see that E, P, and T(V) each present a different text: E — T(V) — P, which duplicates the picture at the end of C1, and in fact P is arguably closer here to the SRed. than to ET(V); compare Pot. 21925–34 (Roach vol. IV p. 5) with A 9465–74. This in fact suggests the only change from

C1 VI is that AS have joined LMQU, or perhaps the reverse. The importance of this fact will be made clear later.

The differences in the EPT(V) group diminish substantially in ep. 1, although PT(V) form a sub-group, and we see: E,PT(V) / AS,KU,MQ —L. This pattern is the same in ep. 3, except that at E 20069–92, PT have the same text as the A group, see Appendix I in Roach vol. IV, and E is isolated. In ep. 4, P moves back to the SRed., at E 20227 (A 10093), but there is really very little difference between the SRed. and the LRed. here, and the pattern is really only: E,T(V) — AS,KU,MQ,P — L. This is the case until E 20368, where ET(V) diverge to some extent,[24] and then at A 10268 (= E 20530), A breaks off short.

We might, then, sum up this section of the text thus: E,T(V) — P — AS,KU,MQ, — L, which would be an accurate enough picture, allowing for minor variations. Subsequently in ep. 5 (E 20529–20619) we have the following pattern, for details of which, see Chapter 4, below: EPS — K,LT(V) // MQU, following which (20620–20687) we have essentially a uniform text, until ep. 6. It should be remembered that Roach makes no SRed./LRed. distinction after E 20530.

Episodes 6, 7, and 8

As we have seen,[25] these episodes are found only in EPS, and are doubtless interpolated, therefore we have: EPS // KLMQTU(V).

Episodes 9–35

From E 21081–30252, approximately, we see several points. Firstly a broad EPS / KLMQTUV distinction is present throughout. The most notable evidence for this is at 23421–34 and 29201–08, present in EPS but not in the rest, in both cases, but we will see further details of this below.

Secondly the most obvious sub-groups are ES, MQ, and TV, but there is also a KMQU grouping, which corresponds to the first section of C2, and a LTV grouping.

Thus, without being too adventurous, we can put forward this picture: EPS / KMQU,LTV which, particularly in the light of episodes 6, 7, and 8, would translate into a *stemma* something like this:

D.

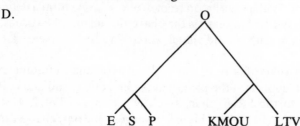

O

E S P   KMQU LTV

From 30253 to the end of C2, a different pattern emerges. The most noticeable change is that we now have a sub-group MS, largely replacing the hitherto constant pairing MQ. This is in fact a sub-group of EMS, itself a sub-group of EMSU and, to some extent, of EMPSU. From this point on, also, M becomes more independent. That there is a division EMPSU — KLQTV is apparent from such passages as 32349–68, present in the former but not in the latter, 32013–51, and 32569 ff., see Roach's note to these lines. However, we also see a division EMSU — KLPQTV, e.g. 31943–44, 31981–84; and a division EMPS — (K)LTUV, in 31209–26, where Q has a different redaction, see Appendix IX.

This last, and the agreement of Q and U in Appendices IX and X, suggest possible contamination, as the simplified *stemma* for this part of the text might well be approximately:

E.

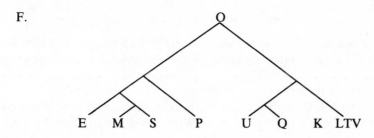

It seems that U is contaminated, since the EMPSU — KLQTV grouping places Q and U on opposite sides of the *stemma*, yet they give the same text in Appendices IX and X, see below. Similarly P and U are shown by that same grouping to be on the opposite side of the *stemma* to KLQTV, yet each is found, independently, with this group, against EMSU and EMPS respectively. It is the evidence of Appendices IX and X which weighs the more heavily in the balance here.

Nevertheless, these considerations, together with the fact that there is evidence for a sub-group LTUV in this section,[26] prompt the thought that, if we accept that U is contaminated, we can assume that the only major change in our *stemma* at 30252 is the shift of M to join S, giving us a *stemma* something like this:

F.

Broadly speaking, then, we have two different *stemmata* for C2 (6–35), which we can portray thus:

20620–30252. ES,P // KU,MQ — L,TV.
30253–end.   E,MS — P / U,Q — K,L,TV.

Manessier

Ivy's *stemma* for CM[27] could be represented thus: P — U / E,Q — MS — TV. If we compare this with the latter part of C2, and remember that K and L break off at the end of that text, we see that, allowing for the fluctuating position of U, there has not been a dramatic change in the manuscript relations, but rather a minor reorganization, a shift in the position of EMS.

We can see from these details, and the overall pattern shown at the start of this chapter, that it would be unwise to conclude that a shift in the manuscript relations, even a fairly major one, necessarily indicates a division in the text. Although some of the major shifts do correspond, more or less, to what we might call natural divisions in the text (thus the shift of PTV at E 7536 is approximately between III/6 and III/7, and the shift of P at E 9786 corresponds roughly to the end of III/10), others clearly do not: it is hard to see the changes at E 16888, in the middle of V/1, or at E 30252, in the middle of C2 episode 30, for example, as marking natural breaks in the text. To put this another way: from simply looking at the changes in the manuscript relations, who could say where the text divides into C1, C2, CM? Thus it would be rash to use the argument that there is a major break at the accepted end of C1 to support the notion that the break does indeed occur there, particularly since the presentation of Roach's edition, as we have seen, lends this change an unwarranted appearance of importance. We will return to the question of the C1/C2 division in the following chapter.

In addition, we see that (a) there is reason to be suspicious of episodes IV/5 and V/5 in C1, on the grounds of the manuscript tradition, that (b) there is good reason to regard both U and the TV pair as contaminated, and that (c) this applies also, to some extent, to P, in spite of the possibility that in IV/5 and V/5 it is P, not A, from the ASP group, which has preserved the primitive text.[28]

THE TRADITION OF THE SECOND CONTINUATION

Let us now examine in more detail the manuscript tradition of C2, which we have seen is not entirely uniform, although it shows much less variation than does C1. For reasons which will be fully explained in the next chapter, we will confine our attentions here to lines 21080 onwards (= episodes 9–35), but the clear EPS — KLMQTUV distinction in episodes 6, 7, and 8 should not be forgotten. While I would hesitate to accept Wrede's suggestion[29] that there are still two redactions in this part of the text, there are a certain number of instances in which there is a clear opposition of one or more MSS to the rest. Many of these are found in the appendices to the Roach edition, and it is easiest to consider these first, to endeavour to ascertain which is the authentic text, in so far as any reasonable degree of certainty is possible.

Appendices VII and VIII require no real attention.[30] Clearly, the former, a lengthy tournament description featuring extensive borrowing from C1, does not represent the authentic text, and it seems unlikely that S should alone have preserved the correct version in the latter, which concerns the danger of trusting women.

Appendix VI, which states that it is paradise to be in the company of women, is more interesting. The only possible way of deciding its authenticity is to consider which MSS have it, and which do not. In this case the fact that only ES omit this passage suggests strongly that it is genuine. Given the EPS — KLMQTUV opposition in this part of the text, the agreement of P with the other MSS against ES seems a strong indication, cf. *stemma* D, *supra*, and the tone of the passage does provide a possible reason for its omission at some stage. Note also the tell-tale presence of a filler line in ES 'Et je, que plus vos conteroie?' (24528) at the exact spot where this appendix occurs.

Appendices IX and X, which deal with Gauvain's meeting with his son, Guiglain, can conveniently be considered together. The basic question concerning these passages is whether Q (with U) has preserved the authentic text, while the bulk of the MSS have a rewritten version, or whether they represent an abbreviation of the authentic text.

In the rather vague realm of literary merits and demerits, it is possible to take either view: on the one hand, a redactor might have been struck by the rather unnecessary exposition of Gauvain's Grail adventure, which (a) was present in C1, and (b) had already been alluded to in episode 28, and so have eliminated much superfluous material. The fact that Q has the Grail automotive and food-providing, while the bulk of the MSS do not (App. IX 57–58, cf. 31207 ff.), merely shows a desire to stick closely to the facts as they are presented in C1, with which the redactor was clearly familiar (App. IX 59–60 = C1 A 7691–92, 8291–92). Equally, however, it is far from unknown for a remanieur to introduce superfluous and often tedious material, so we might just as well suppose that U represents a first expansion of the authentic text (= Q), and LTV, EMPS represent two subsequent reworkings. This latter explanation would explain how U comes to correspond to Q for much of Appendix X, but is difficult to reconcile with the probable *stemma* (see F, *supra*) for this section of the text.

Another small point in favour of the idea that Q(U) have the authentic text might seem to be the fact that, in Appendices IX and X, it is Guiglain who asks his father what is happening at court. This is logical, since Gauvain, as we know, has just left there (ep. 28). In the bulk of the MSS, however, it is Gauvain who asks for news of court. The reason for this, of course, is that it is necessary to prepare the Claudas section of this episode (31300–420). This is done when Guiglain informs his father of the situation, and says that Arthur wishes Gauvain to return to court, to assist him in the war with Claudas and Carras. On the other hand, this point can be viewed in a different light: we know that Gauvain has been away from court for some time, whereas we know nothing of the movements of Guiglain, who may, therefore, have been at court more recently than his father.

Clearly, since the preparation of the Claudas section is entirely omitted by Q(U), their version can only be the authentic one if they omit that section, or if they have some explanation of it prior to l. 31304. This is not the case, so we must assume that Q(U) is a reduction of the common version.[31] This still leaves the problem of how Q and U, which apparently belong to different branches of the *stemma* in other places, have a common text which differs from that of the other MSS. As we have seen, however, the most probable explanation is that the scribe/model of U exploited different versions, see *stemma* F, *supra*.

It is of course important to know which is the authentic text, when considering whether or not episode 32, which corresponds to these appendices, is an interpolation, as Wrede and Lot suggested.[32] This is especially the case because, in the printed text, Gauvain asks his son when he last saw the king, and is told it was two weeks ago (31078–79). However, Gauvain himself only left court a short time before, perhaps two weeks! This small problem of chronology would not have arisen, of course, if Q(U) represented the authentic text, where Guiglain is the one who asks for news of court.[33]

Appendix XI, which contains K's rather unsatisfactory conclusion of C2, in which Perceval is crowned and the Fisher King dies, is of some interest, but I doubt whether it is the original conclusion of C2. It shows clear signs of the influence of the *Didot-Perceval*,[34] unlike the remainder of the text, and the evidence of MS L, and of CG and CM, clearly suggests that C2 was left unfinished. Would two authors, independently as it would seem, have amputated the end of the text in order to prolong the story by 10,000 or 17,000 lines, and have done so at the same point? It seems more likely that whoever detached C2 from C1, in MS K, also added this brief conclusion, to make it a complete independent text. A small point to note is the statement (33–37) that Christ's blood was collected after he was taken down from the cross. This is in contradiction with 25791 ff., where it is said that the blood was collected while he was on the cross, but it corresponds to the *Joseph* (550 ff.).

Besides these appendices, there are other passages where there is a distinct divergence in the manuscript tradition. Of these, some show a difference in only one MS, for example K 21785–86, where K adds 20 lines, which do not appear to be authentic, and which contain an inexact rhyme, *s'engranie: ire*.

These lines do not correspond to anything in any other MS, although the second couplet is similar to Appendix VII TV 553–54. It is certainly possible that K has preserved the original text here, but I think it highly unlikely. This is generally true where only one MS is involved. Several of these passages again involve MS K, which omits 22589–600, perhaps to lighten the text, and 26085–100 in error; the text in K makes no sense here,[35] and replaces 27395–435 by a clumsy abbreviation of seven lines. I do not think we need pay much heed to the reduction in TV of 27533–620, or the frequent and similar omissions in, for example, MS Q. For MS S 29684–762, the same applies as to Appendix VIII, which is found in this section. For M 30280 ff. and 30540 ff., see Roach's notes to these lines. Here again, given particularly the fact that one MS is opposed to the rest, the editor is doubtless correct to consider these divergences as reductions due to the redactor of M or M's model. The omission by U of 32167–218 appears to be an error (see Roach, note to 32167).

In several instances, where we find EPS opposed to the other MSS, the question is more complex. Since episodes 6, 7, and 8 show this to be an aspect of the manuscript *stemma*,[36] it is not possible to say on this basis which is the primitive text. The fact that those episodes are clearly not primitive suggests that the same will be true for any other passages found only in EPS. However, we cannot assume that that is necessarily true, since it is perfectly possible that the forerunner of these three MSS contained an interpolated passage in one place, but retained authentic passages elsewhere which where omitted by the forerunner(s) of the other MSS. The passages in question are found at 23421, 23947, 26172, 28895, and 29201, where EPS contain lines not found in the other MSS (also 29147); then at 22522, 22848, 23960, 26090, 28550, and 29492, where the reverse is true. To these we may add two cases of inversion, at 24833 and 24875.

Taking first of all those instances where EPS lack lines contained in the other MSS, or where there is an inversion, I would say that it is impossible, and unimportant, to decide which is the authentic text at 26090, 28550, 24833, and 24875, while at 22848 and 29492 I would say that EPS have omitted four authentic lines, but this is essentially a subjective judgement. The other two instances are more interesting. At 23960, the reading of K[37] is:

Et si com il avoit esté	23960
Ciés son oncle en la forest	a
Tot li conta sans nul arest	b
Des eschés et de la pucelle	23961

It is clear that the interposed couplet ab can only refer to the famous Good Friday episode in the *Perceval*, since Perceval is currently talking to 'son oncle en la forest'. The question is whether the model of EPS took this to be an absurdity, assuming this to be the same uncle, and so suppressed the couplet, or whether the other MSS, or their model, realizing that this uncle is a paternal, the other a maternal, uncle, inserted this reference to what they considered an important event between the hero's Grail visit and the stag's head adventure. This point is not without importance, as the question of the Good Friday episode is a significant one, and although no certainty is possible, I would incline to the view that the couplet is authentic, and was omitted by the model of EPS, partly on the grounds that if a redactor thought it necessary to insert this reference, he might equally have inserted a reference to the 'Sire du Cor' episode also.[38]

The final instance is of lesser significance, but curious, as the reading of KLMTU is clearly erroneous, in so far as these MSS contain an extra line. This is the reading of K:

Congié a pris a la pucelle	22522	
Qui grant honor li ot portee	a	
Li chevalier sans demoree	b	
Sor les destriers monté se sont	c	(Q om.)
Le pont passerent et la porte	22523	
Qui assez iert et grans et forte	22524	
Chevauchant vont parmi la pree	22525	

It seems very odd that five MSS should contain an error of this sort.[39] There is only one logical explanation for this error. The text must originally have contained line c, and 22523 must have read 'La porte passent et le pont' (= 21472, 29975). This line was accidentally transposed, and a scribe added the banal 22524 to rhyme with it, but omitted to suppress line c, left as a singleton. This error was noticed, and corrected, by the scribes of Q and the ancestor of EPS, the latter also suppressing the couplet ab. There can be no guarantee that this is what happened, but it seems the most likely explanation, and again suggests that EPS do not present the primitive reading. However, in this case, nor do any of the other MSS, strictly speaking.

This brings us to the six instances where EPS contain a passage not found in the remaining MSS. There is one other, at 20587 ff., which will be discussed in Chapter 4. In the case of 23947–50, 28895–96, and 29147–54, it is not really possible to say which is the authentic text, and I would say not very significant. However, I would incline to think that the text presented by L etc. is the authentic one, at least in the second and third cases. The presence of the inexact rhyme *ainme: peine* in these MSS at 29147 might suggest the opposite view, but cf. 22669, 26395, and 28869, as well as 21581.[40]

There is little to help us in the other three passages either. At 23421, the presence of 'lou Sauveor' (23426) is suspicious, as it is otherwise found only in episodes 6 and 8, i.e. in EPS. The monosyllabic form *el* (23431) might have been an indicator, since it is rare in C2, but it is only in E. Certainly 23435 would follow 23420, as in KLMQTUV, with no loss of sense.[41]

Lines 26172–93 could as well be an expansion in EPS as a reduction in KLMQTUV, although the text Roach prints might seem to run better. Once again, though, I would suggest that the K text is primitive. In a way, this is a pity, as the overall picture suggests that EPS do not represent the authentic text when there is a divergence, and this would then apply to 29201–08, which, were they genuine, would be of interest in that they imply a written source, *l'estoire*, which is unrhymed (29205), but too bulky to be included entirely in this rendering of the story. Neither is it very clear, admittedly, why these lines should have been interpolated.

It would seem, then, that EPS do not in all probability represent the original text of C2, after 21080, just as they do not before that point. However, leaving aside episodes 6, 7, and 8, I would scarcely say that EPS represent a different, or Long redaction, in a major sense, any more than do TV, for example.

The EPS grouping is revealed again in several more passages where there is a divergence in the manuscript tradition, but these passages occur after the re-organization of the manuscript relations at 30252, and the simple EPS versus the rest pattern has disappeared. The passages in question are principally these: 31209–12 and 31215–26; 32115–51; 32227–30; 32323–28; 32349–68. The essential manuscript division in these passages is EMPS — KLTV(Q), cf. *stemma* F, *supra*. The position of U varies.

We may consider 31209–12 and 31215–26 together. In each case, we have EMPS, the printed text, versus LTUV (K has a lacuna, for Q cf. Appendix IX). Gauvain is relating to his son Guiglain his experiences in the Grail Castle, cf. C1 V. It would be helpful to see exactly what this passage amounts to in the shorter version of LTUV:

Mais une autre chose veoie	31205
Par coi je me reconfortoie,	
Car avec ce ot un Graal,	
Mais onques hom ne vit ital	31208
Si le portoit une pucelle	31213
Qui molt iert avenanz et belle;	
Par toute le table servoit	
Et pain devant le roi metoit.	
Ce regardoie volantiers;	
Li rois a dit: "Biaux amis chiers	31228

The most curious aspect of this passage is that the essential difference one might expect to find between the two versions: that the Grail is carried in one (= *Perceval*, C2 ep. 35), auto-motive in the other (= C1 V), is not present. It is not implausible that 31209–10 may have been added to the original text (= LTUV), which was subsequently further expanded (= EMPS), but there is no manuscript evidence to support this idea, and in the light of this essential identity between the two versions, I can see nothing that would enable us to choose between them. One is longer, one shorter, but is this an expansion or a reduction? Subjectively I would suggest the former, but objectively we cannot say.

With 32115–51 there is rather more of a difference between the versions, and it is therefore easier to arrive at a positive conclusion. Here is the version of KLTV (that of Q is essentially the same):

Mais sor l'autel, mien escïent,	32102
Gisoit uns chevalier ocis.	
Sor lui ot estendu et mis	
Un riche samit de color,	
U d'or avoit tamainte flor;	
Devant lui uns cirges ardoit	
Ne plus ne mains n'an i avoit.	32108
Percevaux molt s'en esmervelle,	
Molt sovent escoute et oroille	
Se il orroit venir nului.	
Longuemant sueffre cest annui,	
Car molt envis s'an departoit;	32114
Tant que mïenuis aprocha	(cf. 32148)
De la chapele s'en torna	(= 32147)
Por son cheval oster le frain	
Mais ne fu mie bien de plain	
Ensus d'enqui deus piés alés	
Quant estainte fu la clartés	
Qui la chapele enluminoit	
Perchevaus bien s'en aperçoit	
Onques por ço ne s'esbahi	
Ne ne tranbla ne ne fremi	
Montés est ne s'atarge mie	
Tost ot la chapelle esloignie	32152
Et l'arbre ausis, don je vos dis	

This passage does not appear to add anything very significant to the narration of the incident, so we are left to ask what it omits, and whether the elements omitted are more susceptible of having been put in, or taken out. Essentially, the elements left out in this shorter version of the passage are (a) a great light, (b) a great noise (*escroiz*), and (c) a black hand which appears from behind the altar and extinguishes the candle. It is clear that these are basically elements which feature, in the various redactions, in the account of Gauvain's visit to the Black Chapel in C1 V/3. It is difficult to see why a redactor should eliminate such elements, but easy to see why they should be inserted, linking as they do C2 to C1, and creating a clear Perceval — Gauvain parallel. This clearly suggests that KLQTV have preserved the more authentic version of this passage, since the version which is not harmonized with that of C1 must surely be the more primitive.

In addition to this major point, there are smaller pointers which might support or contradict this assumption. For example, the fact that in the E version, Perceval leaves the Chapel just before midnight, whereas in the K version he is just leaving it at that same time, so that in K the sudden disappearance of the light in the Chapel seems to occur at midnight, a very appropriate hour for strange events, whereas in the E version it must have occurred at perhaps 11.45, which is not a very significant moment. Furthermore, in the E version we find two inexact rhymes: 32127 *autel*: *cler* (in EPU; MS eliminate this),[42] and 32149 *monte*: *ancontre*. These rhymes are not found in the K version. While we shall see that dialectal and inexact rhymes are to be found in C2, the latter are not so frequent that the occurrence of two precisely where there is a manuscript divergence should be dismissed as mere coincidence. Against these points, we might ask why, having gone to unbridle his horse, Perceval then rides off, but I should have thought that the possibly supernatural disappearance of the light might be sufficient reason, even though we are told that Perceval was not afraid.

Lines 32227–30 and 32323–28 are directly linked to the previous passage, in that they both concern Perceval's subsequent relation of the events at the Black Chapel. In 32227–30 the distinction between EMPSU and KLQTV is exactly the same: the three elements, light, noise, and black hand, are mentioned in the former, absent from the latter. In 32323–28 the same applies, but the fact that KL and TV have only similar, not identical, readings, while Q omits, might cast doubts on their authenticity. However, I do not think we should place too much importance on this, as the authentic version of this passage must be the same as that of the two previously discussed. Note also that the E version contains the rhyme *ot*: *ot* here, although a rhyme of *i avoir* with *avoir* was one of the more commonly accepted identical or grammatical rhymes.

For 32349–68 the problem is slightly more complex. Once again we have EMPSU versus KLQTV, although in this case the passage is simply present in the former, absent from the latter. In this passage, Perceval tells the Fisher King how he saw an illuminated tree near the Chapel, as was related in episode 34. If there were no reference to the illuminated tree in KLQTV, we would naturally assume that the E version had been inserted by a remanieur who felt that Perceval should have mentioned this phenomenon, the more so, as in EMU we find an inexact rhyme, 32355 *adés*: *divers*. However, KLTV retain lines 32381–82, where the tree and the candles are mentioned, although 32382 is not the same as in EMPSU, and in fact the K version does not have the inexact *chandoilles*: *voires*, which must be suspect. This couplet is omitted by Q. The question then is this: why should a remanieur decide to omit this logical and apparently necessary passage? It is surely more probable that he would insert it, precisely because it appears logical and necessary. After all, Perceval refers in 32381 to the tree, which he has not yet mentioned to the Fisher King (in KLQTV). This slight anomaly is easily resolved by the scribe of Q, who omits 32381–82, whereas someone else apparently resolved it by adding the twenty-line passage in question. If the passage were authentic, the only acceptable explanation for its absence from KLQTV would surely be that the scribe of their ancestor skipped a twenty-line column in his exemplar. While this is possible, and eliminates the need to account for the presence of such an anomaly in the original text, I am inclined to accept the anomaly, and, especially in the light of the passages discussed previously, to assume that 32349–68 are not primitive.

In addition to these passages, where we have concluded that the MSS group EMPS(U) is inferior to the group KLTV(Q), there are several other passages, or couplets, where there is a similar division of the MSS, but this time with P aligned with KLTV(Q). These passages occur at 31680, 31789–90, 31943–44, 32498–500.

At 31680, LPTV add 8 lines; this part of the text is missing from K, while Q, like EMSU, omits these lines. The lines are trivial, and it is impossible to deduce from their content whether they are more likely to have been interpolated or omitted. However, the fact that they contain a possible hint of innuendo regarding the services a young lady can offer might have constituted a reason for their omission. The rhyme *services*: *riches* found here is dialectal, rather than inexact, and of a sort which is a feature of C2, and as such it is doubtless less significant than those mentioned above. All in all, the evidence of Q carries no great weight when set against that of P, and given the nature of the probable *stemma* for this part of the text, and bearing in mind that coincidental omission is possible, not so coincidental interpolation, I would conclude that these lines are primitive.

At 31789–90, we are again dealing with an addition, or rather a substitution, this time of six lines for two, found in LPQTV (K has a lacuna). While L has only four of the six lines, which = TV, P and Q change the last line or couplet slightly. However, all the other evidence suggests that these lines are primitive: the balance of the MSS and the *stemma*, (K)LPQTV versus EMSU; the fact that the E version contains a quatrain, which are not common in C2, and also that the 'or m'escoutez' of 31789 is so similar to the 'or m'antandez' of 31791.[43] Add to this the fact that so far, in every case, we have been led to conclude in favour of the authenticity of the version furnished by (K)LTV, and once again we must suppose that these lines are authentic. This applies equally to the omission of 31943–44 by KLPQTV, which is interesting, although probably not significant, and to the omission of 32498 and 32500, and the alteration of 32497 and 32499, in the same six MSS. This of course, is of very limited interest.

There is one further point to be examined on the subject of the manuscript relations and the probable authenticity of the different traditions. The editor has based his edition of C2 on MS E, which is not a decision we would lightly criticize. Nevertheless, in those places where EPS diverge from the other MSS, we have concluded that their text is probably not primitive. Now, there is a close relationship between E and S more or less throughout the text, and certainly until the second manuscript reorganization at 30252, where the group becomes rather EMS (or E,MS). There are a substantial number of lines found in or omitted from all, or nearly all, the remaining MSS, including P, but not in E(M)S, or in the latter when omitted by the other MSS. In the interests of forming a clear picture of the primitive text, we should try to establish whether or not the lines in question are likely to have been a part of the original text.

We have seen that the evidence of episodes 6, 7, and 8, and certain other passages, shows us a clear EPS versus the rest division. This indicates, broadly, one of two *stemmata*:

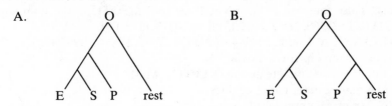

Now, B can only represent the true state of affairs if the passages in EPS are authentic, whereas we have concluded that they are not, cf. *supra*, and must therefore choose A (= D, p. 16). This being the case, and adopting *stemma* F as correct in the latter part of the text, any lines present in P, as well as the bulk of the MSS, but absent from E(M)S, must be assumed to have been omitted from the latter, rather than inserted by the former.[44] The reverse would also apply: i.e. lines in E(M)S, but not in the rest, would be added by the former; nevertheless, this is less certain, cf. my remark *supra* on coincidental omission and interpolation.

The following list of lines involved will show that, in general, the model of E(M)S shows a tendency to lighten the text, removing lines which were clearly considered superfluous. The majority of these additions/omissions are of a fairly trivial nature, the sort of lines which might well be omitted by a scribe who wished to rid the text of some unnecessary verbiage. Where the lines are of no interest, I will simply give line-references, but where there is some linguistic or other point of interest, I will quote the lines. The reading given, both for the additions and for the lines before and after, is that of MS. L, for reasons of uniformity, given the large lacuna in K.

21405 KLMPQU add 4 (not T); 22620 KLMPTU add 2 (not Q); 22760 KLMPQTU add 2; 22764 KLMPQTU add 2; 22776 KLPTU,MQ add 2.

22886 Et grans torz faire et maçoner
  (a) Tot si le fis sans nul mentir (KMQU,LPT)
  (b) Comme a vos oex poés veïr
22887 Or vos ai tout conté et dit

This is of interest because of the presence of the infinitive *veïr*, as opposed to *veoir*, cf. Chapter III note 13.

23020 KLMQTU add 4, P adds 2; 23528 KLMPQTUV add 2; 23638 KLMPQTUV add 2; 23700 KLMPQTUV add 2; 23820 KLMPQTUV add 4; 23938 KLMPQTU add 2; 23978 KLMPQTU add 4; 24298 KLMPTU,Q add 4; 24484 KLMPQTUV add 4; 24506 KLPTUV,MQ add 2.

24514 Et vestues d'une color
  (a) De samis vers bendés d'orfrois (LPTUV,MQ; not K)
  (b) Et si vuel bien que vos sachois
24515 Que toutes samblent d'un aaige

This is of interest for the occurrence of the second person plural verb-ending -*ois*, which is also found in all but ES at 21432 (= KMPQTU, L om.), and in KLMPQTUV at 25360. Note that 24514b = 26310, cf. 31001.

24524 KLMQTUV,P add 2; 24564 KLMPQTUV add 2 (cf. 29965–66.).

24576 Lus et saumons fres et noviaus
  (a) Et poissons de mainte matire (KLPTUV,MQ)
  (b) Des vins ne quier parler ne dire
24577 Nule rien car anuis seroit
24578 Qui tout lo voir vos an diroit
  (a) Mais tant en orent sans mescroire (KLMPQTUV)
  (b) Com se la grans cités d'Aucoirre
  (c) Fust la dame demainement
  (d) Et quanqu'a Vergelai apent
24579 Quant ont mangié par grant loisir

This mention of Auxerre and Vézelay is of little significance for the question of the authorship of C2, for we cannot assume that an author would only mention in this way places near to his place of origin or place of work. Auxerre and Vézelay were well known in medieval France, the former for its wines, and the latter as a site of pilgrimage to the tomb of St Madeleine, from the 10th century onwards.

24622 KLMPQTUV add 2; 24956 KLMPQTUV add 2; 25107–08 KLMPQTUV om.; 25360 KLMPQTUV add 2 (cf. 24514); 25452 LMPQTUV add 2 (not K); 25726 KLPTUV,MQ add 2; 25864 KLMPQTUV add 2; 25884 KLMPQTUV add 2; 25996 KLMQTUV,P add 2; 26387 KLMPQTUV add 4; 26684 KLMPQU,TV add 2; 26780 KLMPQTUV add 2; 26823–27 LTV,KMPQU have 3 lines for 5; 27006 KLMQTUV,P add 2; 27278 KLMPQTUV add 2; 27392 KLMPTUV add 2 (not Q); 27428 LMPQTUV add 2 (K different in this section); 27706 KLPTUV,MQ add 6; 27783–89 KLMPQTUV have 3 lines for 7; 28086 LMPQTUV add 4 (K om.); 28126 KLMPQTUV add 2.

28526 Qui molt de grant biauté estoit
  (a) Et molt plaine de cortesie (KLMPQTUV)
  (b) S'i fu li rois Loth d'Orcanie
28527 Li pere monsegnor Gauvain

28526ab were presumably omitted by the model of ES, who realized that Loth was supposed to be dead, according to *Perceval*, and who changed 28527 accordingly. Might this indicate a primitive independent existence for the first part of episode 28? It is not inconceivable. Similar eradications of Lot's name, which is not in QU here, occur at 28793 and 30089, again in ES only.

29326 LPTUV,MQ add 2 (K lacuna); 29390 LMPQTUV add 2 (K lacuna); 30161–63 LPTV,MQU have 5 for 3 (K lacuna and if Roach's variants are correct, M lacks one line here); 30314 LPQTUV add 2 (K lacuna); 30976–80 LPQTUV have 3 lines for 5 (K lacuna), which is only of interest in that it suggests the slightly obscure 30978 (E) may be the result of scribal confusion; 31788 P,Q,TV add 6, L adds 4 (K lacuna, cf. *supra*, p. 26); 31982–83 KLPQTUV om.; 32172 KLPQTV add 2 (U om. this section); 32388 KLP add 2 (QTV om. U = EMS).

It may be noted that the E(M)S versus P with other MSS criterion applies frequently to readings which are found in the text (= E(M)S), but which are contradicted by the bulk of the MSS, including P. Some of these are of interest when we consider the frequent repetitions of certain lines in the text, or when we look at linguistic and stylistic features. A small example which is interesting is found at 30174, where ES read '(Que par sus l'arçon de la selle) A fait Kex la torneboëlle'. This line has clearly been altered by a scribe who recalled *Yvain* 2256, which is identical.[45] The reading of the remaining seven MSS is 'Jus del bon destrier de Castele' (Q is similar, not identical), which is an exact duplicate of 22046. Without the evidence of the manuscript relations, it could easily be argued that an opposite process might have taken place, but we can see here the influence of Chrétien's work, not on the author, but on a scribe.

To sum up, we have concluded that, in 20630–30252, KLMQTUV(P) have the more primitive text, when faced with ES(P). After 30252, we have concluded that the best version is that of KLTV(Q)(U), and we have concluded against QU, where those MSS confront the others. Thus it is clear that overall, the manuscript group which seems to be most faithful to the original is KLTV, and it might be of interest to see an edition of the text based on that group, with L as base MS.[46]

Finally, the effect of using E, rather than L, as the base MS may be illustrated by two passages in the text, 29514–19 and 32561–75.

29514–19

Eus is the usual spelling, in MS E, of *oés*. I interpret 29514–17 thus: 'And so devoted to them (the knights) That, if they (the ladies) could have whatever (= whoever) they wished for, They (the knights) thought they would be above (= preferred to) everyone, King, count or emperor'. The reading of LMQTUV at 29516 is much clearer than that of EPS, which was probably introduced because the scribe of their model used the form *peüssent* as opposed to *poïssent*.

Lines 29518–19 present more of a problem. A possible interpretation might be 'Even though they (the knights) had no land But (only) themselves, etc'. However, the *eüst*, where we would expect *eüssent*, and the use of *ja tant* with the subj., which usually means 'however much', suggest that 29518 qualifies 29517, which makes perfect sense, but leaves the *s'eus non* of 29519 isolated, and somewhat baffling. It clearly troubled the scribes also. The solution is clear: we must restore the reading of LMQTUV at 29516, which leaves *s'eus non* dependent on that clause, i.e. 'they (the ladies) would not choose King, count or emperor (Be he never so rich) But (rather) them (the knights), etc.', or 'Instead of them, in their place.'

32561–75

The editor's note to 32569 perfectly expresses the problem of sense and syntax in 32569–75. However, he ignores the fact that, as the text stands, the *Mais* of 32564 makes little sense. Both problems are resolved if we adopt the reading of KLQTV 32569. The Fisher King then says that Perceval has done many feats of arms, but, while he (the Fisher King) accepts that Perceval is without peer as a warrior, he has not yet attained the degree of perfection where he can be said to be the best knight in every sense. While I can offer no explanation as to why or how the reading of KLQTV (32569) should have been altered to that of EMPSU, it is impossible to make sense of the latter, and the superiority of the KLQTV reading underlines the fact that these MSS offer the more primitive version of the text.

CHAPTER 2

THE STRUCTURE AND UNITY OF
C1 AND THE C1/C2 BREAK

I have briefly indicated, in the preceding chapter, that I believe the text should be divided, or can be divided, at the end of C1 I (= C1 I/5, not I/10), at the end of C1 III/15, and at A 10268 (= E 20530) in C2. Before looking at C2, though, it will be necessary to consider, in some detail, the text of C1, from the point of view of its structure and unity.

The structure and unity of C1

The episodic nature of C1, accurately reflected by Roach's division into six branches, has long been recognized. The very fact that the text consists of six separate adventures, or sets of adventures, featuring three different heroes, Gauvain, Caradoc, and Guerrehés, prompts the question of how many authors might be involved. Lot considered that there were probably three, possibly four. His divisions correspond to (a) Branches II and IV/1–15, also possibly Branch I; (b) Branches IV/16, V and VI; (c) Branch III, the 'livre de Caradoc'; of the Roach edition.[1] Detailed study of the text has led me to conclude that, while Lot was right to suggest that the text was the work of several authors, he may well have been misled, by the somewhat vague criteria he adopted, as to the distribution of the various parts. I will attempt here to show briefly how the text seems to divide up, and how it may have come to assume its present form.

The simplest and clearest indication that the text is not homogeneous, taking homogeneity to mean single, as opposed to multiple authorship, is the proportion of rich rhymes to be found in the different sections. In the MS L redaction of Roach's edition, Branch I yields 26.5%, Branch II, 21.3%, Branch III, 20.8%, Branch IV, 14.1%, Branch V, 12.6%, and Branch VI, 12.3%. While these figures might suggest a bipartite division into Branches I–III, and IV–VI, a careful examination of the text leads me to propose a division into three sections, Branch I, Branches II and III, and Branches IV–VI.[2] Let us now consider the evidence on which this assumption is based.

The fact is that Branches IV–VI, or rather III/16–VI, (=C1ii), contain certain expressions and stylistic features which are largely, or wholly absent from Branches II and III/1–15 (= C1i). Branch I must be left aside, partly because of its higher rich rhyme proportion, partly for reasons gone into below, though the same features are also largely absent from this branch. These features strike the reader at first sight, let alone after a detailed study. Now, it is clear that the presence of the same expression in two different texts is of no significance, if that expression can be considered a cliché, or formula, but if one text contains a series of clichés and another does not, I believe we may reasonably conclude that the two texts are probably not by the same author, assuming the two texts are of the same type, e.g. two romances. The essential point here is that the absence of a particular cliché is generally more significant than its presence. I will now attempt to show that the same characteristic features, while they are found all through C1ii, are almost wholly absent from C1i.[3] I have selected eight of these stylistic features, which I give here with their distribution in MS L. I have used MS L because, as indicated in the last chapter, I am inclined to think, with P. Gallais,[4] that this is the more primitive version of the text. However, while the pattern does vary, it is rare that any of the following features is markedly less frequent in MS A than in MS L. Where this is the case, I will indicate it, but it should be said that, in general, all the features are slightly more frequent in L than in A, and that the incidences in L often coincide with those in A and, when they do not, often with P, U or S, also variously with E and TV, and of course with MQU in the latter part of the text, cf. Chapter 1.

1. The *formule de conteur*, addressed to the audience or reader: 'Que vos iroie plus contant?'. Such formulae are extremely common in verse romances. However, it is noticeable that each author tends to have a preference for one or two in particular. Thus the author of *Meriadeuc*, for example, often uses the line 'Mais ke feroie plus lonc conte?'. One thinks also of *Méraugis*, which contains more than twenty formulae of the type 'Qu'en diroie?'. This particular formula 'Que vos iroie plus contant?' is not one of the most common.[5] It is not, admittedly, over-frequent in C1ii (L 3503, 3891, 6031, 6999), but it is not found at all in C1i.

2. The line, or hemistich, of padding, ending with 'se Diex (Damediex) m'aï(s)t', used to provide a convenient rhyme for 'di(s)t'.[6] There is one occurrence of this Branch I, L 37; there are two in C1i: 1263, 2815; and there are sixteen in C1ii: 3127, 3311, 3697, 3799, 4535, 5485, 5779, 6507, 6631, 6801, 6869, 7893, 8707, 8791, 9209, 9301, of which the first five are in III/16–IV/6.[7] It is not necessary to go into proportions to see that this feature is rare in C1i, common in C1ii.

3. In C1ii, knights who are fighting tend to attack one another, or strike blows, 'menu et sovant' or 'sovant et menu': L 4883, 5024, 6281, 7147. This expression is not found in III/16–IV/6, but then the only combat description in this section is that by Gauvain himself of his fight with Bran de Lis. There is one line of this type in C1i, L 1901.[8]

4. The use of a rhetorical 'Savez . . .?', addressed to the audience, is common in C1ii, where there are eleven instances of it: L 3170, 3772, 4417,

5887, 6066, 6133, 6473, 6698, 7458, 8424, 8908; cf. also 5071, 8386. It is not found in C1i.[9]

5. Another fairly banal expression found in C1ii is 'Son escu et sa lance prent' or 'Puis prent sa lance et son escu'. What more natural, in effect, than that a knight should perform this action? Yet there are no lines of this sort in C1i, while there are six in C1ii: L 4613, 4747, 5098, 5389, 6171, 9009.[10]

6. In C1ii, there are a number of lines which start with an apostrophe addressed to the audience: 'Seignor . . .'. In all, there are twenty-three such lines, of which one has 'seignor' in the middle of the line, rather than at the beginning. There are only four instances of this feature in MS A, but many of those in L are supported by P,U, PU or even SPU. There is also one isolated occurrence in C1i, L 2063.[11]

7. Another stylistic trait of the author of C1ii, apparently fairly banal,[12] is the hyperbolic affirmation which assures us that 'Ainç si grant joie ne veïstes Puis cele eure que vos nasquistes', or something similar. There are several such affirmations in C1ii: L 3819, 4499, 5211, 6457, 7229, 9335, but none at all in C1i.

8. The most strikingly repeated phrase in C1ii must be 'Estrangement se merveilla' or 's'esmervella', 's'en mervella'. It occurs nine times, at L 4010, 4563, 6940, 8041, 8369, 8512, 8870, 8951, 9399. This line also occurs in P IV/5 (App. II 490). Nowhere is it found in C1i. In C1ii, A has three instances, and two of 'Estrangement s'est merveilliez'.[13]

Thus we have divided C1 into three sections, Branch I, Branches II and III (less III/16), and Branches IV–VI (plus III/16). The eight features we have just looked at, although each might be insignificant by itself, constitute together a strong argument for this division. We should remember also that this view would appear to be supported by the figures for rich rhyme proportions in MS L, although the figures in MS A might argue against it. There is admittedly considerable variation in the proportion of rich rhymes in Branch IV, but not enough to seriously undermine the view that the whole of C1ii is the work of one author. Overall, Branches IV–VI yield 13.4% of rich rhymes.[14] There is a certain amount of purely linguistic evidence to support this analysis,[15] and little to contradict it.

At this point I will briefly attempt a hypothetical reconstruction of the process of formation of C1 as we know it. Naturally, this hypothesis is influenced by the evidence I have just exposed, but at the same time, that evidence is entirely independent of the hypothesis, and rejection of the latter would in no way invalidate the former.

Clearly, the first part of the text to be joined on to the unfinished *Perceval*, although not necessarily the first to be written, since several of the branches may already have existed as self-contained stories, must have been Branch I, which takes up the adventures of Gauvain where Chrétien left off. I would suggest that initially only this branch was added to the *Perceval*.

Let us look at the evidence for and against this hypothesis. First of all, it is clear that the pronounced difference in rich rhyme percentage between Branch I and the rest of C1[16] would appear to indicate some kind of change: the author of Branch I clearly attempted to imitate Chrétien in this respect, and the author(s) of the remainder did not, or could not. It is possible, of course, that we are dealing with only one author, who simply could not sustain such a high level of rich rhymes, but I do not lend much weight to this possibility. Secondly, and this is crucial, one manuscript, R[17] breaks off just before the end of Branch I in MS A (1130), at a point which corresponds almost exactly to the end in MS L, although the final line of R, 'Ou il par force ou par amor' is not found in L. Thus we actually possess an extant version of the C1 which merely concludes the *Perceval*, or more accurately, the adventure in progress when Chrétien broke off. It is true that the version of Branch I contained in MS R is somewhat inflated; it consists of 1405 lines, whereas A has 1172 lines, and L 1070, and that this might cast doubts on the authenticity of its evidence as regards the existence of this short form of C1. However, there are two equally plausible answers to this objection: firstly, the tendency of the scribe of R, throughout the *Perceval*, is to pad out his model,[18] and once free of the inhibiting effect of copying the Master's work, he may have given free rein to this penchant; secondly, if R really represents the first stage in the formation of C1, there is no logical reason why it should not contain the original version, subsequently revised and slimmed down by the remanieurs responsible for the versions represented by A and L. We may add to this that there is no obvious reason why the scribe of R should not have copied the rest of C1, if it existed, nor is C1 the last text in the manuscript, which would rule out external factors such as illness. Finally, there is one detail which might be significant: prior to his combat with Guiromelant, Gauvain sends two messengers to him. Now, in MSS R,L,SP, these messengers are Yvain and Girflet le fils Do,[19] but in MS A, although Yvain is still one messenger, the second is one Gui(n)gan de Dolas, a knight unknown elsewhere in verse romance. It is clear that the scribe of A, or his model, has made a change here. Guiromelant says he has always wanted to meet these two; why should he wish to meet the unknown Gui(n)gan? Logically, although not necessarily, the answer could be that in the original short version of C1, there was no reason why Girflet should not be present. Later, when Branch IV had been added, the scribe of A's model, realizing that Girflet should really be imprisoned in the Chastel Orgueillous, or at least on his way there, instituted this minor change. On the other hand, if no short version ever existed, the scribe may not have been troubled by this small anomaly, owing to the bulk of material, and also the large amount of time in Branch III, with its condensed time-scale, separating Branches I and IV.

To sum up, the first stage in the development of C1 would seem to have been the addition to the unfinished *Perceval* of Branch I, concluding the Guiromelant episode. The manuscript evidence for this is provided by MS R.

We come now to the second stage, and also the less firm ground. I feel that the next element to be added to the *Perceval*-C1 corpus was a large, composite one: the whole of III/16, IV, V, VI, and C2i, i.e. that part of C2 which is preserved in MS A, in other words up to A 10268, see *infra*. This compilation, it seems to me, is the product of one author who almost certainly reworked or rewrote existing stories. That he used source material is suggested (a) by the autonomous nature of the various parts of this corpus, and (b) by the existence of analogous lai-type material, in the case of III/16 (*Lai du Cor*), VI (*Guingamor, Vengeance Raguidel*), and C2i (*Tyolet*).

It is admittedly impossible to explain why the short episode III/16, involving Caradoc, should have been included with the rest, unless it was simply a case of collating several works by one author. The addition of Branch IV, at least, is logical enough, in that it concerns an expedition to rescue Girflet from the Chastel Orgueillous, where he stated that he would go in the *Perceval*.[20] However, I do not believe that Branch IV was composed on the inspiration of this brief reference to the Chastel, but rather that an extant story was here cobbled onto the *Perceval*-C1 corpus, probably bringing with it a number of works by the same author, or assembled by a remanieur (although then the reason for the inclusion of Guerrehés' adventure is hard to see), including a Gauvain Grail adventure,[21] and culminating in an attempt to continue Perceval's adventures.

Of course, the main objection to this theory is that we have no extant text of the C1 in which Branches II and III (1–15) are lacking. Yet, if we are dealing with different authors, as the rhyming and other stylistic criteria would seem to indicate, it is highly improbable that all the elements of the C1 should have been assembled simultaneously.

The next and final stage of the formation of C1 as we know it would then have been the addition of Branches II and III (1–15). The insertion of these two sections, which could well be attributable to one author, judging by the versification, has adequate motivation. In the case of Branch III, the story of Caradoc Briébras, the presence of the short *Lai du Cor*-type section (III/16), with Caradoc as its hero, is the factor which draws this other story, composed possibly at an earlier date, to explain the epithet Briébras.[22] The motivation of the inclusion of the 'cor' episode itself is, of course, open to doubt. In the case of Branch II, the siege of Branlant and Gauvain's adventure with the 'pucelle de Lis', the motivation was presumably to include an episode related by Gauvain further on in the text (IV/5), and which may, in spite of the time supposed to have elapsed, have been thought to be lacking in the otherwise linear narration of his adventures.

How far can the hypothesis that the insertion of these adventures followed the addition of Branches IV–VI to the rump of the *Perceval*-C1 be justified, and if this was the case, which was included first? As to this second question, it would seem logical that the Caradoc section was the first to be included, rather than Branch II, as otherwise the latter would have been in very close proximity to Gauvain's account of the same events in IV/5. However, it is equally possible that one author was responsible, both for the composition of Branch II, and for the composition/redaction of Branch III, and that they were added simultaneously. In either case, it seems possible that the presence of one Ysave de Carahés in both these sections is due to a borrowing from Branch III during the composition of Branch II, unless the character is borrowed by one or both from Branch I.[23]

What of the arguments in favour of the idea that these sections were added last of all? Apart from the indications that Branch II is based on Gauvain's account in IV/5, rather than the reverse,[24] there is little,[25] except for a certain amount of circumstantial evidence provided by the chronology.

There are certain chronological inconsistencies in the first four branches of C1. These anomalies were pointed out by Heinzel,[26] although he did not draw the relevant conclusions from them. Gauvain's adventure with the 'pucelle de Lis' takes place during the siege of Branlant, in Branch II. After it he convalesces for six months (L 1996, A 2006). Thus his son by the pucelle should have been born shortly after the end of the siege. When we first encounter the son, in Branch IV, he is four or five years old (L 4902, A 5036, cf. A 4395, App. II PU 1). It is true that MQ have ten years old, cf. E 14774, and the figures are not attested by the rhyme, but the boy's actions are better suited to a younger child, and four or five is clearly more appropriate. However, between Branches II and IV we have Branch III, the 'Livre de Caradoc'. A long period of time elapses in this branch, which covers the marriage of Caradoc's parents, his conception and birth, his growth to manhood, a spell of illness, his subsequent marriage and accession, and so on. Altogether, the events of Branch III could scarcely be condensed into less than twenty years.[27] Furthermore, a year elapses between III/16 and IV/1, from one Pentecostal feast to the next (L 3115, A 3099; L 3373, A 3329). Thus Gauvain's son, in Branch IV, should be around 25 years old. That is, of course, assuming that we are dealing with a linear narrative, which the III/15–III/16–IV/1 transitions seem to suggest is the case. However, if Branch III was not originally in the text, these inconsistencies would disappear, and the statements about the length of Girflet's captivity — three, four or five years, according to most of the MSS (PU 3676, PU 3677, cf. EMQ 12768, 12786, 12790) although AS are less precise — would also be more consistent. Since Girflet was present at the end of the siege of Branlant, except in MS A, cf. my remarks on Gui(n)gan de Dolas, his captivity must have begun since then. However, the siege took at least seven years (L 1140, A 1219), which would mean Girflet was not made captive for at least seven years after he stated, in the *Perceval*, that he would go to the Chastel Orgueillous. Logically, and judging by what King Arthur says in IV/2 ASP, the fact that Girflet is a prisoner in the Chastel implies that he was captured there, or near there. If Branch IV was originally an independent story, which is perfectly possible, there is no reason why this should seem odd, yet if an independent Branch IV was joined on to the existing C1, it seems probable that the C1 did not yet contain Branch II. The reasoning is this: the events of Branch I take place shortly after Gauvain left court, in the *Perceval*, and there is no real reason why Girflet should not still be there. Then an unspecified period of time elapses, during which Girflet could be assumed to have set off for the Chastel Orgueillous, as he had said he would. Then Arthur and the others set out to look for him, when he has been a prisoner for some years. Logically, Girflet would have gone to the Chastel soon after he promised to do so, not seven or more years later. A passage straight from Branch I to Branch IV would contain no real chronological anomalies, and it seems to me that the *Perceval*-C1 corpus would have been more likely to attract to itself the Branch IV story, if C1 consisted only of Branch I.

In conclusion, it must be reiterated that as long as we have no trace of a MS containing C1 Branches I and IV–VI, but not II and/or III, all this remains pure speculation, however plausible it may or may not seem to the reader.

I have suggested that the addition of Branches II and III was the final stage in the formation of C1 as we know it. This is not strictly true, however, as I believe, with Gallais,[28] that Gauvain's narration of the events of Branch II, as found in IV/5, may well have undergone a recasting, subsequent to the introduction of Branch II. Thus, as I suggested in the previous chapter, the primitive version of IV/5 would be that of PU-EMQTV. Finally, of course, came the LRed. of C1, attempting to make the text into more of a genuine continuation of Chrétien's work than the pot-pourri it had now become, by introducing several new episodes, linking it more closely with the events of the *Perceval*. No-one, surely, still clings to the belief that the LRed. preceded the SRed., and the crucial question is that of the relative chronology of the C1 LRed., C2, and CM.[29]

The C1/C2 break

It is now time to turn our attention to the break between C1 and C2. As I have briefly indicated, I consider that the first part of C2 (C2i, or A 9457–10268 = L 9509–10404) forms a part of the C1ii corpus and, it should be said, is thereby distinct from the rest of C2. My contention is that the first break we can define in C2 comes at A 10268 of the SRed. (LRed. E 20530).[30] From this point on, until E 20620, the manuscript tradition is extremely confused, as we saw in Chapter 1.[31] Subsequently, it is necessary to exclude the three episodes, 6, 7, and 8, which appear to be interpolated in MSS EPS; otherwise the text is fairly uniform in all the MSS, although there are variations, interpolations, and reductions, as we saw in Chapter 1. We have seen that there is little to support the idea that this text, 20620–32594, represents, as has been suggested, notably by Wrede, a LRed. based on a previous redaction, the SRed., thus continuing the situation seen in C1 and the first 800 lines of C2.

For the moment, let us compare C2i with, on the one hand, C1ii, and on the other, the remainder of C2. For the sake of convenience, we will consider only episodes 9–35 (21080–32594, = C2ii). This obviates the necessity to extract 20620–20686 from the surrounding confusion of interpolation and differing redactions.

The first pointer to consider is whether there is a difference in the proportions of rich rhymes. In fact, there is no marked difference between C1ii and C2i, and C2ii, although the overall average in the latter text is slightly higher. This does not, of course, imply that we are in the presence of one text, by one author, but nor does it help us decide whether C2i belongs with C1ii or C2ii, so we must have recourse to other criteria, perhaps more fruitful. Before looking at other aspects of the versification, let us consider those stylistic features which we have already had occasion to note in C1ii. Clearly, though none of them constitutes an important pointer by itself, if a number of them were found in C2i but not in C2ii, this would be a strong indication that C2i belongs with C1ii, and not, as has hitherto been supposed, with C2ii. We will consider these features in the same order as before.[32]

1. 'Que vos iroie plus contant?'. This *formule de conteur* occurs only once in C2i, L 9981,[33] but it is not found at all in C2ii, whose author uses different expressions of the same type, see for example 23718, 24212, 24528.

2. The filler line '. . . se Diex m'aï(s)t', rhymed with 'di(s)t'. This occurs once in C2i, at L 9841, or twice, if we include 9619 (= *Perceval* 4066). This gives a proportion of about one occurrence per 225 rhymes. Compare this with C1ii, where the proportion is about 1:200. With such a proportion, we would expect to find this rhyme at least twenty-five times in C2ii, theoretically. In reality, we find it seven times, at 21751, 24011, 27527, 27867, 29843, 30999, 32507, which is about once per 820 rhymes.

3. The expression 'menu et sovant'. This occurs three times in C2i, at L 9801, 9831, 10395. The author of C2ii does not use this expression. The only line which resembles it is 26909 'Or josterent menüemant'. cf. *Erec* 888.

4. The rhetorical question, prefaced by 'Savez . . .' is not found in C2i. Curiously enough, it does occur once in P and ET, in the confused section of text following the end of MS A.

5. The line 'Son escu et sa lance prant'. Although this feature occurs only once in C2i, and that in MS L only (10291), we may contrast this with C2ii, where the knights tend rather to ride around 'L'escu au col, au poing la lance' etc., cf. 21162, 24711, *et passim*. Even the line which is closest to the expression in question, 25370 'L'escu au col, la lance prant', is only a variant of this latter expression.

6. The apostrophe 'Seignor . . .'. This is found four times in C2i, L 9613, 9814, 10043, 10111. It does not occur in C2ii, although there is one instance (20752) in the interpolated episode 6.

7. The 'veïstes/nasquistes' type of couplet. There is one such in C2i, at L 10029. Although the reading of L is slightly different, the other MSS all contain the line in this form. This feature is absent from C2ii.

8. The line 'Estrangement se merveilla' is found at L 9642, while C2ii, which contains several similar lines, has no instance of this particular line, with 'Estrangement'. Here are some examples: 'Percevaux molt se merveilla' 24274; 'Percevaux molt fort se merveille' 24487; 'Percevaux molt s'an esmervoille' 24707; also 26172, 26729, 27583, 32133. This last line would be perfectly suited for the phrase under consideration.

To these features we may add one more, not included in the discussion of C1i and C1ii only because it is not found in C1 III/16–IV/6.

9. Among the most characteristic features of C1ii are the two mentions of the Moors. At L 5929, we read 'Les pendans avoient fait Mor', and at 8719 'La cote pointe en fisent Mor'. Neither of these lines is found in MS A, but the second is in P (var. 8681–82), and both are well supported by the other MSS (EMQ 15931, TV 11851; MU 18765, TV 14511). In C2i, we find 'Par molt grant savoir furent (read: firent) Mor' L 10114.

This association of the Moors with craftmanship is doubly interesting, since not only is there nothing comparable in C2ii, but that is equally true for CG and CM, for our eight romances (*Inconnu* excepted), for *Lancelot* and *Cligés*, for the *Vengeance Raguidel*, for the *Lais* of Marie de France, for the *Tristan* of Beroul and for that of Thomas, and, as far as I know, for the anonymous lais.[34] The exception is *Le Bel Inconnu* 3952 'Par grant engien le fisent Mor'; this line is essentially identical with the reading of MQ in C2i, cf. A 10018. In both cases it may have been imitated from *Partonopeus* (846), although such supposition runs into the quicksands of relative chronology.[35] There is also a very similar line in *Ipomedon* (2740), and cf. *Galeran de Bretagne* 4784.

Although I feel that the presence of eight of these nine features in C1ii and C2i, combined with their absence from C2ii, is sufficient to show that we should divide the text not at A 9456, but at A 10268, I will attempt to consolidate this evidence by studying other, more general criteria. This, essentially, means the versification. I have already mentioned that the proportions of rich rhymes tell us nothing. It is useless to study the repeated rhymes, after the fashion of M. Delbouille,[36] given that C2i contains only some 800 or 900 lines. There are, however, other aspects of the rhyming which may help us, notably the use of inexact and dialectal rhymes, and of grammatical or identical rhymes, to which features we may add the use of enjambement.

The rhyming in C1ii generally is fairly careful and correct. However, while we may discount L 3477 *voir*, where the evidence of MSS EMQ,TV presents a satisfactory, indeed, superior, alternative (see Roach's note), there remain eight identical rhymes, at L 3503 *eüst*, 3701 *aler*, 3889 *li*, 4175 *non*, 4667 *ont*, 5565 *avront*, 6213 *convoient*, 8085 *mie*. Of these, several could be conjecturally removed, and 5565 could be edited out by reference to MS P; only the *mie* of 8085 is supported (by MQ). There is also one inexact rhyme in C1ii, L 7745 *aciever: vet*, and two apparent errors, cf. 8355 *tendus: encortinés*, and the curious *Graï: mi* 7739, although all of these could be eliminated by reference to MQU, which here follow the same redaction as L.[37] However, there is also an inexact rhyme in C2i at L 10097 *desus: tos*, where we have no point of comparison. This is also true for the one identical rhyme in C2i, L 10193 *lui*.

We can therefore see that there is no marked difference between C1ii and C2i, as regards inexact, dialectal, and identical rhymes. By contrast, rhymes of this sort are found in abundance in C2ii. Here are some examples: there are fourteen instances of the *blanche: lance* type of rhyme, generally considered dialectal, rather than inexact, 21997, 22301, 24445 *et passim*. The poet frequently rhymes *-s* with *-z* which is dialectal, 21515, 24461, *et passim*. Note also *departirent: tindrent*, 28007, cf. 28183, 29913, 30721;[38] *ainme: peine*, 22669, 26395, 28869, cf. *demeine: reclainme*, 24895, *prime: fine*, 21581; *forés: mes*, 25354, *forest: aprés*, 27639; and *mule: obscure* 27581. There are other inexact rhymes, mentioned above, often of doubtful authenticity. Grammatical rhymes are less frequent, but not scarce: 22505 *avoit*, 24995 *fere*, 26101 *avant*, 26423 *mestier*, 26679 *estoit*, 28637 *ot*, 30649 *mie*, 31163 *non*, 31691 *autel*, 32325 *ot*.

Not all of these rhymes, dialectal, inexact, or identical, are in all the MSS, but there are enough which appear to be authentic to underline the difference between C1ii/C2i and C2ii, in this respect. It may well be, though, that the dialectal rhymes are the best indication of this difference, given the dubious authenticity of some of the inexact rhymes. We may note, also, that C2i contains no dialectal rhymes, unless we are to include such as 9701 *ot: cevaucot* and 10365 *pertrus: enclus*, both essentially western.[39]

Now, let us look at the use of enjambement in the three sections. Needless to say, any definition of enjambement is open to debate, and I have simply noted the cases of what I would call pronounced enjambement, where the enjambement is clearly indicated by the punctuation.

In C1ii, there are seventy-six examples, at L 3217, 3301, 3358, 3426, 3636, 3827, 3868, 3896, 3924, 4191, 4196, 4585, 4630, 4646, 4653, 4686, 5018, 5208, 5216, 5325, 5538, 5574, 5603, 5617, 5683, 5686, 5718, 5730, 5776, 5792, 5899, 5901, 5945, 6014, 6224, 6344, 6470, 6492, 6618, 6621, 6637, 6741, 6758, 6781, 6782, 6790, 6794, 6971, 7078, 7191, 7200, 7419, 7784, 7837, 7846, 7850, 8100, 8256, 8347, 8369, 8478, 8591, 8778, 8786, 8831, 8974, 9062, 9095, 9129, 9162, 9180, 9295, 9303, 9378, 9426, 9434. The proportion is about one instance per 85 lines.[40] This compares with about one per 100 lines in C2i, where there are nine instances, at L 9545, 9551, 9565, 10137, 10151, 10170, 10256, 10285, 10296. The tiny difference between C1ii and C2i is put into clear perspective, when we see that C2ii contains seventeen instances of pronounced enjambement, at 21654, 22014, 22376, 23410, 23423, 24558, 24659, 24871, 25770, 26230, 26259, 26534, 29443, 30163, 30918, 31598, 32363, or about one per 680 lines.

All in all, I think there is sufficient evidence to warrant the conclusion that C2i forms a part of a C1ii/C2i corpus, rather than a part of a unit C2i/C2ii, and that as regards authorship, the division should be made at A 10268.

As regards the manuscript evidence for this idea, we have seen that the shift at the end of C1 is substantially less important than Roach's presentation suggests.[41] As for the shift at A 10268 (E 20530), however, one has only to read Roach's edition to see that there is indeed a change at this point, the end of MS A. The evident, and considerable,[42] confusion among the MSS in this fifth episode is indication enough. Does this indicate a change of author or perhaps a change of model? For the scribe of S, at least, there is a change of model: throughout C1, and up to A 10268 of C2, S is fairly close to A, but after that, it joins with E. Why this change?[43] It is an accepted fact that, sometimes, scribes simply changed their model,[44] but it is a strange coincidence that the scribe of S chose to change precisely at the point where A (not the direct model of S, but at least a member of the same family) broke off. Then the question arises, why did A break off at this point? I suggest it was because the scribe, Guiot, had no further model. That is also the opinion expressed by M. Roques in his article on this MS.[45] Roques also believed that C2, in spite of its position at the end of the MS, was not necessarily the last part that Guiot copied: if it was not, then Guiot did not stop at A 10268 for reasons of health, for example. The evidence of MS A is crucial. The fact that MSS BCH break off at the end of *Perceval* is accepted as evidence of the end of Chrétien's work, and similarly the end of KL marks the end of C2, and, to my mind, the evidence of R marks the end of a stage in the formation of C1, although here, as in K, there are other texts in the MS afterwards. Why should the fact that A breaks off be any less significant?

Briefly, then, our conclusions are these: (a) C2i belongs with C1ii (which is separate from the remainder of C1), and should not be considered apart from it, as far as authorship is concerned; (b) this means that in considering C2, we must bear in mind that there is a division Intro.-5 (C2i)/9–35 (C2ii), remembering that 6, 7, and 8 are interpolated, and ignoring, for convenience, the fragment of episode 5 which belongs with 9–35.

CHAPTER 3

THE STRUCTURE AND UNITY OF C2

Having established that C2 can be divided into C2i and C2ii, with episodes 6–8 interpolated, we can now study the structure and unity of the text, where the structure applies to the whole, but the unity, necessarily, applies only to episodes 9–35 (C2ii). We will in effect be considering whether, beyond the C2i/C2ii division, the text is a homogeneous unit, or the work of two or more authors, remanieurs, etc.

Structure

First we will consider the overall structure of the text, the interdependence of the various episodes, and the coherence of the whole.

Wrede believed that C2 boasted a particularly tight, close-knit structure, and produced a complex schema to support his assertion.[1] Three themes, or leitmotiven, form the basis of Wrede's schema, and it is undeniable that, as he suggests, there is a series of references, throughout the text, to these main themes. The themes are Perceval's dual quest, for the head of the white stag and the 'brachet', the motif of the Grail Castle, and, as the third focal point of his intentions, the Mont Dolereus.[2]

The Grail Castle theme is initiated in the Introduction, although clearly it follows on from the *Perceval*, and terminates in episodes 34 and 35. In between, there are references to it, of one sort or another, in episodes 2, 3, 16, 18 and 19, 23 and 24, 25, 26, 28, 32, and 33. Wrede says that there is also a reference in episode 15. In fact, Perceval merely alludes to the *voie* (22895) or *afere* (23095) he has undertaken, without specifying what it is, and could in fact be referring either to the Grail-quest, or to the search for the dog and stag's head. Certainly, though, episode 15 is linked indirectly to the Grail quest, via the *Perceval*. The Mont Dolereus motif is initiated in episode 1, with references in 25, 28, 32, while 27 might be considered a link in the adventure, which terminates in 33. The stag's head and 'brachet' theme is initiated in 4 and 5, with references in 9, 16, 22 and 23, 24, while 21 is a major link in the adventure, which terminates in 26. For episode 15, see *supra*.

According to Wrede, this series of references is part of a careful plan, and shows the tight, coherent structure of C2. I take the diametrically opposite view: the text is more of a patchwork than anything else, made up of a collection of disparate episodes, some of which are dependent on others, and many of which are loosely connected by these themes, even though the episodes are in no way related to the theme(s) in question, nor, in many cases, to each other. It would be easy enough to insert a reference to the Grail Castle, or one of the other main themes, into any episode, however irrelevant that episode to the theme in question. Provided an interpolator remember that, up to episode 21, Perceval is engaged in a triple quest: (stag's head, Mont Dolereus, Grail Castle), then that for 21–26 he is carrying the dog and stag's head with him, that up to 33 he still intends to go to the Mont Dolereus and the Grail Castle, etc., then the scope for expansion of the text is almost unlimited, in that another episode, or more, however little related to any of these leitmotiven, would pass unnoticed.

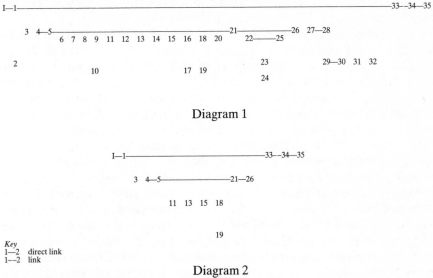

Diagram 1

Diagram 2

In fact these three themes, and the episodes necessary to their completion, can be depicted in a schema which is vastly simpler than that of Wrede, and serves to demonstrate how little the bulk of the episodes of C2 have to do with any of the three. In this schema, see diagram 1, I have linked together those episodes which are genuinely linked by the action, i.e., where the later episode is a logical and necessary complement to the earlier. It can be clearly seen from this diagram that there is a direct link between the Introduction (in the SRed.) and episode 1, which is in fact a continuation of it. In turn, episode 1 gives rise to episode 2 (found only in the LRed.), although this is not a necessary follow-up, and supposes that at some point Perceval will go to the Mont Dolereus. This he finally does in episode 33. Following which, he at last goes to the Grail

Castle, which is of course justified, regardless of the events of C2, since it is the ultimate reason for his wanderings, generated by the *Perceval*. In this sense, although there is no real link between episodes 33 and 34/35, the latter are linked, like episode 33, to the Intro./episode 1, which in turn provide the transition from the *Perceval*.

In the meantime, our hero has become involved in, and brought to a successful conclusion, another quest, that of the stag's head, contained in episodes 4, 5, 21, and 26. This sub-plot, entirely self-contained, i.e. independent both of the *Perceval* and of the other events in C2, is unrelated to the Mont Dolereus and Grail Castle themes, but is coherent and well-constructed; there are clear links between all the episodes. Perceval finds the Chessboard Castle, and the adventure starts (ep. 4), after which he hunts the stag, but the head and the dog are stolen (ep. 5), so Perceval has to find and recover these (ep. 21) and then return to the castle and claim his promised reward (ep. 26).

Of the remaining episodes, although some are inter-connected (10 follows 9, 17 follows 16, 19 follows 18, while 22 and 25, 23 and 24 are linked, as are 27 and 28, which could be said to lead to 29–32, of which 29 and 30 are a pair), none is necessary or relevant to any of the three main themes. Admittedly, one might expect some adventures between episodes 5 and 21, although none are necessary between 21 and 26, and there are a number of allusions to one or other of the main themes, but these are not important or necessary links in the chain of the action. In addition, several of these episodes raise expectations or questions which are not subsequently fulfilled or answered. For example, there is the promised quest for Perceval in episode 2, and one might expect to learn the identity of the knight killed in episode 7, although we may conveniently disregard these, as these episodes are clearly interpolated. Similarly in episode 11, we would expect Perceval to find the killer of Odiniaus, killed with sword and lance, therefore presumably not by the giant of episode 12, who uses a club. Perceval's promise to return and, presumably, marry Blancheflor (ep. 15) is not fulfilled, nor are his promises to his sister (ep. 18) and the lady of the Chessboard Castle (ep. 26). We might also expect to learn more of the Knight in the Tomb (ep. 25),[3] and one would also anticipate the return of the questing knights to court (ep. 28), possibly after at least one, perhaps Gauvain, had met Perceval, while episode 32 clearly reinforces the suggestion (ep. 28) of a second Grail-visit by Gauvain. Naturally, it may be argued that all these loose ends are due to the incomplete state of C2.[4] However, they hardly reinforce the picture of a tightly-knit structure, and there are also one or two anomalies which are harder to explain.

In episode 9, Perceval says that he has seen King Arthur not long since, 'Oanz assez pres de cinc jors' (21345); the variant readings differ, and might suggest corruption of the text, but are no clearer. However, Perceval's last meeting with the king was, in the *Perceval*, at least five years ago.[5] More importantly, in episode 19, Perceval says he wishes to discover the truth about the broken sword, at the Grail Castle (24012 ff.), yet, unlike Gauvain, who underwent the broken sword test in C1, he should not know anything about it. Another anomaly is created by the visit of Keu to the Mont Dolereus, from where he returns in a state of temporary insanity (28310 ff.), from which he subsequently recovers (28497 ff.). However, in episode 33, the damsel tells Perceval that anyone who goes to the Mont Dolereus, except the best knight in the world, will suffer the ill-effects 'a tos dis' (31547).[6]

All in all, it would be easy to draw up a second schema, containing essentially only those episodes necessary to the development of our three main themes. Such a schema is shown in diagram 2, where the interpolated episodes 2, 6, 7, and 8 have been eliminated, as have those enclosed by the start and finish of the stag's head adventure. However, for interest's sake, I have retained some episodes between 5 and 21, to provide some of the trials and tribulations our hero is supposed to undergo. On a purely arbitrary basis, I have included approximately every second episode, with any dependent episodes, on the 9–20 line. Subsequently, I have eliminated all the other unnecessary episodes, leaving only those directly concerned with the three leitmotiven, while episode 3 has been retained, as a transition between 1 and 4. This second schema is not intended to demonstrate any specific point, other than the fact that many of the episodes of C2 could be removed without fundamentally affecting the development of the main themes, and also, by contrast, that the real C2 does not have a tight, close-knit structure. In fact, it would be as easy to insert new episodes as it would be to remove those I have excised, or others.

Unity

Had Wrede's assertion that the structure of C2 was particularly tight been correct, there would be scant reason for examining the question of the text's unity. As it is, having seen that it could easily contain interpolated episodes (other than those which we concluded are indeed interpolations, i.e. 2, 6, 7, and 8) in so far as the structure is concerned, it seems a legitimate exercise to examine the homogeneity of the text, particularly in the light of the small anomalies mentioned above, and the fact that, as we shall see, there is some evidence to suggest that the text is not a single, homogeneous unit. It will be remembered that 'homogeneity' is used here to denote single authorship.

Let us consider first the evidence which suggests that the text is homogeneous, which, after all, is what one would assume, *a priori*.

Looking first of all at the versification, and specifically the distribution of rich rhymes, we find that, although the overall average is quite low (15.3% for 21081–32594), there is a relatively high degree of fluctuation from episode to episode. Discounting episodes of less than 200 lines in length, the highest proportion of rich rhymes is 20.6% (ep. 23), the lowest 11.5% (ep. 33). Although the difference between 15.3% and 20.6% may seem small — it is, after all, only 5.3% — it is of course equivalent, proportionally, to the difference between, say, 50% and 70%. However, the fluctuation in C2 (or strictly speaking what we have designated C2ii) does not appear, statistically, to be significant, taking a standard value of 0.05 as the significant value of P. Looking at the text as a whole, and using groups of 400 or 600 lines, we get values of P of about 0.175 and between 0.1 and 0.05, respectively;[7] these are not significant values.

It might be thought that this picture is due to taking too low a value of P as significant, and that a value higher than the standard 0.05 would give a more accurate idea of whether C2 is probably homogenous or not. Nevertheless, using the standard value, we find that several other texts do yield a value of P which suggests they are not homogeneous.[8] These texts include *Yder*, *Hunbaut*, *Erec*, *Thèbes*, C1ii/C2i A, CG, *Lancelot* and Beroul's *Tristan*.[9] Texts which do not show a significant value of P include *Inconnu*, *Cligès*, *Eneas*, *Ipomedon*, *Protheselaus*, and *Yvain*, while *Méraugis*,[10] *Meriadeuc* and C1ii/C2i L show a significant value for groups of 400 lines, but not for groups of 600 lines. It is worth pointing out in this context that the only significant value of P arrived at in studying C2 is obtained by comparing the central section (episodes 22–25, or, equally, 21–25, 20–25, 20–26)[11] with the preceding and following sections. However, even here the only significant figure is that resulting from a comparison of the central section with the last section; comparing the first section with the second or third does not yield a significant figure. Since, in effect, such a comparison involves taking the group with the highest proportion of rich rhymes, the central section, in isolation, and comparing it with the remainder of the text, we should not lend too much weight to the results.

In brief, then, while there is considerable fluctuation of rich rhyme proportions in C2, it is not statistically significant, and, while this does not necessarily mean that the text is homogeneous, it does mean that we are not authorized to conclude, from the variations in rhyming, that it is not. Thus, in a negative sense, it may be considered a positive piece of evidence.

Having ascertained that the versification does not weaken the idea of single authorship, let us look at the style and language of the text, confining our attention, as always, to episodes 9–35.

From the linguistic point of view, there are features in C2 which might be thought to reinforce the argument in favour of homogeneity. Essentially, these are all features characteristic of the northern or north-eastern dialects, and which would seem clearly to indicate a picard origin for our text. Firstly, there is the abundance of rhymes in *-iee* reduced to *-ie* (21499, 21573, 21625, 21716, etc.); there are some fifty-six of these rhymes in C2. Secondly, there is the regular occurrence of the mixed rhymes of the *lance*: *branche* type, which are sometimes held to be characteristic of northern texts.[12] Rhymes of this type are much less frequent, but well distributed throughout the text. There are sixteen in all (21179, 21589, 22301, 22633, etc.), and if one or two are of doubtful authenticity, e.g. 21179, there are others, found in the variants, which could offset this, e.g. var. 26023. Other linguistic features found throughout C2 are rhymes of -s with -z (21515, 24461, etc.), infinitives of the type veïr, cheïr (22174, 23009, 24407, 24498, etc.),[13] the northern possessive pronouns no, vo (21809, 23661, 25193, 25267, etc.),[14] and the accusative personal pronouns of the mi type (21894, 23560, 25080, 26420, 27796, 32243).[15]

In addition, there are one or two linguistic features which are not so widespread, but which are also fully compatible with the idea of a north-eastern origin for our text: (a) the elision of the object personal pronoun in expressions of the type 'laissiez m'ester',[16] found in 25182 (E only) and 24425, as well as episode 7 (20853); (b) the non-enclisis of the masculine definite article in 'a lou matin', found in 24431, 25584, 25990, 27335, cf. Roach note to 24431.[17] It is interesting that these two features are found exclusively in episodes 20, 22 and 24, with the exception of 25182 (ep. 21), whose authenticity is highly doubtful. On the same note, it is curious that of the seven features mentioned previously, not one occurrence is found in episodes 16 and 17, which form an essentially autonomous unit. This is not true of any other episode, however short, for the section 9–35.

To this phenomenon may be added another, the fact that, of several lines which are repeated at fairly frequent intervals in C2, none is found in episodes 16 and 17. The lines in question are the following:

1. 'Ne sai que plus vos an devis'. This line occurs 9 times, 21398, 25319, 26314, 26688, 28028, 29584, 30314, 30930, 31330, also PT 20032, cf. A 9885. More often than not, it forms a couplet with asis. The problem with any line of this type, as we have seen for C1, is to decide how much importance we can attach to it when trying to define authorship. In this case, this line is found in C1 (P(U) 4182) and also in the LRed. (E 7080), but most notably, it is found in Troie, where there are seven instances.

2. 'Certes, fait Percevaus, amie' or 'amis', cf. Roach, note 21765. This line occurs eleven times, 21765, 21782, 21895, 22893, 23836, 25520, 31702, 32217, and (amis) 22079, 24942, 27340. Roach also mentions 23787, 24356 and 24601, which are similar lines, but not 31973 (cf. 24601) or 26450, where all the MSS but ES reproduce 21765.[18] Here ES have 'Certes, fait il, ma doce amie', possibly under the influence of the identical line in Yvain 1555.[19] This line, by its very nature, cannot be considered a cliché, but conversely, could easily be imitated, consciously or unconsciously, by a remanieur, particularly as it contains the hero's name. There is no similar line in the Perceval.

3. 'Que vaut que vos esloigneroie?', cf. Roach note 29454. This is found at 24212, 29454, 30224, 31334, 32272, while 28708 is very similar; it is undoubtedly a cliché as regards the sense, but as to the wording, that is less certain.

4. 'De toz iceus qui ore (i) sont'. This line, invariably forming a couplet rhyming with 'mont', recurs several times, 19740 (EPT), where the couplet is an adaptation of A 9817–18, cf. *Erec* 4061–62, 22146, 27552, 31550, 31622, 32566. It is certainly a cliché-type line, but I have found it only in *Protheselaus* 11421.

5. 'Qui molt ert avenanz et belle'. cf. Roach, note 21366. As Roach suggests, this is the most common line in C2. It occurs fifteen times in roughly this form, and there are several similar lines. To those mentioned by Roach from Chrétien, we may add *Perceval* 5820 (reading of MS A), also C1 A 4452, and *Eneas* 7410 and *Ille* 2838 which are similar.

6. 'L'escu au col, au poing la lance'. This line occurs often, in various forms, and also each hemistich is found independently, or they are together, but in different lines. Altogether, I would include the following lines in this section (some have similar hemistiches, such as 'l'espee çainte', or 'l'espee au lé', etc.): 20301 (ET), 21823, 22018, 22019, 22277, 23761, 23763, 24711, 24956 (EPS), 25370, 25715, 25957, 26871, 27238, 28466, 29089, 30118, 30175, 32001, 32002, 32004. Lines of this type must be considered genuine clichés, and, on their own, no great importance should be attached to their presence. Line 30175 reappears at *Erec* 141, while there are at least twenty-four lines in *Troie* containing one or two hemistiches of this type, and they are also to be found in the chansons de geste (e.g. *Raoul de Cambrai*, *Couronnement de Louis*, even the *Chanson de Roland*), cf. also *Thèbes* 3560, 3561, 5791; *Ille* 1914; *Protheselaus* 5446, 7186.

7. 'Hardiz et coraigeus et fiers'. Lines of this type, combining *coraigeus* (also *combatanz*) and *fiers*, occur at 22142, 25124, 27142, 29404, 29728, 30060, 30156, 31775, 31998. In nearly every case, the line provides a rhyme for *chevaliers*, the exception being 25124. The line is also found in the var., KU 21214, and Appendix VII TV 210. Again, I think this can be considered a cliché, or at any rate of slight significance, cf. notably *Erec* 32, 3391; *Cligés* 65; *Ille* P 671, P 1630.[20]

8. 'Que ce n'iert se mervoille non'. This line, which occurs eight times, 20112 (= A 9982), 24573, 24721, 25618, 27676, 28106, 28854, 31163, may be considered a genuine cliché. It occurs in *Troie* 15915, 20483, in *Ille* (P 1039), and in the C1 SRed. L 6222 = PU, A 8210 = PU, and the C1 LRed. 8844, 10183, 12017. It also appears in the *Elucidation* 312, the *Enfances Gauvain* 367, and *Meriadeuc* 9814, which are possibly later than C2, in *Durmart* 10653, which most probably is, and in CG 16323, which certainly is.

9. 'An ce qu'il iert an ce pansez/pansé/panser'. This line, which we will have occasion to note again, see below, occurs six times, 25454, 25608, 27614, 30564, 32070, 32115, cf. also 29272. I would not describe this as a cliché.

10. Lines of the type 'Et si que ja n'an mantirai', usually forming the second half of couplets with '. . . dirai' (or '. . . conterai'), are reasonably frequent: 20936, 23338, 24600, 25108, 27786, also Appendix XI K 4. This can be counted as a cliché, cf. *Erec* 6316; *Thèbes* 2070, 7476, 7961, 9980, 10142; *Ipomedon* 6758; C1

L 1626, A 7384; also C1 E 11846. This is the only one of these eleven expressions which occurs in episodes 16 and 17 (23338). Lines 25108 and 27786, as we saw in Chapter 1, are only found in ES. In passing, we might note that 24599 reproduces *Erec* 2541, 5388.

11. 'Desoz un grant aubre foillu'. This line occurs at 22257, 25689, 27228, 29174, 31918, cf. also 24701, also 32334, 29275 and 32351. This is merely banal, rather than a cliché.

We have, then, a number of expressions which occur fairly frequently in C2, some of them clearly clichés, and therefore of lesser importance, others whose importance is less easy to define. The problem that confronts us, then, is this: broadly speaking every expression which we may consider is either totally banal, and therefore might be considered negligible, or in some way striking, and might therefore be considered susceptible of imitation. In this instance, therefore, I intend to consider some more evidence, although it is of a similar nature. Here, the material consists of a large number of expressions which occur, more or less in the same form, at least three times in the text.

1. 'Onques mes nons ne fu celez'. 22375, 29324, 30683, 31062. = *Perceval* 5622, 8831. Manessier uses this line, 42003.

2. 'Qui de biauté resambloit fee'. 23756, 28131, 29726, and in all but EMS, 30946, also Q 25511. = *Guigemar* 704.

3. 'De par Perceval lou Galois'. 21343, 21524, 23469, 28613; 25060 is similar. This line occurs five times in CM, also.

4. 'Ne meschine ne damoiselle'. 28249, 29309, 29907, 30483; cf. 23019.

5. 'N'i ot sergent ne escuier'. 21738, 21883, 24560, 28144; 28107, 28123 are similar.

6. 'Qui iert plains de religion'. Similar lines occur at 23841, 24006, and 25804.

7. 'Et la pucelle coloree'. 26464, 27576, 29725; 26390 is very similar.

8. 'Atant ez vos une pucelle'. 24345, 26647, 31640.

9. 'N'ot plus belles tant qu'a Limoiges'. 21086, 29556, 29732, cf. Roach, note 23304.

10. 'Mais ce li torne a grant annui'. 21134, 22266, 23541, 24276. = *Erec* 5870, cf. also *Eneas* 10019.

11. 'Et som cheval pestre leroit'. 25686, 27592, cf. Roach, note 21726. There are similar lines, as Roach points out, at 25693 and 31039, at 31528 and 32164, and almost identical couplets at 21725 and 22259.

12. 'Qui toute estoit ovree a lambre'. 21108, 22788, 24506, 26360, cf. Roach, note 21108. Roach points out that this also occurs in C1 E (14322–A 4678), and cf. E 4584 (also E 7124).

13. 'Le bon chevalier, le loial'. 22718, 28700, 31424.

14. 'Tant com il dure a la reonde'. 22100, 25136, 25936, and 26052, 26782. = *Yvain* 6286. The line is also found in C1, T 13388, E 44.

15. 'Se je lou voir vos an disoie'. 22730, 29438, 30648, cf. Roach, note 29282.

16. 'Jusqu'au matin a l'anjornee'. 21405, 26963, 28445, 31245, cf. *Erec* 3120. The line is also found in LU 27594.

17. 'Tant ont chevauchié et erré'. 26315, 26522, 26825, cf. 29990. Similar lines occur in: *Troie* 6493; *Eneas* 3581; *Erec* 3667. It is also frequent in CM: 36917, 38923, 40349, 40504, 41321, 42106, and cf. 39032.

18. 'Parmi forés et parmi plaignes Par vallees et par monteignes'. This couplet, 23399, is very similar to two others, 28515, 31875. A very similar couplet occurs in C1 E 3635, cf. *infra.*, and also Appendix VII TV 1256 = 23400 (= 28515 = C1 E 3635 = *Troie* 2428). More importantly, there are similar couplets in *Thèbes* 621, 9947 (and cf. 10180, 10189), and in *Eneas* 365, cf. also CM 41611.

19. 'Qui molt estoit et belle et grande'. 25164, 25226, 25298, 30700, 31717, cf. also 24735.

20. 'Sus un molt grant chevau baucent'. 23205, compare 31049, 32204.

21. 'Qui basse estoit par terre aval'. This is not actually the reading of MS E at 21093, but cf. 27295, 28609.

22. 'Les blans hauberz ont andossez Et les chauces de fer chauciees'. These lines, 22194–95, may be compared with 24183–85 and 27023–25. Lines 22195 and 27023 recall *Brut* 9275.

23. 'Ne vos i faz autre devises'. 22166, 27682, 30326.

24. 'Or a il molt de son voloir Or n'a son cuer de coi doloir'. This couplet, 22751–52, may be compared with 25923–24 and 23674.

25. 'L'erbe i estoit et vers et drue'. 21984, 25721, 27030. In addition, 21981–84 are similar overall to 27027–30.

26. 'Formant s'am prant a merveillier'. 26288, 26632, cf. also 29690, and, from episode 5, 20563.

27. 'Tout lou jor tant qu'a la vespree'. 26081, 27377, 30511. In addition, 26082 = 30512, and the following line is similar in each case.

28. 'Ainz iert la terre si hideuse D'espines et si annïeuse'. This couplet, 23151–52, is very similar to 27511–12 and 28245–46, which are essentially identical.

29. 'Et quant ce vint a l'anuitier'. 22248, 30382, also 28251. However, in 30382 it is only found in ES, while in 28251 it is in all the MSS except ES. It is borrowed, perhaps consciously, by CM 40990 and CG 2680, 6094.

30. 'Car molt fu lassez et deliz'. 24671, 25697, 26472.

31. 'Es blans hauberz mailliez menuz'. Lines of this type occur at 22360, 23251, 26890, and in all but ES at 23820. Similar lines occur in *Troie* 8345, 11154, 11209, 11252, 15626, 17580; in *Thèbes* 4783, 9723, cf. 6209; in *Ille* P 2547; in *Perceval* A 2210 (of doubtful authenticity); in *Partenopeus* 2985.

32. 'Vasaux, fait il, trop grant posnee'. This is 21196; 30604 is identical, 31304 very similar.

33. 'Pres iert li solaux esconsez'. Similar lines occur at 21242, 23863, 26104, 29916, 30282, cf. *Troie* 11656, 19303; *Thèbes* 1523, = C2 30282; *Eneas* 10037.

34. 'Percevaux, li preuz, li senez'. 23864, 26332, 27096, cf. 27504. We may also compare these with 30230, 30387 and 30912; line 30230 = *Cligés* 4917 (in ES; the var. = 30387).

35. 'Parmi la grant forest ramee'. This is 21583; 21955 is identical, while 23967, 29245, 29991, all identical to one another, are very similar. In addition, 29992 = 21956, cf. also 23986, 25165, 30267, 32010.[21]

There is also a series of other lines which are repeated, and which, like 3 and 34 above, contain the hero's name, and are therefore likely to have stuck in the mind or, equally, simply to have been duplicated by accident, so plentiful are the instances of 'Percevaux'. There are two which are found frequently in more or less the same form: (a) 'Percevaux molt fort se mervoille', which occurs at 24487, 24707, 32109, 32299 (cf. also 22382, 27583, and 24274), and (b) 'Percevaux l'a mont esgardé', which occurs at 21131, 21631, 21999, 25478, 26209, 26545, 28293, 31445 and 31536 (cf. also 21327). There are thirty-three others,[22] some of which occur as many as four times, and two of which feature the name 'Gauvains', rather than 'Percevaux'.

It is easy to see from these extensive lists that there are a large number of expressions which recur in C2, often many times. Some of them might be left out of the reckoning, dismissed as clichés, others cannot, and yet others are more or less borderline. The important thing here is their number; even if all were to be considered simple formulae, forty-eight[23] expressions of this sort would constitute a substantial body of evidence that C2, or some parts of it, is the work of one author. The next question is whether it is only some parts, or whether the whole text is involved in this mass of examples. The answer is that every episode, from 9 to 35, is involved. We could look at the density of these common expressions in each episode, proportionately to the length of the episode. However, it would be more to the point to add first that a further block of evidence can be adduced, in this case consisting of expressions which occur at least twice, after 21080, in C2. These will not be listed *in extenso*, for the simple reason that there are over 150 of them, see note 22.

Certain things are immediately apparent from this mass of examples. There is a very substantial amount of verbal duplication in the text, and it does not in general consist of blocks of lines occurring together, which might have implied borrowing, i.e. multiple authorship, but rather of scattered similarities.

Other points are less obvious: all the episodes are represented to a certain extent, but if we take into account the length of each episode, those with the highest proportion of common lines[24] are 9, 10, 12, 13, 14, 20, 22, 23, 24, 29, 30, 31, 33, 34. Those with the lowest proportions are 11, then 15, 17, 27, 32, and 35. The remainder, 16, 18, 19, 21, 25, 26, and 28, are in between. None of this points to any firm conclusions, however, other than a general impression of homogeneity.

Now, in order to try to consolidate this impression, we may attempt to build up a pattern of linked episodes — that is, episodes in which the same lines occur — using four identical lines as the criterion for a link, and working on a triangular basis, e.g. 9–10 linked, 10–12 linked, and 9–12 linked gives us a triangle 9–10–12, all linked. This process produces the following pattern:

(a) 9 14 31. 9 23 31 = (b) 9 14 23 31
(c) 13 24 30
(d) 14 20 31
(e) 20 22 23
(f) 20 22 28
(g) 20 28 33
(h) 20 31 33 (e) + (f) + (g) + (h) = (i) 20 22 23 28 31 33
(j) 21 22 23
(k) 21 23 31
(l) 21 31 33 (j) + (k) + (l) = (m) 21 22 23 31 33
(n) 22 24 28
(o) 22 28 33 (n) + (o) = (p) 22 24 28 33
(q) 24 28 33
(r) 26 29 30
(b) + (d) = (s) 9 14 20 23 31
(i) + (m) + (p) = (t) 20 21 22 23 24 28 31 33
(s) + (t) = (u) 9 14 20 21 22 23 24 28 31 33

To this we can probably add 19 (and therefore 18) and 29 (and therefore 30, and perhaps 26), as there is a fairly clear 9–19–29 pattern.

Two points now become apparent. Firstly, the episodes missing from this pattern are 10, 11, 12, 13, 15, 16, 17, 25, (26), 27, 32, 34, and 35; yet it is difficult to separate, for example, 22 and 25, 21 and 26, while 13 is linked to 24, 30, see (c), above.[25] Secondly, there is a very imperfect correlation between these episodes and those with the lowest concentration of common lines; indeed, 10, 12, 13 and 34 are among the higher group. Were this not the case, we might assume that those episodes, broadly speaking, represented an original C2, and the episodes in (u), above, represented an interpolation or remaniement.

All this is really intended to show that, while one could attempt to show that these common lines divide up in such a way as to suggest interpolation and borrowing, such an attempt, which would require a computer, would be swimming against the current. The bulk of these examples, which involve at least 450 lines, and their spread, are such as to suggest fairly positively that we are in fact dealing with a single author.[26]

Now, it may seem to the reader that an inordinately large amount of evidence has been put forward to prove the obvious. However, there are points which might suggest that the text is not homogeneous, and we may now examine them.

The first indication that the text might contain interpolations lies in the presence of certain couplets, or groups of lines, which are repeated verbatim at precisely those points where the editor feels the text divides naturally into sections, i.e. at the beginning of various episodes. The most obvious example of this is the couplet 'D'eus vos voil ore ci lessier A Perceval voil repairier', which first occurs at the start of episode 16 (23121–22), and is repeated almost word for word at the start of episode 18 (23533–34). It occurs again at the start of episode 27 (28239–40). It is the first and second occurrences which particularly arouse the reader's instinct that we may be dealing with an interpolation, since they neatly enclose episodes 16 and 17, which form a complete, and wholly independent, unit.

Needless to say, the use of the same couplet in two places does not necessarily mean that the text in between is interpolated, cf. the evidence alluded to above, but the process is by no means unknown. For example, in the LRed. of C1, at the beginning of the interpolated episode I/6, we find these lines:

Si vos conterons de Gauvain	1957
Qui s'an vet par bois et par plain:	
Par plains, par landes, par bruieres,	
Primes avant et puis arieres,	1960

the first couplet occurring in EMQU, the second in EU only. At the beginning of episode I/7, that is, at the end of the interpolation, we find these, very similar, lines:

Par vallees at par monteignes	3635
Et parmi bois et parmi plaignes,	
Primes avant et puis ariere	
Tant que vint a une riviere	3638

the latter couplet occurring in MQ as well as EU. Note that 3637 corresponds to 1960.

A more striking example is found at the end of CG, where not only are the last fourteen lines of C2 repeated verbatim, but roughly one half of the last 140 lines were borrowed, or adapted, doubtless by the remanieur who inserted CG between C2 and CM, from episode 35 of C2 (CG 16946 ff.; C2 32268 ff.).

There is another instance of this type of duplication in C2. In the opening section of episode 22, we see Perceval asking God to guide him to the castle 'Ou il vit lou bel eschaquier Et les eschas, qui tant sont chier' (25445–46), shortly followed by the line 'Antre qu'il iert an ce pansez' (25454). This pattern is repeated at the beginning of episode 26, where Perceval again prays to be guided to the Grail Castle, or to the castle 'Ou il vit le bel eschaquier Et les eschas qui tant sont chier' (27609–10) and, four lines later, 'An ce qu'il iert an ce pansez' (27614). Again, it seems suspicious that these two sets of lines neatly encapsulate episodes 22–25, which form an unnecessary pause between episodes 21 and 26. That is not to suggest that episode 26 need follow immediately after episode 21, only that it might perfectly well do so.

So far, then, we have enough to arouse our suspicions as to the authenticity of episodes 16–17, and 22–25. By removing these, 23121–23532 and 25455–27614, we would, of course, obtain a LRed. and a SRed., of 11514 and 8942 lines respectively, from 21080 onwards, but that hardly proves Wrede to be correct. However, we are still basically in the realm of pure hypothesis. Let us now see if there is any other evidence in favour of the idea of dual or multiple authorship, remaniement, etc.

There is one more argument that can be put forward in favour of the possible duality, or plurality of C2. This argument, not without importance, is essentially a straightforward comparison of C2 with the very similar *Didot-Perceval* (D-P). In my opinion, the D-P is probably based entirely on C2 and the *Perceval*,[27] and never had any existence independently of these two texts. Admittedly, it contains one or two short episodes, notably concerning appearances of Merlin, which are found in neither text, and there are some divergences in those episodes common to the D-P and C2 or *Perceval*.[28] Nonetheless, a rapid inspection of Roach's edition of the D-P shows us the following pattern:

D-P episode	Corresponding to:
B	*Perceval*
C	introduced or preserved as link to *Merlin*?
D	*Perceval*, C2 11 and 12; *Erec*?; *Inconnu*?
E1	C2 4 and 5
F	C2 18 and 19
G	C2 16 and 17
H	C2 13
J	C2 33
K	as C
L	*Perceval*
M	*Perceval*
E2	C2 21 and 26
N	*Perceval*
O	*Perceval*
P	as C
Q	C2 35

If we look at this in terms of which episodes of C2 are represented, we find the following episodes are involved: 4, 5; 11, 12, 13; 16, 17, 18, 19; 21; 26; 33; 35. Curiously, this corresponds very closely to my structural diagram 2, given that the choice of episodes retained (from 9–20) between 5 and 21, in that diagram, was essentially random, and could just as well have been represented by episodes 11–13, 16–19. Naturally, the fact that episodes 14 and 15, 20, and 22–25, 27–32 (and 34) do not have any equivalent in the D-P does not mean that C2 ever existed without them, but it is an interesting coincidence that many of those episodes we originally qualified as superfluous are missing, notably 20 and 22–25. The omission of episodes 29–32, which concern Gauvain, would cause no surprise in the D-P, which is essentially devoted to Perceval, but why should the compiler of this text use episodes 11–13, for example, which are basically isolated incidents, and omit 23–25, which show Perceval overcoming obstacles which add to his prestige? This is the most notable omission, in that the D-P has Perceval return to the Chessboard Castle as soon as he has recovered the stag's head, and we have seen that this could easily be made the case in C2, simply by omitting 25455–27614, which are encapsulated by two sets of similar lines.

All things considered, there is not enough evidence to imply clearly the existence of a shorter version of C2 than the one we know. Faced with the large number of lines repeated in different parts of the text, the lack of any close correlation between them and any other pointers, and, most importantly, the lack of any text which does not contain all of episodes 9–35, we must conclude in favour of the idea that this part of C2 is a single, homogeneous unit, and should be treated as a whole. This makes a difference to our view of the text itself, in that, for example, instead of saying 'this passage is odd, therefore it must be interpolated',[29] we might say 'this passage is odd; why has it been included, what is its function?'

The importance of this conclusion in a broader sphere is also clear: in order to fully explore the development of the Grail legend, it is necessary to have as clear a picture as possible of which elements definitely belong to a given text. While it is not always possible to be so precise, particularly with prose works, the more positive information available the better. In C2, this concerns, for example, episode 22, where there is a reference to the Grail as a Holy Blood-relic (25791 ff.). F. Lot thought these lines were interpolated,[30] but there is no reason to suppose this, unless the whole episode, or unit 22–25, were interpolated. As I have indicated, while there is some evidence to suggest this, it cannot be shown to be the case, and indeed, should be assumed not to be the case.

CHAPTER 4

EPISODE FIVE

The fifth episode of C2, the one in which the SRed. comes to an end, is, from the point of view of the manuscript tradition, the most interesting in the text. It is also of particular interest because of the implications of that tradition for the remainder of the text. The sudden confusion in the manuscript relations, which, as we have seen, is one reason for locating the C1/C2 distinction at A 10268, as regards authorship, is such that we can justifiably discern three separate redactions of this one episode. These redactions are represented by the MSS groupings EPS, KLT, MQU. This is excluding A, of course; were V present, it would naturally follow KLT.

These groupings, it should be noted, apply to the text from 10268 onwards, and when we compare them with the groupings prior to that point, some interesting facts emerge. The previous groupings were essentially AKL-MQSU-EPT, then AKLMPQSU-ET, cf. Chapter 1, as the editor's page-headings indicate. However, the major group AKLMQSU may be subdivided thus: L-AS, KMQU, cf. A 9463, 9471, 9481, 9559, 10019–28 (K 10021–28), 10089–90, with L fairly independent, until 10161, and MQ forming a close-knit sub-group. Following 10268, then, we might expect K to remain with MQU, rather than to join L and T; and why has T joined L, or the reverse, while S joins E? It is simplest to disregard the comings and goings of P, which in any case is closer in some respects to ET than to the larger group, see below. As well as suggesting that there is a break at this point, the shifting of the manuscripts makes it virtually impossible to use the manuscript relations to help us decide which is the primitive version of the text in the section following 10268.[1]

Let us consider the events of episodes 5 as related in the various redactions, beginning with lines 10162–10268 (= E 20304–20530), which may be sub-divided as follows:

(a) Perceval enters the park, and kills the white stag. He cuts off its head, but while he is so doing, a maiden rides up and carries off the *brachet* (10162–10181; 20304–20321).

(b) Perceval gives chase, with the stag's head, and after a discussion, agrees to go to a nearby tomb to ask a painted knight what he is doing there. In return he will be given the dog (10182–10224; 20322–20368).

(c) He goes to the tomb, and in response to his challenge, a black-armoured knight appears[2] (10225–10240; 20369–20447). In this section ET contain a digression, describing the tomb, and relating, though not in great detail, the circumstances of the knight's residence there (20377–20425). It is tempting to suggest, although without any clear supportive evidence, that this passage must have been largely borrowed from P, see Roach's Appendix V, and placed here in what seems a more apposite context. On the one hand, the borrowing of a combat description, from C1, by the model of ET accords with this possibility, and on the other, it is more logical than that P should borrow the same passage — but only part of the ET digression — and insert it in a less appropriate spot. Nevertheless, no certainty is possible on this point.

(d) A combat ensues, and here ET expand it substantially by means of a borrowing from C1, cf. Roach's note to 20465–524. While the two are fighting, a third knight makes off with the stag's head and the dog, leaving Perceval much put out (10241–10268; 20448–20530).

Thus far, there is really only one version of the story, although there are two clearly distinct redactions. From this point on, however, we have two very different versions of the plot, one of which we can divide into two redactions.

The first version, A, is represented by the redactions EPS, KLT.

(e) Perceval, furious at the loss of his dog and his trophy, swiftly brings the fight to an end, cutting off his opponent's ear, and pursuing him back to his *arcel*, into which he disappears (20531–20561). At this point P inserts Appendix V.

(f) Perceval calls him in vain, and returns to his horse (20562–20586). Up to this point, although K is fairly independent, EPS corresponds to KLT, but now there is a substantial, albeit brief, divergence.

(g) In KLT, we are merely informed that Perceval

i Poignant s'en vait parmi la lande
ii Que nule rien plus né demande
iii Molt par s'en vait grant aleüre
iv Et lués en la forest oscure
v En est entrés sans atargier
vi Durement siut le chevalier
vii Qui son brachet en va portant.

In EPS (20587–20619), meanwhile, there is a section reporting Perceval's thoughts on his problem: he has no dog and no head, and consequently no reward, therefore he had better follow the knight who took them, rather than return empty-handed. This is followed by a section similar to lines i–vii above. It might be as well to discuss the relative authenticity of these two versions at this point. Several points are relevant: firstly, 20609–10 are similar to i–ii; secondly, there is an inexact, although acceptable, rhyme at 20611, *lors*: *esclos*; thirdly, the passage i–vii also occurs in MQU at the same point, i.e.

immediately before 20620. In my opinion, these points[3] suggest that i–vii are primitive, 20587–20619 an expansion.

From 20620 to 20687, and from 21081 onwards, all the MSS give essentially one version, with the exceptions which we have already considered.[4] However, we must now return to consider the version B of MQU between 20530 and 20619, the text of which is found in Roach's Appendix IV.

(h) The knight who appeared during the fight appropriates the stag's head and the *brachet* (1–16). The word *garder* is used, but cf. (j) below.

(i) Perceval is annoyed, and rapidly defeats his opponent, who says he would rather die than be defeated, as defeat would mean losing his lady, for whom he has been there three years, fighting regularly (17–47).

(j) Perceval sees the other knight make off with the dog and the trophy, and accuses him of breaking his word; he was supposed to guard them, not take them (48–61). This must presumably correspond to the knight's statement 'Or garderon Le brachet et la venoison' (15–16), although Perceval's reaction to that statement seemed to suggest a sense of 'keep', rather than 'guard'.

(k) The knight's only reply is that Perceval will never recover them, and that he should get on with his fight; he adds a reproach concerning Perceval's visit to the Grail Castle, and rides off (61–73). This is intriguing, in that it seems to tie in with episode 8, found in EPS, and not MQU, where it is related that this knight was sent by the daughter of the Fisher King, as a punishment for Perceval's remissness, in asking no questions about the Grail (20960–21007).

(l) Perceval now threatens to kill his beaten adversary, and the latter relates his story. He, like Perceval, was sent by the maiden in the Chessboard Castle to hunt the stag. Events fell out the same way as for Perceval, but when he had defeated the knight of the tomb, and found his trophy gone, he returned empty-handed to the maiden. She told him to spend three years in the rock, and if he could defeat all comers in that time, he would have won her love. Today was the last day of the set period (74–124).

(m) He entreats Perceval to surrender his shield to him, which will enable him to claim his reward. He will give Perceval another shield. Perceval agrees, having warned him never to say that he overcame him in battle, for 'Sachiez de voir que ma vertu Est grant, onques meillor ne fu' (147–48) (125–50). This recalls Gauvain's chivalrous action in C1 IV, as, to some extent, does (i) above. The heroic arrogance of Perceval's last remark is something which we would not usually associate with this modest hero, although elsewhere he displays confidence in his own prowess, cf. episode 21, 24911–17.

(n) Perceval surrenders his shield, and decides to inspect the knight's residence in the rock before choosing a replacement. The rock is beautifully decorated (151–80).

(o) Perceval chooses a shield similar, or even identical to his own, and asks if the knight can give him any information about the trophy-thief. He replies that the thief is from the Roiaume Destruit, and could direct Perceval to the court of the Fisher King, whom he calls Noc (Q- Not, U- Nor). He sets Perceval on his way, and tells him his name is Sagremor. Perceval in turn reveals his own name, and they part company (181–230). Several points emerge here. Perceval's shield must be the same colour as before (192) if he is to be recognized in episode 8 (20928 ff.), but again, that is EPS, this is MQU. The Roiaume Destruit must be the Waste Land, and the name of the Fisher King, who is not named anywhere else in the verse Grail texts, is of interest; *la cort Noc* also evokes echoes of *cor(bo)noec*. The identity of the Black Knight is curious. Surely only a primitive text would identify him with such a well-known Round Table knight as Sagremor, especially as Perceval and Sagremor met in the *Perceval*, and there is no indication of recognition here. However, this might be over-assumptive, and the reading of Q 225 (*Seguin*), although the line is hypometric, may suggest that Sagremor is a scribal rationalisation, due in part perhaps to a desire to correct a metrically defective line.[5] Finally, 231–237 are identical to i–vii (g) in KTV, and bring us back to 20620.

The first thing which strikes the reader of these 230 lines, leaving aside 231–37, which we assume are primitive, cf. *supra*, is that they present a serious anomaly, or series of anomalies. While the above-mentioned reference to an agreement between Perceval and the knight who stole the dog and stag's head is possibly not significant, the whole episode with the Black Knight is in opposition to the facts later presented to us in episodes 21 and 26. Indeed, in episode 21, we learn that the Black Knight is the half-brother of the trophy-thief, and he is not called Sagremor. He never went through the stag-hunt-damsel-tomb-combat routine that Perceval performed, and in fact lives in an invisible castle with his lady-friend; a far cry from the decorated vault of Appendix IV.[6] Furthermore, if the Black Knight was able, thanks to Perceval, to claim his reward, which seemingly was of a permanent nature (App. IV 106–07), it seems odd that Perceval is then able to claim his reward, in episode 26. The contradiction between the Black Knight's story and the Chessboard Castle lady's statement that 'ainz mes d'amer ne fui requise' (A 10123, also in L) may, I suppose, be dismissed as mere female duplicity, and I leave aside the varying lengths of time the Black Knight is supposed to have spent in the tomb, from three to ten years, given the general unreliability of numbers in medieval manuscripts.[7]

This blantant discrepancy between the narrative of Appendix IV and that of episode 21 leaves us with two clear possibilities: either, Appendix IV represents the original text, and episode 21 is a reworking, in which case Appendix IV would have been suppressed by a discerning scribe in the model of EPS, KLT,[8] or episode 21 represents the original, and Appendix IV is merely a hopelessly bungled interpolation, perhaps introduced to avoid the mysterious disappearance of the Black Knight and completely at odds with the facts given further on in the story. This latter alternative is perfectly plausible, yet it would be such an inept piece of work that it leads us to examine closely the first alternative. Were Appendix IV the original version of Perceval's encounter with the Black Knight, we would also need to consider the possibility that A 10268 does not after all mark a break in the text, and that this passage in MQU might be linked to C1ii/C2i.

If we look first at the proportion of rich rhymes in Appendix IV (1–230), we get an indication that, at any rate, it does not belong with C1ii/C2i, as the figure is 20.9%. This cannot be considered conclusive, in a text of this length, although it does suggest a difference between this and the rest of episode 5. In MQU we find 14.4%, with a higher proportion before Appendix IV than after it. The difference between Appendix IV and C2ii is even less conclusive, given the great fluctuations in rich rhyme proportion in that text.

There are various other features of this passage which are of interest, and they fall roughly into two categories: (a) linguistic or stylistic features; (b) verbal reminiscences of C1ii/C2i or C2ii.

Under (a), we find the grammatical and identical rhymes *avoir*: *avoir* (103, 111), *aler*: *aler* (215), the formula 'se Diex m'aïst' (61), and several instances of pronounced enjambement (60, 98, 114, 160?,[9] 197, 222), all of which could equally well come from C2ii or from C1ii/C2i, cf. Chapter 2. The rhyme *estre*: *metre* (7) would accord best with C2ii, cf. e.g. 23478, 27603, as would the *-z*: *-s* rhyme and the conditional second person plural verb-ending *-oiz* in *savroiz*: *Galois* (227), cf. 20191, 23282, 23453, etc. (although the *-oiz* ending also occurs in C1ii/C2i), while the western dialectal first person plural verb-ending *-on* (15) is common in C1ii, but does not occur in C2ii. The use of *cestui* as a nom. (191 MQ) and the final *-t* of *respondit* (12) cannot really be assigned to either text. The evidence of these features does not suggest conclusively that this passage belongs either with C1ii/C2i or with C2ii. Note that the verb-ending *-on* also occurs at 20752 (ep. 6).

Under (b), the following lines recall lines in other parts of the text:

1	Sor un grant destrier pommelé	= 30710 (ep. 31)
20	Et sachiez qu'an molt petit d'eure	cf. 20880 (7), 25006 (21)
63	Que jamais jor de vostre vie	} cf. 10204–05 (C2i)
64	Ne l'avrez en vostre baillie	
72	Quar onques n'enqueristes rien	cf. 9499, 9502 (C2i)
74	Et Perceval tout a droiture	= 23758 (18)
96	Par cele foi que je vos doi	= 26022 (22), cf. 26790, etc.
136	Ostez!. .	cf. 10038 (C2i)
149	Cil dist: Sire n'en doutez mie	cf. 23223, 23748, etc.
153	L'escu li baille et il le prent	= C1 L 5763; cf. 23101 (16)
161	La grant biauté ne la noblece	— 28083 (26)

162	Ne le deduit ne la richece	— 28084 (26)
163	Qui ert leanz ne porroit dire	cf. 22767, 26135 (15,22)
164	Nus hom ne nes un hom escrire	cf. 22768, 26136 (15,22)
178	Perceval a mout esgardee	= 25478 (22), cf. 21131, etc.
195	Or me dites, se vos savez	= 25103 (21)
198	. . . Par Saint Simon	= 27781 (26)
221	Seignor . . .	cf. C1ii/C2i
228	J'ai non Perceval le Galois	— 19959 (2), = *Perceval* 4562.

Unfortunately, the fact that there are certain verbal reminiscences, in Appendix IV, of the remainder of C2 (ii), is not very helpful. After all, there are only a few possibilities. In the first place, Appendix IV may not have been written by the same person(s) as C2ii, in which case whichever was written first may have provided material, perhaps unconsciously, for the other. In the second place, the author of Appendix IV may have been the same as the author of C2ii, in which case we would really have to postulate more than one author, because of the discrepancies between Appendix IV and episodes 21 and 26 mentioned previously, and we have already concluded in favour of single authorship for C2ii, so this can be ruled out. The fact that Appendix IV 195 corresponds to 25103 (21) provides a further problem, for we can hardly envisage these two passages being by the one author, but a mutual borrowing from or influence by *Erec* (583, 5386) is probably the solution here. We would also have to assume a substantial recasting of episode 21 (and perhaps 26), for which there is no evidence. In the third place, the author of Appendix IV could be the author of C1ii/C2i, and there is not nearly enough evidence in favour of this to counter that which we have seen as indicating a break at 10268.

It must also be said that each of these resemblances is, in itself, fairly trivial. However, there are two tiny pointers which are of interest. The verb-ending *-on* is only otherwise found, in C2, in 20752, episode 6, and the same line contains the apostrophe 'Seignor . . .', found in Appendix IV (221), but nowhere else after the end of C2i.[10] These two minute links between Appendix IV and the three episodes 6, 7, and 8, added to the correlation I have mentioned, concerning the Fisher King's daughter, etc., intriguingly evoke the idea that, if not actually by the same author, which is a possibility, if one considers the relatively high rich rhyme proportion in both passages, episodes 6, 7, and 8 may have been written into, or as a part of, a text containing the MQU version of episode 5. We might then suppose that they were mainly written out at the same time as Appendix IV, although this need not have been the case.

The fact that 20553, found in the episode 5 section where KLT,EPS conflict with MQU, corresponds to 21869 (and K 20554 = 21870) (ep. 12), while at the same point K contains a passage (20545–52) essentially borrowed from episode

9 (21267–74), may be seen either as supporting or as undermining the idea that MQU have the primitive version of episode 5, while the other MSS represent a recasting; it depends on whether we envisage borrowing or repetition as the more likely explanation for these similarities. My feeling is that the presence of these similar lines in no way rules out the possibility of MQU having the original text, and might be seen as supporting it. The further resemblances between this section of episode 5 and the remainder of the text (20558 = 20979 (= 25073 = 27847), 20569–70 cf. 23159–60, 20563 cf. 29690, 20575 = 27851), do little to alter this view, although again there are two opposing arguments. In the first place it is odd that of this passage of fifty-eight lines in KLT, seven should coincide with other parts of the text (sixteen in K). In the second place, it is odd that those parts of the text with which they coincide should be so widely separated (from episodes 8, 9, 12, 16, 26, and 29), suggesting merely that one man wrote the whole text. In the light of the evidence in Chapter 3, this must seem the more likely.

We might assume that K has the original version of the recasting, subsequently recast again by LT, EPS, but this shows how confused the text of episode 5 really is; any close analysis of it begins to suck the unwary scholar into a vortex of recasting and writing-out, interpolation and borrowing, and all of it hypothetical. Once again, we can draw no firm conclusions as to the status of Appendix IV, and of the various versions of episode 5. What is clear, however, is that we have a situation similar to that in C1, with the two versions of Gauvain's encounter with the Pucelle de Lis. There are two versions of the Black Knight's story (= App. IV, episode 21), mutually contradictory, yet found together in some MSS. One must have preceded the other, and while it is impossible to say which, common sense suggests that no sensible person would have added Appendix IV to the text if he had read episode 21 in its present form.[11] This in turn suggests that there may have been a primitive redaction of C2 which has been lost to us, or simply several abortive attempts to continue the story after 10268. Certainly episode 5 boasts multiple redactions, but it presents such a tangled web that it is difficult to do more than state the facts, as any attempt at disentangling these redactions, from a chronological point of view, is liable to founder in a welter of idle conjectures and vague, unsubstantiated hypothesis. Nevertheless, all things having been considered, and allowing for the fact that remanieurs do frequently produce anomalous texts, it cannot be said that there is any positive reason for supposing that Appendix IV is primitive, and given that KLT-EPS present a coherent and largely uniform version of episode 5, their version should be accepted as primitive, and that of MQU rejected as an interpolation, in any assessment of C2.[12] We may note that, like episode 8, Appendix IV seems to attempt to link the stag's head adventure with the Grail, cf. (k) *supra*, which might constitute one reason for an interpolation, and that the idea of the knight fighting all comers for a set period, to win his lady, might have been adapted from episode 13, where the knight in question was also approaching the end of his allotted time; he had been there more than six years (22073), out of the allotted seven (22144).

Although that resolves the question of Appendix IV, albeit in a somewhat negative and unsatisfactory manner, we have not quite finished with episode 5. It is not irrelevant to consider the evidence of the *Didot-Perceval*, although the most this can really tell us is with which version the author of that text was familiar, the relevant section being (Roach) E 540–631, D 522–605. A cursory inspection shows us that the version nearest to that of the *Didot-Perceval* is that of KLT, and this brings us to one final point concerning the text of episode 5.

In MS T there is a short passage (Roach's App. III), in which we learn that a second pucele, rather than a knight, makes off with the head and the *brachet*. She says nothing to Perceval or the Black Knight, cf. the similar statement in the *Didot-Perceval*, E 608–09, D 583–84, nor to the first pucele, whom she may or may not know, depending on how we interpret the statement that she gave no sign of recognizing her. Yet T subsequently includes the lines 'Durement siut le chevalier Qui son brachet en va portant' (vi–vii, *supra*). Possibly the reason for this passage is that the scribe[13] linked this pucele with the one found in episode 21, whereas the general impression given by the MSS is that the latter was the first pucele.[14] Once more, this little deviation from the common version, if we may speak of such a thing, raises intriguing questions, as does the fact that in the *Didot-Perceval* the equivalent of the first pucele is an old woman, and further, the difference between the story told to Perceval in episode 21 and the equivalent in the *Didot-Perceval*.[15] However, this is not the place to start a close comparison of C2 with the *Didot-Perceval*, and we will conclude by repeating that the variety of redactions in episode 5 strengthens the idea of a break at 10268; while also suggesting that there may have been a more primitive redaction of C2, after that break, than the one which is known to us.[16]

CHAPTER 5

THE AUTHORSHIP OF C2

> Gauchiers de Dondain, qui l'estoire 31421
> Nos a mis avant an memoire, '
> Dit et conte que Perceval . . .

The question of the authorship of C2, hinging on these lines (31421–23), has been long and widely discussed, but since the article of F. Lot on the subject,[1] the attribution to Wauchier de Denain, known as the translator of a series of *Vies des Pères*,[2] has been abandoned, until G. Vial's recent re-establishment of it.[3]

Lot himself destroyed most of the arguments put forward by M. Wilmotte,[4] who wished to see the whole corpus as the work of Chrétien, Gerbert and Manessier, and a series of interpolators/remanieurs, such as the idea that the use of the past tense *a mis(e) avant* evoked an event in the distant past,[5] although he added that 'Il reste que l'expression *mettre en avant* s'entend mieux d'un auteur dont on invoque l'autorité que d'un auteur qui se nomme'.[6] He also clearly made the point[7] that the silence of Gerbert and Manessier on the subject of any previous continuator meant nothing, since it is certain that neither these nor Chrétien wrote C2. Lot concluded that Wilmotte was correct to suggest, as had Potvin, that l. 31421 referred to an authority, not to the author, but that 'Cette autorité, quoi qu'il dise, est incontestablement celle de Wauchier de Denain'.[8] Wilmotte's other main argument against the attribution to Wauchier, that such a pious hagiographer could not have written the mildly licentious C2, has been effectively countered by Vial, who points out that if a single patron (Jeanne of Flanders, see below) was interested in such disparate works, there is no real reason why one author should not have produced them.

Let us now consider this crucial passage, for which the text given above is the reading of MS E. There are two issues to be resolved here: firstly what is the precise meaning of the much-debated l. 31422 'Nos a mis avant an memoire', and secondly is the gentleman in question actually Gauchier, or Wauchier, de Denain?

As to l. 31422, there is little or no doubt: Vial is correct in suggesting that this is a straightforward statement of authorship, not an invocation of Gauchier as an authority, or anything else. The famous expression 'metre avant an memoire' is simply a combination of two well-known expressions, 'metre avant' and 'metre an memoire', both meaning 'tell, relate'.[9] We can safely disregard the isolated 'A mis chi aprez en memoire' of MS T.

There remains the question of the identity of 'Gauchiers de Dondain'. Here are the various readings of the nine MSS containing this passage:

E Gauchiers de Dondain[10]
L Gauciers de Donaing
M Gauchier de Doudain
P Gautiers de Dons dist
Q Chanter dou douz tanz
S Gauchier de Dordan
T Gautiers de Denet
U Gauchier de Doulenz
V = T

We can probably disregard the reading of Q altogether, and as far as the choice between *Gauchier* and *Gautier* is concerned, the fact that the EMS group have the former, as does L from the LTV group, combined with the ease with which the *Gaucier* of a picard text could be miscopied as *Gautier*, although the reverse is also possible, suggests that *Gauchier* is the original form. Note that P, T, and V, all giving *Gautier*, are all northern-flavoured MSS.

The localization of our poet is more difficult. We have on the one hand the *Dondain* of E, which is effectively indistinguishable from the *Doudain* of M. The *Dordan* of S is similar, as we might expect from the close filiation of these three MSS, and all these three show a *-d* in the second syllable of the name, as, in a sense, does P. On the other hand, the isolated *Donaing* of L is supported to some extent by TV (*Don-* or *Den-*, no second *-d*); the *Doulenz* of U is completely isolated.

The issue is complicated by the fact that, faced with a proper name he did not recognize and, or, could not read, a scribe might well insert the name of a locality which he did know, in his particular region. Thus we can probably explain the *Dordan* of S, the only reading lacking the *Don-* first syllable, to which I regard *Den-* and *Dou-* as equivalent,[11] as a rationalization by this francian scribe, since Dourdan is south-west of Paris, in the department of Seine-et-Oise, about twenty kilometres from Rambouillet.[12] We might explain the *Doudain* of M, also francian, in the same way (*Doudain* for *Dourdain*).

This leaves *Dondain* (E), *Denet* (TV), *Dons* (P)?, for which I can find no actual equivalent,[13] *Donaing* (L) — the Denain of the Gauchier in question, which is just outside Valenciennes — and *Doulenz* (U), presumably Doullens in the Somme, about thirty kilometres from Amiens. Of these latter, Doullens is in one sense more probable, since U is a francian MS, not a northern one like L, and therefore the scribe of L might be deemed more likely to have substituted the name of a town in his region, especially as Gauchier de Denain was a known literary figure.[14] On the other hand, the transmission of proper names is, overall, slightly superior in L to that in U. Compare for example U's readings for Taulas (de Rogemont): Rolliart (21503), Calas (26843), with L's Taillars and Tallas, both closer to the standard form. This is only one example, but in general I consider L superior, though not to the extent that we can reject out of hand the *Doulenz* of U. Note that Roach, in his note to 31595, says 'L and V are particularly faithful in the preservation of proper names.' We may note also that the dialectal flavour of C2, essentially northern,[15] accords with a localisation at Doullens or Denain, and argues against Lot's idea[16] that the author was from Champagne or northern Burgundy.[17] Of course, Lot accepted, as we have seen, that this passage refers 'incontestablement' to Wauchier de Denain.

The only other source of evidence relating to the question of whether Gauchier, or Wauchier, de Denain wrote C2 is the collection of intercalated comments in octosyllabic couplets, found in his translations of various *Vies des Pères*.[18]

These are, unfortunately, of limited value, in that there are only 138 verses which can be positively attributed to Gauchier, plus a further 134[19] which can be tentatively attributed to him. A sample of this size tells us little about the author's use of rhyme, the more so as these verse passages are in short sections, the longest of which is only sixty-six lines, i.e. thirty-three rhymes. They offer little in the way of linguistic evidence, either, for the purposes of comparison with C2.[20]

Probably the most positive link between Wauchier and C2 lies, not in the verse portions of the *Vies des Pères*, but in the prose, where we find the following passage:[21] 'Dex! con[22] il sunt ore poi de gent qui a ce preignent garde; l'essample en a oblïé et deguerpi tote criature (118a) fors solement le livres en qui est escrit, qui vos le[23] met avant en memoire'. The presence of the identical expression, 'metre avant en memoire', which occurs in the relevant passage in C2, and which has been so much discussed, cannot be dismissed as mere coincidence, in the light of the apparent rarity of the expression.

Finally, there is one point of circumstantial evidence to consider. Wauchier undertook his prose translations for Philippe of Namur, son of Baudouin of Flanders, and may also have worked for Jeanne of Flanders,[24] the same Jeanne for whom Manessier worked, and the great-niece of that Count Philip whom Chrétien mentions in the prologue of *Perceval*. This coincidence, upon which Meyer remarked,[25] seems to point a decisive finger at Wauchier as the author of C2.

To sum up, it seems to me that, given the well-attested existence of a Wauchier, man of letters working for the ruling family of Flanders in the relevant period (c. 1200–20), the link between Manessier and Chrétien, and therefore the Continuations, and that same ruling family, and an express statement in C2 that this Gauchier is the author of that text, albeit there is identity of names only in one MS, it would smack of prejudice to suggest that Wauchier/Gauchier de Denain could not have written C2. Although no absolute certainty is possible, the onus of demonstration must lie with those who reject the attribution; their arguments seem thin, and, like Vial, I would re-establish this controversial attribution.[26] It is noteworthy that Roach, who earlier deemed it prudent not to ascribe C2 to Wauchier,[27] says in the preface to CM (p. xi) that 'the question of Wauchier's authorship of the Second Continuation has been solved decisively' by Vial.

CHAPTER 6

SOURCES, INFLUENCE(S), AND PLACE IN THE CYCLE

Sources

The question of sources for C2 (episodes 9–35) is an interesting one, but one to which there are few positive answers. Nevertheless, we may review the situation, and assess what answers there may be, positive or otherwise.

It is clear that the two positively identifiable sources used by the author of C2 are the *Perceval* itself, and C1/C2i. Perceval furnishes the basis, though not the details, for episodes 15, 18–19, and probably 35.[1] That is to say, given the elements of the *Perceval*, it would require no great imagination to produce these episodes. C1 is clearly a source of C2, in so far as Gauvain's Grail-visit is concerned, since that is evidently the basis of his accounts in episodes 28 and 32. It is possible also that C1 V/3 (Branch V, episode 3) was a source of episode 34, or even the only source, but we have seen that the version of that episode (the Black Chapel) which is closest to C1 V/3 appears to be a reworking,[2] and there are sufficient differences of detail, e.g. the transposition of the dead body from the Grail Castle to the Chapel, to cast doubt on, though not to rule out, the idea that episode 34 was engendered simply by C1 V/3 and the author's imagination. As to C2i, it is manifest that, since C2 continues it, it must have served as a source for that continuation. To what extent this was the case, however, we can only surmise. The two elements furnished by C2i for the author of C2 were the projected visit by Perceval to the *Mont Dolereus* (9830–39), and the quest for, and recovery of, the stolen dog and stag's head, coupled with the return of our hero to the Chessboard Castle to claim his promised reward (episodes 4 and 5). No matter that episode 5 was left unfinished, it required little imagination to suppose that Perceval was intended to recover his stolen property, and claim his recompense. Thus the framework of the plot of episodes 21 and 26 was there, although not the details, and there is no reason to assume that the author had access to a source-work containing these elements.[3]

As for episode 33, that could be the result of the slightly sketchy indications in episode 1 (9819–29), and the author's imagination; it would not be hard to associate any such magical feature as the pillar with Merlin, the great Arthurian magician. Indeed, the probable transformation from hooks or nails (*cros, clos*; 9823–19919) to crosses (31589–91, 31598–605) would appear to stem from episode 1, where the same mistake[4] is found, cf. Roach's note to 19919. Thus there is no real need to postulate a Mont Dolereus story as a source, and the apparent *cros* — *croiz* confusion even argues against it.

Of the remaining episodes, one other, episode 9, could be seen as stemming from *Perceval* and C1. The basic framework of episode 9, where the hero enters a castle, finds it deserted, goes into a garden where he finds a knight and a lady, and has to fight, is essentially that of Guerrehés's adventure in C1 VI, and the lion might have been borrowed from Gauvain's visit to the Castle of Wonders in *Perceval*. However, we have seen[5] that the mysterious axe in episode 9 might suggest that some other source was involved, as might the disappearing horse, and I am inclined to think this slightly more probable than the C1 VI — *Perceval* solution.

Episode 10 can be considered a part of episode 9, from which it stems directly, and Episode 11 echoes *Perceval* (and *Peredur*), where the hero finds his cousin (foster-sister) cradling the headless body of her lover (*Perceval* 3430–55). Again, though, as I have pointed out, the detail of who killed Odiniaus is missing, and possibly suggests a garbled source.

Episode 12 is banal, in that combats with giants are a commonplace of arthurian literature, cf. *Brut*, *Erec*, *Yvain*, *Inconnu*, and there is no need to postulate any specific source, although any one of the first three texts mentioned, and perhaps even *Inconnu*, may have contributed the idea.

In episode 13, there is little which might not have come from the author's imagination, although the detail of the 'Galois' and the 'serpent crestu' is curious (21962–67).

Episodes 14 and 32 may be considered together, as they pose similar problems: do they presuppose the existence of *Inconnu*, are they mutually contradictory, and what is their relation to C1 V/7–8? I cannot answer the latter question, but I do not think too much importance should be attached to the name 'Lionel' in C1. If these episodes stem from *Inconnu*, it is only in a very loose sense, i.e. they are references to a well-known tradition, represented by *Inconnu*. We cannot rule out the possibility that a prior version of the Fair Unknown story is involved, but why suppose it, and further, as does Wrede, that *Inconnu* post-dates C2, when *Inconnu* provides the relevant details, few as they are? Of course, we may then ask who, in relation to *Inconnu*, is the *amie* of Guinglain in episode 14 (perhaps the same as in C1 V/7–8), and where is she in episode 32? I feel that these are unimportant details, as is the fact that in episode 14, Gauvain's son calls himself 'Li Biaus Desconeüs' (LiBD), and in episode 32, Guinglain. In my opinion, Wrede's stress on this point, and the fact that Guinglain first says that 'li Breton' call him LiBD (22387–88), then later that the name was given him by King Arthur (31070–72), and his suggestion that this represents a progression, and means that episode 32 is interpolated, because later than *Inconnu*, itself later than C2, is essentially absurd. Particularly, be it said, since he assumes, wrongly in my view, that Guinglain does not use his proper name in episode 14, but rather his epithet, because he does not yet know the former. There is no reason to assume that this is the case, given that Guinglain might be better known to Perceval as LiBD than by his real name.

Episodes 16 and 17 present a case for a distinct source used by the author of C2. Somehow this incident has a traditional ring to it, which suggests it is not the product of our author's imagination, and nowhere else do we have any reference, except for the bare name 'Le Biau Coart' (or 'Mauvais', as here, cf. *Erec* 1696), which might have prompted this episode. However, the change from ugliness to beauty, undergone by the Biau Mauvais' *amie* (23529–32) is perhaps the only positive hint at a source.[6]

Episode 20, at first sight, strongly suggests a source-work, yet closer examination shows that this is not necessary. The castle full of ladies recalls the Castle of Wonders in *Perceval*. The empty, then populous, castle, a hallmark of celtic tradition, is found in C1 VI and perhaps C1 IV, and, in reverse, in *Perceval* and C1 V. Similarly, the awakening alone in the open countryside, similar to *Perceval*, corresponds closely to C1 V/6, and there is no other element in this episode which the author might not simply have made up, adapting the table from similar incidents involving a horn, e.g. *Erec*.

Episodes 22 and 25, like 16–17, do suggest a source, what with the mule controlled by a ring, the Glass Bridge, and the Knight in the Tomb. Nonetheless, it is only the latter which is hard to explain, other than by a source, since there are enough strange bridges in earlier works to inspire the Glass Bridge, cf. *Mule, Lancelot*.[7]

This last point applies equally to episodes 23 and 24, and these contain no other element which requires more than a touch of imagination from the author. For the story of the origin of the unfinished bridge, cf. *Guigemar*, etc.

Episode 28, as I have suggested,[8] might have had an independent existence —at least, the Bagomedés section might — in which case episode 27 would be a back-formation from it, although this need not be the case. As to the rest of episode 28, as we have seen, it shows the influence of C1 V.

Episodes 29 and 30 pose a slightly different problem from the others we have looked at, in that we need to decide whether a Gauvain source was used, as opposed to a neutral, or Perceval source, since the incident in episode 29 is clearly of the type associated with Gauvain, cf. *Perceval*, C1 II.[9] However, that very point indicates that there is no positive need to assume a source. Further, the Petit Chevalier could be drawn from C1 VI, and the magic shield could easily be adapted from such well-known stories as those of the *Cor* and the *Mantel*. Nonetheless, it is here that we find the clearest statement that a source was used, a point to which I shall return.

Episode 31 would pose few problems for the author's imagination, especially since the famous reverie in *Perceval*, and we have already seen that episode 33 is essentially based on episode 1, but the child in the tree might suggest a further source. There is also the link with episode 25.[10]

Thus far, a great deal of the subject matter of C2 can be explained as resulting from the author's imagination, combined with hints from C2i and elements adapted from, or inspired by, *Perceval* and C1, but there are also some small indications that he may have had a source for some of the episodes, in which case he may have had a source for all of them. Let us see what he has to say on the subject.

There are numerous references to 'le conte' or 'l'estoire', (many of which seem to have been suppressed by the model of ES), most notable of which is the slightly enigmatic passage at the end of episode 28 (29201–08), whose authenticity is in some doubt, as it is found only in EPS, cf. Chapter 1. We cannot attach too much importance to these allusions, even that to 'li contes . . . Qui a Fescamp est toz escriz' (31594), given that this might indicate precisely that the author was making up this part of the text, cf. the *cros — croiz* point discussed earlier. There is one other such intervention, though, which merits close attention, and that is the famous 'Bleheris' passage in episode 29, 29351–57. I will not reproduce the various versions of this passage here, as Roach has done so in his note to these lines.

What are we to make of this reference to 'Bleheris' (MS. L) or 'li escriz' (EMPQSTUV), and to the count of Poitiers (in LMQTUV, not in EPS)?[11] The overall impression we gain from the MSS is that the latter reference is primitive, and this might suggest that that in L to Bleheris is primitive also. However, M also gives a fairly coherent reading, without the reference to Bleheris, and the unanimity of the other MSS on this point argues against the reading of L. Nevertheless, the coherence of L is such that we cannot entirely discount the possibility that this is the only uncorrupted reading. In addition, we note that if, as it would seem, Wauchier de Denain is really the author of C2, only L has correctly preserved his name, in 31421. All in all, I am inclined to believe that the reference to Bleheris may be authentic, and that that to the count of Poitiers undoubtedly is. Whether our author is here alluding to a genuine, rather than a mythical, source, is open to question. Given the unexpectedness of an allusion to Poitiers in this text of northern origin, I would favour the idea that the reference is genuine. The source alluded to need not be a source for more than this one episode (i.e. 29–30), but it could be, and if a source was used for one part of C2, the same might apply to other parts. The overall impression that we have already formed is that either explanation is possible, either a source (or sources), or pure imagination and the use of *Perceval*, etc., plus standard elements. However, while some episodes of C2 would be more easily explained by a hypothetical source, there is really nothing which positively requires this.

Literary influence(s)

By literary influences, I mean those texts which influenced C2, and by literary influence, those which were influenced by C2. Regarding the former, we have just seen possible or definite influences on the content of C2, but we need to consider the form, the actual wording of the text. I shall limit my remarks on this point to indicating some of the many verbal resemblances to other, earlier, texts, which were doubtless imitated, consciously or unconsciously, by the author of C2, and which show with which texts he was most familiar.

We have already seen (p. 47 ff.) a number of points of similarity between C2 and other texts, which show, more or less, what we might expect: a basic familiarity with the three great 'romans d'antiquité' (but especially with *Troie*), and with the works of Chrétien de Troyes, in particular *Erec*, *Yvain* and *Perceval*. A look at some further similarities will largely confirm this pattern:

21086 etc. cf. *Erec* 2624; *Lancelot* 5804; *Perceval* 3076
21106 = *Erec* 3961
21199, 25597 = *Troie* 19664; *Erec* 2538; *Guillaume d'Angleterre* 644
21206 = *Yvain* 204; cf. *Erec* 391–92
21377 = *Cligés* 5028
21393 = *Thèbes* 939
21397, 29593 = *Troie* 19457
21472 etc. = *Erec* 5494
21577–78 = *Perceval* 8125–26
21651 cf. *Troie* 16363, 16464, 19278, 21753; *Thèbes* 2394
21767 = *Erec* 1055; cf. *Thèbes* 2983
21924, 25545 cf. *Troie* 14509; *Protheselaus* 4199, 10906; C1 L 7046
22026 cf. *Thèbes* 5674, 5718, 6364
22187–88 etc. = *Yvain* 5871
22349, 24971 = *Troie* 1836, 12163
22381 cf. *Erec* 3858
22401–02 = *Erec* 2619–20, cf. 1388
22475 = *Perceval* 562 (Roach notes)
22706, 27783 cf. *Troie* 94; *Protheselaus* 5046, 11919
22727 cf. *Lancelot* 5273
22747, 24571, 29915 cf. *Erec* 3266

24752 = *Troie* 2478; *Eneas* 1467
24902 = *Eneas* 3870
24921 cf. *Thèbes* 3011
24946 = *Eneas* 6708
25103 cf. *Erec* 583, 5386
25127 = *Perceval* 6236
25501, 27707 cf. *Troie* 14790
25584 = *Troie* 6219, 12759, 13234, etc.
25622 cf. *Thèbes* 332, 1006; *Troie* 15300, 17608; *Erec* 3729
25742, 26506 = *Erec* 128
25759 cf. *Erec* 5050
26582, 31925 cf. *Brut* 9881; *Troie* 2102, 4339
26868 = *Troie* 17097
26884, 28819 = C1 L 1366, 1856
26931 = *Troie* 24974
27237, 27453 cf. *Erec* 4301
28276 = *Yvain* 4660
28145 cf. *Erec* 487; *Perceval* 2072
28483, 31893 cf. C1 A 2193, 3304
28750 = *Troie* 2845 (proverb, cf. Morawski 2351)
28978, 29860 = *Troie* 12382, 12630
29757, 32583 = *Lancelot* 596
29812 cf. *Yvain* 5144

22811 cf. *Thèbes* 1005
22819 cf. *Perceval* 2070
23197 = *Erec* 739
23244 = *Troie* 2486
23249 cf. *Erec* 882; *Troie* 2404,
  19050[12]
23759 (ES) cf. *Cligés* 3979
24339 = *Troie* 8338
24377, 31563 *Troie* 2692; *Thèbes*
  167; *Ille* 5586
24719, 29553 cf. *Erec* 3671
24732 = *Eneas* 370

29828, 31475 cf. *Troie* 29277; *Erec*
  6243
29966 = *Erec* 1860
30173–74 (ES) = *Yvain* 2257–58
  (Roach notes)[13]
30694 cf. *Perceval* 5229
30768 cf. *Erec* 4432
31203–04 cf. *Thèbes* 961–2; *Erec*
  1755–56
31563 = *Troie* 2695[14]
32392, 32456 = *Erec* 3315

There are, in addition, some similarities which are common to a large number of texts, and which cannot really be pinned down to one or two possible sources; and also a certain number of resemblances to specific texts, e.g. *Ille*, but none in any real quantity, nor sufficient to suggest a definite knowledge of the texts in question, although since our author appears to have been quite well read, it is quite possible he was familiar with them.

What then of the influence of C2 on other texts? First of all, let us look at CM and CG, the two texts we might expect to be most influenced by C2, particularly with regard to content. To some extent, this will also throw light on the attention to detail, or lack of attention, shown by these two continuators.

Manessier's continuation shows the influences of C2 at several points.

1. The Fisher King tells Perceval that the Grail was used to receive Christ's blood as he hung on the cross:

Biaux filz quant Jhesu Crit pandi   32698
An la sainte croiz glorïeuse
Qui seur totes est precïeuse
Et il ot percié lou costé
Puis que li fer an fu osté
Qui fu estaichié an l'espié
En corut li sanc jusqu'au pié
Mais Josepf de Barimacie
Ot de duel la color nercie
Por Dieu que il vit ou martire
De li s'am prist corrox et ire
Ce saint vaisel ne s'an deçut
Tandi et le saint sanc reçut.   32710

This corresponds to what we are told in episode 22 (25792–96), rather than to Robert de Boron's *Joseph*, where the blood is collected after the body is removed from the cross (*Joseph* 555–574).[15] This same piece of information is contained in C1 V/5, the *Gralvorgeschichte*, which may or may not have been known to Manessier, but we can be sure he knew C2, though we cannot positively say this detail was taken from there.[16]

2. Perceval meets Sagremor, who tells him that forty knights left court to look for him (CM 33254–67). This is based on episode 28 of C2, although there are minor changes in CM, e.g. the knights leave Camaalot, rather than Garadigan (C2 28518), which is a mechanical change due to Manessier's extensive use of the prose *Lancelot* and the *Queste*,[17] in which Camaalot is King Arthur's principal residence.

3. The fact that Gauvain is at court when Silimac's sister comes to look for him (CM 35051 ff.) might imply that Manessier was aware of episode 32 in C2, where Gauvain, who had set off to look for Perceval, and to try to find the Grail Castle (29113–16), returned to court, in order to assist King Arthur in his war with the brothers Claudas and Carras. Equally, if one takes the view that episode 32 is interpolated,[18] it could be argued that the prime reason for the presence of episode 32 is to bring Gauvain back to court, as his next appearance in the corpus, in CM, requires his presence there.

4. The presence of the Castle of Maidens in CM (34103 ff.) might show the influence of C2 episode 20, but the details of the Castle are totally different, and its presence might as well be due to the influence of the *Queste*, in which it also appears.

5. Manessier has a whole section devoted to Perceval's encounter with a coward knight (CM 39577–969, 40975–41317), called the Biaus Mauvais (41272) and whom he rechristens the Biaus Hardi (41278). The similarity to episode 16 in C2 is obvious, but the details in CM are much the same as those in the *Perlesvaus* (pp. 241–43, cf. also 78–80, 189).

6. The fact that a hermit tells Perceval he should not go around indiscriminately killing knights in both C2 (episode 19 24001–09) and CM (37795–834) may be due to the influence of the former text, but this is not certain.

7. The fact that Perceval states he has not returned home since leaving for the first time to go to court (CM 42003–4) shows a lack of influence, cf. episodes 18–19 in C2. This is typical of the lack of attention to detail shown by Manessier.[19]

8. As regards the Grail procession, CM shows the influence both of C2 and *Perceval*. The procession consists of a maiden carrying the Grail, a maiden carrying the Lance, and a youth carrying the broken sword[20] in C2 (32396–410), while Manessier adds to the first two a *tailleor* (32619), carried at first by a damsel, and later by a youth (41955); in fact, later still, the Lance is carried by a youth, the *tailleor* by a maiden (42493–500). The broken sword, originally taken over from C1, also plays a role, in the sense that it is involved in the Fisher King's story of his maiming, etc.

9. The only major element in CM which is based on C2 is the Black Chapel adventure, which Perceval brings to a successful conclusion (37194–726).

We thus see that there is little trace of influence of C2 on the content of CM, and indeed a certain lack of attention in the latter to the details furnished by the former.

The continuation of Gerbert shows the influence of C2 to a much greater extent than does that of Manessier.

1. Perceval comes across two maidens hung up by the hair (913 ff.). This is a result of a visit by Agravain and Sagremor to the Mont Dolereus, which has resulted in their madness; they hung up the maidens, their *amies*, and then fought to a standstill. This much, and the fact that the source of madness is a pillar, surrounded by fifteen crosses, placed on the Mont by Merlin, shows the influence of C2, notably episode 33. However, here the problem is due to the fact that there is a demon inside the pillar, and the question 'Quist laiens?', addressed to it, is what brings on the insanity.

2. We find King Arthur and his knights hunting 'le blanc cerf au Noir Chevalier' (1211), possibly under the influence of C2. Although the White Stag was killed by Perceval in episode 5 of C2, such animals can be assumed to be replaceable, as in *Erec*, where hunting the white stag is a regular custom, although we are not told positively that the stag has ever been caught and killed, and in Appendix IV of C2 we are told a knight had hunted, and apparently killed, the stag before Perceval did so. The Black Knight's white stag also appears in the *Vengeance Raguidel*, where 1564 corresponds to 1211 here.

3. In CG, Perceval remembers his promise to his sister, and returns to take her away (2613–21). There is also a reference to the hermit, and the hermitage where Perceval's mother was buried (2707–09, 2732–34), based on episodes 18 and 19 of C2.

4. In this text, as in CM, we encounter the Castle of Maidens (3008 ff.). Here, Perceval returns to the castle, which he recognizes, and the details correspond closely to those given in episode 20 of C2.

5 Perceval's return to Biau Repaire (6191 ff.) shows the influence of episode 15 of C2, not so much in that the description of the castle's magnificence is similar (contrast the desolation of Biau Repaire in *Perceval*), but in that, while Gornemant is surprised by this magnificence,

> Car ainc puis n'i avoit esté
> Que Clamadeus avoit gasté
> La terre et le païs d'entor.   6215–17,

Perceval, on the other hand, 'Bien a reconut le païs' (6213) because he has already been back and seen the restored state of the castle and lands. The fact that in the same passage (6268–70) Blancheflor repeats the sentiments she expressed in episode 15, that she has waited for Perceval a long time, but will go on waiting if it suits him, is another small point of influence.

6. Perceval's encounter with a 'worm', i.e. serpent, in a marble *perron* (14368–556) is reminiscent of the Knight in the Tomb (ep. 25 of C2), especially in that both eventually are returned to captivity, although the circumstances are rather different.

7. The references to Perceval being happier in the forest than in the open (15732–35, 16156–59, cf. 16860–61) may well have been inspired by 22233–34 and 22249–52 in C2 (ep. 14),[21] but no certainty is possible.

8. Perceval meets a giant, who is looking for him because he had killed his brother (16161–221). This is a reference to C2 episode 12, as the precise details contained in 16275–77 show beyond doubt:

> Dist Perchevax: 'Par Saint Nichal,
> Ausi ochist il mon cheval
> En un vergier, devant sa porte'.

9. As I have mentioned previously,[22] the last section of CG (16946 to the end) draws heavily from episode 35 of C2. The reference to the serpent seems curiously out of place here (16991–98) for precisely that reason, but one would not conclude from that that the serpent episode was originally part of C2. The reference to the child in the tree[23] (17001) relates to the first part of episode 33, just as 1. above related to the latter part of that episode.[24]

This brief comparison of CM and CG with C2 shows us that, while Gerbert made use of C2, and kept fairly closely to the facts given in that text, the influence of C2 on Manessier seems to have been slight, in so far as the content of his work is concerned, with the exception of the Black Chapel incident. In addition, C2 clearly influenced *Durmart le Galois*. There is no need to go further into this question, already much discussed, but let us note that J. Gildea accepted the C2-*Durmart* filiation.[25] It is doubtful whether any other influence of C2 on subsequent texts is demonstrable.

On the level of form, little is demonstrable either. Certainly, CM, CG and *Durmart*, the texts we know were influenced by C2, all show some verbal similarities to the latter, with CM having the most, and *Durmart*, the least.[26] Many of these are trivial, however, and this influence should not be thought to be considerable, at least for CG and *Durmart*. It does exist, but it would be tedious to cite examples here.

Apart from this, it is possible that *Yder* 802 (= 21220, 21446) is borrowed from episode 9, while *Meriadeuc* 11075–76 (= 22249–50, 23143–44) seems more appropriate to C2, that is, to Perceval, and is perhaps slightly reinforced by the fact that *Meriadeuc* 3534 = C2 27557, but these are minor points, and hardly amount to clear influence.[27]

Place in the cycle

In discussing the place of C2 in the cycle, I should make it clear that I mean the cycle of *Perceval* and the Continuations, rather than the Grail cycle as a whole.

First of all, on the most basic level, that of narrative line, it is clear that C2 comes between C1 and CM/CG. Chronologically, there is no doubt that C2 follows C1ii/C2i, and precedes CM and CG. If my theory concerning the formation of C1 is correct, C2 could pre- or post-date C1 II and III, but I would suggest the latter. The question of the relative chronology of C2 and the LRed. of C1 is more complex. Broadly speaking, I am sure that C2 pre-dates the LRed., but the LRed. is possibly made up of several elements and probably at least two authors are involved, even leaving aside C1 I/6 and I/8,[28] and it is difficult to be certain whether C2 precedes all of them. However, as far as the Grail episodes are concerned, I have no doubt C2 precedes C1 I/7.

As regards the Grail Castle and the phenomena inside and outside it, including the Grail and Lance, C2 shows an apparent desire to blend the elements of *Perceval* and C1 into a single unit, and this process includes the retention of the broken sword, and therefore, implicitly, the theme of vengeance, of prime importance in CM. How much this is a deliberate and conscious effort to reconcile *Perceval* and C1, is, of course, impossible to determine.

As far as the development of the cycle is concerned, if C1 V/5 is interpolated, as it would seem, cf. Introduction, Chapter 1, then episode 22 (25792–96) would seem to mark the first equation of the Grail with a Holy Blood-relic. The casualness of the reference there, though, and the fact that, interpolated or not, C1 V/5 could have been present in the version of C1 known to the author of C2, mean we cannot be certain. The statement in episode 22 that the Grail was used to collect the Holy Blood is perhaps too offhand to be the first exposition of this important idea, but it may well be the first in the *Perceval* cycle.[29]

There is one final and important point about the place of C2 in the cycle, and the development of the Grail cycle generally: it is the last text in the *Perceval* cycle which shows no positive signs of the influence of the *Lancelot-Grail* cycle, since CM and CG both show signs of such influence.[30] This means that while any consideration of CM or CG cannot ignore the Vulgate, this is not the case for C2.[31]

NOTES

INTRODUCTION

1. See Bibliography for details of this and other editions, articles, etc.
2. Vol. III/2 contains L. Foulet's glossary for the whole of C1.
3. All except K contain the *Perceval*, though not always in its entirety.
4. Wilmotte, 'Gerbert de Montreuil'.
5. Ch. François, 'Etude'.
6. A. W. Thompson, 'Elucidation'. The *Elucidation* is also printed by Potvin, 1–484, and by Hilka, in appendix, pp. 417–29.
7. See Bibliography.
8. Wilmotte, 'Poème du Gral', Chap. II.
9. Including, apparently, the *Bliocadran*, but not the *Elucidation*.
10. Wilmotte did not commit himself on the identity of the author of the rest of C1 and C2, saying only that it was not Wauchier de Denain. It would be surprising if he believed Chrétien to have written the remainder, up to the end of C2. Roach, at least, believed that Wilmotte attributed C2 to Chrétien, see 'Romans du Graal', p. 108.
11. For this attribution, due to P. Meyer, see H.L.F. 33 (1906), 290–92. The attribution is discussed in Chapter 5, below.
12. According to F. Lot, Gerbert 6980–84 suggest that that poet believed Chrétien wrote at least up to 23070; see Lot: 'Auteurs', 122. I consider the lines in Gerbert too ambiguous to be interpreted in such a positive way.
13. See CG 6980ff., CM 42638–68. The variants given by Wilmotte for the end of CM in MSS TU ('Poème du Gral', pp. 71–72) contain numerous inaccuracies. The end of the poem is missing in EQS.
14. F. Lot, 'Auteurs'.
15. G. Vial, 'L'auteur de la deuxième continuation'.
16. This was the opinion of J. D. Bruce, for example, see 'Evolution' I, 291.
17. H. Wrede, 'Die Fortsetzer'.
18. B also contains an *explicit*: 'Explicit li romans de Perceval'. Wilmotte asserted that MSS A and B were closely related, and of little value, 'Poème du Gral', p. 35.
19. *Perceval*, rich rhymes 16.5%, leonine rhymes 14.5%. C1 I, rich rhymes 18.8%, leonine rhymes 12.2%.
20. For the opinion of Lot on this question, and on that of the provenance of the different parts of C1, see 'Auteurs', 128ff.
21. See W. Roach, 'Conclusion of the Perceval Continuation', also Appendix XI of his edition of C2.
22. CM 42660–61. Gerbert also says that he began at this point, see CG 7008ff.
23. The Roach numbering here refers to MS. A, since the numbering of C2 continues with A, rather than L.
24. H.L.F. 30 (1888), 27–28.
25. art. cit. p. 136.
26. Lot was perfectly aware of this; idem, p. 126.
27. Idem, p. 136.
28. This episode has come to the general attention of scholars partly because it contains a name for Perceval's father.
29. In the sections preceding and following E's lacuna, the text of E is some 10% longer than that of MQ(U). We would thus expect the 2560 lines missing from E (two quaternions, = 16 × 160 lines) to correspond to some 2300 lines, not the 2428 found in MQ(U) in the relevant section of the text. The 226 lines of V/5 would more or less account for this difference.
30. For details, see Chapter 4, *infra*.

CHAPTER 1

1. In other words, the basis for comparison is which lines are in the text, rather than precise verbal correspondence within those lines.
2. In general, I will try to avoid constructing a series of hypothetical *stemmata*, which would necessarily be simplified, and very possibly would not represent the real state of affairs, and will confine myself to indicating broad manuscript groupings. The following symbols will be used: // = different redactions; / = substantial difference; – = difference; A,B = sub-groups.
3. I have omitted those MSS which are of no concern to us in the Continuations.
4. This is an approximation of:
    E 19607–19656. E – T(V) – P / AS,KU,MQ – L.
    E 19657–20226. E,PT(V) / AS,KU,MQ – L.
    E 20227–20368. E,T(V) – AS,KU,MQ,P – L.
    E 20369–20530. ET(V) / AS,KU,MQ,P,L.
5. 'Tradition manuscrite', p. 233.
6. Or, more precisely, lines 1959–3636 and 3959–4828.
7. In general, the indications of where a shift occurs should be taken to be approximate.
8. *Romania* 83 (1962), 400–07.
9. For the text of P, see Roach III Appendix I.
10. Note that E has a lacuna, 12577–736; we may also note that the version of IV/2 given by ASPU is actually longer than that of the LRed.
11. That is, the incident in which Gauvain recounts his adventure with the sister of Bran de Lis, and his subsequent combats with her father and brothers.
12. P. Gallais, 'Gauvain et la Pucelle de Lis.'
13. In fact, the text of E could be allowed to stand uncorrected, but that of L is preferable.
14. The unusual form *tailloër* cannot be considered an error; it occurs in MS U, var. to E 3850, as well as the instance noted by Foulet, U var. to E 3795.
15. Except, as I stated, in IV/5.
16. Roach might have made more use of MQU in order to make his rare emendations to L, in this part of the text (i.e. Branches V and VI). Note that, in the introduction to vol. II, Roach hints that in this part of the text MQU do not follow the same redaction as E, but have been classed with it because of E's lacunae.
17. For this episode, and E's position, see *supra*, Introduction.
18. See *supra*, p. 5–6.
19. It is interesting to compare this with the provisional *stemma*, attributed to Roach, given by Brugger (*ZRP* 65, 380), though it should perhaps be stressed that Roach never put this, or any other *stemma* in print.
20. It should be remembered that Roach divides C2 simply into 35 episodes, not into Branches and episodes, as in C1.
21. K contains only the text of C2, while V has a lacuna at this point. However, V always forms a pair with T, throughout the corpus.
22. See *supra*, p. 6.
23. This variation in L disappears at A 10162, but note that the erasure in L at that point shows that this was not originally the case, see *infra* Appendix II, note 3.
24. Note that P contains a passage corresponding to ET (E 20391–422), but slightly later in the text, see Roach IV App. V, and chapter 4, *infra*.
25. See *supra*, p. 6.
26. Due to the lacuna in K and the idiosyncrasies of Q, this could well simply be equal to U + the KLQTV sub-group.
27. Ivy, 'Manuscript relations', p. 65.
28. There is a theoretical possibility that in E 7537–9786, P has preserved the best text, and that episodes III/7 and III/8 have been suppressed by LAS, while III/9, like III/13, has been added by EMQTUV. However, I think even a cursory inspection of the versification in the relevant parts of the text will show that this is not the case. The rich rhyme proportion in III/7–8 is in excess of 40%, while in P III/1–6 and III/11–15 it is about 20%.
29. Wrede, 'Die Fortsetzer', pp. 116–119. In the opinion of Wrede, the primitive C2 could be more or less reconstructed, and he considers the evidence of MS K to be particularly important. We do not yet have Roach's definitive ideas on this question. In 1954, he seemed to agree with Wrede, see 'Romans du Graal', p. 111. Since then, his edition of C2 has appeared, but he has hardly expressed his opinion more clearly; in the introduction to C2, he simply says that after the end of MS A 'the Short Redaction ceases to exist' (p. xiv), but on page xvi he says 'To the extent that the Short Redaction survives. . .', which seems to

suggest that it must have existed in a longer form than that of the 800-odd lines which have reached us intact.

30. Appendices III, IV and V will be dealt with later, in Chapter 4.
31. The rhyming is also inferior in Q and U; note the identical rhymes *non* : *non* (Q 27, = U 25), *dire* : *dire* (Q 31, = U 29) and *estoit* : *estoit* (U 17). The *lit* : *loisir* of Q 61 is a scribal error; read *lit* : *delit*, as at 31244.
32. Lot described the episode as 'postiche' (Etude, 357). In his article on the authorship of the Continuations, he suggested that the whole of episodes 28–32 might be an interpolation, and that episode 32, at least, is posterior to the prose *Lancelot*, see 'Auteurs', p. 126 note 1.
33. For further discussion of the theory that episode 32 is interpolated, see Chapter 6, note 20.
34. Rather than Robert de Boron's *Joseph*, in which Alain is not called 'le gros', although he is in the prose *Estoire*. Note also the fact that, in Appendix XI, as in the *Didot-Perceval*, the Fisher King dies three days after Perceval's arrival at the Grail Castle.
35. The non-sense of K is important, since without it the presence of two inexact rhymes in the passage K omits (*escoutent* : *montent* 26091; *acroire* : *fere* 26099) might suggest that K's version was authentic.
36. For 20621–30252.
37. This is a reconstruction from Roach's variants, not the actual reading of MS K. This applies equally elsewhere.
38. In theory, of course, it is possible that EPS have the authentic text, and that there was no Good Friday episode in the original *Perceval*. However, it is unlikely; even if that episode were interpolated, it was almost certainly in the text of the *Perceval* by the time C2 was composed.
39. KLMTU. V has a lacuna here.
40. These four rhymes are clearly primitive; only L does not have that at 21581, only MP that at 28869.
41. There is no passage equivalent to 23421–34 in the *Didot-Perceval*, which contains the same episode, but this does not necessarily mean the passage is not authentic.
42. This is of course an acceptable rhyme, insomuch as *auter* is an attested form of *autel*.
43. Add to this the confusion in 31791, where only MS have *m'antandez*, clearly a change introduced to eliminate the repetition of *m'escoutez*.
44. Naturally, this does not mean that the editor is wrong to suggest, as he does periodically, specifically in his notes, or tacitly in his edition of the text, that ES sometimes preserve the best reading, when they are in conflict with the other MSS. That would only be the case if the reading of P were identical with that of the other MSS, in opposition to that of ES, and if that reading were not one which may easily have been arrived at independently by different scribes.
45. The same line occurs in C1 (A 6814), cf. Roach's note to 30173–74.
46. Given the lacuna in K and the divergences in TV (such as Appendix VII).

CHAPTER 2

1. Lot, 'Auteurs', pp. 130–33.
2. In fact, as I have indicated, I would group III/16 with IV – VI, rather than with II and III/1–15. In MS L, III/16 has a rich rhyme proportion of 14.5%, cf. III/1–15, 21.7%, and IV, 14.1%; III/16 also contains some stylistic features characteristic of IV – VI, as we shall see. It is of course virtually impossible to demonstrate that a passage of about 160 lines belongs with one group of several thousand lines rathr than with another. The overall rich rhyme figures for MS A are: Branch I, 30.9%; II, 19.3%; III, 19%; IV, 17.1%; V, 14.4%; VI, 12.4%. These suggest a more positive difference between I and the rest, but also point rather to a II – IV group, than a IV – VI group. See, however, the evidence presented below.
3. To give some idea of the banality/rarity of each feature, I will give its incidence in each of the following works: *Erec*, *Yvain*, and *Perceval* (chosen as representing the beginning, the middle, and the end of Chrétien's work), *Méraugis de Portlesguez*, *Le chevalier aux deux épées*, *Le Bel Inconnu*, and the two short romances *Le Chevalier à l'épée* and *La Mule sans frein*.
4. P. Gallais, 'Formules de conteur', p. 187ff.
5. It occurs once in *Yvain*, where the speaker is a young lady, rather than the author, and three times in *Inconnu*; there is also a similar line in *Mule* 'Ne sai que j'alasse acontant'.
6. This type of filler line is found once in *Erec*, 3 times in *Yvain*, 9 times in *Perceval* (to which we may add 3 others, where the rhyme is *redit* : *aït*) twice in *Méraugis*, 8 times in *Meriadeuc*, and once in *Mule*. Some of these lines have '*se (Dame)Dieux t'aït, vos aït*', etc.

7. I confess to a lingering doubt as to whether III/16 – IV/6 belongs with the rest of C1ii. It does have a higher rich rhyme proportion in MS A, perhaps the result of reworking. In any case, I shall treat C1ii as one unit, cf. Note 15, *infra*.

8. Chrétien uses this expression once in *Erec*, 1459, and once in *Yvain*, 4121, and it is also present in *Meriadeuc*, 9851, but the only use which corresponds to that in C1ii is in *Inconnu* 1152.

9. This rhetorical device occurs 3 times in *Erec*, 2802, 5792, 5924, once in *Yvain*, 2399, twice in *Perceval*, 313, 2351, *Méraugis*, 1174, 5668, and *Chevalier*, 558, 752. More often than not, it is used by a character rather than the author. It is also found in C1i, according to Potvin, 11787; however, the variant Roach gives for MS P here (= A 1357) is 'Saciés'. I have not been able to check the MS reading, but allowing for printing errors, etc., it is probable that Roach gives the correct reading.

10. Banal though this action is, expressions of this sort are not as frequent as one might expect: *Erec* 'La lance et l'escu prist aprés' 3965, 'Son escu a pris et sa lance' 4304; *Meriadeuc* 'Et si prist son escu et sa lance' 7909, 'K'il ne mont, et prent son escu' 2691; *Inconnu* 'Son escu a pris et sa lance' 687; *Chevalier* 'Lor escuz et lor lances pristrent' 127.

11. This type of apostrophe is surprisingly rare in romances; except when a character is speaking, which is clearly a different case. I have found only one instance in the eight romances, in *Méraugis* 33, and that in the most logical place, at the beginning of the story. The feature is, however, very frequent in Béroul's *Tristan*.

12. Nevertheless, it does not appear once in any of our eight texts.

13. Although this phrase may seem banal, it is not in fact found anywhere in the eight romances we have used as a basis for comparison. Indeed, I have found it nowhere else except in the romances of Hue de Rotelande and in *Fergus*.

14. 15.5% in MS A.

15. Notably the following features, found in C1ii, but not in C1i: (a) first person plural verb-ending *-on* L 4469, 5251, 5736, 6386, 6430, 6521, 6665, 7458, 7897, 8117. (b) the rhyming of *nos*, *vos* with *-ous* L 3747, 4578, 5224, 5246, 5475, 6027, 6367, 6891, 7975, 9436; also with *seus* (from SOLUS), *deus* (DUOS) L 6122, 7311, cf. 5391, 8928. (c) third person sing. imperfect in *-ot* L 5933, 9044. (d) second person plural verb-ending in *-oiz* L 4129, 5124, 8930. It is worth noting that many of these examples come from III/16 – IV/6.

16. Pronounced in A and R, less so in L. The percentage for Branch I in R is 39.4% as against 31.5% in A, and 26.5% in L.

17. The text of MS R is given in full in Roach's edition of C1, at the end of vol. III/1.

18. See Micha, 'Tradition manuscrite', pp. 310–15.

19. In R 647 he is called *li fils al roi Yder*, but elsewhere in this MS (277, 693, 800) he is, as usual, the son of *Do(e)*. The remaining MSS, EMQU,TV, also have *Girflet*.

20. Hilka ed. 4721–23. MS A actually has 'fils de *Nut*', but the majority of the MSS have the correct reading 'fils de Do'.

21. Again, an understandable addition to a story which is essentially about Perceval's Grail quest, and which Chrétien entitled the *Conte del Graal*.

22. As is well known, 'Briébras', misunderstood as Short-arm, is a corruption of Breton *Brechbras* (Welsh *Vreichvras*), or Arm-strong. It is possible that the story also sought to account for the epithet attributed to Caradoc's wife, who, although the only attestation is of later date, seems to have been called Tegau Eurvron, or Tegau Breast-of-Gold.

23. She is simply called 'ma dame Ysaje' in the shorter version of Branch II contained in MSS MQ; it seems probable in any case that this is a reduction of the common version, rather than that the latter is an expansion of the MQ text. The treatment of Ysave is a marked anomaly in C1. She is first found in Branch I (A 85, L 83) as a lady of Arthur's court; then, in Branch II (A 1235, L 1165) she is among the besieged at Branlant, only to reappear in Branch III (A 2057, 2066, L 2051, 2060) as Arthur's niece.

24. See Gallais, 'Gauvain et la Pucelle de Lis'.

25. It will not have escaped the notice of anyone who has read C1 that there is a marked similarity between the beginning of episodes III/3 and IV/1. Not only are the scenes and action essentially the same, but there is enough textual similarity to indicate clearly a borrowing. What is less obvious is which passage is borrowed from which.

26. R. Heinzel, 'Gralromane', pp. 32–34.

27. This was also the opinion of Heinzel, who said these events must take 'mindestens zwanzig Jahre', op. cit., p. 33.

28. See note 24, *supra*.

29. It would appear that there was still one more stage in the formation: the addition to the LRed. of the two long passages in Branch I, found only in EU, see Introduction, p. 6.

30. Lot, who saw similarities between Branches IV and V of C1, and C2 (art. cit., 127), might have reached the same conclusion, had he had the benefit of using the Roach edition, rather than that of Potvin, which gives only the text of MS P.
31. It must be remembered that Roach prints the SRed. and the LRed. in parallel text, up to the end of MS A; subsequently he prints the LRed., i.e. the text of E. Mainly because of the difference in length between C1 SRed. and LRed., 10268 of the SRed. corresponds to 20530 of the LRed.
32. The redactions in MSS A and L are fairly different, although they both represent the SRed.; I propose to consider the version of L, as in C1ii. The picture would not be radically different if we were to look at MS A. For the text of L, see the transcription in Appendix II, *infra*.
33. The numbering refers to the transcription in Appendix II, *infra*.
34. These are the mentions of the Moors which I have found, none of them resembling the expression we are concerned with here: *Yvain* 288, *Mule* 515, CG 8944.
35. Note though, that the line in *Partonopeus* is identical to the reading of A and L, here, not that of MQ/*Inconnu*.
36. M. Delbouille, 'Rimes familières'.
37. In spite of Roach's classification, see Chapter 1, *supra*.
38. For fuller discussion of this type of rhyme, see Chapter 3, note 17.
39. We have seen that the third person imperfect verb-ending *-ot* occurs in C1ii, and of the other features found there, the second person plural verb-ending *-oiz* is found in C2i, L 10155, 10257, as are rhymes of *vos* : *-ous*, L 9753, 10217, 10379 (also *vos* : *sos* 10185). These features do not markedly distinguish C2i from C2ii, however. What does is the absence in the former of predominantly northern dialectal features; note the rhymes cited from C2ii, and also the fuller survey of these features, in Chapter 3.
40. The proportion of enjambement, like that of everything else, is affected in the C1ii/C2i corpus by the presence in MSS L and A of episode V/5, which we have seen is probably an interpolation. However, as this episode contains only 226 lines, or 3.1% of the total length of C1ii/C2i, and the proportions would also be affected if the PU version of IV/5 were the primitive one (it is considerably longer than IV/5 L or A), I have simply based my figures on the text as Roach prints it.
41. See Chapter 1.
42. See Chapters 1, 4.
43. One assumes it is a change, regardless of A simply breaking off, in that E did not = A, so if S = E, S would not = A.
44. Cf. MS M at C2 30252, for example.
45. M. Roques, 'Le manuscrit fr. 794.'

CHAPTER 3

1. Wrede, 'Die Fortsetzer', p. 128.
2. For the following section, reference may be made to the useful summary of the events of each episode in Roach IV pp. xviii–xxxix.
3. Indeed, he tells Perceval he will learn his name within the year (27501–03).
4. In fact, many of them are tied up in CM and CG, see Chapter 6.
5. Another detail of episode 9 is mystifying, and seems to hint at source material: the Danish axe which Perceval finds, and takes wth him (21102–07), but of which there is no further mention, since Perceval fights the lion with his sword (21162–76).
6. The fact that in episode 14, Gauvain's son calls himself 'Li Biaus Desconeüs', while in episode 32 he calls himself by his proper name, Guinglains, is a small point which might point to different authors for these two episodes. However, I feel that Wrede attaches too much importance to this point, and that the two facts are by no means irreconcilable.
7. Using the Brandt and Snedecor method. A significant figure of $P = 0.05$ means that there is only a 1:20 chance that the sample is homogeneous, i.e. that probably it is not, although this need not mean it is the work of more than one author. A standard table for the accumulative distribution of Chi-Square was used. A statistical analysis has the advantage that the proportion of rich rhymes in a text is not relevant.
8. Both for 400 and for 600 line groups.
9. *Yder* does not show a significant value if we discount 5000 ff.; *Hunbaut* does, even when we discount 3200 ff., where the proportion is *c.* 33.5%, as opposed to *c.* 84% up to 3200; the figure for *Erec* can be explained by the steadily increasing proportion throughout the text, perhaps the mark of an early work (the first 1000 lines yield 24.8%, the last 1000, 37.8%); that for *Lancelot* (1–6000) is more intriguing, especially as eliminating the *Nouauz* episode

makes little difference; CG yields the most interesting figures, since even if we discount 1–5000 and 15000 ff., thus eliminating the Tristan episode, with its very low proportion, perhaps due to the source, and the contamination at the end of the text, we are still left with a significant value of P. As for Béroul's *Tristan*, if we split the text at 2800 or 2600, and compare the two halves, we get a significant figure again, but the internal figures for each half are not significant, which strongly suggests, statistically, dual authorship or remaniement.

10. *Méraugis* does not yield a significant figure for 600 line groups, if we discount the first 800 lines, where the proportion is noticeably higher: *c.* 54%, compared with *c.* 34% for the remainder.

11. Or even 20, + 22–25, since removing these episodes in no way harms the structure of the text.

12. Cf. Ch. Th. Gossen, 'Grammaire de l'ancien picard', p. 97; G. Wacker, 'Dialekt und Schriftsprache im Altfranzösischen', p. 67.

13. Alongside the standard forms *veoir, cheoir*, etc. The latter are slightly the more frequent in C2ii (counting only those at the rhyme, of course), although there are some instances in the variants which might be authentic, and would make the numbers about even.

14. There are also examples of this feature in the variants, very possibly authentic, e.g. 27164, 27329.

15. Also a northern feature.

16. See Foulet, *Petite Syntaxe* § 212–13, 169.

17. We also find, for example, *-u* (from *-OCU*) 31331, 31917; *-ain: -ein* 21319, 22081, 22301, etc.; introduction of interconsonantal *e* in *averai*, etc. 30495, 30692, 30773, also LPTV 26945, KLPTV 27876, etc.; 4th person ending *-omes* 25218, 26945, 29468; occasional consonantalisation of *i* in hiatus in 5th person cond. and imperf. 24203, 28737, 31469, 31565, although in general, the disyllabic form is commoner, cf. 22859, 22909, 22910, 25830, 25928, 27733, etc.; the northern form *bos* (from BOSCUM) 27644, 29162. The northern dialect would also explain the rhymes of the type *departirent: tindrent*, found at 28007, 28183, 29913, 30721. The reduction of *-nr* to *-rr* to *-r* is well attested in the north, cf. Roach, note to *Perceval* 2929, and to CI T 6500. Since this area also has forms *vinrent, tinrent*, etc. (for francien *vindrent, tindrent*), these rhymes are clearly equivalent to *-irent: -ir(r)ent*. Rhymes of this type figure fairly widely in northern texts, cf. *Rigomer* 7695, 12855; CM 34149; *Floire et Blanch.* 3291; *Jehan et Blonde* 5277, and perhaps *Bel Inconnu* 5069, and also *Guill. d'Angl.* 2089, 3125. There may well be others, relegated to the variants of modern editions. On the other hand, C2 also contains features characteristic of the western area, such as *vos: -ous* 22069, 23347, 23909, 25713, etc; the imperfect in *-ot* at 31503; and the suffix *-al* (from *-ALIS*) 22667, 24079, 25274, etc. Whereas, the survival of the 5th person *-oiz*, cf. 23282, 23453, 26310, 28975, etc. is essentially eastern. It is reasonable to assume that a northern author would be sufficiently conversant with other dialectal features to use them at the rhyme when it suited him.

18. For reasons which were gone into in Chapter 1, I am inclined to favour readings found in all but ES, as probably authentic, and to dismiss those only in ES, as probably not.

19. And also *Durmart* 3291.

20. The *Ille* references prefaced by the letter P are to the Löseth edition, all others to the SATF Cowper edition.

21. In addition to these, there are 3 expressions which are found frequently in C2, forming a single hemistich. 'Dont n'i ot/a plus', as a first hemistich, occurs 8 times, 23059, 26876, 27017, 27274, 27430, 28844, 29580, 30151. The similar 'Or n'i a/ot plus' occurs 6 times, 22935, 23377, 26016, 29332, 31710, 31910, all in direct speech. Besides these, there is 'plus n'i atant', which occurs, as a second hemistich, 9 times in isolation, 21095, 22372, 24904, 25956, 27450, 28462, 29465, 30456, 31038 (to these we may add 22511 'plus n'i atandent'), and 3 times linked to the first hemistich of the line, at 9524, 20766, 21660.

22. For details, see the equivalent chapter of my unpublished doctoral thesis, Edinburgh 1983.

23. Excluding the 33 just mentioned.

24. For this I have counted only those lines which I consider identical, and have discounted all those which contain the proper names Perceval and Gauvain.

25. While episode 10 requires episode 9, the reverse is not true, so I have discounted this link, to some extent. Equally, 27 and 28 do not require one another at all; indeed, the variant of QT 28606 'Atant es vos un chevalier' might hint at an independent existence for the Bagomadés section of episode 28, with 27 added on the basis of Bagomadés' account of his brush with Keu and the others, cf. my remarks in Chapter 1, p. 29.

26. There are some lines common to C2ii and to episodes 1–8. However, their number is not such as to suggest either that episodes 6, 7 and 8 are not interpolated, or that there is no break at A 10268.

27. This view is shared by Wrede, and was adopted by Bruce, following W. Hoffman.

28. While these differences might be explained by postulating an earlier version of C2, or a verse work by Robert de Boron, as for the *Joseph* and the *Merlin*, one is naturally reluctant to add to the plethora of lost models which seem to abound in the field of medieval literature. In reality, it is only episode H which differs radically from its counterpart, episode 13.
29. This has tended to be the case with episode 32, for example; see Chapter 1, note 32.
30. 'Etude', p. 161 note 4.

CHAPTER 4

1. Cf. note 12 below.
2. For the link between the Black Knight and the white stag, cf. Chapter 6, p. 75.
3. Plus the fact that line i is closer than 20609 to line 20685, for example.
4. See Chapter 1.
5. Cf. my remarks on Gales li Caus, Chapter 6, note 24. The original reading may have been *Segurain*, or something similar, cf. West 'Prose' for Seguran(t), Senigran-Segrain.
6. Note, though, that the facts given in episode 21 do not accord with those in EPT, either, in that the latter show the knight living alone, and in the vault, as in App. IV.
7. The Black Knight's story, authentic or not, conjures up an intriguing picture of a somewhat circular situation (due to enchantment), in which a knight solicits the love of the lady of the Chessboard Castle, hunts the stag, loses the dog, fights the previous suitor, who is now in the *arcel*, and takes his place, then is defeated and displaced by the next suitor. Perceval's arrival would (of course) have brought all this to an end.
8. The discrepancy between the EPT version and episode 21 might support this idea, see note 6. It must be said, too, that the best way to eliminate the Black Knight's troublesome revelations would have been to have him disappear into his *arcel*.
9. I would punctuate with a full stop after 160, and a comma for the semi-colon in 161, hence no enjambement.
10. The high proportion of rich rhymes precludes the possibility that episodes 6, 7 and 8 belong with C1ii/C2i. While odd little points may hint at remnants of a SRed. after 10268, such as the 'Savez . . .?' of ET 20392 (= App. V P 2), the balance of evidence is clearly against such a possibility.
11. However, experience tells us that interpolations in medieval texts do not always increase the coherence of the narrative, besides which, a scribe could have added App. IV without having read episode 21.
12. This view would also conform with the fact that, while before and after episode 5 there is a KMQU sub-group (see Chapter 1), MQU here confront KLT (+ EPS). This would of course suggest that MQU do not give the primitive text, but it is not a very positive piece of evidence, given the shift in the MSS that occurs at A 10268.
13. We see elsewhere how the scribe of T inserts lines to make his text conform with earlier or later events; the addition at 28137, for example, is probably due to the presence in T of CG.
14. In the *Didot-Perceval*, the old woman who first takes the *brachet* is a fairy, sister of the lady of the Chessboard Castle, and the same one who built the invisible castle for the Black Knight. This fact, and the passage in T, might seem to suggest that the other MSS have rationalized the situation, and eliminated a maiden or old woman. Yet how could T have retained this one fragment of a previous version, yet elsewhere kept to the idea that a knight stole the dog and the stag's head?
15. See note 14.
16. The state of MS L at the break is also intriguing, see App. II, note 3.

CHAPTER 5

1. F. Lot, 'Auteurs'.
2. See P. Meyer in H.L.F. 33 (1906), 258–92.
3. G. Vial, 'L'auteur de la deuxième continuation'.
4. M. Wilmotte, 'Poème du Gral', pp. 38–73.
5. Lot, 'Auteurs', p. 123.
6. Idem, p. 124.
7. Idem, p. 122.
8. Idem, p. 136.
9. This appears to be more or less how the redactor of the 1530 prose version understood it, for he says: '. . . Gauchier de Doudain, qui ceste hystoire nous a comemoree et mise en avant . . .' (f° 177 r°).

10. The 1530 prose version agrees with M, see preceding note; K has a lacuna here.
11. Note that the original latin name of Denain appears to have been DONINCUM, see H.L.F., 30, 290. Wilmotte (op. cit., p. 67 note 3) cites the following forms of the name: Donain, Donen, Doneng, (all from the 12th century), and Denen, Denaing, Deneng (all c. 1190–1210); see also the series of forms given by M. Gysseling, *Toponymisch Woordenboek van België, Nederland, Luxemburg, Noord-Frankrijk en West-Duitsland (voor 1226)*. Brussels 1960, p. 261–2.
12. There is also a Dordan in the Nièvre, but it is a small village, and probably negligible.
13. There are possibilities for these locations, but nothing very convincing. Wilmotte suggested, very plausibly, that *Denet* might have been a miscopying of *Denent, Denen(g)*.
14. Although we cannot say to what extent his name would still have been known when the MSS were copied.
15. See Chapter 3, pp. 46–47.
16. Art. cit., p. 126.
17. For the reference to Vézelay and Auxerre, see my comments, Chapter 1, p. 28. As for the reference to 'le petit village de Ronay', only P has this reading: *rosnais* 22964.
18. Cf. note 2.
19. This figure includes some verses hypothetically restored by Meyer, and if we count the four obvious octosyllables found in the prose, p. 283: '(car) par (le) bien savoir et retenir / puet l'en sovent a bien venir. / Qui bien ne seit ne bien n'entent / de bien faire n'a nul talent', we have 138 lines.
20. The same is true for the compilation of ancient history (see P. Meyer, *Romania*, 14, 36–63), where there are rather more verse passages, including one of more than 280 lines, but whose attribution to Wauchier is purely hypothetical.
21. Carpentras MS ff° 117d/118a.
22. MS. *con con*.
23. *vos le* is not entirely clear.
24. See H.L.F., 33, 288.
25. Idem, 290.
26. As a footnote, let me add that there is a further question relating to the author of C2; was he also responsible for the LRed. of C1? Although the LRed. is a complex text, possibly the work of more than one author, see Chapter 6 n. 28, and although no positive answer can be given without undertaking a closer examination of C1 LRed. than would be appropriate here, I would say that the answer to this question is no, and that Wrede may well be correct in suggesting that the C1 LRed. post-dates Manessier.
27. Roach I, p. xv.

CHAPTER 6

1. See Chapter 3 note 2.
2. See Chapter 1.
3. The enigmatic allusion to the stag's head as a subsequent cause of strife at King Arthur's court (28232–38) might hint at a source, only partially used.
4. Assuming it is a mistake, as seems probable.
5. See Chapter 3 note 5.
6. The apparently parallel traditions represented by the CM and *Perlesvaus* 'Handsome Coward' episodes, see below, make a source seem fairly plausible.
7. If episode 33 had a source, of course, the relevant part of episode 25 could be a back-formation from there, which would explain why Perceval relates in episode 33 the events of episode 25 at some length, instead of the narrator saying 'si li conta . . . ainsint con oï avez' or somesuch, as for example in episode 19 (23969–77). It would also explain the fact that 31624–27 do not correspond to anything in episode 25.
8. See Chapter 1, p. 29 and Chapter 3 note 25.
9. I wonder if the statement that Gauvain did not force his attentions on the girl (29864–70), might not suggest that the author was familiar with a tradition in which he did, cf. C1 IV in the version given by PU, EMQTV.
10. Cf. note 7.
11. P's reading is so obviously corrupt that we must needs disregard it; therefore we have ES versus the rest, which makes their reading suspect, cf. Chapter 1.
12. This is a 'combat-cliché' par excellence.
13. This resemblance, in ES, appears to be due to a scribe, cf. Chapter 1, p. 29.

14. In this section, for *Troie* I have indicated only identical or near-identical lines, since there are so many similarities between C2 and *Troie*, which is by far the best represented text in this respect, and with which the author of C2 was obviously very familiar. To be more precise, I have omitted at least 27 points of resemblance of the sort indicated by 'cf.' for other texts.

15. Cf. my remarks concerning App. XI, Chapter 1, p. 20.

16. The casual reference in episode 22, with no sense of revelation, suggests one of the following: (a) the author of C2 (or episode 22) knew C1 V/5, which is possible, but unlikely, in that we have concluded that V/5 is probably an interpolation; (b) he knew CM, in which case episode 22 would have to be an interpolation; (c) it was common knowledge (since the appearance of the *Joseph?*) that the Grail was a Holy Blood-relic. Of these, I would favour (c).

17. The argument of J. Marx (*Romania*, 84 (1963), 451–77) that the author of the *Queste* (and the *Agravain*) and Manessier used the same material, is based to a great extent on his assertion that, had Manessier known the prose *Lancelot*, he would doubtless have made extensive use of it, and that this is not the case. This argument is entirely spurious, given the fact that the three elements quoted by Marx as common to *Agravain-Queste* and CM (combat between Hector and Perceval; combat between Boort and Lionel; importance of Agloval) are not, as he would have us believe, the only ones. For example, there is the episode involving the diabolic black horse, the rock, and the false Blancheflor (*Queste* 91–112; CM 37919–38354), but, more importantly, there are several elements in CM which we might attribute to the direct influence of the prose *Lancelot*. Thus the incident in which Gauvain rescues a damsel from the stake, and in the ensuing combat knocks his antagonist into the fire (CM 35389 ff.) corresponds precisely to the similar incident involving Lancelot in the *Lancelot* (ed. Micha (II), chap. XLIX 26–31). The incident in which the *Sore Pucelle* sends the son of King Margon back to him, fully-armed, by catapult (35809–65) is the doublet of that involving Boort, the *damoiselle de Hongrefort*, and the knight sent as a captive by the former to the latter (Micha (II), XLIV 31–32); note also the white pennon given to Boort, which he bathes in his adversary's blood (Micha (II), XLV 2–6), cf. Gauvain in CM 36155–62, 36723–32. For further details, see MLR 81 (1986), 574–91.

18. See Chapter 1, note 32, and note 20, below.

19. Compare the fact that, when Gauvain sets off from court to finish the task of Silimac, the knight killed in his conduct in C1 (V/2), he puts on Silimac's armour (CM 35257–58, 35295–96, 35785), although all the MSS of C1 agree in stating that the armour was taken away by a stranger, following Gauvain's return from the Grail Castle (C1 A 8243–50), and no mention is made of Silimac's sister having brought it with her.

20. Although the sword is arguably not a part of the procession; it does not return, 32422 ff. In episode 32, Gauvain mentions a youth carrying the Lance, and another carrying the sword — again, not part of the procession — (31188–95), and a maiden carrying the Grail (31207–14). Again, the contradiction between episode 32 (youth carrying the Lance) and episode 35 (maiden) can probably be explained away, as can the fact that Gauvain's two accounts differ, by the confusion resulting from an attempt to harmonize the elements of *Perceval*, C1 and the imminent Perceval visit in C2. The very fact that the broken sword is carried by a youth in episode 32, on which Wrede placed so much importance, surely indicates, not the influence of episode 35, exactly, but rather a preparation for it. It might seem harder to reconcile the fact that in episode 28 Gauvain said the broken sword was on the bier (29124–25), while in episode 32 it is brought by a youth, but having seen the changes the procession undergoes in CM, who can doubt the confusion the differing traditions caused the continuators? In fine, Wrede's argument that episode 32 must be interpolated, being posterior to the LRed. of C1, itself posterior to CM, is severely weakened by the fact that those elements he says are borrowed from C1 LRed., notably the Lance carried in procession, are found in the *Perceval*.

21. Also 23143–45 (episode 16); note that CG 16861 = C2 23145.

22. See Chapter 3, p. 53.

23. '*soz l'arbre*' in the text.

24. In passing, we may note that in 3072 of CG, Perceval says that his father was Gales li Caus. This suggests that Gerbert knew C1 V/5 and that this is a scribal rationalization of the name found there (Gulle Genelax, A 7633; Guellans Guenelaus, L 7671; other forms in MQU) to that of a recognized Arthurian character. This impression is strengthened later on, when Perceval fights with one Gollains li Chaus, who is doubtless the same as Gales. It is noteworthy that Perceval says he knows his father's name because the Fisher King told him (3073). This does not correspond to anything in any known text, and puts one in mind of the similar error in C2 episode 19, where Perceval seems to know about the broken sword, cf.

Chapter 3, 45). I would ascribe both these anomalies to inattention, rather than assume a Perceval Grail-visit corresponding to that of Gauvain in C1.

25. *Durmart* II, 60–63.
26. In CM, most of the verbal resemblances fall into the category of clichés in C2, listed in Chapter 3. In CG, many of them are also clichés of this sort, while others are less so, for example those mentioned in points 7 and 9, *supra*, and also such as CG 14738–39, cf. C2 23296–97.
27. There are a number of other textual similarities between C2 and *Yder, Meriadeuc*, but they are essentially clichés, which could be attributed to the influence of other texts. In general, there are more similarities between *Meriadeuc* and C2 than between *Yder* and C2, and they are sufficiently numerous to suggest the author of *Meriadeuc* may possibly have been influenced by C2.
28. These episodes are found in EU only, see Chapter 1. I believe that C1 I/6–10 and III of the LRed. may be due to different authors, but this is not the place to explore such a possibility.
29. I would be inclined to think episode 22 was based on C1 V/5, on this point; yet, if that were the case, why is there no mention in C2 (episodes 28 and 32) of Gauvain having learnt anything of the Grail's nature? Cf. note 16.
30. It is accepted that Gerbert used at least the *Estoire*. See note 17, *supra* for a discussion of Manessier's use of the Vulgate.
31. There is the possibility that Claudas de la Deserte (episode 32) is taken from the Vulgate, but this is not demonstrable, and, I feel, probably not the case.

GLOSSARY

As is generally the case, it has been considered necessary and prudent to include here only a selection of the words found in the Second Continuation. The basic criterion for this selection has been the exclusion of any word which, (a) is readily comprehensible to someone with a knowledge of Modern French, or to someone with a basic knowledge of Old French, and (b) which presents no real linguistic interest. Clearly, there is a substantial element of subjective judgement involved in such a process of selection, and probably no two scholars would agree exactly on which words merit inclusion. Further, some words which appear to be errors have been included, on the principle that they might have a genuine, though unattested, existence. On a statistical note, while the glossary contains some 1,800 headwords, nearly the same number of words have been omitted.

All orthographical variations found in the text are given. The first form given is generally the more frequent, otherwise that which occurs first in the text. However, an exception has occasionally been made, to place the entry under the better-known form of a word, e.g. *eslaissier*, not *alaissier*. Normally, variant spellings are not given, but if a word occurs only in the variants, it has been treated as a main text entry, i.e. all spelling variations are given.

The meaning given first is always that which occurs first in the text, with the variants afterwards. In general, all meanings are given, but in some cases it has been thought necessary only to include the less usual meanings of a very common word.

Apart from exceptional cases, a definition is given, followed by line-references. Quotations are preceded by line-references, and followed by definitions. Three instances of each meaning have usually been cited, where possible, but this was not considered necessary in occasional cases involving very common words. References are given in the order: text, var., individual MSS, where the abbreviation var. indicates the reading of more than four MSS. Readings of up to four MSS are indicated by the *sigla* of those MSS. References consisting of two line-numbers separated by a dash (10115–20130) are to equivalent lines in the Short (A) and Long (E) Redactions, up to A 10268. In some instances, MSS *sigla* have been given with line-references, e.g. 20119 (ES), to indicate that a reading is only in the MSS so indicated. This is to give a clearer picture of the degree of rarity of such words in the text.

The abbreviation Pot. before a line-reference refers to the Potvin edition, and designates the short passage in MS P at the very beginning of the text, unnumbered by Roach, although printed in full, pp. 3 and 5. Similarly, the numbering for MS K in Appendix VII has been continued from 74, although the editor has not numbered the lines.

Apart from current abbreviations, the following practices might be pointed out:

coll. = collective	part. = particle
ind. = indirect	rej.r. = rejected reading (= MS A or E)
lit. = literal(ly)	temp. = temporal
loc. = locution	var. = variant(s), see *supra*

A

A.   prep. 1. (in order) to. 9588; 2. for. 20414. 9720 *a ce que* — because, cf. 23391 *A ce, fait il, ne dites mie* — now, he says, do not say; 3. with. 20679, 20699, 23349; 4. from. 21002; 5. on. — apparently the sense of S 10028, cf. 20985 *a la terre* — on the ground. With inf. 20354 *Force a fere n'est mie droiz* — it is not right to use force.

AARBRER.   see *arbrer.*

AATE.   adj. nimble. 23997, 27941.

AATIE.   n.f. 1. condition, obligation. 29628; 2. ardour. *par aatie.* keenly, eagerly. App. VII TV 1059.

(AATIR, AHASTIR).   v.tr. attack, provoke. var. 26583, cf. *anhastir.* v.refl. 1. be provoked. 21854 *De bien ferir s'est aatis* — he set about striking great blows; 2. (+ *a*) attack, provoke. 26575 *A lui s'ahasti de bataille* — he challenged him to fight; 3. mutual refl. attack one another, fight. var. 27120, cf. *anhastir.* This word and *anhastir* seem to be interchangeable.

ABAISSIER.   n.m. (inf.). lowering of lances (and so = the coming together of the tourney). App. VII TV 308.

ABANDON.   n.m. 32586 *Je vos met tout an abandon* — I put all (I have) at your disposal. var. 28560 *Et qui n'avoit a abandon Son cors par sa proësce mis* — and who had not put himself at risk by his prowess.

(ABELIR).   v.intr. please. 28058.

(ABONDER).   v.intr. 1. abound, be abundant. 9618; 2. App. VII TV 345 *Mesire Gauvain qui abonde* probably 'be strong, powerful', cf. T-L I 58, 23. However, if we were to read *qu'i abonde,* the sense might be 'rush, dash'.

(ABONIR).   v.refl. give o.s., devote o.s. TV 28926 *Au roi de trestout s'abonist* — he should put himself entirely in the king's hands in this matter.

ABOSMEZ.   adj. (p.p.). downcast, upset. 20662.

ABRIVÉ.   adj. (p.p.). in a hurry, quickly, flat out. 9637–19770, 10188–20326, 10266. The verb seems to have been applied mainly to horses, then the use of the p.p. was extended to the rider, and eventually to persons not on horseback, e.g. 29571.

(ACEINDRE).   v.tr. surround. Q 27647.

(ACENER).   v.tr. beckon. 22663, P 22662.

ACESMÉ.   adj. (p.p.). well-armed, well-dressed, well-turned-out. 19769, 30946. In the variants we find numerous other senses of the word, 'prepared, equipped, adorned', but all contain implicitly the idea of elegance.

ACEUDRE.   v.tr. join on, add. P 24298, cf. God. I 83a. Not in T-L, AND.

(ACHACIER).   v.tr. chase, harry. 32180.

ACHENAL. adj. K 32100. mortal, of flesh and blood? This is not found in the dictionaries, and may well be an error. The scribe may even have intended this as *a cheval*, though that would make little sense.

ACHERIE. adj.f. reduced, diminished. 31414. Only E has this spelling, MS give the more usual *escherie*, and none of the other MSS has this reading, see Roach, note to 31414.

ACHOISON, ACHEISON, OCOISON. n.f. 1. cause, reason. 9503, 24810; 2. facts, circumstances. 24013, 25822; it is sometimes hard to differentiate between these two meanings, e.g. 22106; 3. delay. 25290 *sans achoison* — immediately, or 'freely', from a basic sense of 'impediment, obstacle'?; 4. inducement. L 20672, cf. 1.

ACLERIER. see *esclairier*, cf. Roach, note to 25662.

(ACLINER). v.refl. (also intr.). 1. lean over, stoop. 27387. 24768 *Qant vint a l'uis, si s'aclina Et vit* — when he came to the entrance (of the tent) he stooped to look through, and saw; 2. lie down? var. 27596.

ACOËR. see *aqueer*.

ACOILLABLE. adj. agreeable, pleasant. Q 27924.

ACOILLIR. v.tr. 1. take. (road). 28394. 21040 *Atant aquiaut chascun sa voie* — then each one goes his way; 2. corner, round up. 26603, 31333; 3. gain, acquire (from the sense 'take hold of, seize'). var. 25114; v.refl. start. 9894. (refl. in A only).

ACOINTIER. v.tr. 1. tell, make known to. 24018; 2. make the acquaintance of, get to know, possibly with connotations of physical love. (inf. as n.m.) 21635.

(ACOISIER, ACHOISIR?). v.refl. quieten, calm down. LPTV 25576. The *achoisi* of V, suggesting an inf. *achoisir*, is probably an error, cf. TV 25660 *racoisie* with a picard -*ie* for -*iee*.

(ACONSUÏR). v.tr. strike. MQU 21269, also K 20545? — see *consuïr*.

ACONTE. n.m. enumeration. 22465.

(ACONTER). v.tr. 1. enumerate, relate, recount. 9909, 22776; 2. assess, consider. App. VII TV 212 *Por esprover se acontez Porroit estre avec les prisiez* — to see whether he might be counted among those held in high esteem.

(ACORDER). v.tr. reconcile. 9796, 25042, 31364. v.intr. agree. M 31366 *Seroit a lui tout acordant* — he would agree with him entirely, i.e. do just as he wished.

(ACORER). v.tr. kill. QU 23668.

ACORSÉ. adj. (p.p.). swift, rapid. LTV 32183.

(ACOSTER). v.refl. approach, draw near (to). 27418.

(ACOUVENIR). v.intr. (impers.). be necessary. S 28449.

ACOVIERS. adj. (p.p.). covered. P 23929.

ACREANTER. v.tr. assure (of), promise, agree (to), grant. 26279, 27338, 27602. 30448 *Mais ne li veust acreanter La demorance* — but he would not agree to stay (with him).

ACROIRE. v.tr. *fere acroire* (*q.ch. a qn.*). make (s.o.) believe (s.th.). 25546, 26099, 27557. This word seems to imply a belief in something which is not actually true.

ACROSE. adj.f. horrible, awful. Q 25545, cf. God. *acrous*. Not found in T-L, AND.

ADEIGNIER. v.tr. (intr.). 20996 *onques nou vost adeignier De dire*. In EP this verb is tr., and the meaning seems to be 'she would not favour (or respect?) him enough to tell him'; in S, where the verb is intr., the meaning would simply be 'deign, condescend'.

ADELAIER. v.tr. leave, give respite?. T 23300. Not in T-L, AND, but cf. God. *adelaissier*.

ADEMIS. adj. (p.p.). keen, eager, lit. 'head-down, precipitate'. 21822, 27112.

(ADENTER). v.tr. knock (s.o.) down (on his face). App. VII TV 352.

ADÉS. adv. 1. unceasingly, always. 9836, 28500; 2. straightway, directly. 29207; 3. many, in abundance. 32355.

(ADESER).   v.tr. touch, go near. 19869, 24273.

(ADESTRER).   v.tr. 1. ride on the right-hand side of. 23419; 2. (more loosely) ride with, accompany. 23459.

ADIREEMENT.   adv. TV 26075. frantically, wildly, quickly? This word is not found in the dictionaries. Might the root be *adirer*, 'lose', and so *adiré*, 'lost'? It is more likely to be an error for, or variant form of, either *atireement* 'regularly', or *atirieement* 'elegantly'; cf. CM 33589, where PT have *atiree* for *adiree*.

ADOS.   n.m.pl. App. XI K 49. The usual meaning of this word is 'armour or equipment'; here, the meaning is probably the vestments (and accessories?) required for the coronation.

ADRECIER, ADRESCIER.   v.tr. 1. direct, aim. 25332, 28801, 32263; 2. make good, redress. 28629. v.refl. make one's way, go. 23146, 27440.

ADRESCE.   n.f. path. 21972, 24131. In the first of these examples, the sense could be 'direction', the other common meaning of this word. TV 23774 *Dalez l'adrece d'une angarde* would appear to mean 'beside the path leading to a look-out post'.

ADRESCEMANT.   n.m. amends, redress. 31380. M has *adroitement*, the only example of this word I have found. God. and T-L have *adroicement*, perhaps wrongly, among the variant spellings of *adrescement*, and God. has one example of *adroitier*, with the meaning 'amender', so there is clearly no difference in meaning.

ADROITEMENT.   see *adrescemant*.

AERDRE.   see *aherdre*.

(AESMER).   v.tr. aim a blow at. P 19845.

AFAITEMANT.   n.m. courtliness, courtesy. L 10102. This is the only example of the word in the text, and the meaning could be an external quality, such as elegance.

AFAITIEZ.   adj. (p.p.). courteous, courtly. 21537. The exact meaning of *afaitieemant* (adv.) is less clear; most probable is 'quietly, decorously'. 26075.

AFAUTRÉ.   adj. (p.p.). saddled, harnessed. 9928–20060, 31535. The lit. sense of *afautrer* is to put on the saddle-cloth or saddle-blanket.

AFENIR.   n.m. (inf.) end. S 30350. The usual spelling of this word is *afinir*; God. has one example of *afenir*.

AFERE, AFAIRE.   n.m. 1. thing. 20229. 24591 *por nul afaire* — for anything, at any price; 2. matter, business, situation. 20850, 23095, 24646.

(AFERIR).   v.intr. (impers.). be fitting, relevant. 20002, 22902, 26421.

AFFLIT, ASFLIT.   adj. (p.p.). distressed. KQTU 24671, U 29138. In both these instances the word would appear to denote a physical, rather than an emotional, state; E has *delis* in each case.

AFFRENÉ.   see *enfrené*.

AFICHIER.   v.intr. declare, affirm, promise. 19691, 21238, 27060. v.refl. promise one self, say to one self 25638, 32067. In both cases, the thought is probably unvoiced, as the thinker, Perceval, is alone.

AFÏENCIER.   v.intr. promise. 25748.

(AFÏER).   v.tr., intr. promise, assure (of). 20848, 23320, 28163.

(AFILER, AFFILER).   v.tr. sharpen, whet. p.p. (as adj.) App. VII TV 428. The meaning in MQ 29426, clearly fig., would seem to be 'quick, keen, ready'.

(AFINER).   v.tr. bring to an end, finish. 19880. v.intr. come to an end, die. 23668, 26801.

AFOLER.   v.tr. wound, harm, kill. 19853, 28824, 31964.

(AFONDER).   v.intr. Q 21666. Although the editor prints *a fonde*, we should perhaps read *afonde* 'is tired, weary'? Even this would make doubtful sense, and an error is more probable.

(AFUBLER).   v.tr. dress (in, with), put on. a) when the person dressed is also the dresser, the article of clothing being dir. obj. 29455, 30292. b) when another party does the dressing, the article of clothing being dir. obj., the person dressed, ind. obj. (+ *a*) 22164, 22660. These rules of syntax are broken in 26340 (E only) and var. 24495. Note also in S,U 26340 *afubler* (*qn.*) + *de* (*q.ch.*); *afublé de.* dressed in, wearing. 28636, 29880.

(AGASTIR).   v.tr. lay waste, ravage. 22853. *agastie.* deserted, bare. 24613.

(AGREER).   v.intr. please, be agreeable to. 20531, 24790, 25508. v. impers. 22690, 24370, 26700. The unusual syntax of 21804 *Mais li jeanz, qui molt agree De ce qu'il l'a aparceü* might suggest an intr. use, where *qui* is not dative, with the sense 'be pleased', but this seems a little unlikely.

AHAN.   n.m. hardship, trouble. 23401, 26579, 29053.

(AHANER).   v.tr. plough, cultivate. 22556. U has the alternative form *enhaner*, which has the same meaning.

AHASTIR.   see *aatir*.

AHÉ, AÉ.   n.m. life. 9553–19675.

(AHERDRE, AERDRE).   v.tr. catch, seize. imp. 6, P 20792, Q 31971.

AIESE.   see *ese*.

AIESIER, AAISIER, AEISIER.   v.tr. make comfortable, put at ease. 19903, 24657, 24727. inf. as n.m. 21364. v.intr. 1. make o.s. comfortable, be at one's ease. 24552; 2. rest. 25694, 27197, 28118. v.refl. 10116 *De tant con pot s'an aeisa* — he took what pleasure he could from her. *aiesiez* p.p. (as adj.) 1. comfortable, agreeable (to ride). 9848; 2. comfortable, well-endowed. 22492, 29559.

AIGLIERS.   see *egliaus*.

AIGREMANT.   see *aygremant*.

AIGROUSE.   adj.f. TV 23151. Not found in the dictionaries, but the sense, 'rough, unpleasant', is fairly obvious from the context. cf. *acrose*.

AINÇOIS, EINÇOIS.   adv. 1. (but) rather. 20626, 20644, 20665; 2. first (of all). 30679. 31132 *con je poi ainçois* seems to mean 'as quickly as (as soon as) I could'; cf. *cant ainçois* in T-L. prep. before. 30067, 30394. conj. (+ *que*) before. 19613, 19622, 20959. 9852 *Einçois que je plus sejort* — rather than stay any longer.

AINSI, AINSINS, AINSINT.   see *einsint*.

AINZ (1).   adv. before, first (of all). 19944, 20674, 21333. conj. (but) rather. 19956, 20417, 20479. *a l'ainz que.* as soon as, as quickly as. 20505, 21532, cf. L 10090 *com il ains pot.* On one occasion (19944) this word is spelt *ains*.

AINZ (2), AINS, EINZ.   adv. 1. ever. 22971, 25757; 2. (+ *ne*) never (before), sometimes with the sense 'not at all'. 19831, 9806–19906. 23784 *ainz ne li dist fors desreson* — all that he said to him was unreasonable. 31346 *qu'ainz ne pot plus* — since he could not do otherwise; 3. (+ mes. . . + *ne*) never yet. 9553, 19979. This word is more usually spelt *ainc*, but the scribe of E never uses this form.

AÏR.   n.m. ardour, violence. This word is almost invariably used in expressions such as *par (molt) (grant) aïr* 9623, 21200, *de tel aïr* 9689, *d'aïr* 9939, with a range of meanings: 'violently, quickly, with great force'.

AIRE.   n.m. or f. The basic meaning of this word, 'origin, extraction, race', cf. C1 M 8435 was extended to 'nature, character'; thus *de bon aire (ere)* or *debonaire* (adj.) denotes good qualities, and is used as a general term of approval, with a range of meanings from 'noble' to 'kind, charming' and simply 'good'. 20650, 22786, 32305, cf. also *debonairemant, deboneremant* adv. generously. 30972, 31981, MQT 26487. The corresponding expression, *de mal(e) aire (ere)* or *de mal(l)aire*, means the oppposite, 'rude, bad-tempered, spiteful' etc., and is a general term of disapproval. 10176–20318, 27790, 28328 (E), cf. also *deputere*.

AÏRIER, AÏRER.   v.intr., refl. become angry, upset. 20070, 21812, 24837. inf. as n.m. anger. 23800, 26770, 30786. *aïris* (P 29534) is a curious form of the p.p.

AIS.   n.f. one of the strips of wood which composed a shield. 20517, 30167, 30798. These were apparently glued together, cf. 30798, and were frequently covered with leather, cf. 20517, also *Erec* 3778. In the first example, this word could be n.m., which is perhaps less usual; in the other two, it is definitely n.f.

AJAMBEE.   see *jambee*.

AJOSTER, AJOUSTER.   v.tr. assemble, draw up. TV 26865. v.refl. join (with). var. 26861. inf. as n.m. joining (in battle), joust. P 29701.

ALAINE, ALAINNE, ALEINE.   n.f. 1. breath. 21651, 33301. 20523 *an la grosse alainne* — out of breath, breathing heavily. 23295 *molt ont cortes les alainnes* — they are very short of breath; 2. blast (on a horn). 19746. Similarly, *a grant alaine* 'loudly'. 20077 (voice), 26323, 32171 (horn). cf. *alegier*.

ALASCHIER, ALASQUIER.   v.intr. tire, weaken. KUV 23299.

ALEGIER.   v.tr. make lighter, easier. S 23301 *Que s'alaine puist alegier* — until he should get his breath back.

ALER.   v.tr., intr., refl. A frequent use of *aler* is with pres.p., sometimes with a sense equivalent to Eng. 'go seeking, go galloping' etc. cf. 19629, 20686, but more usually expressing an action or a state which in Mod.F. would be expressed simply by the verb here in the pres.p., but in the tense of *aler* used here (thus *va chevauchant* = Mod.F. *chevauche*); 9909, 20378, 20437. Other uses worthy of note are: v.tr. take, follow, travel along (a road). 22541, 22542. 23829 *s'an va son santier*, cf. Eng. 'go one's way'. 26116 *La quelle voie aler devoit* — which way (the mule) should go. v.absol. move about, travel. 9582–19703, 9836, 9857. v.intr. 1. progress, go on. 21281. 27305 *Car la nuiz estoit molt alee* — for the night was far advanced. 28995 *ja iert auques li jors alez* — the day was almost over; 2. (impers.) happen, turn out. 22835, 26622. 25912 *conmant qu'il aille* — come what may. 20472 *tost alant* (pres.p. as adj.) fast, rapid. 21008 *Se parti de moi an allant* — he left me and went on his way. inf. as n.m. 20810 *Ainz esploita dou tost aler* — but rather strove to go fast, cf. *errer*. 20824 *de si tost aler (s'avance)* — so quickly, at such a speed. Note the dissimilated cond. form in 29675, see Roach note.

ALERÏON.   n.m. large eagle. KQU 9666.

ALÉS.   see *eslés*.

ALEVER.   see *eslever*.

ALIE.   n.f. sorb-apple. 29528. This word is commonly used to denote a minimal value.

ALOIGNANCE.   n.f. prolongation, extension, perhaps with a suggestion of tedium, as in Mod.F. 'longueur'. S 29595. cf. God. *alongance, esloignance*. cf. *alonge*.

ALOIGNIER.   see *esloignier*.

ALONGE, ALOIGNE, ESLOIGNE.   n.m. (sometimes f.) 1. lengthening, prolongation. 28087, 32306, var. 24298. 23332 *sanz alonge* — briefly. The word usually implies a needless and boring expansiveness; 2. delay. 29664, P 31268. It is not always possible to distinguish clearly between these two meanings, particularly in expressions such as *sanz alonge*. cf. *aloignance, alonguement*.

ALONGUEMENT.   n.m. 1. prolongation, extension. 29006; 2. delay. P 22682. T-L has only the latter meaning, and only one example, but God. has several examples with the first sense. cf. *alonge*.

(ALOSER).   v.tr. praise, esteem. p.p. (as adj.) esteemed, renowned. 20968, 30230. v.refl. gain renown. S 26787.

AMANDER. v.tr. 1. avenge, make up for. 25410; 2. repay. MU 28970; 3. make good. 30691; 4. help, assist. 31982 *se Diex et foi m'amant* cf. Eng. 'so help me God'. v.intr. improve. 29208 (EPS). The context makes this the most likely meaning, although one might expect the verb to be refl. Otherwise, the meaning could be 'grow, increase in size', which is a normal sense of the intr.

(AMANTEVOIR). v.tr. mention, speak of, tell. 31784. This word is also found quite frequently in the var., when E has *ramantevoir*.

AMANTOIRE. n.m. (inf.) mention, reference. 23022.

(AMASSER). v.intr. assemble, gather (together). 26252, 31160.

AMATIZ. adj. (p.p.). tired, weak. S 24671, S 24680.

(AMBARRER). v.tr. 1. stave in, dent (helm). 20514; 2. drive in (sword). 22358. cf. *ambatre*.

(AMBATRE). v.tr. 1. drive, chase (into). 20311; 2. drive in (sword) 22030, 24973. cf. *ambarrer*. v.refl. thrust o.s., rush. 27101, 30241, S 27492.

(AMBELIR). v.tr. 1. embellish, make beautiful. 22738; 2. (or intr.) please. MSU 28058. cf. *abelir*.

AMBLER. v.intr. amble. 23999, 26074, 26152. This word has a less restricted meaning than in Mod.F.

AMBLEÜRE. n.f. amble. 20636 *Anforciee avoit s'ambleüre* — she had increased her speed. 23778 *Percevaux erre s'ambleüre* — P. goes along at an amble. Used adverbially *l'ambleüre*. at an amble, ambling. 20922, 30712, 31655.

(AMBRACIER). v.tr. put (s.th.) on one's arm, put one's arm through. 20468. This example, in ET only, is a borrowing from C1; the author of C2 does not use this word.

AMBRASÉ. adj. (p.p.). lit, alight. 22735, 25610, 32324. fig. S 29817.

(AMBROIER). v.tr. drive in, thrust in. 21594, 22031. cf. *ambarrer*, *ambatre*.

AMBRUNCHIER. v.intr. bend over, lean over (forwards). 22044 *Si qu'il le fist tout ambrunchier Devant sus l'arçon de la selle* — so that he knocked him face-down over his saddle-bow, cf. S 20546, S 20871. The p.p. is used to denote any physical or mental state in which the head droops: tiredness, thoughtfulness, shame, sadness, etc.

AMEEMENT. adv. willingly. M 23524.

AMENDEMENT. n.m. reparation, amends. var. 31379.

AMENEVIZ. adj. (p.p.). adroit, skilful. 29796, TV 30820.

(AMENUISIER). v.intr. dwindle, diminish. 32084.

AMESURER. v.refl. calm o.s., control o.s., be reasonable. 27803, 28756, S 21670.

AMONT. see *aval*.

AMONTER. v.tr. increase. 22863.

(AMORDRE). v.refl. apply o.s. 24073. *amors* (+ *a*) p.p. (adj.) inclined, given to. 24088.

AMOREUS. adj. lovely, charming, delightful. 22296.

AMOUREES. adj.f.pl. (p.p.). U 29513. The meaning and root of this word are unclear. Is it 'prepared with love', i.e. 'filled with love, loving'? cf. T-L *amorer* from Lat. *amor*. Or is it simply an error, possibly caused by a var. spelling *amerees* (for *esmerees*) in U's model? cf. T-L, God. *esmerer*, and Roach, note to 25662.

AMPIRE. n.m. army. 30964.

AMPIRIER. v.tr. hurt, injure. 22367, KMQU 9738 (also rej.r. 21314). v.intr. deteriorate, (decompose). 25380.

(AMPLOIER). v.tr. spend, use (time). 25127.

AMPOINDRE, EMPEINDRE. v.tr. 1. strike, hit, knock. 9735–19851, P 22048, App. VII TV 271, where *lance* is dir. obj.; 2. imprint, inscribe? S 25260. v.refl. hit one another. 23294 (fist). P 23246 *A la terre s'empaingnent jus* — they knock each other to the ground.

(AMPRANDRE). v.tr. 1. undertake. 21051, 23095, 24207; 2. take, seize. LT 20652; 3. take on, gain. App. VII TV 870 *Por lui tel hardement emprisent* — they took heart so much because of him. (it could also = 1., with *hardement* meaning 'great deeds', rather than 'courage'.) v.intr. (+ *a* + inf.) start. 31874 (E). T-L has only refl. examples with this sense, but God. has comparable examples.

ANANZ. prep. into? rej.r. 21595, 21921. T-L, AND have *enenz* as adv. Might this be a prepositional use? We also find *anz anz*, cf. Roach, note to 21595, and add 21139 to his examples.

ANARME, ENARME. n.f. (usually pl.). strap(s), loop(s) by which the shield is held. 9668, 20468, 22196. unusually sing., 29520. These straps, sometimes of (twisted?) cloth, cf. 9600–01, are used to hold the shield for combat, as opposed to the *guige*, a longer strap used to hang the shield round the neck, usually for transport. *anarmé, enarmé.* adj. (p.p.). 9601–19723 *anarmez de* — with straps made of. 32004 *bien anarmé* — with good straps.

(ANASTELER, ENASTELER). v.tr., intr. splinter, 22027, 30204.

ANCERCHIER. see *encerchier.*

(ANCHANTELER). v.tr. hold ready for combat (shield). 23240.

(ANCHAUCIER). v.tr. chase, harry. 30264. U 31284 is probably an error.

ANCHAUS, ANCHAUX. n.m. 1. fight, combat. 26929; 2. chase, pursuit. 27186, LP 27098.

ANCLAVEÜRE. n.f. lock. (L 9558–) 19681. This appears to be the only attestation of this meaning; the word usually means 'enclosure'.

ANCLIN. adj. bowed, stooped. 9473, 25284. In the first of these instances, the word probably indicates tiredness. cf. *ambrunchier.*

ANCLINER. v.tr. bow to. 26377, 31660, 31690. v.intr. lie down? Q 27596, cf. *acliner.* p.p. as adj. bowed (head). 30543, 30570. cf. *anclin.*

ANCOLORIS. adj. (p.p.). brightly coloured, bright. 27697, LPTV 31042 (sun), K 28033. cf. *coloris.*

(ANCOMBRER). v.tr. 1. trouble, bother, hinder. 30475, MQ 10146, MQ 22924; 2. fill (up). 28085 (E) — a curious fig. use; the room is filled with *biauté, richesce*, etc.; the dictionaries have no comparable examples. Perhaps 'crowded' is nearer the sense here, cf. AND (*encombrer*[1]).

ANCOMBRIER, AMCOMBRIER. n.m. 1. trouble, bother, difficulty. 20596, 25389, 26015; 2. troublesome person (or thing). var. 23222. An unusual sense of the word, yet clearly the original reading, found in 7 out of 10 MSS, including S, which usually = E, and also the *lectio difficilior.*

ANCONTRE. n.m. meeting, encounter. 20497, 27057. 22647 *Li sont a l'ancontre venu* — they came to meet him. *mal ancontre.* mishap. 32150.

ANCONTRER, ENCONTRER. v.tr. 1. clash, collide with. 9688; 2. meet, come across. 20046, 20622, 20913. inf. as n.m. clash, encounter. 19803, 9744.

ANCONTREVAL. adv. down, downwards. 30208, 30579, U 30543. cf. *contreval.*

ANCOR, ANCORE, ENCOR. adv. 1. yet, still. (+ *ne*) not yet. 9903, 21047. 20594 *Ancor me vient miauz . . . Que j'aille* — better (yet) that I go. 23239 *vostre merci, Qant vos ancor me desfïez* — I thank you for challenging me all the same (= in spite of your anger); 2. again, as well. 21494, 28391; 3. (+ subj.) although, even though. 23772, 25680, 29405. see also *ancui.*

ANCORTINEE. adj.f. (p.p.). draped, hung. 9802, 24482, 26361.

ANCOSTE. adv. sideways. var. 24484 *encoste et en lé* — in all directions, everywhere. 27679 (E) *d'ancoste* — sideways, i.e. round the walls. prep. beside. 21480, 21513, 25539.

ANCUI. adv. today, this day. 20083, 23404, 27159. 9620 *encor ancui* — this very day.

ANDEMANTIERS.   see *endemantiers*.

ANDROIT.   n.m. 23861 *an nul androit* — in no wise. var. 31452 *Jo ne suis pas de (en) vostre endroit* — I am not your equal; here the sense seems rather to be 'you are not my equal', which is unusual. adv. (reinforcing adv. of place), also *androites*. 24373 (EP) *ici androites* — (just) here., cf. 28398, P 21146. prep. 1. near, level with. 9681; 2. (temp.) about, near. 20911, 25718.

ANFERMETÉ.   n.f. illness, infirmity. 29035. The var. forms include *anferté, enferté, enfreté*.

ANFERMEÜRE.   n.f. 27762 (E). Normally this word means a fortress, or fortified place, but here it seems to indicate a 'strongroom' or 'armoury'.

(ANFORCIER).   v.tr. 1. increase. 20636; 2. step up. U 26908. v.intr. (grow larger), involve more people. M 26908. cf. *angreignier*. v.refl. exert o.s., make an effort. LM 23156. adj. (p.p.). PS 28891 *enforcie (feste)* — rich, sumptuous. The forms *anforcier* and *esforcier*, theoretically different verbs, seem to overlap; not the only example of an alternation of the prefixes *an-* and *es-*.

ANFORESTÉ.   p.p. well into the forest, hidden by the trees. 26521. I know of no example of this word other than the 3 recorded by T-L: *Erec* 3535, 3611, *Mule sans frein* 130, and that in C1, T 14439. The sense attested by AND is quite different.

ANFOSSEZ.   adj. (p.p.). sunken, deep-set (eyes). 23184.

ANGARDE.   n.f. hill, eminence; sometimes a fortified look-out post situated on one of these. 23774, 28563, 31046. see also *garde*.

ANGART, ENGART.   n.m.? QU 27739. A var. form of *angarde* or an error? Not found in T-L, God., but cf. AND *agard, enguard*, etc.; the sense 'vision, sight' is possible, but unconvincing.

ANGIGNIER.   v.tr. 1. trick, deceive. 9959–20089; 2. harm, shame. 23489.

ANGIN, ANGIEN.   n.m. 1. artifice, trick, deception. 26596, 27725, 28713; perhaps with connotations of magic, 26714; 2. skill, ingenuity. MQ 10018.

ANGOISSEUSEMANT.   adv. keenly, violently. 19698, 19825.

(ANGOISSIER, ENGOISSIER).   v.tr. press, urge. 9957–20087.

ANGOISSOS, ANGOISSEUS.   adj. 1. worried, anguished, distressed. 9749, 10110–20246, 28951; 2. (over-) eager, hurtful, harmful? Q 10244. Although such meanings as 'cruel, causing distress' are not uncommon, the dictionaries have no attestation of such a use where the word is applied to a person.

(ANGREIGNIER).   v.intr. increase in size, (involve more people). 26908. cf. *anforcier*.

ANGRÉS.   adj. violent, fierce, savage. 28936, var. 23412, App. VII TV 799.

(ANHASTIR).   v.tr. attack, provoke. 26583 *Qu'il anhasti celui de guerre* — that he declared war on him, attacked him. v.refl. 1. mutual refl. attack one another, fight. 27120. 2. be provoked. M 21854., cf. *aatir* refl. 1.; 3. attack, provoke. M 26575., cf. *aatir* refl. 2. The variants suggest that this and *a(h)a(s)tir* are interchangeable.

(ANJENOÏR).   v.tr. beget, engender. 29352.

ANLUMINER.   v.tr. 1. illuminate, make bright. 21932, 22806, 22956; (fig.) MU 29817; 2. make beautiful, enhance. 25138, 27705, 32467; 3. decorate (usually with gold). 27964, 30817, 32284.

ANMI, ENMI.   adv. in the middle. 10016–20150, 21121, 21604. 21475 *Et une croiz avoit enmi* — and there was a cross in between (the roads). prep. in the middle of. 9532, 9560, 9686. As in Eng., the word is occasionally reinforced; *droit anmi* — right in the middle. 20698, 24740. In C2, the scribe of A uses *enmi* exclusively, the scribe of E, *anmi* except at 32073.

ANMUSELEE.   p.p.(f.) veiled. 27522.

ANN'. interrog. part. Used in a question expecting an affirmative answer. 24361 *Ann'estes vos am bon ostel?* — are you not well lodged?

ANNEUR, ANNOR, ANOR. see *honor.*

ANNÏEUX, ANUIOX, (ANÏEUSE, ANNÏOSE). adj.(f.). 1. annoying, vexatious. 20852; 2. disagreeable, unpleasant, often with a sense close to 'difficult'. 23152, 26158, 27512; 3. listless, downcast. Q 9473.

ANNUI, ENUI. n.m. 1. nuisance, irritation, displeasure. 19634, 24577, 26346; 2. trouble, difficulty. 20356, 26996, 27657. *fere annui (a).* cause (s.o.) trouble. 9717, 19886, 20536.

ANNUIT. adv. 1. tonight. 20744, 21672, 21808; 2. last night. 23619, 24715, 25774. These two meanings occur with about equal frequency. There seems to be no clear difference in the meaning of *annuit mes*, except that it is used exclusively for the coming night, cf. Roach, note to 29385. 24697 (E) *Percevaux toute annuit dormi* seems a curious usage, and may well be an error.

ANORER. see *honorer.*

ANROSINEE. adj.f. (p.p.). covered in dew. 32168, KL 27593, where M has *arosinee.* I feel the editor is perhaps a trifle over-conservative in retaining the *anracinee* of EU, here.

ANSEIGNE, ANSAIGNE. n.f. 1. news, tidings. 9656–19788; 2. banner, standard. 26868, 27020, LTV 30144.

ANSEIGNIER, (ENSEIGNIER). v.tr. 1. point out, indicate, show (the way to). 19939, 20714, 21021. 23561 *Lou chevalier qui m'anseigna Lou roi Artu* — the knight who directed me to King Arthur; 2. tell, instruct. 20769, 20995. *anseigniez, anseignie* p.p. (f.) as adj. 1. courteous, well brought-up. 27484, 28379, 30998; 2. (+ *de*) learned, educated (in). 27913, LTV 29015. In var. 27954 *ensegnié* apparently means marked, i.e. inlaid: absent from T-L, AND, but cf. God. III 232b, and Roach, note to 24982. cf. also *saignié.*

ANSERIR. n.m. (inf.). evening, dusk. 30350. V has *eserir.*

(ANSERRER). v.tr. shut in, imprison. 20434.

ANSEURQUETOT. adv. what is more, besides. 27480.

ANSON, ANSONC. adv. high up, at the top, at the tip. 24014, 32407, 32453. prep. up on, on top of, high up. 24252, 31494, 32377.

(ANSORCETER). v.tr. (E) 23431. If this word is genuine, the meaning is clearly the same as that of P's *ensorceré* — 'enchant, cast a spell on'; however, my reading of the manuscript would be *ansorceré.*

ANSTEE. n.f. lance-length. LTV 28863. cf. *hante* (1).

ANSUS. see *ensus.*

ANTALANTEZ. adj. (p.p.). pleased, content. 10171. This is not the usual meaning of the p.p., which is 'eager, willing', cf. *entalentis.*

(ANTAMER). v.tr. cut, pierce. 20554, 26891.

ANTANDRE, (ANTENDRE), ENTANDRE. v.tr. 1. listen to, hear. 20829, 21009, 21909; 2. understand. 32132 *riens fors Dieu n'i antendoit* — he saw in all this only the hand of God? v.intr. (+ *a*) 1. concentrate on, give one's attention to, think about. 10175–20317, 10264–20525, 21741, with the sense of 'aspire to, hope to gain' 30494, Q 10133; 2. hear, listen to. 22053, 22087, 27622. Also v.refl. rej.r. 32130, cf. intr. 1.

ANTANTE, ANTENTE, ENTENTE. n.f. 1. effort, application. *metre s'antante (a).* apply o.s., devote o.s. (to). 20343, 22227, 26080; 2. thought(s), intention. 29546, 32130.

ANTECHIEZ, ANTEICHIEZ, ANTESCHIEZ. adj. (p.p.). 1. afflicted (with sin). 23888, 32448, S 24098; 2. endowed (with good quality). 24051, 29015.

ANTENCION. n.f. mind, thoughts. 32137. cf. *antante.*

ANTENTIS. adj. attentive. 31240 *A autre riens fui antentis* — my mind was on other things. *ententiue* (: *piue*). KLTV 32062.

ANTIER. adj. 1. fair, favourable. 21468; 2. whole. 21771, 26173, 26185.

(ANTR'ABUICHIER) (?). v.refl. rej.r. 30162. Possibly 'come together (in combat)', cf. T-L *abochier*, and FEW I 583b. Although the reading of E is the *lectio difficilior*, it is isolated, and the fact that the scribe of E normally spells *trebuchier*, *trabuichier*, suggests that this may be *s'an trabuichent*, and therefore an error.

(ANTR'ANCONTRER). v.refl. encounter one another, clash, collide. 9673, 20491. cf. *entrecontrer* U 9673, *entr'acontrer* Q 24958.

ANTRE. prep. frequently used with v.refl., often in compounds, cf. *antr'ancontrer*, etc. 1. mutually. 9796, 23256; 2. between. (E) 22177 *antre ces diz* — meanwhile. (also T 21365); 3. together. 22656, 30123. *antre que*. temp. conj. while. 25454.

ANTREDONER. v.refl. give one another (blows). 10258–20520, 23244, 23249.

(ANTREFERE). v.refl. 23703 *molt grant joie s'antrefont* — they make much of one another.

ANTRELAISSIER. v.tr. leave (off, aside), abandon. 26550, 28755, LPTV 29597, although the meaning of PTV is not satisfactory. KL also have *entreloier*, *entrelaier*.

ANTREMANTRES. see *entremantres*.

ANTREMETRE. v.refl. (+ *de*). devote o.s. (to), occupy, busy o.s. (with), engage (in). 10233–20429, 21377, 21936. Exceptionally, in 23423 (E), the verb is used with *por*, which slightly alters the sense.

ANTREPRIS. adj. (p.p.). put out, at a loss. 23442 (ES).

ANTRESEIGNES. n.f.pl. insignia, device of a knight (on his horse's trappings). 27019.

(ANTRESEIGNIER). v.tr. mark, decorate. 27954. cf. *anseignier*.

ANTRESEING. see *antressoinz*.

ANTRESET, ANTRESAIT. adv. completely, definitely. 22016, 26706.

ANTRESSOINZ, ANTRESEING. n.m. sign, mark. 9865–20013. The following spellings occur in the var.: *entresaing*, *entresains*; *antreseing* itself is in fact introduced by the editor.

(ANTREVENIR). v.refl. come together, attack one another. 9667, 20509, 24957.

ANTULLES. adj. stupid. 29870 (ES).

ANUIERE. adj.f. MU 23506. disagreeable, vexatious (?). Not found in the dictionaries, but cf. FEW IV 702, *enoiere*.

ANUITIER. v.intr. 1. fall (night). 28138, var. 25551, S 28103; 2. (impers.) become dark, become night. 28354, 30412, 32044. inf. as n.m. nightfall, dusk. 22248, 26769, 27895.

ANVEILLIR. n.m. (inf.) growing old, old age. 23035.

ANVERS, ENVERS. n.m. back, inside (shield). 28276. adj. on one's back, supine. 9686. *a envers*. adv. back to front. 9517. prep. 1. compared with. 9714; 2. against., with different senses, var. 22371, M 9669; 3. towards, before. U 9788; 4. (temp.) towards, near. Q 20687.

ANVIE. n.f. 1. desire. 25840, 26220, 30862; 2. envy, ill-will. 26864, 29020, 31940. It is not always possible clearly to differentiate these two meanings.

(ANVIRONER). v.tr. go around, circle. 21078 (E).

ANVIZ, ENVIZ. adv. Invariably *a anviz* in E, but not always in the var. unwillingly, reluctantly. 28735, 29077, 32113.

(ANVOISIER). v.refl. be pleased, happy. 25560.

AOIRE. v.tr. enlarge, increase (in size). LP 26100.

AORER, (AOURER). v.tr. worship, pray to. 19623, 29131 (E), 31689. v.intr. pray. L 23845. cf. *orer*.

(AORNER). v.tr. supply, provide for, endow. K 21712, M 22556.

APARAILLIER, APAROILLIER (1). v.tr. 1. prepare, make ready, (sometimes simply 'make'). 23103, 24283, 26485; 2. fit out, equip, dress. 24950, 25484, (fig.) 28664. v.refl. 1. dress. 21461, 24708; 2. get ready. 29960. At 27281 we find *aparaillerent*: *laverent*, but only in EMU.

APARAILLIER, (APAROILLIER) (2). v.refl. be equal, compare. 28316, 31620.

(APARLER). v.tr. speak to. KLTV 27722. v.refl. (mutual refl.) speak to one another. var. 22843.

APARMAIN. adv. directly, immediately. 30744. *ore aparmain*. right now. 23091.

APAROILLIER. see *aparaillier* (1), (2).

APAROIR. v.intr. appear, come into sight, be visible. 21073, 22766, 24249. *aparant*. pres.p. visible. 25574. v.refl. appear. 32127.

(APARTENIR). v.tr. be related, be close. 23350, 30243.

(APENDRE). v.intr. belong. var. 24578.

APERTEMANT. adv. openly, clearly. 31110.

APLAIDEÏCE. adj. formal (joust). 20477 (ET). see Foulet's glossary to C1, from which this is a borrowing. The two examples of *de / a plaideïces* given by T-L from *Guillaume le Maréchal* raise the question of whether we should not read *a plaideïce*. Meyer, in the glossary of that text, defines such jousts as ones 'dont les conditions étaient débattues et réglées d'avance'. It is curious that T-L has not noted the instance of this word in *Troie*, l. 17131.

APLAIDIER. v.intr. speak. 27290.

APLANOIER. v.tr. 1. stroke, caress. 25441, 27719, 31669; 2. smooth, make smooth, plane. 29304, Q 27021.

(APLOVOIR). v.intr. abound. Q 22766.

APOIER. see *apuier*.

(APOIGNIER). v.tr. grasp. T 20468.

(APOINDRE). v.intr. spur (and hence 'gallop'). 27991.

APRESTER. v.tr. 1. prepare, make ready. 19931, 20299, 21425; 2. equip, dress. Q 22330, Q 23654. cf. *aparaillier* (1).

APRIS. adj. (p.p.). 1. well brought-up, sensible. 22587, 24208, 29757; 2. skilled, learned, capable. 27484, 27921. 30464 *Trop suis aprise a male escole* — I have made a great mistake, been very foolish.

(AQUEER, ACOËR). v.intr. become still, quiet, peaceful. KLTV 32046.

AQUI. U 27146. Probably an error, unless it represents *ce qui* (= I think).

AQUIS. adj. (p.p.). tired, (physically) distressed. P 24671, PQ 29138.

AQUITER. v.tr. 1. free, liberate. 22719, KMQU 9506; 2. (+ *foi*) keep, make good (promise), discharge (obligation.) 28134, 30956.

ARAGON. n.m. (adj.) (Aragonese) horse. var. 24956.

ARAISONER. see *aresnier* (2).

ARAUMANT. see *errannmant*.

ARBALESTEE. n.f. the distance one can shoot a crossbow bolt. 24245, 26125. cf. *archie*.

ARBRE. n.m. T 22604 *dusc'al sec arbre* — as far as the Dry Tree, i.e. to the ends of the earth.

(ARBRER, AARBRER). v.intr., refl. rear, prance (horse). L 26871, L 9938. see note on this word at end of Glossary.

ARCHEL, ARCEL. n.m. arch. 10217, 10226, 25073. It would appear that the tomb of the Black Knight is situated under a man-made arch. The scribe of A uses *arcel*, that of E, *archel*. cf. *archet*.

ARCHET. n.m. arch. 20558, 20562, 20979. cf. *archel*. This word is used only in these three instances; elsewhere, in episodes 21 and 26, *archel* is used.

ARCHIE. n.f. bowshot, the distance one can shoot an arrow. 20628. cf. *arbalestee.*
ARCHOIER. v.intr. bend. 20487 (ET). A borrowing from C1.
(ARÇONER). v.intr. bend. 10254. cf. *archoier.*
ARDURE. n.f. heat. 25351, App. VII TV 1079.
ARESNER, ARESNIER (1). v.tr. tether by the reins (horse). 9825–19920, 9987–20117, 21142. (fig.) hold back? U 21249.
ARESNIER (2), (ARAISONER), ARESONER. v.tr. (sometimes also mutual refl.) speak to. 21248, 21636, 21962. 25089 *sans aresnier* — without saying a word.
AREST. n.m. pause, halt, delay. Used exclusively in phrases such as *sanz (nul/plus d')arest.* 20685, 21450, 21646.
ARESTEE. n.f. pause, halt, delay. 20616, 24140, 28142.
ARESTEMANT. n.m. pause, halt, delay. 25369, 26047, 28461.
ARESTER. v.tr. stop, catch. 20624, 24880, 28823. v.intr. 1. stop, tarry, stay. 20288, 10242, 20679; 2. stay, reside. 22109, 22133. v.refl. stop, tarry, stay. pret. 3. 9864, 20490, p.p. 21225. inf. as n.m.? rej.r. 28125, supported by L. 30540 *aresté.* adj. (p.p.). motionless, immobile.
ARESTOISON. n.f. pause, halt, delay. 22246, 24219, 26478.
ARESTUE. n.f. pause, halt, delay. V 31272. The rarest of this family of words; T-L has one example, God., AND have none.
AREVERTIR. v.refl. K 25668. Not found in the dictionaries. Probably the same as *ravertir.* cf. *arevenir* for *revenir,* God. I 394c?
(ARGUËR). v.tr. press, urge. 32421.
AROUTEEMANT. adv. rapidly, without pause. 20619 (EPS).
(AROUTER). v.refl. go, move. Q 21156.
(ARREER). v.tr. make ready, prepare. S 27318.
ARREMANT. n.m. ink, blacking. 23183, 25082, 30161 (ES).
ASAMBLER. v.tr. 1. gather together, assemble. 19941, 29651, 30964; 2. join together. 32528. v.intr. 1. gather together. 23083, 24620, 27027; 2. meet, come together, clash (in combat), joust. 23811, 26898, 27041.
ASAVOIR. v.tr. *fere asavoir.* tell. S 10080.
ASAZEE, ASSAZEE. adj.f. (p.p.). rich, prosperous. MQ 22850, TV 31858.
ASENER. v.tr. 1. hit (a target), strike. 20544, 21841, 24875; 2. direct. 21507, 27620, 31463. It is possible the obj. of 20544 is the *cop,* which would modify the sense. v.intr. 1. arrive. 23556, 27695; 2. strike. LT 22357.
ASENS. n.m. 1. way, manner. 26426; 2. direction. var. 31558.
(ASEOIR). v.tr. besiege. 22854.
ASERIR. v. impers. become dark. 31224 (M only). inf. as n.m. Q 30350. cf. *anserir.*
(ASEÜRER, ASSEÜRER). v.tr. 1. reassure. 22250, 23144; 2. (+ *de*) assure (of). 29856. v.refl. 1. (in neg. phrases) linger, tarry. 10186 *De rien nule ne s'aseüre,* cf. 21105, 24187; 2. be reassured, be calmed. 21670, 29644, S 22869; 3. persist in. 23496. The editor could have retained *esseüre* in 21670.
ASFLIT. see *afflit.*
(ASOUPER). v.refl. trip, slip. App. IV Q 26.
(ASSENTIR). v.tr. hit, strike. P 24875.
(ASSERER). v.intr. become dark, evening. S 30412.
ASSEÜR. adj. assured, sure. S 22868, Q 24363, M 31601. adv. certainly, indeed. var. 31601. The adv. use is also attested by AND. cf. *seür.*
ASTELER. v.intr. splinter, break. P 30204. (cf. *anasteler.*)
ASTIS. see *hastis.*
ATACHES. see *estaiches* and Roach, note to 26363.

ATAINDRE, (ATEINDRE). v.tr. 1. reach, catch, catch up (with). 10133–20267, 10167–20314, 20611; 2. hit, succeed in hitting. 9721–19845, 20517, 21266. (cf. *asener*); 3. land (a blow) on. with *cop* as dir. obj., and ind. obj. for the person struck. 21833 (this syntax in E only). v.intr. (+ *a*) attain, reach. M 10133.

ATAÏNE. n.f. attack, offensiveness. 31114.

(ATALANTER). v.intr. (impers.) please. 22976, 29545.

ATAMPRER. see *atramper*.

ATANDANCE. n.f. wait, delay. 32480.

ATANDUE, ATENDUE. n.f. wait, delay. 25534, 26520, 30128.

ATARDIER. v.intr. delay, linger. 10220, 24173 (E only, var. have *atargier*), 28269. cf. *atargier*.

ATARGEMENT. n.m. delay. LTV 27673.

ATARGIER. v.intr. delay, linger. 19950, 20219, 20362. inf. as n.m. delay. 29974; also 22065, where the final *s* suggests the word is seen as n.m. cf. *atardier*.

ATENEMENT. n.m. U 23218. Not found in T-L, AND. God. has one example meaning 'riches, possessions', cf. *atenir* = possess. Might the meaning of *par atenement* be similar to that of *par contenemant*, 'to cut a figure', related to the sense 'be suitable, apt' of *atenir*?

ATENIR. v.refl. hold one self back (from), keep from. S 25208.

(ATILLIER). v.refl. make ready, equip one self M 31322.

(ATIRIER). v.refl. make ready, equip one self S 31322.

(ATOICHIER, ATOUCHIER). v.tr. touch, reach to. 24464, 24747, 25620. The *atouchoient* of 20792 is conjectural, see Roach, note; in my opinion, the manuscript reading is clearly *acroichoient*.

ATOR. n.m. 1. ornament, decoration. 21922, var. 24484. 20110 *de riche ator* — fine, beautiful. 29748 *Et molt par i a bel ator* — and there are many beautiful things; 2. attire, equipment. 24513, 31645, 31813.

ATORNEMANT. n.m. 1. equipment, things. 22592; 2. furnishings, decoration. 27674.

ATORNER. v.tr. 1. decorate. 9566; 2. prepare, make ready, equip, dress. 9602–19724, 22457, 22519; 3. (usually with *mal*). cause trouble for, maltreat. 21946, S 24962. 10044 *Que de barat fu atorné* — that he was being tricked, cf. *barat*; 4. arrange. 29514 *a leur eus si atornees* — so well-disposed towards them, cf. *eus*. v.refl. make ready, equip o.s., dress. 20632, 21453, 21933. *atourné* 30431, is the reading of P, not E.

ATOUCHIER. see *atoichier*.

(ATRAIRE). v.tr. assemble, gather together. 30302.

(ATRAMPER, ATAMPRER). v.tr. 1. temper (steel). 23262; 2. moderate, temper. 30853.

ATRAVER. see *estraver*.

AUCENT. n.m. story, tale. S 26432. cf. God. I 494c; not found in T-L, AND.

AUQUES. adv. 1. somewhat, quite, rather. 22250, 22304, 23144; 2. a little, at all. 26973.

AUQUETON. n.m. acton, thick tunic worn under the hauberk. 21547.

AUTEL. adj. such. 19791, 22599 (ES), 31692. For the almost pronominal usage in 31691, see Roach, note to that line.

AUTR'AN. (*l'autr'an*). temp. loc. some time ago. In 22907, the moment referred to is some years ago; in 30645, it is not stated, but seems to be more recent.

AUTRESI, AUTRESINT. adv. 1. also, likewise. 10035, 22478, 22545; 2. equally. 10040–20176; 3. (+ adj.) as. 31593, 32050, 32076. 27642 *autresint con s'* — as if.

AUTR'IER. (*l'autr'ier*). temp. loc. recently, not long ago. In some MSS it is used where the text has *l'autr'an*. 22407, 22412. cf. *autr'an*

AVAL, AVAU. adv. 1. down, downwards. 20495, 20871; 2. (down) across. 20528; 3. down below (in). 28547. *(basse) par terre aval* seems to designate a *salle* which is at ground level, rather than raised up and reached by steps; thus both Perceval and Bagomadés enter such halls on horseback. 27295, 28609, var. 21093. *amont et aval.* up and down, to and fro, hither and thither. 19615, 31212, 32099.

AVANCIER. v.tr. 1. help, further. 20747, M 32190; 2. advance, move forward. MQ 27952. v.refl. advance, go forwards. 20824, 26245.

AVAU. see *aval.*

AVENANMANT. adv. pleasantly. 25869, 29813, P 24282.

AVENIR. v.intr. 1. happen, come about. 9527, 19921, 19947; 2. suit, be fitting, appropriate. 9639–19771, 20447, 27776; 3. reach. 31435.

AVERE. adj.f. reticent, reluctant. 29930.

AVERSIER. n.m. devil. 23222.

AVERTIR, (AAVERTIR?). v.refl. recall, decide. MQSU 25668. The *aavertir* of M seems to be a *hapax.*

AVÏERE. n.m. opinion. P 25615 *lor est avïere* — it seems to them, in their opinion. cf. *avis, vis.*

(AVIRONER). v.tr. go around, circle. PS 21078. cf. *anvironer.*

AVIS. n.m. opinion. 20651, 23343, 23362. *ce m'est avis* or *li est avis*, etc. — it seems to me, to him, etc., in my opinion, I think, etc. 9546, 19790, 21643. cf. *il iert avis.* — it seemed to him, etc. 25499, 29263; *m'iert avis.* — it seemed to me, etc. 26174. cf. *avïere, vis.*

(AVISER). v.tr. look at, consider. 23212, 30064, Q 10116.

AVOIER. v.tr. lead, guide, direct. 20864, 28165, 29184. v.refl. make one's way, travel. 32017, TV 31914.

AVOIR. v.tr., aux. have. 20735 *ce n'i a pas* — there is no question of that. 22365 *N'i a celui son per ne doute* — each of them fears his adversary. 22381 *conquis m'aiez* appears to indicate a desire or suggestion, not the statement of fact we might anticipate. We may note two uses of the imp. subj., seeming to imply a thwarted desire: 20394, 22254. n.m. riches, possessions. 21918, 22896, 23364.

AYGREMANT, AIGREMANT. adv. sharply, keenly, violently. 20509, 24853.

(AYGRÏER). v.tr. goad, spur. 20539, App. VII TV 668.

B

BAER, (BAIER). v.intr. 1. be open (mouth). 24850; 2. (+ *a*) think about. 25566 (EPS), 30494.

BAICHELER. n.m. young man. 23486.

BAILLE, BAILE. n.m. or f. (sometimes pl.) 1. bailey, outer wall surrounding a castle or house. 9888–20033, 26616; 2. the space enclosed by such a wall? 9978–20108.

BAILLIE. n.f. power, control, possession. 25158, 25519, 27555.

BAILLIER. v.tr. 1. give (to, into the care of). 10148–20282, 21447, 22452; 2. take. 27454, 31349, var. 24943.

BAILLIR. v.tr. possess. 24943 (E only; the other MSS have *baillier*, for which this may be a miscopying.)

BALANCE. n.f. 29278 *am balance* — in doubt, uncertain.

BALANCIER, BALLANCIER. v.tr. throw. 10061–20195.

BALOIER, (BALIIER). v.intr. dance (of banners dancing or fluttering in the wind, in each case). 26868, App. VII TV 226, TV 476.

BANDE. n.f. head-band, hair-band. 24518, 32206.

BANDÉ. adj. (p.p.). 1. banded, circled. 9565–19689, 26131, 26902; 2. edged, bordered? MQ 10066, P 24676.

BANDON.   n.m. always *a bandon*. 1. freely, rapidly, impetuously. 21848, 22219, 24640; 2. at risk, in danger. 29784. cf. *abandon*.

BARAT.   n.m. trickery, ruse. 10044, Q 25547. cf. *atorner*.

BARBACANES.   n.f.pl. barbican, outer fortification, across the moat from the main gate. 22628.

BARBARINE.   adj.f. barbarian. 22606.

(BARGAIGNIER).   v.refl. S 28762 *Que de honte ne me bargaigne Se nus la me veust metre sor* — that I will not talk myself out of any accusation that I have acted shamefully.

BARNAIGE.   n.m. knightly reputation. 22152.

BARONIE.   n.f. 1. (coll.) barons. 28542, 28793, 28892; 2. vassalage, and therefore land (held in vassalage)? P 22605.

BASETURE.   n.f. Q 26529. I have not found this word anywhere; it appears to be a *hapax*. Could it be a mis-spelling of *basteüre*, also unattested, with the sense 'how something is built'?

BASSET.   adj. small-built (horse). S 9479.

BATAILLE.   n.f. one of the groups into which each side is divided, prior to a tournament or battle. 26831, 26865, 31311.

BATAILLIE.   adj.f. (p.p.). battlemented, crenellated. 27652, 32195. These are Picard forms; the verb is *bataillier*.

BATESTAL.   n.m. noise. 22790. The manuscript actually has *bastestal*.

BATIR.   v.tr. create, make. 20596.

BATRE.   v.tr. 1. (+ *a or*) decorate (cloth) with (beaten?) gold. 21172, 22970; 2. reach (to), wash against. 22579, 27654, KMQU 25620; 3. beat, strike. (straw, to soften it) 24151, 24478; 27460, 28693; (gold) S 24152. mutual refl. 26912. *batue*. p.p.f. well used (road, path). 22536, 23148, 29983.

BAUCENT.   adj. piebald. 9479, 23205, 29095.

BAUDOR.   n.f. joy, rejoicing. 22771, 28579, M 28382.

BAUT.   adj. joyful, lively. 9482, Q 21358. *baudemant*. adv. 26610.

BAUTESTIRE.   n.m. baptism, christening. 22063, 31064.

BEL.   adj. *estre bel* (+ *a*). please. 22684, 22915, 24504. also *estre bon et bel* 22880. The expression is frequently impers., but not always, e.g. 24504, 24830, 30968.

BENEÜREZ.   adj. fortunate. MSU 25453, MSU 25946, S 27548.

BERSEREZ.   n.m. 9482 (AL) *Un berserez tot baut au sanc. au sanc* must qualify *berserez*: this is a tracking-dog of some kind, cf. *Rou* III 522 *chien a sanc* (glossed 'limier'), and var. III 10526 (not 10556, so T-L) *brachet a sanc* (glossed 'limier?'), also *Eneas* 3608 *chien a sanc*. The *au* of A is supported by L, the only other MS which contains this line.

(BESTORNER).   v.tr. turn around, confuse. T 20244.

(BETER).   v.intr. clot, coagulate. 32003.

BRUEL.   n.m. Q 26319. This is probably an error, caused perhaps by the presence of *bruoil*, a variant spelling of *Briol* in MQ, in the next line of Q's model, cf. Q 26236.

BLANC.   adj. On occasion this word is applied to silver, as it used to be in Eng. 23076 (E), M 25726, Q 27150. also *blanc a argent* 21996.

BLAZONS, BLASONS.   n.m.pl. shields. 20469, 26885, 28816. Perhaps the arms painted on these, 22033.

BLÏAUT, BLÏAU.   n.m. female over-garment. 22309, 29437, 29453. In the latter instance, it is apparently worn over a *peliçon*, cf. 29289.

BLOI.   adj. 1. fair. 22988, 24491, L 29365; 2. a pale shade of blue. 27517, 30705, LP 22990.

BLOÏE.   adj.f. (A) 9959–App. I P 23. troubled? Although this seems to be the only attestation of this word, the editor prints it without comment, as there are no notes for MS A. It is presumably cognate with Mod.F. 'éblouir', cf. FEW I 404, **blauÞ*-. The wide range of var. suggests this word also troubled the scribes. cf. *bleuir*, in Foulet's glossary to C1.

BOCIAUX. n.m.pl. small barrels, kegs. 30298, M 21642.

BOFU. n.m. sort of cloth. 24152.

BOIDIE, BOISDIE. n.f. trickery, falseness. 28713, 32522.

BOISE. n.f. piece of wood. TV 31615.

(BOISIR, BOISSIR). v.tr. 1. disappoint? KU 9959. It is possible that we have here a Picard *-iee* → *-ie*, and that the inf. should be *boisier*, as in the dictionaries. However, there is no such doubt in 2. deceive, be false to. Q 31677.

BONAIRETÉ. n.f. kindness, goodness. K 27570. Not found in T-L, but God. has several examples, and AND lists one, with the definition 'gentleness'.

BONDIE. n.f. sound, noise. S 26645.

BOQUERANZ. n.m.pl. sort of cloth. rej.r. 22589.

BORDE. n.f. small house, hut. 9533–19657, 20738, 24722.

BOUCLE. n.f. boss in the centre of a shield. 22039, 22359, 23245.

BOUT. n.m. *tot de bout* (adv. loc.) entirely, altogether. 20594 (EPS).

BOUTER, BOTER. v.tr. push, shove, thrust. 9735–19851, 21876, 23294.

BRACE. n.f. arm, i.e. the force of one's arm. S 30168.

BRACIE, BRACIEE. n.f. 1. span of the arms. 21593, 26888, Q 31588; 2. armful, bundle. 30300.

BRAICHET, BRACHET, BROICHET, BRECHEZ. n.m. hunting-dog. 10138–20272, 10141–20275.

BRANDIR. v.intr. stagger, reel. K 27177.

(BRANLOIER). v.intr. shake. 24344 (EPS).

BRET. n.m. screech 26797.

BRETESCHE. n.f. wooden fortification. 22633.

BRICON. n.m. fool. 20343.

BRIEMANT. adv. briefly, in short. 20600, 22291, 26555.

(BRIVER). v.intr. run fast, gallop. Q 28852. God. has four examples of this word.

BRONCHIER, BRUNCHIER. v.intr. lean, bend over. 20546 (ELPT), 20871 (EP).

BROON. n.m. brawn. 21846. The var. mainly have the more usual form *braon*.

BRUESE. n.f. K 22245. Probably the same word as *broce*, *broisse* (see T-L I 1154, 10), 'bushes, underbrush'.

BRUILLEZ. n.m.pl. thicket, copse. 9472 (A)

(BRUIRE). v.intr. 1. rush (noisily). 21845; 2. make a noise, be noisy, 22727, KMQU 26871.

BRUN. adj. 1. dark, gloomy. 25569, 29246; 2. burnished. 29790.

BRUNCHIER. see *bronchier*.

(BRUNIR). v.tr. polish, burnish. 9993–20123, 28279, 30815.

(BRUNOIER). v.intr. look dark. 26542.

BUIES. n.f.pl. chains, fetters. App. VII TV 1069.

BUISINES. n.f.pl. trumpets. 31319.

(BUROIER). v.intr. P 26542. be turbulent? Apparently a *hapax*, see T-L, *buriier*.

BUSCHIE, BUISSIE. n.f.? scrub, brush? App. VII TV 1160. Not found in the dictionaries. Were *ermitaige* feminine, we might read *embuschie*, 'in the woods'. There is a curious similarity between this and the *ambeschiez* of (CM) E 34106, where the diversity of the readings suggests that, if this line is an error, it is not due to the scribe of E, cf. Roach's note to that line, where he remarks that *embuschier* does not seem to be applied to buildings. Note also that, in that passage, Sagremor has *left* the forest when he comes to the castle.

C

ÇA. adv. 1. here, hither. 19709, 10201–20339. used as a command: 9921 *or ça* — come with me. 10148–20282 *ça le brachet* — give me the dog, cf. 21220, 21446; 2. (temp.) 19632 *ça devant* — before now, earlier. 26557 *au tans ça an ariere* — in the past.

CAISANS. adj. (pres.p). cutting, keen? L 9732. T-L has only one example of the verb *caisir*.

CAMBERIELE. n.f. small chamber. P 24383.

CARRÉ. see *quarré*.

CARREL. see *quarrel*.

CARTIER. see *quartier*.

CASSIAUS. see *tassiel*.

CAUMOIS. see *chammois*.

CAURE, CAURRE. n.f. heat, warmth. KLP 25710, PTV 28446, LPTV 29254.

CELÉ. n.m. ceiling. 32283. P has *celee* n.f., the only example of this given by T-L.

CELEE. adj.f. (p.p.). panelled. 22455.

CELLEE. n.f. *a cellee*. secretly, covertly. 22664.

CELOISON. n.f. *fere celoison*. conceal. S 22702.

CEMBUE, CENBUE. n.f. lady's saddle or saddle-covering. 25461, 25480, 27942.

CENDAL. n.m. thin silken material. 22589, 24777, 29371.

CERCHIER. v.tr. 1. search (through). 19988, 20721, 24382; 2. search for, seek. 19998, 24635, 31864; with a sense of 'seek successfully, find' 10015. v.intr. search. 23006, 24314, 26206.

CERTAIN, CERTEINE. adj.(f.). 1. (of things) real, true, pure. 22929, 29928, 31787; 2. (of people) sure, certain. 10126, 26988, 29674. *certenemant*. adv. surely, with certainty. 19946, 9866, 30576.

CERZ, CERTE. adj.(f.). 1. (of people) *estre cert de*. know (s.th.) definitely. 24617, Q 22901; 2. (of things) certain, definite. 32364.

CHACEÏZ. n.m. hunt, pursuit. Q 26603. The sense of *an un chaceïz* seems to be 'during the hunt, while hunting'.

CHACEOR. n.m. hunter (horse). 9479, 20705.

CHACIER. v.tr. 1. chase, pursue, hunt. 10132, 10165, 26601. *chacier (la) follie*. behave foolishly, waste one's time. 20579 (ES), 27435 (EPS); 2. seek, look for. rej.r. 23006.

CHAISTIS. see *cheitis*.

(CHALONGIER, CHALANGIER). v.tr. 1. claim, demand. 23803; 2. hinder, oppose. 30251.

(CHAMBRILLIER). v.tr. panel, wainscot. Q 22455. cf. *lambroisiee*.

CHAMMOIS, CAMOIS, CAUMOIS. n.m. open ground, heath. S 9472, App. VII TV 548.

CHAMP. n.m. (judicial) combat, dispute. 28904.

CHANGIER. v.tr. App. II L 78. The context suggests 'lose the track of' which, although unattested, is close to meanings deriving from CAMBIARE, such as 'give up (one thing) for (another)', in this case, one stag for another, cf. Mod.F. 'donner, prendre le change' and, crucially, the expression *cure a(l) change* in Thomas's Tristan, and its gloss in AND (I 89b), 'to chase a different quarry'. The brachet will not be thrown off the track of the White Stag on to that of another beast. cf. also K 26895, and 28168 *changier la voie* which essentially means 'lose one's way'. v.intr. 23634 *ne me puet li cuers changier . . . que ne* (+ subj.) — I cannot help but. cf. *müer*.

CHANTEL. n.m. *an chantel*. held across the body, in the combat position (shield). 22022. cf. *anchanteler*.

CHARGENZ. adj. (pres.p.). violent, unpleasant. 9732.

(CHARGIER). v.tr. 1. burden, weigh down (with blows) 21274, (fig.) 28271, 28846; 2. give. 27048. *chargié*. adj. (p.p.). laden, covered. 22526, 22557, 23167.

CHARRIERE.   n.f. 1. ferry. 9944, 9961, 9963; 2. track, road. 24244, T 21664, T 22533. The instance at KMSU 21102 must be an error.

CHASTELIERS.   n.m. small castle or fortified building. (A) 9902–PT 20043 (also KLMU 9898), TV 25409. Not found in the dictionaries, cf. Roach, note to 20031–44. For comparable forms, see FEW, *castellum*.

CHASTI.   n.m. advice, warning. S 24029.

(CHASTOIER).   v.tr. 1. reproach. 23510; 2. exhort, admonish. 23935, 24004; 3. advise, warn. 29711; 4. punish. (fig.) Q 9757; 5. control, dominate. var. 25145. v.refl. improve o.s., learn. 29714, 30778.

CHEITIS, CHAISTIS.   n.m. unfortunate, wretch. 9494. adj. wretched, unfortunate. 27394.

CHENES, CHIENNE.   n.f.pl. (sing.?) grey hair. App. IV MQU 2.

CHEVEÇAILLE.   n.f. collar, neck (garment). 20788 (EPS).

CHIEF.   n.m. 1. head. 19696, 10004–20136, (= hair) 9914–20048; 2. end, edge, extremity. 20129, 25165. *au chief del tor*. finally, in the end. 10047–20183, 28680, 28842. *de chief an autre, de chief an chief*. from top to bottom, from head to foot. 21270, 23759 (ES), 27759. *venir, traire a chief* (+ *de*). reach the end of, achieve. 22430, 31199. 30941 *je n'an sai a quel chief traire* — I do not know where to go, which direction to take. *a chief de foiz*. from time to time. 23950 (EPS).

CHIENETEES.   adj.f.pl. (p.p.). App. VII K 29. The dictionaries have no such word. I think we should read *chievetees*, perhaps meaning 'edged, bordered', cf. *cheveté*, T-L II 370, 41; God. II 116a.

CHIERE.   n.f. face, expression. 31204. *faire chiere morne*. look unhappy. 20290, 24906. *faire chiere de*. show sign(s) of. 22947, 29981, 31357, cf. *samblant. faire belle chiere a*. treat kindly, welcome. 25883. *a belle chiere*. happily. App. IV MQU 98.

CIÇAMUS.   n.m. fur of the spotted suslik or souslik, a sort of ground squirrel. 24677.

CITOAL.   n.m. zedoary, an aromatic root similar to ginger. 22594, 23027.

(CLAMER).   v.tr. call. 10174, 25766, 28207. *clamer (q.ch) quite (a qn.)*. release, free (s.o. from s.th.). 9789, 22220, 30973. *clamer (qn.) quite*. acquit, release (s.o. from an obligation). 23522 (EPS). v.refl. complain. 28568 (E).

CLARÉ.   n.m. spiced wine. 24055.

CLAVEÜRE.   n.f. lock. 9558 (AS).

CLINER.   v.tr. bend, lower (head). 30549. v.refl. bend, lean over. 26040.

(CLORE).   v.tr. 1. enclose. 21083, 31345 (EMS); (= contain) Q 25936; 2. close. 24272, 24639.

CLOS.   n.m. enclosure, close. MT 23868.

CLOSURE.   n.f. enclosure, fence. 21669.

COI, QUOI.   adj. 1. still, motionless. 21146, 23215, 23828. *tenir coi*. hold still. 23554, 25527, 27126. *se tenir coi*. stand still. 31636, 32119; 2. quiet, calm, silent. 25781, 27270, 30358. *se taire coi*. keep silent. 23063. *laissier coi*. leave in peace, alone. 30614. 23797 *La pucelle me laissiez coie* — let me have the maid peacefully. *coi de parler*. silent. 28047.

COIEMANT.   adv. quietly. 22663.

COIFE, COIFFE.   n.f. hood of chain-mail, worn under the helmet. 9740, 20551, 21296.

COILLIR.   v.tr. 1. take, collect, acquire. 23730, 25114. 29863 *Que Gauvains la fleur an coilli* — that G. plucked her flower, i.e. took her maidenhead; 2. catch, corner. M 26603. cf. *acoillir*.

COINTE (1).   see *cote*.

COINTE (2).   adj. 1. elegant. 19769, 22180, 22281; 2. clever. 25826.

COINTEMANT.   adv. elegantly. 9602, K 23217.

COINTISEMENT. n.m. elegance, or possibly affectation of elegance. MQ 23218. This appears to be a *hapax*, cf. God. II 176a.

(COISIER). v.intr. become calm, quiet. 25576.

COITIER. v.tr. 1. chase, harry. 10166; 2. press, urge on (horse). 28802. v.intr. hurry. 28491 (or refl.?), 31518, V 25643. v.refl. strive, hurry. T 21136, T 25643.

COL. n.m. 27265 *lou col de som pié* — his ankle.

(COLLER). v.intr. 1. flow. 24988; 2. slide. M 23266.

COLLIERES. n.f.pl. the front part of a horse's harness, going around the neck. 30139.

(COLOIER). v.intr. turn one's head, look around. 25664.

COLONBELLES. see *coulombes*.

COLOR. n.f. 1. colour. 22527, 22574; 2. colour of the face, complexion. 22551, 22693. *de color(s)*. coloured, bright. 22513, 30377, 32105.

COLOREE. adj.f. (p.p.). 1. ruddy, rosy. 21632, 25511, 26390; 2. coloured, bright: like 1., applied exclusively to the face, in E. 22297, 24531, 29296.

COLORIS, COULORIS, COLORIE. adj.(f.) (p.p.). bright, coloured. KMQ 27697, LMQU 28033. cf. *ancoloris, encolouree*.

COMBEL, COMBLEL. n.m. T 25079, T 25251, TV 25252, also T 25262. While these forms would appear to be errors, or misreadings, for *tombel* (we find *tomblel* in V 25251, V 25262, also), the fact that this word is several times written in T with the abbreviation for *con/com* might raise doubts on this point. Nevertheless, while *comblel* exists, cf. God. II 187b, and *combel* puts us in mind of *combe* and *combele* 'little valley' cf. T-L II 585, 33; 586, 18, we are left with the feeling that an error is the most likely explanation.

COMBLE. n.m. upper part of the shield. 29237, S 25014. This word is still used in Mod.F. heraldry.

COMBRER. v.tr. seize, grasp. U 21302.

(COMPASSER). v.tr. make, build, construct. 21687, 24304, S 24283.

COMPLIE. n.f. hour of compline, the last service of the day. 21626 *des ier complie* — since yesterday evening.

COMPLOT. n.m. group. Q 29162.

(COMPORTER). v.tr. carry. Q 25896, Q 32047.

CONCÏENCE. n.f. consciousness, inner thoughts. 24092. 23067 *N'aiez triste la concïence* — do not be sad.

CONCILLE, CONSILLE. n.m. meeting, council, assembly. T 23086, U 30964.

CONCLUS. adj. (p.p.). defeated. 26784.

CONCORDÉ. adj. (p.p.). agreed, in agreement. 29861.

(CONDER). v.refl. actually *re-condez*, with the part. *re-* contained in the auxiliary *rest*. U 26806. This word is not found in T-L, God. I suggest it may actually be *re-çoudez*, that is, a form of *resouder*.

(CONDUIRE). v.tr. 1. conduct, lead. 21807; 2. escort, give safe-conduct. 24910, 24917.

CONFEZ. adj. confessed. T 24101.

CONFONDRE. v.tr. destroy, ruin. 24440, 28342, U 21294. v.intr. collapse, crumble. 24417.

(CONGENOÏR). v.tr. conceive, engender. Q 29352.

CONIN. n.m. rabbit. 25305, 26690, 30297.

CONISSANCHE. n.f. insignia, badge. App. VII TV 84.

(CONJOÏR). v.tr. welcome, make much of. 27269, var. 25063, KLMT 21287.

CONJURER. v.tr. ask, conjure. 28922, 30627, 30633.

(CONMANDER). v.tr. 1. order. 22215 *a desarmer le conmande* — he orders that he should be divested of his armour. cf. 23519; 2. entrust, commend. 25067, 25329, 30458.

CONMUNAL.   adv. (adj.). all together. 23028, 30111.

CONMUNEMANT.   adv. all together. 19983.

CONNOISTRE, (CONOISTRE).   v.tr. 1. recognize, know. 9648–19780, 22475, 23595; 2. get
• to know, realize. 9709–19833, 9866–20014, 10054; 3. welcome, accept. 21287, 25063.

CONQUESTER.   v.tr. gain, win. 24210, 30758.

(CONREER).   v.tr. 1. equip, arm. 23654, 27820, 29799; 2. prepare. 26831; 3. endow.
Q 22556. v.refl. prepare, get ready. 31322.

CONROI.   n.m. 1. care. 20744, 20759; 2. equipment. 30948; 3. troop, battalion. var.
30133, L 30134. cf. *bataille*, *eschieles*.

CONSEILLIER, (CONSOILLIER).   v.tr. counsel, advise, help. 27398, K 24806. v.refl. 1.
(+ *a*) consult, take counsel (of). 22882, 26589, 31376; 2. decide. 25622. 30621 *Ne s'an
set conmant conseillier* — he does not know what to do; 3. reflect, consider. App. VII
KTV 68.

(CONSER).   v.intr. sink, set (sun). Q 29916, Q 30282. A rare word, if we are to judge by
the dictionaries.

CONSILLE.   see *concille*.

(CONSUÏR).   v.tr. 1. strike, hit. 21269, 30796, 30814; 2. catch (up with). P 26603.
K 20545 and MQU 21269 could be either *consuïr* or *aconsuïr*.

CONTANZ, CONTENS.   n.m. opposition, resistance. var. 30276.

CONTEMENT.   n.m. enumeration, account. App. VII TV 1168.

CONTENEMENT.   n.m. demeanour, appearance. 10101–20237. 23218 *par contenemant* —
in order to cut a figure, to look elegant.

CONTENIR.   v.tr. conclude, finish? P 23528. v.refl. conduct o.s. var. 23938, M 27190,
M 27194.

CONTRAIRE, CONTRERE.   n.m. 1. trouble, annoyance, harm. 10214–20356, 23305, 24192;
2. antagonism, ill-will. P 20973.

CONTRAITE.   adj.f. crippled, deformed. 23195.

CONTREDIRE.   v.tr. 1. refuse, deny (s.th. to s.o.). 21880, 22840, 29338; 2. deny, dispute
(s.th.). 28977.

CONTREDIT.   n.m. opposition, resistance. 10137–20271, 27661.

CONTREFERE.   v.tr. copy, depict? U rubr. 23196.

CONTREMOIER.   v.tr. 21838 *Mais ne le pot contremoier* — the sense appears to be 'but
he could not reach to strike him a good blow'. The *contrenoier* of U is doubtless an
error.

CONTREMONT.   adv. 1. upstream. 21685, 24244; 2. up, upwards. 21828, 23185, 26534.

CONTRESTER.   v.tr. 1. withhold, keep from. 25366, T 29662 (V has *contre ester*); 2.
oppose, withstand. 29659, P 24652, M 30244.

(CONTRETENIR).   v.tr. refuse. S 22840.

CONTREVAL.   adv. 1. down, downwards, down below. 20515, 21845, 31220; 2. throughout. 21093. prep. throughout. T 22958. 21675 *contreval l'eve* — downstream.

COPLES, COUPLES.   n.m.pl. 1. pairs, couples. 9484; 2. leashes. 9992–20122.

CORAIL, COROIL.   n.m. bolt, bar. 9558–19681.

CORBE, COURBE.   adj.f. bent, crooked. var. 23196.

CORBINNE.   n.f.(?). Q 23183. Although this word is not found in the dictionaries, it is
clearly a variant form of *corbin* 'raven'.

COROIL.   see *corail*.

CORON.   n.m. corner. 32413.

CORRE.   v.intr. 1. run. 21165, 21378, 21963. *corre seure*. attack. 9704–19822, 20879,
21263. *laissier corre*. charge (lit. 'let one's horse have its head'). 22024; 2. run, flow
(water). 21679, 22580, 23682; 3. be current? U 10044.

CORRECIER. v.tr. anger, displease, sadden. 22924, 23490, 28590. inf. as n.m. anger. 31350.

CORS. n.m. body. 10072–20206, 20235, 20400. This word is frequently used with the sense of 'person, self', thus 9700–19818 *mes cors* = I, myself; 21622 *lou cors de son ami* = her lover, cf. 27141, *passim. cors sains.* holy relics. 23125 (ES), also var. 27706?, or perhaps 'holy being'. 30759 *cors a cors (am bataille)* — in single combat.

CORSUS. adj. big, strong. TV 30659.

COSTAU. n.m. slope, rise. 20474 (E).

COSTE. see *cote.*

COSTIERE. n.f. slope, rise. 27646.

COSTUMIER. adj. used, accustomed (to). Usually this word is used with *de*, cf. 26631. The absolute usage such as we find at 9933–20065 is not unknown, but neither is a use with *a*, and I wonder if we should not read *La mule qu'i fu costumiere.*

COTE, COSTE, COUSTE, COUTES. n.f.(pl.). quilt, quilted bed-covering, or possibly cushion. 21188, 22658. also *cote pointe.* 22179, 24152, 30725. The *cointe* of Q 22179 is an unusual var. of the form *coite.*

COU. enclitic form. = *qu'il le.* 20273 (E), 21543 (EQ), cf. Roach, note to 20273.

COULOMBES. n.f.pl. pillars, columns. 24285, 24301. Also *colonbelles, coulombelle.* n.f.(pl.). There is apparently no difference in meaning. 24279, 24309.

COURBE. see *corbe.*

COUSTE, COUTES. see *cote.*

COUTURE. n.f. cultivated land. 22558.

COUVENANCIER. v.intr. promise. S 25748.

COVANT (1). n.m. promise, agreement. *metre an covant.* promise. 23130, 30994, S 24027. *avoir an covant.* have promised. KU 22905, PTV 25921. *par (tel) covant que.* on condition that. 9790, 25030. cf. *covenant.*

COVANT (2). n.m. convent, here used loosely to designate a company of women. 24536.

COVENANCE. n.f. promise, agreement. 27530. *tenir covenances.* keep one's word. 25752.

COVENANT. n.m. promise, agreement. 26273 *Et qu'avec lui par covenant ira.* — and (on condition) that he would agree to go with him. 26750 *Carimedic son covenant Demande de l'eve passer* — C. asked her to fulfil her promise to help him cross the river. cf. 27870. *avoir (an) covenant.* promise, have promised. 20399, 22905, 25921. *metre an covenant.* promise. 24027, Q 23130. *par couvenant (que).* on condition (that). MQ 25030. This last use is probably due to contamination with *covant* (1).

COVENIR. v.intr., impers. (often absol.) 1. be necessary, needful. (often giving a sense of 'must'). 9469, 19649, 23315. 29435 *meillor ne covenoit* — no better was needed, there was none better; 2. suit, be fitting. 22182. 24434 *miauz me covient a estre ci* — it is better for me to be here; cf. *miauz.* The range of syntactical constructions in use with this verb is considerable; there are eight or nine different ones, including dir. or ind. obj., with *a* and inf. or simply with inf.

COVERTURE. n.f. roof, roofing? T 19716.

(COVESCLER). v.tr. Q 32283. A var. of *covercler* (T-L has *covescle* = *covercle*) which usually means 'cover with a lid', or 'cover' more generally. If *sa* were here taken to be an unusual, picard influenced, enclitic form (*si la*), the line would make sense: '(whoever looked up) could see it (the roof) ceilinged'. This seems probable, cf. *tronçoner* and Roach II, note to E 5668.

COVINE. n.m. situation, affair. 25228.

CREANTER. v.tr. 1. promise. 9795, 25154, 26004; 2. agree (to), grant, 26730, 28025, 28927. It is frequently hard to distinguish these two meanings.

CREMIT.   see *criembre.*

CREMOR.   n.f. fear. T 31463.

CREMUZ.   see *criembre.*

CRENU.   àdj. Q 21966. Although usually this word means 'long-haired, long-maned', here it is a var. for *crestu*, and presumably has the same sense, 'maned', or 'crested'.

CRESTU.   adj. crested. 21966.

CRETEL, CRETIEL.   n.m. battlement, crenellation. LT 22568, LT 24258, LTV 31152. also *cre(s)telé.* var. 24720, LPT 22628, LPTV 29554.

CREVEÜRE.   n.f. crack. 32558 (EMQS), P 19716.

(CRIEMBRE).   v.tr. fear. *cremuz* p.p. 26563, *cremit* imp.subj. 3, 32523.

CRIEME.   n.f. fear. 26170.

CROISSIR.   v.intr. break. 28818, 30164, KL 26887.

(CROISTRE).   v.intr. grow, increase in size. 21054, 21948, 32161. M 21966 *creü* probably = 'large', cf. *parcreü.*

(CROLLER).   v.tr. shake. MSTV 31200. v.intr. shake, tremble. App. VII TV 622.

CROMBE.   adj. crooked, bent. KP 23196.

CROS.   n.m.pl. hooks. (L 9823–) 19919 (E). cf. Roach, note to 19919.

CUER.   n.m. heart. Most often used to denote the emotions, and thereby the self, thus *mes cuers* effectively = I, myself. 22873, 22938; *son cuer* = he, himself (she, herself), 22752, 22931; etc. 22780 *An son cuer panse —* he thinks to himself, cf. 30588, 32133. 24118 *Ne cuer ne lou porroit panser —* nor could anyone imagine it; cf. Q 22768. 30477 *Qui ne li tient de riens au cuer —* which does not touch him at all closely. *de bon cuer.* 1. willingly, cheerfully. 19638, 21886, 23894; 2. deeply. 23886; cf. 23062, 23918. 22934 *de cuer dolant —* sadly. see also *esclairier, esleecier. cuer* is also used to denote courage. 23814, 29501, 30115. *prandre cuer.* take heart. 9724. Also 'intent, interest', 32312, KLU 26435; 'pride', 23508, cf. *desanflez.* See also *changier, müer, retirer.*

CUEVRECHIERS.   n.m.pl. nightcaps. U 24156. T-L has one example of this slightly unusual form of *cuevrechief;* AND has one of *cuvercher.*

CUIDIER.   v.intr. 1. expect (to), think to. (sometimes giving a sense of 'wish to'). 9525, 9999–20131, 21271. Note 21819 *De mautalent cuide anraigier —* he nearly goes mad with anger. inf. as n.m. 29853 *au mien cuidier—* I expect, I presume; 2. think, believe. 19839, 9782–19884, 20606. 31687 *sans cuidier —* without speculation, i.e. truly.

CUL.   n.m. App. VII TV 527 *de cul et de pointe.* T-L has 4 examples of this expression, three under *cul* and one under *pointe*, of which the last is very similar to this one. God. (IX 264c) has one of *de cul et de teste*, which appears to be a variation of the same expression. The range of meaning, judging from these examples, would seem to be 'headlong, vigorously, willy-nilly', any of which could fit the example here. *Cul* and *pointe* are applied in O.F. to the two ends of a needle, and possibly of other objects.

CULIERES.   n.f.pl. cruppers. U 30139.

CURE.   n.f. interest, attention, care. Usually *avoir cure* (with *de*). be interested (in), concerned (with), desirous (of). 21637, 24923, 25554. *metre sa cure* (with *a*). concentrate (on), devote one's energies (to). 30168. Q 21923 *sanz nule autre cure —* without worrying about anything else.

CUVERS.   n.m. villain. 30695.

D

DAHÉ.   n.m. curse. 30752. *Orer dahé.* curse, wish ill. 30212. 9489 *Des dahez qu'il li volt orer —* of the curses he wished to heap upon him.

DAMAGE.   see *domaige.*

DANOISE, DANESCHE.   adj.f. danish. 26850. 21103 *haiche danoise* — danish axe, a long-handled, single-bladed war-axe.

DANZ, DAN.   n.m. form of address, roughly equivalent to 'sir'. 9947–20078, 10232–20428, 25264. Used ironically in 9702–19820.

DAREAINS, DARRÏENE.   see *derrïens*.

(DEBATRE).   v.refl. (mutual refl.) hit, strike one another. 23290, KQ 26911.

DEBOISSIER.   v.tr. carve, shape (wood). 19678, Q 10006. Q 21928 might imply the sense 'decorate by carving'.

DEBONAIRE, DEBONERE.   see *aire*.

DEBONAIRETÉ.   n.f. nobility, goodness. 23372.

(DEBOUTER).   v.tr. push, hit. 30605 (EQ), K 9735, MS 23294.

DECLIN.   n.m. *traire, torner a declin.* draw to a close (day). 31508, var. 25476, TV 23834.

DECLINEMANT.   n.m. *aler a declinemant.* fade, dwindle (light). 31740, 32085.

DECORS.   n.m. 25571 *la lune estoit retornee An decors* — the moon was on the wane.

(DEDUIRE).   v.intr., refl. occupy o.s., amuse o.s. 30730, M 22841.

(DEFENDRE).   v.tr. split, cleave. P 22345.

(DEFINNER).   v.intr. end. Q 30351.

(DEFOLER).   v.tr. trample. 30226.

DEGRÉ.   n.m. (usually pl.). step, stair. Always applied to steps leading up to or into a building, not inside it. 9990–20120, 10159–20296, 21158.

(DEGUERPIR).   v.tr. leave. var. 32240.

(DEHURTER).   v.tr. push, shake. 30606, L 23294.

DELA.   adv. over there, yonder. 22542, 23648. also *par de dela* 31556. prep. across, beyond, on the other side of. 22091, 31763. also *par dela* 32330.

DELAIANCE.   n.f. delay. TV 27441, TV 27453, LSU 30031 (where S has *deloiance*, cf. *delaie*.)

DELAIE.   n.f. delay. U 21662 (: *voie*). *metre an delaie.* put off, delay. 30052.

DELAIEMANT.   n.m. delay. 27673 (EMS), 31146, 31379 (E).

DELAIER.   v.tr. Q 30052. put off, delay? (this passage is corrupt in Q). v.intr. delay, waste time. 20556, var. 21324, Q 26693. v.refl. delay, waste time. 23300, 25010, 26794. *sanz delaier.* without delay. 9830, 21778, 26512. S 24709 has *sanz deloier*, cf. *delaie, delaiance.*

DELASKIER.   v.intr. T 23299. give way, weaken? Not found in T-L, AND; cf. God. II 603b *deslachier*.

DELESSIER.   v.tr. leave aside, ignore. S 30366.

DELIIE, DELÏEE.   adj.f. fine, delicate. 21716, 30308.

DELIS.   see *deliz*.

DELISTABLE.   adj. pleasing, delightful. 24300, 24406, 27708.

DELIT.   n.m. 1. pleasure, delight. 29933. *par, a grant delit.* very pleasantly, agreeably. 24149, 26459, 31244; 2. that which delights, causes pleasure. 28084.

DELITEUSE.   adj.f. pleasant, delightful. 29211.

(DELITIER).   v.tr. please, delight. 24105, 26394.

DELIVRE.   adj. free. 21776, 25033. *a delivre.* freely, completely. 23125, 25363, 28844. In the var. of 23125 this expression seems to mean 'free, healthy'.

DELIVREMANT.   adv. freely, without hindrance; most often with the sense 'rapidly'. 9523, 20374, 20549.

DELIZ, DELIS.   adj. (p.p.). exhausted. 24671, 25697, 29138.

(DEMANTER).   v.intr., refl. lament. 25455, 30462, Q 29136.

DEMEINE.   adj. own. 22986, 24895.

DEMEINEMANT, DEMOINEMANT.   adv. 1. (EPS) 19945 *A icel jor demeinemant* — on that very (same) day, cf. 31236 (EPS); 2. in person. 28710 (EQ), var. 24578.

DEMENER.   v.tr. 1. manifest (emotion). *joie demener*. show joy, be joyful. 22399, 23030, 23715; 2. mistreat, maltreat. 23293, L9718; 3. do, perpetrate, pursue. 24093. 31389 *L'an ne doit pas la grant folie Tant demener* — one should not take folly to such an extreme. v.refl. get upset, get excited. 20071, P 24093.

DEMENOIS.   adv. 1. immediately, now. 23454, 24032, 26322; 2. with one's hand(s). 27169 (= at close quarters). cf. *manois*.

DEMENTRES, DEMENTRUES.   adv. (+ *que*). while. KLTV 27795.

DEMETRE.   v.tr. omit. *sanz demetre*. without omission. MS 31614.

DEMEURE, DEMORE.   n.f. delay. 22351, 28764. *faire demeure* seems to mean 'dwell on a point', as opposed to getting on with the story. 19821, 26692.

DEMORANCE.   n.f. 1. delay. 9684, 20302, 21179; 2. the act of staying. 30449. *faire demorance*. stay. 27345. This word occurs slightly less often than *demoree*.

DEMOREE.   n.f. delay. 19974, 21160, 21406. cf. *demorance*.

DEMORER, (DEMEURER).   v.intr. 1. delay, tarry. 9916, 21221, 21454. *sanz demorer*. without delay. 9574, 19932, 22960; 2. stay, wait. 19733, 10154, 21408. inf. as n.m. (EU) 30447 *Li Petiz Chevalier li prie . . . dou demorer* — the P. C. begs him to stay. v.impers. be delayed, take a long time. 24084 *que qu'il demore* — however long it may take. 32402 *Gaires aprés ne demora* — shortly afterwards; cf. 32527; 2. (with *en*) be hindered, prevented. S 22836, T 28137. cf. *remenoir*. v.refl. delay, tarry. 21429, 27369.

DENÇONS.   n.m.pl. (little) teeth. P 22299. T-L has no other example.

(DEPANDRE).   v.intr. hang down. (E) 20791.

DEPARTIR.   v.tr. 1. divide, separate. 9750–19860, 23367, 28882; 2. give, dispense. 26920, 27094; 3. distribute, divide up. 30150; 4. cut up? Q 10128. inf. as n.m. separation. 19850, MQ 9744. v.intr. 1. (+ *de*) go away (from), leave. 22233, 22907; 2. separate, part. 22546, 26931; with the sense 'come apart from' P 20791. v.refl. 1. (+ *de*) go away (from), leave. 19637, 21977, 22136; 2. separate, split up, divide. 21476, 22535, 22795.

DEPENER.   v.tr. M 27326. Although the dictionaries have no attestation of such a word, this must be derived from Lat. *poena* and signify 'punish, overwork', or something similar.

DEPORTER.   v.tr. amuse, divert. 28687. v.refl. divert o.s., amuse o.s., pass the time. 20726, 22638, var. 22176. inf. as n.m. distraction, amusement. T 20212.

DEPUTERE.   adj. vile, ignoble. 21761, 25401. cf. *aire*.

DEREAINS.   see *derrïens*.

DERESNIER.   v.tr. enumerate, recount. MQU 24038. v.intr., refl. talk, speak KQS 24729.

DERESONÉ.   adj. wild, unjustified? 21815. or perhaps 'great, terrible', cf. *desmesuré*.

(DEROMPRE).   v.tr. 1. tear (to pieces). 20790; 2. break, smash. 21294, 22345, 23288; 3. break off, interrupt (conversation). 22396.

DERRÏENS, DAREAINS, DEREAINS, DARRÏENNE.   adj.(f.). last. 32377. *au derrïens* — finally, in the end. 25294, 27949, 28643.

DES.   prep. 1. from. 10073–20207; 2. (temp.) since. 20732, 21581, 21625. *des lors*. a) since then. 21908, MQSU 22913, cf. 23944. b) then. 25088, 25518. *des donc*. since then. 22913, 23673. *des ier*. yesterday. 25305. *des or an avant*. henceforth. 31365. *des que*. once. M 10139. *des ore*. now. S 21832.

DESABITEES.   adj.f.pl. uninhabited, deserted. var. 22244.

DESAFUBLEZ, DESAFUBLEE.   adj.(f.)(p.p.). Not wearing a cloak or mantle. 23197, 24517, 26203. cf. *desfublé*.

(DESAGREER).   v.intr. displease. T 20531. cf. *agreer.*

(DESAICHIER).   v.tr. pull (about). 30606, M 23294.

DESANFLEZ.   adj. (p.p.). deflated. (fig.) 23508, where *cuer* has more or less the sense 'pride'.

DESAORNEZ.   adj. (p.p.). bereft, devoid (of the qualities in question). M 29494.

(DESAPAROILLIER).   v.refl. differ (from), not be the same (as). 24488.

DESAVENANT.   adj. ugly, displeasing to the eye. S 27516.

DESBARAT.   n.m. defeat. (KL 10044–) 20180.

DESBARATEES.   adj.f.pl. (p.p.). waste, deserted. 22244.

(DESBRONCHIR).   v.intr. Q 28359. Although this appears to be a *hapax*, it is clearly the opposite of *bronchir* (God. I 742a) or *embronchir* (T-L III 74b), and means 'rise', or possibly 'be uncovered, shine through the clouds', cf. FEW I 565a.

DESCHEVAUCHIER.   v.intr. be unhorsed, lose one's seat. 28839, App. VII TV 1116.

(DESCOICHIER).   v.intr. detach itself, come loose. Q 26804

DESCONEÜE.   n.f. shame, mishap? P 28945. cf. (CM) 36937, where P again has *descouneüe*, against the *descovenue* of the MSS. It is not uncommon to find these two words as variants one for the other. It is not easy to gloss them precisely, however, and they do not appear to be synonymous. *Desconeüe* seems to imply shame, whereas *desco(n)venue* suggests injury, misfortune, or even misdemeanour. see also *desonües*.

(DESCONFORTER).   v.tr. make disconsolate, sad. 10268, 20587. v.refl. be disconsolate, sad. 20530, var. 23638.

(DESCONOISTRE).   v.tr. not recognize, fail to recognize. var. 27046.

DESCONSOILLIEZ.   adj. (p.p.). at a loss. 27584.

DESCORDELMENT.   adv. fervently. U 31920. A var. form of *descordement*, just as *escordelment* corresponds to *escordement*; it is not *descordaument*, God. II 556a.

DESCOVENUE.   n.f. 1. injury, wrong. 20552; 2. shame, mishap? 28945. cf. *desconeüe.*

DESCOVRIR.   v.tr. reveal. 23608, 24510, KMQU 10073. *a descovert.* openly, without protection. 22361.

(DESDIRE).   v.tr. 1. contradict. 28714; 2. refuse. PQ 22840.

DESDIT.   n.m. contradiction, objection, refusal. 24814, 25025, 31367.

DESEMBLER.   v.tr. separate. S 28798.

DESERTE.   n.f. payment, that which is deserved. 30694.

DESERTINES.   n.f.pl. deserted region. 24799.

DESERVIR (1).   v.tr. 1. deserve. 31006; 2. promote, pursue? U 31389.

DESERVIR (2).   v.tr. serve badly, not serve as one should. Q 31678.

DESEURE.   n.m. *estre au deseure.* have the upper hand, be in control. 31010, P 23125. adv. *de desoure.* above, on top. P 32354. see *desoivre.*

DESEVRER, (DESSEVRER).   v.tr. 1. cut off. 21870, K 20554; 2. separate, part. 9853, 23958, 25633.

DESFÄÉ.   adj. wicked, dreadful. var. 21815, P 25648.

DESFAIRE, DESFERE.   v.tr. 1. cut up (dead animal). 10175–20317, 20974; 2. bring to an end. 24009.

DESFERMER.   v.tr. 1. open. 19759, 20104, 21090; 2. untie, unmoor. 9932–PT 20064, 28194.

(DESFERRER).   v.refl. free o.s. from a lance-point. 20506 (ET).

DESFUBLÉ.   adj. (p.p.). Not wearing a cloak or mantle. 21358, cf. *desafublez.* In LT 22284, we have *deffubler* v.tr., 'take off'.

DESGARNIZ.   adj. (p.p.). bare, without armour. 23287.

(DESGUISER). v.tr. S 24772. It is difficult to be certain of the sense of this, as the line is corrupt.

(DESHAITIER). v.tr. sadden, depress. 31008. v.refl. be discouraged, downhearted. 21260.

DESHET. n.m. distress. 29936.

DESIRREE. n.f. desire, longing. P 21046.

(DESJOINDRE). v.intr. come apart. L 30166.

(DESJOINTIER). v.tr. separate, split. 30166.

DESJOINTURE. n.f. crack. SU 9594.

(DESJONCHIER). v.tr. U 30166. Not found in the dictionaries. Probably a var. of *desjointier*.

(DESJOSTER). v.tr. rej.r. 30166. separate, split. T-L has only one example of this word, God., AND have none. The emendation of this word, as opposed to the whole line, is justified by the rhyme.

DESLAIER. see *deslïer*.

(DESLOIGIER). v.intr. break camp. 31324.

(DESLIC(H)IER). v.tr. separate, split. App. VII TV 269.

(DESLÏER). v.tr. untie, unfasten. 21324. p.p. as adj.(f.). with (her) hair untied, loose. 23197. The form *deslaie* is unusual, cf. Roach, note to 21324.

(DESMANEVER). v.tr. lose. 20602 (ES).

DESMELLEE. adj.f. (p.p.). P 29937. beside o.s.? cf. T-L II 1649, 51.

(DESMENTIR). v.tr. damage, break. App. VII TV 866.

DESMESURE. n.f. lack of moderation, excess. 30849. *a desmesure*. extremely, excessively, immoderately. 10069–20203, 21789, 22369.

DESMESURÉ. adj. (p.p.). 1. great, excessive. 20543, 25648, 32541; 2. immoderate. 24933.

DESMOINTURE. n.f. L 9594. Probably an error for *desjointure*. Nevertheless, a link with *desmenture* is conceivable, with the sense being 'break, gap', cf. *desmentir*, and FEW VI/1 744b.

DESOIVRE. P 32354. Professor Roach kindly informs me that this is a ghost word, and that the variant would be better printed *desoïure*. He suggests that the *i* is an error, pointing out that reading *desoure* would make P's version equivalent to the *par desus* of EMU.

DESONÜES. adj.f.pl. rej.r. 29196. Probably an error for *desconeües* 'out-of-the-way', although this would give a hypermetric line.

DESOUNESTÉ. adj. (p.p.). dishonourable, degraded. P 24933.

(DESPENDRE). v.tr. give out. MU 21522. Although it might be possible to make sense of T 30493, it is probably an error.

(DESPIRE). v.tr. despise, scorn. 20438 (ET), 20866 (EPS).

(DESPONDRE). v.tr. set forth, tell. KLT 21522, K 22396.

(DESPRISIER). v.tr. despise, scorn. P 20866. cf. *despire*.

DESRAISON, DESRESON. n.f. 1. wrong. 25027, 27478, KU 22922. *a desraison*. wrongfully. 23309; 2. unreasonableness, unreasonable thing. 23784.

DESREEZ. adj. (p.p.). wild, unmannerly. 20859, Q 21815.

DESROI. n.m. wildness, impetuosity. 28668, 29060, S 31541. *a, par desroi*. wildly, impetuously. 24968, S 20808.

(DESROIER). v.refl. be impatient. 26867 (ES), QU 26072.

(DESSASFRER). v.tr. spoil the finish (of a hauberk). App. VII TV 599.

DESTANDRE, DESTENDRE. v.intr. run, rush, charge. 26881, 27074, LT 22019.

(DESTINER). v.tr. T 26650. say, declare. The v.refl. of V, if it is not an error, would have a similar meaning.

(DESTONBIR). v.intr. App. VII TV 377. Although this appears to be a *hapax*, it is clearly cognate with *estomir*, *estombir* (T-L III 1406, 42) and *destomir* (T-L II 1773, 12), cf. FEW XIII/2 409. The meaning is 'come to, recover from being dazed'.

DESTOR, DESTOUR. n.m. *sanz destor*. straight. MQS 9967. Used fig. KMU 9868 = certainly.

(DESTORBER). v.tr. hinder, harm. 10146–20280.

DESTORBIER. n.m. harm, bother. 20668, K 10146.

(DESTOUNER). v.tr. P 21274. Not found in the dictionaries, although it is in Potvin; if this is not an error, the meaning must presumably be much the same as *estoner*, 'stun'.

(DESTRAVER). v.intr. break camp. 31324.

(DESTREINDRE). v.tr. 1. press, urge. 20471 (ET); 2. harrass, annoy. P 25656.

(DESTRÏER). v.tr. prevent, keep (from). 27130. v.intr. delay, tarry. 26106, P 30188, U 30454. v.refl. delay, tarry. 26887.

DESTROIT. n.m. 1. trouble, distress. App. VII TV 911. *an destroit*. a) troubled, distressed. 22931, b) in dire straits. 28397, K 27186. *a grant destroit*. hard-pressed. 27844 (var. have *al g. d.*); 2. power. 31452. adj. (*destroiz*). anguished, distressed. 30666, 32502, Pot. 21922.

(DESVER). v.refl. go mad, wild. 30787. *desvé*. adj. (p.p.). mad, furious. 21850, 28323.

DESVERIE, DIERVERIE. n.f. madness, wildness, stupidity. ST 20580, P 30777.

(DESVOIER). v.intr. go mad, be beside o.s. 9752. v.refl. go the wrong way, make a mistake. 26072. *desvoiez*. p.p. (adj.) lost, off the right road 21022, 26661.

DESVOLEPEES. adj.f.pl. (p.p.). unrolled, unfurled. App. VII K 78–TV 108.

DESVOLOIR. v.tr. not want. L 22918.

DETENIR. v.tr. 1. hold back, stop. 10064–20198; 2. pull on, tighten (bridle). 20375, 28790; 3. detain, keep from leaving. S 22920. v.refl. refrain, keep (from). 25208 (E).

DETRIERS. adv. behind. TV 30574.

DETRIT, DETRI. n.m. delay. U 27528 (:*contredit*), U 30696 (:*toli*).

(DETRÖER). v.tr. pierce, make a hole in. L 21254.

(DEVALLER). v.tr., intr. go down, descend. 20296 (E), 26819.

DEVINAILLE. n.f. *sans devinaille*. straightforwardly. S 21332.

DEVIS. n.m. 1. description. 21380; 2. 27976 *par tel devis* — in such a way; 3. T 24213. conversation, disposition, intention? 4. (pl.) U 28084. beauty? cf. God. II 701b; there are other possibilities, such as 'blazon', 'design'. cf. *devise*.

DEVISE. n.f. 1. way, manner. 9821 *par tel devise* — in such a way; 2. description. 22166, 23718, 27682; 3. care, skill. 27965; 4. arrangement, conditions. 30048, 31627. *a devise*. altogether, in every way. 22619. cf. *devis*.

DEVISEMENT. n.m. description. M 29006.

DEVISER. v.tr. 1. tell, recount, describe. 9814, 9885, 10046–20182; 2. divide, organize, arrange. 26865, 27040; 3. specify. 28135; 4. devise? P 19678. v.intr. 1. relate, tell. 22620; 2. tell, order. 30063.

DEVOIR. v.intr. The most noteworthy use of *devoir* is with the sense 'be going to, intend to'. 30577, 31931, L 9941.

DIERVERIE. see *desverie*.

DIS (1). n.m.pl. days. 31764, 31869. *toz dis*. always, unceasingly. 27625. *a toz dis*. for ever. 31547.

DIS (2), DIZ. n.m.pl. that which is said, conversation. 24213, 27010, 27622. *antre ces diz*. meanwhile. 22177, T 21365.

DIVERS. adj. strange, wonderful. 32356.

DOBLIER.   n.m.pl. tablecloths. 22764.

DOIS.   n.m. table. 28524, Q 22764.

DOIZ.   n.m.pl. *doiz a doiz*. hand in hand. Q 24032.

DOLEREUS.   n.m. (adj.). wretch. 9512.

DOLOSER.   v.intr. weep, lament. 29136.

DOM.   see *dont*.

DOMAIGE, DAMAGE.   n.m. harm, hurt. 19794, 21387, 28660.

DONGIER.   n.m. reluctance. Usually *sanz dongier*. freely, abundantly. 20417, 21381, 32587. *faire dongier*. be reluctant. 26686.

DONT, DOM, DON.   adv. 1. of, from, for, about, with which. 9463, 9871, 20413; 2. from where. 20928, 21013, 21016; 3. because of which, whereby. 23144, 32230, 32488. There are also frequent examples of *dont* or *donc* meaning 'then, so'.

DORMANT.   see *table*.

DOUTANCE.   n.f. doubt, uncertainty. var. 29278. Usually *sanz doutance*. 'without doubt, certainly'. 26024, 28350, 31736. Sometimes the sense might be 'fear, hesitation'. 26166, S 21180.

DOUTE, DOTE.   n.f. 1. fear, anxiety. 21155, 25746, 26170; 2. doubt. 31687.

DOUTER, DOTER.   v.tr. fear. (sometimes with a sense of 'healthy fear, respect'). 19837, 9719–19843, 22365. v.intr. doubt. 23223, 23748, 24881. *sans douter*. without doubt, certainly. 30871, S 22870. v.refl. 1. be afraid. 21757, 22865, 28198; 2. doubt. 24726.

DOUTOR.   n.f. M 27574. doubt, fear, hesitation? Not found in God., AND or FEW; one example in T-L: II 2047, 7.

DOUTOUS.   adj. doubtful, hesitant. 32020.

DRECIER.   v.tr. 1. pitch (tent). 24750; 2. direct, turn. L 20680; 3. place together, join?. U 31197. v.intr. realign o.s., take up one's position. 10051–20185.

DROIT.   n.m. right. 10058–20192, 10212–20354, 27806. adj. 1. right, correct. 9775; 2. straight. 22303. also frequently with *chemin, voie, santier*, giving a sense of 'right, correct'. 9855, 23749, 25972. adv. 1. straight. 20371, 20476, 23768; 2. (qualifying prep.) right. 20698, 21128, 30723; 3. (qualifying adj.) fully, properly. 21193. *a droit*. correctly, properly. 25765, 26721, 32553.

DROITEMANT.   adv. straight, directly. 9683, 20037, 20963.

DROITURE.   n.f. 1. right, justice. 23741. *tenir droiture* (+ *a*). do justice (to). 28625; 2. right, claim. 29706; 3. duty. 29892. *a droiture*. adv. a) immediately, forthwith. 20980, 21638, 22782, b) straight. 23572, 24130, 32208, c) certainly. 24236, 26294. It is not always possible to distinguish clearly between these meanings, of which a) is the most common.

DROITURIER.   adj. 1. rightful. 30037; 2. right, just. 30501.

DRU.   n.m. (close) friend. 21536. adj. 1. (always f., always applied to grass). thick, lush. 21984, 24894, 25721; 2. high-spirited, wild. TUV 28306.

DRÜERIE.   n.f. love, intimate friendship. 23384. *par drüerie*. in friendly fashion? U 26977.

DURER.   v.intr. 1. extend. 26059. *Tant com il dure a la reonde*. to its (the world's) furthest extent. 22100, 25136, 25936; 2. (often with *vers*) endure, resist. 22370, 30661, 30881; 3. last, endure. 23032, 24994, 31605; 4. live, survive. 29017.

DÿASPRE, DÿAPRE.   n.m. fine cloth (usually patterned), or garment made thereof. 25503, 32405, K 25495.

E

EBENUS.   n.m. ebony. 9542–19666.

ECE.   see *ez*.

EFFORCEMENT.   n.m. P 31442. effort, exertion?

EFFORS.   n.m.pl. army, forces. var. 31346.

EGLIAUS.   n.m.pl. eagles (painted on shield). 30158. The *aigliers* of Q is not found in T-L, AND; cf. God. I 183c.

EINÇOIS.   see *ainçois*

EINSINT, EINSIN(S), AINSINT, AINSINS, ENSI, EINSI(S), AINSI(S).   adv. 1. thus, in this way. 19624, 9529, 19731; 2. (qualifying adj.) so, such, 19840, 20085, 21749; 3. (with *con/ com*) a) as, as though. 10150–20284, 21612, 21783, b) (conj.) while. 20696, 20982, c) so that, in such a way that. 32327; 4. (with *que*) a) in that, because. 29851, b) how. Pot. rubr. 21917, P rubr. 22637, P rubr. 23121.

EINZ.   see *ainz* (2).

EL.   pron. anything else, something else. 22421, 24049, 24319 (ES). 10062 (–T 20196) *N'i avoit el fors del lancier* — he was about to throw them. 21205 *non por el* — for no other reason. 21395 *si vont parlant Et d'un et d'el* — and (they) speak of this and that, cf. 22160, 26284. 29876 *qu'il n'i ot el* — for there was nothing else to do, cf. S 20733.

ELLÉS.   see *eslés*.

EMPAINTE.   n.f. blow, attack. App. VII TV 272.

EMPEINDRE, (EMPAINDRE).   see *ampoindre*.

EMPRISE.   n.f. undertaking. *avoir en emprise*. have undertaken. Q 22895. This expression is not attested in the dictionaries, but there is no reason to suppose it is an error.

(ENAMER).   v.tr. fall in love with. P 22831.

ENARME.   see *anarme*.

ENASTELER.   see *anasteler*.

ENBARNIE.   adj.f. (p.p.). large, strong in numbers. App. VII TV 93.

(ENCERCHIER), ANCERCHIER.   v.tr. ask (s.o. about), try to discover (s.th.). 26373, 27157. At 26373 L has *escherquier*.

ENCHARGIÉ.   adj. (p.p.). filled. TV 28846.

ENCLOS.   n.m. enclosure. LQU 23868.

ENCLOSTRE.   n.m. enclosure. K 23868.

ENCLUS.   n.m. L 10230. closed room?, cf. T-L III 220, 20.

ENCOLOUREE, ENCOLOREE, ENCOULOREE.   adj.f. (p.p.). rosy, red-cheeked. P 22297, KMT 24531, LTV 25511. cf. *coloris*.

ENCOMBREMENT.   n.m. trouble, bother. App. VIII S 18. cf. *ancombrier*.

ENCONTRER.   see *ancontrer*.

ENCOR.   see *ancor*.

ENDEMANTIERS, ANDEMANTIERS.   adv. meanwhile. 31222 (EMPS) with slightly unusual syntax, K 23750. conj. (+ *que*) while. 27795, S 25485.

ENDENTEES.   adj.f.pl. (p.p.). indented. (heraldic) App. VII K 86.

ENDUEIL.   n.m.? U 22635. Not found in the dictionaries. Error?

ENFICHIER.   v.tr. pitch (tent). LP 31781.

ENFRENÉ.   adj. (p.p.). bridled. 30901. TV have *affrené*, with the same meaning.

ENGAIGNE.   n.f. anger. App. VII TV 617. (The *egaigne* of V is a mistake.)

(ENGANER).   v.tr. trick, take in. P 20602.

(ENGARDER).   v.intr. look. K 24253. corresponds to *esgarder*, cf. LM 23156 *enforcier* for *esforcier*.

ENGART.   see *angart*.

ENGEMÉ.   see *esgené*.

ENGOISSIER.   see *angoissier*.

ENGRESSER.   v.tr. attack, press. S 23300.

ENHANER.   see *ahaner*.

ENHERMIE.   adj.f. desolate, deserted. 9468.

ENHERMINEES.   adj.f.pl. (p.p.). ermined. App. VII KTV 30. Not attested by the dictionaries. cf. *ermin*.

ENHEUDEÜRE.   n.f. hilt (sword). PS 20827.

ENJAMBEE.   see *jambee*.

ENMI.   see *anmi*.

ENMOI.   M 21483. var. of *anmi*?

ENOR.   see *honor*.

ENORER.   see *honorer*.

(ENORTER).   v.tr. TV 27555. This may be a deformation of *estorer*. If not, what might be the relationship between this and the instance in Beroul's *Tristan* (2108) quoted by T-L (III 481, 8)? We may also note the reading of E 27421, where a close examination of the MS suggests not *anorre*, as in Roach, but *anorte*, possibly for *anorté*.

ENSEIGNIER.   see *anseignier*.

ENSUS, ANSUS.   adv. away, back. 22372. prep. away, at a distance. 24749, 32091.

ENTAILLE.   n.f. *(fait) a entaille*. cut out, imprinted? MU 25726.

(ENTAILLIER, ENTALLIER).   v.tr. 1. embroider? Q 22991, cf. AND *entaillure* and Foulet C1 *entaillier*; 2. sculpt, work (stone). P 27651.

ENTALENTIS.   adj. keen, eager. TV 30820. cf. *antalantez*.

ENTANDEMANT.   n.m. understanding. Q 24089.

ENTANDRE.   see *antandre*.

(ENTASSER).   v.intr. U 26252. assemble. The dictionaries have no example of an intr. usage.

ENTENTE.   see *antante*.

ENTENTIUE.   see *antantis*.

ENTERCIER, ENTERCHIER, ENTIERCIER, (ENTERCER).   v.tr. recognize. var. 30233 (where L has *rentercier*). v.intr. 1. (+ *de*) ask (about). Q 22844; 2. look, enquire? App. VII TV 307.

ENTRANT.   n.m. (pres.p.). entry, edge. LMPS 27226.

ENTRECIES.   n.f.pl. P 20039. Error.

ENTREDEUS.   adv. in between. P 28883.

ENTREMANTRES, ANTREMANTRES.   adv. meanwhile. 31749 (where L has *d'entrementres*, MQU *endementres*, with the same meaning). conj. (+ *que*) while. 25485 (E), cf. MQU 27795 *endementres*.

(ENTREREQUERRE).   v.refl. (mutual refl.) attack one another. S 10260.

(ENTRESALIR).   v.intr. KU 9920. jump up? Or should we read *en tresali*? This word is not found in the dictionaries.

ENTRETANDIS.   adv. meanwhile. KLQU 21365 (M has *entratandis*), KLTU 22177 (M has *entandiz*, P *entredis*). For all these forms, see T-L X 73, 21.

(ENTR'OUBLIER).   v.tr. forget, abandon. M 26550.

ENTRUES, ENTROES, ENTROS.   conj. (+ *que*). while. var. 25454, var. 25485, LPTV 27614.

ENUI.   see *annui*.

ENVALLISANT.   n.m. S 29528. This appears to be a *hapax*, and is either an error for, or a variant of, *vaillissant*, value.

ENVERSER.   v.tr. knock down. P 28809.

(ENVÏER).   v.tr. call, summon. App. VII TV 725.

ENVIZ.   see *anviz*.

ENVOISEÜRE.   n.f. jest, pleasantry. L 10097.

ERALE.   n.m.? App. XI K 47. I can make little of this, whether it be a picard form of *erable*, or a picard rhyme, with *delitable* (= *delita(u)le*). The only possibility seems to be a corruption of *estalle* 'stall', meaning some kind of room or cupboard. Otherwise, we might surmise that the reading *a son erale* represents an error for *a soue ta(b)le*, although that would not be standard syntax.

ERMIN.   n.m. 1. a heraldic fur. P 19720; 2. ermine. MTUV 29289, M 24514. cf. *ermine*.

ERMINE, HERMINE.   n.m. or f. (often pl.) 1. a heradic fur. 9598–19720; 2. ermine. 22995, 24156, 24493. In 24493, this word is spelt with initial *h*, which contradicts Foulet's observation (C1, see *hermin*). cf. *ermin, hermin*.

ERRANMANT, ERRANMENT, ERRAMANT, ARAUMANT.   adv. quickly, immediately, suddenly. 9491, 20017, 24945.

ERRANT.   adv. (pres.p.). quickly, immediately. 21074, 28628, 30031.

ERREMANT.   n.m. situation, way of life, activity. 23676, 30668.

ERRER.   v.tr. travel along, go along (across, etc.). 19937, 21031, 21066. v.intr. go, travel, ride. 19615, 19639, 9547. 24232 *Dou tost errer onques ne fine* — he does not stop riding quickly, cf. *aler*. 25991 *Si fera molt meillor errer* — when it will be much more pleasant to travel. Sometimes the verb has almost a sense of 'hurry', cf. *errant*. For *eroie* (29675) see *aler*.

ERREUR, ERROUR.   n.f. apprehension, uncertainty. U 23644, S 28162. Curiously, these two lines are virtually identical.

ERSOIR.   adv. yesterday evening. 23985, 25737. The latter use describes a time close to midnight, and corresponds rather to 'last night'.

ESBAREE.   adj.f. (p.p.). startled, alarmed. L 23696.

ESBAUDIZ.   adj. (p.p.). 1. bright, light. 27311, var. 24061; 2. happy, joyful, encouraged. 27636, Q 28170, App. VII TV 523.

ESBENOIER.   v.intr. amuse, divert o.s. 21367, 21485, 23649.

ESBESSIEZ.   adj. (p.p.). M 31559. Conceivably a var. form of *abaissiez*, cf. Roach, note to 25662, with a broad sense of 'in a bad way', but more probably an error.

ESCARTELER.   see *esquarteler*.

(ESCAUCIRER).   v.tr. P 28753. T-L, God., have only one example of this verb used transitively (T-L III 870, 31), where the sense is not appropriate to this context. This is probably an error.

ESCEURE.   v.tr. obtain, garner. P 21055.

ESCHAQUIER.   n.m. chessboard. *a eschaquier*. in a chequered pattern. 24753.

ESCHARNIR.   v.tr. mock, insult. 23231 (EPS), 23500, 28502.

ESCHAVIE.   adj.f. slim. var. 23446.

ESCHELETES.   n.f.pl. small bells. 29461.

ESCHEQUEREZ.   adj.pl. chequered, checked. 30704. U has *eschequetez*, which in my opinion is also the reading of E, with the same meaning.

ESCHERQUIER.   see *encerchier*.

ESCHIELES.   n.f.pl. troops, detachments. 26866, 30133. cf. *bataille, conroi*.

ESCHIS.   adj. shy, timid. Q 22680.

ESCHIVER.   v.tr. avoid. 31326, 31566. At 31326, T has the var. form *esquïer*.

ESCHOIS.   see *escoi*.

ESCÏENCE.   n.f. U 23067. The usual meaning is 'knowledge'. If this is not an error, the sense here must be 'mind'.

ESCÏENT.   n.m. knowledge, learning. 29767. Usually *(au) mien escïent, mon escïent*. in my opinion, as far as I know, I think. 20620, 21708, 27516. similarly *a son escïent*. as far as he knew, in his opinion, etc. 24542, 28660. *a escïent*. consciously. *savoit a escïent* — was aware. 23606. E also has *mien escïentre*, with the same meaning, 19786, rej.r. 19794.

ESCLAIREMANT.   n.m. daybreak. 26264.

ESCLAIRIER, (ACLERIER). v.tr. (+ *le cuer, coraige a qn.*) cheer, hearten, relieve. 21417, 30688. v.intr. 1. (with *cuers* as subject) a) feel better (physically). 21326, b) be cheered, feel relieved. 21959, 25662 (E has *aclere*), 30434; 2. a similar but impers. usage (+ *cuer*). 24526; 3. a) become light, break (day, dawn, etc.). 28358, Q 24169, and perhaps 22270, cf. *esclairir*, b) start to shine (sun). 29252; 4. (impers.) become light. 25601; 5. light the way. S 21923. For the form *aclere*, and references for the expressions with *cuer*, see Roach, note to 25662.

ESCLAIRIR. v.intr. break, appear (dawn). 22270, or is this *esclairier*? inf. as n.m. dawn. 24228.

ESCLARCIR. v.intr. 1. (impers.) get light. 20762, U 25601; 2. a) break, dawn (day, dawn). 24698, 28140, 29954, b) begin to shine (sun). 27014, 28359. inf. as n.m. dawn. 29084.

(ESCLICHIER). v.intr. break, splinter. App. VII TV 270.

ESCLISTRER. v.intr. (impers.) lighten. LTV 32033.

ESCLIZ. n.m.pl. splinters. 30804.

ESCLOZ, ESCLOS. n.m.pl. hoof-prints, tracks. 9516. The *Toz les granz esclos* of E 20612 perhaps means 'quickly, following his tracks'; the reading of S presents no such problems.

(ESCLUMIR). v.refl. lie down, go to sleep. P 22272. a form of *esclemir*, see T-L, God.

ESCOI, ESCHOIS. n.m. boat. LTV 26129.

ESCOLE. n.f. *tenir escole* (+ *de*). discuss. App. VII TV 1184. see also *apris*.

ESCONDIRE. v.tr. (*q.ch. a qn.* or *qn. de q.ch.*) refuse, deny (s.th. to s.o.). 28037, 28053, 29337.

ESCONSER, (ESCONSSER). v.intr. set (sun). 21242, 23863, 29916. also v.refl. 26104 (E).

ESCORCIEZ. adj. (p.p.). with one's garment(s) kilted up. 26204, var. 25491. cf. *secorciez*.

ESCORDEMANT. adv. passionately, in heartfelt manner. 31920 (E). KPTV have *escortrement*; L has *encortrement* which does not seem to be attested, but the alternation of *es-* and *en-* is not unknown.

ESCREBEÜRE. see *escreveüre*.

ESCREMIE. n.f. 1. sword-fighting, fencing. 21859. 21288 *a l'escremie* simply qualifies *lou requiert*, to indicate that the knights are fighting with swords; 2. combat. 24994, 26928; 3. In P 24343 this word would appear to be an error for *estormie*, indeed, Potvin read *estremie*. Note, however, that God. has one example of this word meaning 'noise' (also an error?), and one of *escarmie* which might mean 'noise, rumpus'.

ESCREMIR. n.m. (inf.). sword-fighting, fencing. 23254.

ESCREVEÜRE. n.f. crack. K 32558. The *escreb(r)eüre* of LTV is not in the dictionaries, but would appear to mean the same.

ESCRÏER. v.tr. shout, call to. 20308. v.intr. (+ *a*) cry, call to. 20076, 22122, 23224. v.refl. cry out, call. 21806, 22332, 24350.

(ESCRIRE). v.tr. 32286. The sense here seems to be 'paint' or 'inscribe'.

ESCRISTURE. n.f. written source of the author, real or supposed. 20446, also T 19642? The sense of (E) 19642 *Qui ne sont pas an escristure* seems to be less definite 'which have not been written down'.

ESCRIT. n.m. 1. written source(s) of the author, real or supposed. 29351, LT 23532; 2. inscription. 31614.

ESCRIUTURE. n.f. P 32558. Probably the same as *escristure*, and meaning 'inscription', in which case it is an error.

ESCROIS, ESCROIZ. n.m. crash, crack, loud noise. 32123, 32227, 32323. All these are only in EMPSU, cf. Roach, note to 32115–51.

(ESDIGNER). v.refl. V 25852. eat, breakfast? Not in the dictionaries.

ESE, AIESE. n.f. *a ese*. 1. in comfort. 20761; 2. pleased, content. 27879. adj. comfortable, happy. 28390.

(ESFORCIER). v.refl. strive, exert o.s., make an effort. 9622, 20036, 9946. Also v.tr. increase, quicken (pace). K 20636. v.intr. become larger (involve more people). K 26908. For these latter, cf. *anforcier*.

ESFORZ. n.m. strength, prowess. 27178.

(ESFRÈER, ESFROIER). v.refl. take fright, be frightened. 30545. The spelling *esfroie* is not uncommon. p.p. (as adj.) frightened. 20860, 22312.

ESFROI. n.m. *a grant esfroi*. fearfully, in terror. 20808. *an grant esfroi*. worried, upset, frightened. 24376, 25636, 32414.

ESGARDER. v.tr., intr. look (at), see. 19654, 9552–19674, 9747–19857.

ESGAREE. adj.f. (p.p.). lost, helpless, put out. 31561, MQ 22312.

ESGART. n.m. 9793 *sanz autre esgart* — immediately, cf. L 10035. 10035–20171 *par grant esgart* —carefuly, deliberately. U 27792 *en l'esgart* may mean 'watching'. rej.r. 20698 *anmi son esgart* probably means 'in sight'.

ESGENÉ. adj. (p.p.). injured, hurt. 24961. The *engemé* of S is interesting, in that it seems to reinforce the solitary attestation in T-L, God., from *Foulque de Candie*. I would surmise that the sense is the same as that of *esgené*, cf. T-L III 378, 1.

ESLAVEZ. adj. (p.p.). washed clean. 24052. Given the frequent alternation of *es-* and *a-* in the text, the editor might have retained the form *alevez*.

(ESLEECIER). v.intr. rejoice, be glad. 26822, 29259, var. 24381. cf. *releecier, resleecier*.

ESLÉS, ESLAIS, ELLÉS, ALÉS. n.m. *a, de (grant) eslés*. quickly, running, galloping. 22646, 24856, 32182. For the form *alés* see Roach, note to 20479.

ESLESSIEZ, ESLAISSIEZ, ALAISSIEE. adj.(f.) (p.p.). The usual meaning of this p.p. is 'galloping, quickly' etc. 30240, 31559. In 20479, however, where it is a borrowing from C1, it is rather 'conducted at full tilt'.

ESLEVER, ALEVER. v.tr. increase. MQ 22863. In 26292, might the rej.r. *alevee* (= *eslevee*) mean 'well-developed, full-grown'? cf. T-L III 1090, 39, where the definition is 'aufgeschossen'.

(ESLIRE). v.tr. 1. distinguish, recognize. 28555; 2. pick out, aim for. 28814. p.p. (adj.) 1. excellent, admirable. 23895, 26952; 2. distinguished, select. 28573, 30977 (EMS), 31783.

ESLITE. n.f. *a eslite*. choice, of the best quality. 26393.

ESLOIGNE. see *alonge*.

(ESLOIGNIER), ALOIGNIER. v.tr. 1. level, point forward (lance). 23242, T 20467; 2. ride away, ride back (horse). 23810; 3. prolong, extend. 24212, 26089, 27367; 4. leave behind, abandon. 32152, 32475; 5. throw, knock away. LTV 28863. v.intr. 1. draw out, prolong (with 'story' as understood obj.). 10045, 28708, 29454; 2. draw back, move away. 24955, 30788. v.refl. draw back, move away. 10247–20453, 28799, 28845, cf. Roach, notes to 29454 and 25662.

ESMAI. n.m. *an esmai*. worried, despondent. 22881.

ESMAIER. v.refl. be dismayed, afraid, worried, discouraged. 20555, 21757, 24441.

ESMARRI. adj. (p.p.). upset, disconcerted. 20584, 22860, 30646.

ESME. n.m. *fere esme*. show sign(s) (of). 20502 (ET). A borrowing from C1.

ESMER. v.tr. count. App. VII TV 192.

ESMERÉ. adj. (p.p.). pure, fine. Applied exclusively to precious metals, usually gold, except 29513 *amies esmerees*. 19684, 21714, 28878.

ESMERILLONS. n.m. merlin. 9666, 28412, 28805.

(ESMÏER). v.tr. break (into pieces). App. VII TV 367.

ESMOLUE.　adj.f. (p.p.). sharp. 22029, 30827.

ESMOVOIR.　v.tr. 1. stir to motion. 28262; 2. move. P 21144. v.intr. move forward, start forward. 30154. inf. as n.m. 28803 *a l'esmovoir* — to move, into motion. v.refl. start to move, set off, go. 20608, Q 9673, MQ 27859. p.p. moved, aroused. P 23491.

(ESPANDRE).　v.tr. (ES) 21522 *Puis a sa raison espandue* — then he set forth (explained) what he had to say. The *espondue* of Q is more conventional, cf. *espondre*. The *espendre* of E 27275 would be a possible reading, with roughly the sense of 'spread around' (i.e. they have the candles brought), but the emendation is clearly justified.

(ESPANIR).　v.intr. bloom, open out. 24533.

(ESPARDRE).　v.tr. send out, distribute. App. VII TV 1254. P 23290 seems to be an error, whether it is for *espardre* or *espartir*. v.intr. dissipate. 32040.

ESPARGNIER, ESPARNIER.　v.tr., intr., refl. spare (o.s.). 21175, 22032, 30081. The readings of T are interesting; at 21175 and 22032, we find the form *esparignier*, giving hypermetric lines, while at 30081 the normal form is used, but this leaves a hypometric line.

ESPARTIR.　v.intr. (impers.) lighten. 32033, Q 32040.

ESPARZ.　n.m. rej.r. 32122. lightning.

ESPENOÏR.　v.tr. expiate, atone for. 24104, 29228.

ESPERDUZ.　adj. (p.p.). put out, at a loss, distracted. 21612, 25815, 30820.

ESPERITABLE.　adj. 1. heavenly, divine. 24463, 25501, 27707; 2. spiritual, pious? 31654.

ESPERITAL.　adj. heavenly, spiritual. MQ 24080.

ESPESSE.　adj.f. dark, murky. 31134.

(ESPESSIER, ESPOSSIER, ESPOISSIER).　v.intr. darken, grow dim. KTV 25645. cf. also the *respissa* of L, and the *respescha* of P.

(ESPIRER).　M 29256. v.tr. inspire, brighten? (from INSPIRARE) or v.intr. expire, pass? (from EXPIRARE). If the former, one would expect a reading *toz li mons*, rather than *li mois*.

(ESPLANDIR).　v.intr. shine. Q 27916.

ESPLENDISSOR.　n.m. brightness, splendour. K 24171.

ESPLOIT.　n.m. profit, advantage. Q 26466. *a (molt) (grant) esploit*. quickly, hurriedly. 22170, 23584, 26502. In 31234, the sense is almost 'abundantly'.

ESPLOITIER.　v.intr. 1. gain, achieve. 10210–20352, 26786, var. 31201; 2. (+ *de*) strive. 20810, 22230; 3. get on, succeed. 23664, 28401; 4. hurry. 25467, 31028; 5. ride, travel. 31106, T 24130; 6. act, do. 31962. v.refl. strive. 25471, 30126 (only EL refl.).

ESPÖANTEUSE.　adj.f. horrific, horrible. Q 27512.

ESPOIR.　n.m. *au mien espoir*. I think, it seems to me, etc., cf. *escïent*. 24362, 25063, 29363. The simple form *espoir* is pres. indic. 1 of *esperer*, and has the sense 'perhaps'. It is found only in EPS 20727, 21064, 23438.

ESPONDRE.　v.tr. explain, expound, speak. Q 21522. Also K 25097, although the line is corrupt. cf. *espandre*.

ESPRANDRE.　v.tr. light. 27275. v.intr. 1. (fig.) be inflamed (with a passion). 20874, 24946, 30493; 2. (lit.) catch fire. 25617. The p.p. (as adj.) also has both fig. and lit. senses, 'inflamed'. 28847, 29817, 31103, 'alight, burning'. 26415, 32082, 32094. In KMQU 23696 the sense is almost 'dazed' (with the idea of a rush of blood to the head). v.refl. be inflamed. var. 23491.

ESPROISIER.　v.tr. evaluate, assess. 29704.

ESPROVER.　v.tr. 1. try, put to the test, discover. 9620–19742, 24422, 28352; 2. experience. 26440. v.refl. test one's mettle. 19630, 28348. *esprovez*. adj. (p.p.). proven, tried and tested. 19841, KMQU 27548.

ESPUISIER.　v.tr. plumb, get to the bottom of? S 29704.

ESPUREE.　adj.f. (p.p.). clear. 32046.

(ESQUARTELER, ESCARTELER).　v.intr. break. SU 30204.

ESQUÏER.　see *eschiver*.

ESRÉS.　p.p. (*esrere*). razed to the ground? S 9898. The fact that S reads *de feu esrés* is interesting, cf. God. VII 79b *rere* (2), and the comments thereon in FEW X 15a n. 1.

ESSAMPLERE.　n.f. account, story. M 27889.

ESSAUCIER.　v.tr. 1. exalt, glorify, bring honour (to). 28593, 28907, Q 29630; 2. pursue, promote. 28753, 31389; 3. increase, heighten. T 22118, U 22152. p.p. as adj. sumptuous, magnificent. 28891.

(ESSEÜRER).　v.refl. rej.r. 21670. The emendation is unnecessary; this is an attested form of *asseürer*.

ESSIL.　n.m. *metre a essil*. bring destruction, disaster upon. S 24461.

(ESSILLIER).　v.tr. destroy, devastate. 31353.

ESSOINES.　n.m. hindrance, obstacle. 31268.

ESSORELÉ.　p.p. U 26521. Error? or cognate with *essorer*, in the general sense of 'set off, rush off'?

ESTABLIR.　v.tr. 1. construct, build. 22626, 22630, 26532; 2. organize, arrange. 27040, 30133, 31322; 3. establish, designate. 28796, 32460.

ESTAICHE.　n.f. pillar, column. 26538. This would also appear, unusually, to be the meaning of M's *estage* (n.m.).

ESTAICHES.　n.f.pl. fastening. 26363. cf. Roach, note to this line.

ESTAIGE.　n.m. position, place. 29300, rej.r. 32460. The latter reading would be acceptable, but it is isolated. cf. also *estaiche*.

ESTAL.　n.m. position, place, often that in which one offers combat. 23815, App. VII TV 670. also, therefore, combat. var. 23815, KMQU 10164. *prandre, faire estal*. stop. 24390, 27832, 29032. *movoir, müer estal*. give ground. 24976, 27114. *a estal*. resolutely. M 29114.

(ESTANCELER).　v.intr. MQ 30204. The sense here, 'break, splinter' is not normally that of this verb. Given the frequent confusion of *c* and *t*, this is probably an error for *escarteler* (cf. reading of SU).

(ESTANCHIER).　v.tr., intr. (put a) stop (to). 30333.

ESTANT.　see *ester*.

ESTAT.　n.m. place, position. U 27114. cf. *estal*.

ESTEL.　n.m. jamb, (door-) post, pillar. 21102, T 21723.

ESTELÉ.　adj. (p.p.). decorated with stars. 22991, KMQU 23017.

ESTER.　v.intr., refl. 1. stop. 9487, 9767–PT 19869. The imper. is used exclamatorily in T 20174, 'hold!'; 2. stand. 9937, 21192, 25894; 3. stand, be. 20044; 4. stay, tarry. 22084, 22493, 30669; 5. The sense of *laissier ester* is 'abandon, put aside (s.th.), leave (s.o.) be'. 20853, 21392, 24209; 6. (impers.) 30417 *mal li estait*— all was not well with her, she was put out, (reading of P; E omits). The refl. is found only at 19731 (= intr. 3.), and 10071–20205 (= intr. 2.), and occasionally in the var. *estant*. pres.p and n.m. *an (son) estant*. standing, upright, on one's feet. 10152–20286, 21562, 31636. There is a certain amount of overlap between this verb and *estre*, cf. 9579, 9611.

ESTOIRE.　n.f. (also m.). story. The two principle meanings, not always easily distinguished, are: 1. (the) story which is being told. 19617, 26097, 31421; 2. the source, real or supposed, used by the author. 29190, 29354, 32292. The sense of 29202 is almost 'the material furnished by the source'. In 26089 the meaning seems to be 'short story, episode'. In 32292 this word is n.m.

(ESTONER).　v.tr. 1. stun. 20500, 20870, 21274; 2. shake. P 24396. v.refl. be stunned, stun one another. 22354, M 10254.

ESTORBEILLON.   n.m. whirlwind, swirl. 32030.
ESTORDIE.   n.f. V 24343. noise, resonance? cf. *estormie*.
ESTORDRE.   v.intr., refl. escape, get away. Q 32224, App. IV MQ 118, App. VII TV 983.
(ESTORER).   v.tr. build, construct, create. 26549, 32468, Q 26560.
ESTORMIE.   n.f. noise, resonance. 24343, 24870, 29423.
ESTOUTIE.   n.f. arrogance, folly, rashness. 20841, 31115.
(ESTOUTOIER).   v.tr. 1. harm, ill-treat. 22364, T 28664; 2. frighten, intimidate. 23806.
ESTOUZ.   adj. 1. violent. 20497; 2. proud, arrogant. 28748.
(ESTOVER).   v.tr. P 28187. Although no degree of certainty is possible, particularly as the editor says the MS is unclear, and this hypermetric line is clearly corrupt, we might surmise that the correct reading (still hypermetric) would be *S'i out estoiiee une grant nef*, meaning 'and there was a large boat kept there'. Alternatively, and perhaps more plausibly, *estovee* could be maintained, 'furnished, laden'; the word is commonly applied to ships, cf. AND *estuffer*.
ESTOVOIR.   v.intr. (impers.). be necessary, needful. 9644, 9892, 20488. P 20753 *Grant cose a en fere l'estuet*—necessity is a hard taskmaster. inf. as n.m. necessity, obligation. *par estovoir*. of necessity, because I (you, he, etc.) must. 10130–20264, 10208–20350, 22056. 30762 *par vostre estovoir* — because you are obliged, compelled (to).
ESTRAIERE (1).   n.f. MS 30935. delay, lingering; or does this refer to Gauvain's horse?
ESTRAIERE (2).   adj.f. alone, by oneself. 24202, (m.) var. 23829, var. 31169.
ESTRAIN.   n.m. straw. (used for bedding). 24151.
ESTRAVEE.   adj.f. (p.p.). encamped. 30014 (E only, the var. have *atravee*, cf. PT 31324, which is clearly an error).
ESTRE (1).   v.intr. There is little that is unusual in the use of this verb in C2. Here are some examples: 10038–20174 *ce que sera?* — what can this mean?, also 27463. 22570 *Et s'il est qui le voir vos die* — and were someone to tell you the truth of it, cf. 32249 *se c'estoit que je vos deïsse* — if I were to tell you. 22901 *ne qu'il an iert* — nor what will become of this. 23512 *Ou soit s'anor ou soit sa honte* — whether it be to his honour or to his shame. 24985 *qui qu'an soit let* — regardless of whether anyone is displeased. Note also 25051 *Filz fui le duc de Geneloie*, a specific use of the pret. for a statement of pedigree. see also *ancor*, *ja*.
ESTRE (2).   n.m. 1. state, condition. (often with the sense 'identity', or 'the truth, the facts'.) 9768, 20059, 23138; 2. spot, place. 21705, 22489. 10007–20139 *ci fet boen, bel estre* — this is a pleasant place to be; 3. situation, position. 21113, 22206, 28782. also 28168, perhaps with the sense of 'direction'. There is a certain amount of overlap between these three meanings, and it is not always easy to distinguish them; cf. e.g. 24466 *(Conme celle) qui bien sot l'estre* — does this mean 'who knew her way around', or 'who understood the situation'?
ESTRES.   n.m.pl. (upstairs) living-quarters. 10011–20143, 10093. In 10060–20194 *soz les estres* simply means '(down) below'.
(ESTRIVER).   v.intr. argue. 22394, 25565.
(ESTROUER).   v.tr. pierce. 21254, KM 21274.
ESTROX.   adj. *a estrox*. certainly, without doubt, without fail. 28702, 32573, var. 29030.
(ESVANOÏR, ESVENOÏR).   v.refl. disappear. 31501, 32244, 32336. cf. *resvanoïr*.
EUR.   n.m. side, edge. var. 21270. cf. *eure* (2).
EÜR.   n.m. (good) fortune. 22781, var. 29492. *eürez*. adj. (*boens, bien eürez*) fortunate. 25453, 25946, 29494. cf. *beneürez*.
EURE (1), ORE.   n.f. 1. time, moment. 9956–20086, 30041, 31009. *an meïsmes l'ore*. at that moment. 9703. *d'eures an autres*. from time to time. 24866. 28024 *de quelle eure*

que — when, whenever. 30269 *an icelle eure* — immediately, soon; 2. hour, short space of time. 10205–20347, 23341. *an po(i), petit d'eure.* shortly, quickly, soon. 20880, 25006, 25612. *an es l'eure* (also *enz en l'eure* in var.). immediately. 21456, 30923, L 30269. 26691 *Vïende orent con a telle eure* — they ate the sort of meat appropriate to the time of day; 3. (appointed) time. 27824.

EURE (2). n.f. side, edge. K 20545. cf. *eur.*

EUS. n.m. profit, advantage, disposition. 29514 *Et a leur eus si atornees* — and so well-disposed towards them. This is the usual spelling in E of the more common *oés.*

EUVRE. see *uevre.*

EXAMPLE. n.m.pl. exempla, moral tales. 24064.

EZ, ECE. demonstr. part. (always + *vos*). The basic meaning is 'see' giving rise to two uses: 1. (now) here is/are, and now there arrive(s). 22161, 24134, 24345; 2. (now) see them (= now they are). 22201, 23462, 29038? The *ece* in 27746 is found only in E, while MS have *estes.*

F

FABLE. n.f. falsehood, deception. 31653, S 9940, and P 30224 (the picard form *faule*).

(FABLOIER). v.intr. tell stories. 26087.

FAÇON. n.f. 1. face, countenance. 23194; 2. appearance. 19776, var. 22290, T 22292.

FAEE. adj.f. under a spell, enchanted. 23532 (EP).

FAIERIE. n.f. magic, enchantment. 20580, 24725.

FAILLANCE. n.f. 1. end. 26540 *a la faillance* — at the point where the bridge ended; 2. *sanz faillance.* certainly. Q 21998.

FAILLE. n.f. *sanz (nule) faille.* certainly, assuredly, without fail, without doubt, etc. 9521, 21332, 25915. The primary function of this expression is to provide a convenient rhyme for *bataille*; of the ten occurrences found at the rhyme, only 23174 and 28532 prove exceptions to this rule.

FAILLIR. v.intr. 1. (+ *a*) fail, not succeed (in). 9509, 26824, 29509. When negated and impers., gives a sense of 'be inevitable' — 24084; 2. (impers.) be lacking. 20412, 21715, 25197. 20456 *bataille ne vos faut* — you need not look elsewhere for a fight; 3. fail (s.o.). 27351. 20669 *ja ne li faudra d'aïe* — he will not fail to come to her assistance; 4. miss. 21830; 5. fail to get, lose. 22828, Q 10144; 6. end, come to an end. 23098, 26105, 26535. *sanz faillir.* without fail. 24991. v.refl. *pou s'an faut que* gives the sense of 'almost' 22040. p.p. as adj., n.m. *failliz.* coward. 10216. perfidious, dishonoured. 20358. pres.p. as adj. *faillant.* exhausted. MU 31526.

FAINDRE, FEINDRE, FOINDRE. v.refl. hesitate, refrain, cease. (always used negatively, to denote a positive action). 10134–20268, 10168–20313, 20518. *sanz faindre.* 1. without letting up. 9736–19852; 2. without doubt. (from the other meaning of *faindre* 'pretend'). M 9722.

FAINTIE. n.f. *sans faintie.* assuredly, without deception. P 25855.

FAINTISE. n.f. *sans faintise.* straightforwardly, without any deception. 30047.

FAITEMANT. see *sifaitemant.*

FAITURE. n.f. 1. structure, appearance. 26529; 2. appearance. 29350, 31440.

FAMELLEUS. adj. hungry. 9473.

(FANDRE). v.tr. split, cleave. 22026, 26903. The intr. use in 22019 (ES) *fandant*, seems to imply merely speed, rather than referring to any direction or manner of motion, and as this could apply equally to the two examples given by T-L

(III 1710, 49), I would hesitate to agree with the latter's definition: 'quer durch gehn'.

FARAINS.   n.m.pl. wild animals. 22240, 23840.

FAUS.   n.m. falcon. 26882.

FAUSER.   v.tr. break, damage. Q 9740. v.intr. *sanz fauser.* truly, without deception. 22870, T 20310, MQ 29660.

FAUTRE (1).   n.m. blanket or rug. 10024–20160.

FAUTRE (2).   n.m. lance-rest. 22023, 24956, 28800. There is some doubt as to the exact nature of this feature of the knight's equipment. It seems possible that it may have been a raised support, attached to the saddle bow, cf. expressions such as *lance levee sor le fautre* (*Yvain* 6084). see also Foulet C1.

FAUVELLE.   n.f. *sans fauvelle.* probably 'truly, with certainty'. 19664 (E), though cf. *fere favele.* waste time. P 29381.

FEAUS.   n.m.pl. (adj.) faithful. 32489.

FEINDRE.   see *faindre.*

FELONESSEMANT.   adv. fiercely. 21868.

FELONESSES.   adj.f.pl. terrible, dangerous. 19628.

FENEE.   adj.f. (p.p.). mown, made into hay. P 27593.

FENESTRÉS.   adj.pl. KLU 22299. The dictionaries have no corresponding usage; the meaning might be 'smooth (and shining?)' or 'white'.

FERE, FAIRE, FEIRE.   v.tr., intr. For the most part, the uses of this verb in the Second Continuation require little comment, being common in O.F., and often still current in Mod.F. The basic meaning ranges from 'do, act, make, render, construct' to 'say' and 'finish'. The following selection is intended to represent the more noteworthy uses.

9907 *ci fet mal sejorner* — this is a bad place to stay, cf. *estre* (2). *fere sage (+ de).* tell. 10122–20258. 10206–20348 *Si ferai* — yes, I will, cf. 21430, 25181. *neant feire.* waste one's time. 10233. 20649 *De mon frainc n'avez vos que fere* — you have no business with my bridle (i.e. leave it alone), cf. 24001 *n'an ai que fere* — I am not concerned with that. *faire le bon de qn.* do s.o's will, submit to s.o's wishes. 21773, cf. *fere le voloir, le plesir de qn.,* etc. 21877 *n'i ot plus fet* — and there was an end to it. 22946 *Que a son voil ne feroit mie* — that he would not do as she wished. 23037 *Qui plus an set et plus an fet* — the more accomplishments each person has, the more he does. 23910 *que faites vos?* — how are you? *faire a* + inf. be worthy, deserving of. 26083, 27690, 28970, cf. 24056 *De ce ne faz mie a mescroire* — I am to be believed on this point, also 28604 *n'an faites pas a blasmer* — you should not be reproached for it. 25433 *faites pais* — be silent; but cf. 28958, where *fere la pais* = Mod.F. *faire une prière.* grant a request. 25920, the same sense being found with *volantez* 26726. *le faire bien.* fight well. 27079, cf. 27067. 28112 *ne vos faz novelle* — I will not tell you, cf. *devis, devise, memoire. faire que cortois.* act in a courtly manner. 31709, U 10058, see also *fol,* and cf. *faire folie, corteisie, vilenie* etc. — to behave foolishly, courteously, etc. To these we may add *fere mançonge.* lie. 25547; and *faire honte, contraire, tort (+ a).* 22078, 23305, etc. An interesting syntactical point is the construction in 24413 *Ja por peor ne por proiere Que vos ne autre . . . ne me face* — (I will not desist) for prayers or threats, where *fere proiere* has a difference sense from that in 25920, cf. *supra.* inf. as n.m. fabrication, manufacture. 9644, 22140. v.refl. be. 30099, 31798. For other uses of *fere* see *demeure, demorance, dongier, esme, estal, fauvelle, feste, force, gorge, honor, plet, rebors, retor, samblant, sarmon.*

FERIR. v.tr. (also intr., refl.) strike. 9665, 9679, 9705. with person as dir. obj., but also, frequently one finds *ferir un cop* 'strike a blow'. 20512, 20543, 21862. 28881 *Ja refusent au cos ferir* — they were about to come to blows again. Note also *espee* as dir. obj. in 30826–31, giving *ferir* almost the sense of 'propel', and TV 29628 *Que li tornois ne fust ferus* — that the tournament should not take place.

FERM. adj. strong, solid. M 24364.

FERMÉ. adj. (p.p.). 1. attached. 9560; 2. enclosed, fortified. 26311, 26559, 30520.

FERMEMANT. adv. 1. soundly (sleep). 25210; 2. firmly. M 28821.

FERMEÜRE. n.f. 1. lock. 9557, KQU 9558, MQS 27762; 2. locked room, strong-room? var. 27762. cf. *anfermeüre*.

FERRANT. adj. (iron-) grey. 27992, 28471, LT 22328.

FERRÉ. adj. (p.p.). 1. paved, metalled (road). 9475, 19644, 21027; 2. shod (horse). 9517. Does *a envers ferrei* mean with one shoe on back-to-front?

FERREÜRE. n.f. ironwork, metalwork. KLU 9557, M 9558. This word is found frequently enough as a variant for *fermeüre* or *serreüre*, to suggest that its meaning may have been extended to include 'clasp, lock'. cf. also T-L III 1763, 10.

FERVESTI. adj. (p.p.). armed. 28786, 31310. We also find *fervestu(z)* K 28306, M 29091, cf. the alternative p.p.'s of *vestir*.

FESTE. n.f. 1. pleasure. 10169, 26108; 2. feast, festivity. 23033, 26572, 28431; 3. feast-day. 25222, 28487, 28517. *fere feste*. 1. (+ *a*) rejoice over, welcome warmly, make much of. 26382, 28382, 31670; 2. rejoice. 20315. (+ *de*) rejoice over. 24892.

FESTOIER. v.tr. fête, welcome warmly, make much of. 9811.

FETICEMENT. adv. elegantly, gently. M 26075.

FETIS. adj. elegant, tastefully decorated. S 10012, although this may be a metathesis for *fet si*.

FI, FIZ. adj. certain. 24594, App. XI K 13. *de fi*. for certain. 27723, 29110, 30468. We also find *de fit*, P 29016, P 29390.

FÏENCE. n.f. 1. confidence. 26165; 2. promise, assurance. 29529. *a fïence*. sure, assured. 26030. *perdre fïence*. break one's word. 27346. see also *passer*.

(FÏENCIER). v.tr., intr. promise. 27085, 31778.

FIN (1). n.f. end. 26556. *an toutes fins*. in any case, regardless. 27799. *an nule fin*. in no wise, under no circumstances. 28039. *an la fin*. at length, at last, when all was said and done. 28448, 29074, 31956. *venir a bone fin*. bring s.th. to a satisfactory conclusion, not make a mess of s.th. 28758.

FIN (2). adj. 1. pure, of the highest quality. 9556, 9597–19719, 9899; 2. absolute, complete, veritable. 20592, 20702, 27035; 3. fine, excellent, beautiful. 22551, 23444, 26378; 4. true, genuine, pure (love). 22929, 23359, 29632. *de fin cuer*. with all one's heart, truly. 29928, 30897, 31685. *a fine force*. by force of arms. 9716, MQ 24944. Also, combined with another adj., has an adv. sense, 'finely'. 22773.

FINER. v.tr. finish, bring to an end. 9780, 23012, 24664. v.intr. 1. stop, pause. 19925, 20304, 20910; 2. (+ *de*) leave off, stop. 25860, 27327, 29563; 3. come to an end. 26707.

FIZ. see *fi*.

FLAIREUR. n.f. smell, aroma. L 10011.

FLATIR. v.intr. fall. Q 9690.

(FLERER, FLAIRER). v.intr. smell. (pleasantly or unpleasantly). 21126, 23930, 25377.

FLOREÏS. n.m. 19647 (E). This appears to be a *hapax*. If it is a genuine word, the meaning is presumably 'field covered with flowers' or something similar. However, given the curious metatheses occasionally perpetrated by the scribe of E, cf. note to 28833, this may be an error for *rifleïs*, cf. PT.

FOILLIEZ. n.m.pl. pages. 26432, where KMU have various spellings of the synonymous *fueil*.

FOILLOLÉ. adj. (p.p.). App. VII TV 77. bedecked (like a tree with leaves)? Or perhaps a heraldic term; see the note at the end of the Glossary.

FOINDRE. see *faindre*.

FOL. n.m. fool. 30851. (also 20851, 20855?). adj. foolish, impetuous, careless. 20847, 21824, 23501. 19878 *que fox feroie* — I would be foolish, it would be foolish of me. cf. *fere*.

(FOLOIER). v.intr. behave foolishly, waste one's time. 20678. refl. in var.

FOLOR. n.f. foolish or impetuous behaviour. 22823, 26028.

FONDE. n.f. (shot from) catapult. App. VII TV 346. For Q 21666 see *afonder*.

FONDEÏS. n.m. ruin. (L 9898–) 20043.

(FONDER). v.tr. build. 9902 (A). This isolated reading may be an error; *fondre* would seem more appropriate.

FONDRE. v.intr. 1. melt. 20578; 2. collapse, fall down. 24418, 25649, 26159; 3. collapse inwards, be dented? L 9738.

FONNESTRIELE. n.f. P 22530. This seems to be an error.

FONTEINE. n.f. (spring–) water. 21319.

FORCE. n.f. force, strength. 26719, 28820, 29479. *fere force (a)*. a) rape. 10127–20259, 29868, b) use force on, do violence to, etc. 10212–20354, 10213–20355, 27806, cf. *droit. metre sa force (a)*. devote one's strength (to). 22366. *a, par force*. 1. (hunt) with dogs. 10133–20267, (also 20312?); 2. by force. 21801, 24944, 30644. cf. 30657.

FORCHIÉ. adj. (p.p.). 1. cleft (chin). 22301; 2. forked (road). 22534, 29176.

FORDINE. n.f. sloe. var. 23183.

FORFAIRE. v.tr. do (s.th.) wrong. S 20863. v.intr. (+ *a*) harm, maltreat, do wrong to (s.o.). 25917, 26590.

FORIERE. adj.f. T 22534. As an adj., this word is not found in the dictionaries. Comparing it with *foriere*, cf. T-L III 2100, 7, we would assume that a *voie foriere* is one which runs along the edge of a wood or a field.

FORMÏER. see *fremïer*.

FORNI. see *furnir*.

FORS. adv. out, outside. 21241, 24610, KLTU 21138. with various verbs of motion (usually *fors de*). 9625, 19768, etc. prep. 1. except. 9534–19658, 19789, 9774. 24358 *Je n'i vins fors por herbergier* — I came here for lodging, and for no other reason; 2. (but) only. 9538. *fors de*. except for. 20395, 20734. 27041 *N'i avoit fors de l'asambler* — all that remained was for them to come together (in battle), cf. *el*. 23771 *fors de guerre* — out of trouble. *fors que*. except (that). 21019. *fors tant, itant que*. except that. 20998, 21110. see also *sens*.

(FORSTRAIRE). v.tr. take (away) (from). 20973, P 20974.

FOURS. n.m. fork (road). S 29176.

(FRAINDRE). v.tr. break. 22026, 26903, S 9738.

FRAITE. n.f. break, opening. 20359.

FRANINES. adj.f.pl. ash. 23242.

FRAPIER. n.m. *metre qn. au frapier*. put s.o. to flight. 30279. *se metre au frapier*. set off in a hurry. 31517.

FRASER. see *or*.

FREMAILLES. n.f.pl. clasps, fastenings. K 21317.

(FREMÏER). v.tr. shake. M 24344, MQ 24396. v.intr. 1. boil. 20540; 2. shake, tremble. var. 24344, var. 24396, U 24343; 3. be agitated. var. 26867. Many of these examples have the form *formïer*.

FRES. adj. 1. new, fresh. 20148, 21111, 21402. often in conjunction with *novel*; 2. bright. 21481. also adv. Q 22773. brightly.

(FRESTELER). v.intr. pipe, play the flute. App. VII TV 148.

FRIÇON. n.f. fear, anxiety. 24787.

(FRÖER). v.tr. break, smash. S 30166.

(FROIER). v.intr. (+ *a*) grate (on). 21296.

FROISSEÏS. n.m. breaking, splintering (lances). App. VII TV 546, 823.

(FROISSIER). v.tr., intr. break, splinter. 9678–19806, 23818, 32038.

(FRONCHIER). v.intr. snort. 20071 (E).

FRONT. n.m. *tot a un front*. all together, side by side. 27062.

FRONTÉ. n.m. rej.r. 32283. Although T-L attests *fronté* (= *frontel*) only as adj., I would suggest that this does correspond to *frontel* (cf. God. IV 162b), perhaps meaning an ornamental strip around the edges of the ceiling.

FUER. n.m. Usually *a nul fuer*. (not) at any price, in no wise. 23074, 23340, 23688. *metre a un fuer*. place the same value on, treat all the same. 30478.

FUERRE (1). n.m. sheath. 20879, 22028, 24970.

FUERRE (2). n.m. straw. KS 24151.

FUNS. n.m. steam, breath. 21651.

(FURNIR, FORNIR). v.tr. finish, complete. LMP 27990. p.p. (adj.) big, strong, solid. var. 23189, Q 9993–P 20121, LMTV 26291.

FUST, FUZ. n.m. 1. wood. 9542, 19667, 26531; 2. piece of wood, stake. 27446.

G

GAAIGNAIGE. n.m. 29811. Probably used here with a fairly loose sense, 'business'.

GAAIGNIER. v.tr. 1. gain, achieve. 10192–20330; 2. cultivate, grow. 29221. v.intr. make a profit, (a) gain (usually by tourneying). 26926, 27138, 31382. inf. as n.m. 27066.

GABER. v.tr. mock, make fun of, tease. 21061, 29694, 30330. v.intr. (+ *de*) mock, make jokes about, make sport of. 23234, 26981, 28665.

GAITIER. v.tr. watch (over). 24648. v.refl. (+ *de* + *inf*.) make sure one does not do s.th. 26428. v.intr. P 23236. imper. 'look to yourself, take care!'

GALESCHE. adj.f. of *galois*. welsh. 24763 (cf. *loige*), KMQU 26850. Also n.f. welsh woman. 26849.

GALIE. n.f. rej.r. 24000. galley. The line makes sense in isolation.

(GALIR). v.intr. leap. (fig.) App. VII TV 430. A dialectal form of *ja(il)lir*.

(GANCHIR). v.intr. 1. move aside, dodge. 21831. Q 26892 *au cop ganchir* — in dodging the blow?; 2. (also v.refl) turn aside, turn back. var. 9634.

GARDE. n.f. 1. watch, guard. 10032–20168; 2. care. 10075–20209, 25942. *prandre garde*. pay attention, look out (for). 27051. also refl., P 22092, but error. 24888 *Avez vos eü de lui garde Se bone non?* — has he given you any cause for concern?; 3. 28564. fortress, stronghold?

GARDER. v.tr. 1. keep, take care of, protect. 10078–20212, 22518, 29967; 2. (+ *de*) keep, protect (from). 21492, 25379, 25810; 3. guard, watch over. 22069, 22134, 22144, (28797 with roughly the sense 'oversee'); 4. keep, retain. 28905; 5. care for (medically), make well. App. VII TV 796. v.intr. 1. look. 9593, 21100, 21114; 2. (imper. only) a) know (that), look! 25192, b) make sure (that). 28203. v.refl. 1. be careful, take care. 21832, 24420, 31309, with the sense 'defend o.s.', 22336, 23237; 2. (+ *que ne* + subj., or + *de*) avoid. 29268, 29719; 3. be aware of, on the look-out for. K 27395. 31076 *de vos ne me gardoie* — I was not expecting to see you.

GARIR. v.tr. 1. save, rescue. 21944, 24409, 28343; 2. protect, save. 24797, 26015, 30803; 3. heal, make well. 9792–19895, 28360, 28498. v.intr. 1. save o.s., escape, be saved. 21794, 25034; 2. be at ease, rest easy. 26718. v.refl. protect o.s. 23253.

GARNEMANZ. n.m.pl. clothes. 21462, 21748. In sing. Q 27674 furnishings, fittings, LTV 30142 arms, equipment.

GAS. n.m. Q 9631 *Ou tot a gas ou tot a certe* — whether in jest or seriously.

GAST. adj. deserted. 9545–19672, 24642.

GASTINE. n.f. deserted place, wilderness. 24386, S 31578.

(GASTIR). v.tr. lay waste. U 22853. cf. *agastir*.

GAUDINE. n.f. forest, woodland. 24732, 25716, 31578.

GAUT. n.m. wood. 24820. I see no reason to reject the *gau* of E 22510, since both *gau* and *gal* are attested, and the word is synonymous with *bois*. cf. note to 22510.

GELEE. n.f. frost. var. 22298. Only E has *gelee*, p.p., here.

GEMÉ. see *jermé*.

GENCIULES. n.f.pl. P 23192. gums. Possibly we should read *gencivles* with T-L (IV 238, 15), although we also find *gençures* (IV 238, 2).

(GENTER). v.intr. S 29249. Doubtless an error for *gouter*, 'drip'.

GENTIS. adj. noble (of falcons). 28806.

GESIR. v.intr. lie down, be lying (down), rest, sleep, spend the night. 10235, 20501, 21143. In 23922, the sense is 'be buried'. also v.refl. 22263, 27833, 31244. The scribe of E uses the forms with initial *j* frequently, and not merely in front of *u*.

GEU, JEU. n.m.(pl.). 1. chess-set, chess-pieces. (The sing. sometimes seems to indicate the board). 10023–20159, 20162, 10028; 2. *partir le geu*. make a choice. 30489; 3. game, performance? App. VII TV 1214.

GIRON. n.m. lower front part of a garment, which constitutes the lap when one is seated. 20788.

GIRONEES, GYRONNEES. adj.f.pl. (p.p.). App. VII K 77–TV 107. gyronny (of a banner), divided into between six and twelve triangles, their corners meeting at the central point.

GITER. v.tr. The more interesting uses of this verb are: 1. liberate, free, release. 23118, 24071, 28288, also with the sense 'protect', 29034; 2. push out (tongue). 24849. *giter un soupir*. sigh. 21614, 28283; cf. 26797. *giter hors de son sens*. drive mad. 26180. *giter morz*. kill, strike dead. 28825. Note also v.refl. free o.s. 28745.

GLAS. n.m. App. VII TV 887. *mener (grant) glas (sor)*. probably means 'pursue hotly (as though hunting)'.

(GLATIR). v.tr., intr. bark, give tongue. 20817, 27638, 27717. The tr. form is *moz glatir*, 27638.

GOINDRE. see *joindre*.

GOLES, GUEULES. n.f.pl. gules, red colour (on shield). 9597–19719.

GORGE. n.f. food for a hawk, in *faire gorge a*, feed. Q 9914.

GORT. n.m. stream, current. Q 27653.

(GRÄER). v.tr. grant. 27726, 29867. v.intr. please. PS 20531.

GRANT. adj. well-advanced (day). 22187, 22273, 27599. *an grant* (+ *de* + inf.) keen, anxious (to). 29826. P has the equivalent *en grandes*.

GRE.   n.m. 1. agreement, permission. 24899. *de (bon) gré*. willingly, freely. 20295, 21567, 23319. *mau gré suen*. in spite of him, whether he like it or not. 24927, cf. 29139, 29865. 25412 *outre son gré* — against his will; 2. *savoir (bon) gré*. be grateful, thank. 20659, 21949, 28004. *randre grez*. thank. 26043; 3. *a vostre gré*. as you wish. 27877. 25962 *par mon gré N'an iroiz vos ancore mie* — I do not wish you to leave yet. *venir a gré*. please. 22615, 25886, 30611. *s'il vos vient a gré*. please. 24920, 25850, 30751. *estre gré (a)*. please. 28114.

GREINE.   n.f. red dye. 26345, P 22661.

GRENONS.   n.m.pl. whiskers. 23193.

GREVAINE.   adj.f. difficult, arduous. 26733, S 29152 (m.).

GREVAL.   see *greviex*.

GREVANCE.   n.f. trouble, bother. 29595.

GREVER.   v.tr. 1. harm, wound. 19854, 26595; 2. oppress, harry. 9758–19866; 3. grieve, distress. 24456; 4. annoy, bother, fatigue. 27890, 29598, 29974. v.intr. 1. grieve, distress. 21852, 21934, 22930. also impers. (as is 21934), with a different syntax, 22944, 23044; 2. (impers). bother, trouble. 32370, 32515. p.p. (adj.). tired. 21925.

GREVIEX, GREVAL, GREVOLS.   adj. fierce, hard to bear. S 9732, KL 31852.

GREZOIS.   adj. greek (always applied to cloth). 9600–19722, 19755, 9997–20127.

GRIEF.   adj. difficult. 32415, var. 29147, P 29153.

GRIFAINGNE.   adj.f. menacing, dangerous. Q 31756.

GRIS.   n.m. miniver. 21361, 22588, 31729. adj. grey (or possibly 'of miniver', in some cases). 23520, 27765, 29589.

(GUERPIR).   v.tr. leave, abandon. 23280, 32240, Q 21625. *guerpir place*. give ground, retreat. M 9760. It is worth noting the refl. use in E, rej.r. 28932, meaning 'go away (from), leave'. God. attests one refl. example, with a slightly different sense.

GUERREDON, GUERREDOM.   n.m. recompense. 20868, 31004. 31012 *par guerredom* — by way of recompense. *randre guerredon (de)*. pay back (for). 9729, 32474.

GUEULES.   see *goles*.

GUICHET.   n.m. wicket gate. 23838, 23851, 26956.

GUIGE, GUICHE.   n.f. 1. strap (horn). 9564–19687; 2. strap (shield, for hanging it around one's neck, cf. *anarme*). 9599–19721, 21171, 29988.

GUIMPLE.   n.f. wimple. 22285, 27521, 27527. worn by a knight as a sign of a lady's favour, 30144.

GUINON.   n.m. rej.r. 32413. The dictionaries have no such word. I. Short surmises that this corresponds to *guiron*, in which case it might conceivably mean 'side', cf. AND *gerun*.

GYRONNEES.   see *gironees*.

H

HAITIEZ.   adj. (p.p.). well, in good health, in good spirits. 21538, 26937, 32498.

HANTE (1).   n.f. lance or spear-shaft, lance. 9994–20124, 23105, 27021.

HANTE (2).   n.f. grafted tree. 21512, 22756, var. 32398. It is unusual to find this word with initial *h*, and noteworthy that at 22756 we must read *de hante* as two syllables (unless there is a hiatus *blanchë est*), while at 21512 *une hante* counts for only two syllables.

(HANTER).   v.tr. 1. frequent, live in. 20719; 2. frequent, use. 23150, 29178, L 9898, cf. *anties, hansties* in the corresponding line PT 20040, possibly due to confusion with *antie* 'old'? v.intr. dwell, reside. LQU 30669, TV 30670.

HANTIERS.　n.m.pl. lance-racks, lance-holders. 20121. cf. *lanciers*.

(HARPER).　v.intr. V 26871. prance (horse)? Not in T-L, but cf. God. IX 748a, AND III 351.

HASTER.　v.tr. 1. press, pursue. 9757–19865, 23302; 2. hurry up with, prepare quickly (food). 23617, 24139, 26357; 3. urge (on), make hurry. 24267, 26484, 26826 (ES); 4. press, urge. 29832; 5. *haster sa voie.* hurry on (one's way). 22941, 27044. v.intr. hurry. 26816, 28726. v.refl. hurry, be impatient (+ *de* — for). 28740, 30076, 31522.

HAUBERGIERS.　p.p. T 21240. This must mean 'dressed in his hauberk', and is a p.p. with -*r* added for the eye-rhyme.

HAUT.　adj. 1. noble, important. 23085, 23388, 23393; 2. 23378 *li jors est ancor assez hauz* — the day is still (quite) young; cf. 25343; 3. well padded? (bed). 24151; 4. tall. 25572, 25791 (and others, often applied to trees). *an haut* loudly, out loud. 10231–20427, 22442, 26812. cf. *a haut son.* K 20575.

HAUTEMANT.　adv. loudly. 9576, 20565, 20575. Most often found with *saluer*.

HERBERGIER.　v.tr. lodge. 21808, 22491, 23859. v.intr., refl. lodge, be lodged, spend the night. 20742, 20899, 21672. p.p. well-endowed, comfortable (building). 22610, 24265, 29552.

HERBERJAIGE.　n.m. lodging. 30527, 31032.

HERBOI.　n.m. grass. 23868.

HERMIN.　adj. (of) ermine. 22661, 22816, 29289. It is a moot point whether *hermine* following a n.m. is adj.f. or a juxtaposed n.m., probably the latter, cf. Foulet C1, *hermin*; compare 26649 with 29289. In 24776, E's *porpre hermine* is probably an error; the MSS have *robe h.*

HERMINE.　see *ermine*.

HERMINEZ.　adj. (p.p.). bordered with ermine. M 21359.

HEUT.　n.m. hilt. 21264, 23264, var. 24982. cf. *hodeüre, enheudeüre*.

HODEÜRE.　n.f. hilt, guard (sword). 20827. cf. *heut, enheudeüre*.

HONESTE.　adj. 26571. (properly) sumptuous, magnificent.

HONOR, ANNEUR, ANNOR, ANOR, ENOR, ONOR.　n.f. 1. victory. 9463, cf. *perdre honor.* be defeated. 25189; 2. honour, renown. 9497, 21020, 21346. 31708 *vostre honor Dites . . .* — your words honour you; 3. land(s), fiefs. 19961, 22721, 22891. *faire honor.* 1. (+ *a*) honour, treat with honour. 19888, 9814–19912, 20768; 2. (absol.) behave honourably. 26663; 3. (+ *a*) do justice (to)? 28631. *porter honor (a).* honour, treat honourably. 22985, 23140, 26327.

HONORER, ANORER, ENORER.　v.tr. honour. 9806–19906, 9811, 21551. *la virge honoree.* the blessed Virgin. 24924.

HORDEÏS.　n.m. enclosure, outer wall. T 20043.

HUESES.　n.f.pl. leggings, hose. 26205. The unsupported *huece* of E 29416 would constitute an acceptable reading.

HUICHIER, HUCHIER.　v.tr. call. 25093. v.intr. 1. call (to). 20564, 21318, 22012; 2. call (out). 26637. 20981 *por huchier* — if one calls him.

HUISEZ.　adj. (p.p.). hosed, wearing leggings. 26204.

I

IGAL.　adj. flat, i.e. shallow (river). 29170. *par igal.* on an equal footing. 21279. This is also the sense of *igaumant.* adv. 24974, but *ingalment*, App. VII TV 1125 means rather 'all together, unanimously'.

(IRAISTRE). v.refl. become angry. pret. 3, *irasqui.* App. IV M 53. *irascus.* p.p. angry. App. VII TV 589.

IRE. n.f. 1. anger. 9692, 20325, 20874. *par grant ire.* angrily, violently. 9706–19824, 21855, 21862; 2. anxiety, grief, distress. 9752, 19915, 9872.

IRIEEMANT, IREEMANT. adv. angrily, violently. 10055, 20510, KMQU 20681.

IRIER. v.intr. 21817 *Lors n'ot qu'irier am Perceval* — then P. was very angry. p.p. (adj.). *irié.* 1. distressed. 9529, 19859, 10200–20338; 2. angry. 9697, 23267, 23809.

IROR. n.f. 1. anger. 22350; 2. distress. 23644, KMQU 9651.

J

JA. adv. 1. ever. 9852, 28353, 29012, 20819 (all the time); 2. (+ neg.) never, never more. 19667, 9568–19692, 20669. also + *mes (jamés).* 10057–20191, 20274. also *jamés jor.* 10144, 10204–20346; 3. with a sense approximating to 'however'. 28045, 29026, 29518. 19999 *Ja n'iert an si estranges terre Qu'il nou truissent.* — no matter how far away he is, they will find him; 4. now. 10042, 22326 (indeed?), 23795; 5. already, by then, by now. 10174, 21281, 22969; 6. (+ neg.) not at all, in no wise. 20271, 20394, 21006; 7. straightaway, this minute. 20535, 20868, 24407; 8. at any moment, soon, shortly. 21779, 23418, 24422. *ja soit que.* even if, although. 23350, cf. U 10042 *ja soit ce qu'* — although; 9. because, given that. 25545; 10. at one time, in the past. 29116. *ja mar* + fut. see *mar.*

(JALIR). see *galir.*

JAMBEE. n.f. stride, pace. 25470 (EMQU). KLPV have *ajambee,* ST *enjambee.*

JARONEUSE. see *röeuse.*

JART. n.m. park, garden. 27739, 27792, LPTV 24820.

JEHUIR. adv. A form of *jehui,* 'today'. This occurs at 24489, 24608, 31551, also in C1 E 8283, although there it is rejected without any note. The scribe of E may also have written it at 28877, where a letter has been erased after *gehui.* In addition to the references given by Roach, see note to 24489, *gehuir* is found in MS. A of *Perceval,* at (Lecoy) 7045 (= Hilka 7293) and 8675 (H. 8945), although Lecoy rejects it, and Hilka suppresses it without even noting it in his variants; also in the var. to *Troie* 9365.

JENESTOIS. n.m.pl. piece of land covered in broom. L 9472.

JERMÉ, GEMÉ. adj. (p.p.). set with gems. 21273, var. 23760. 24979 *d'or gemé* — decorated with gold? See Roach, note on the form *jermé* in 21273.

JEU. see *geu.*

(JOINDRE, GOINDRE). v.tr. join, stick together. 30798. v.intr. touch. 30419. v.refl. give o.s. over to. 32476. p.p. (as adj.). 1. swift, keen. 9666; 2. close, tight. 9669.

JOÏR. v.tr. 1. welcome, make much of. 21551. also Q 21287, where one should surely read *nel joït* rather than *ne lioit*; 2. caress. 27718, 30487 (with an explicitly erotic sense, in the latter case?). v.intr. 1. (+ *de*) enjoy, benefit from; 20604. 2. make merry, amuse o.s. 23440 (where *a* must = with).

JOÏSE. n.m. Judgement Day. 25378.

JOLIZ. adj.(pl.) 1. lively. 22296; 2. gay, cheerful. U 30402.

JONCEÏS. n.m.pl. pieces of land where rushes grow. Pot. 21932.

JONCHIER. n.m. patch of rushes, piece of land where rushes grow. Q 29145.

JOR. n.m. 1. day. 9816–19914, 9836. *le jor.* a) on that day, this day. 23535, 30281, b) by day, in the daytime. 25799. We also find the expression *tote jor,* var. 27145, MQ 29258, T 30511; 2. daylight, daybreak. 23880. *au jor.* in the morning. 19986;

but *au jor*, alive, living. 9829. *a toz jors (mes)*. for ever. 10215, 30589. 20953 *de ce jor an avant* — henceforth. *(a) nul jor*. on any day, (not) ever. 9553, 19668, 25350. 27729 *a jor de ma vie* — ever. Also used with *jamés*, cf. 10144 (= never), *ja* 25336 (= not a single day), *mes* 22779 (= never again).

JORNAUX.   n.m. day. 24803.

JORNEE.   n.f. 1. day's ride (as a measure of distance). 22243, 24619; 2. day's travel, journey. 23535, 24241; 3. day. 27245, var. 21415.

JOSTER.   v.tr. assemble, bring together, put together. 27181, 31197. v.intr. joust. 26901, 26909, 27117. v.refl. come together, clash. K 24958. inf. as n.m. Q 9743.

JOVANT.   n.m. youth, youthfulness. 25808, 31442.

JUS.   adv. down. with v.tr. 19809, 9685, 9739. with v.intr. or refl. 20130, 21275, 23266. *la jus*. down there, down below. 21901. *sus et jus*. up and down, hither and thither. 27632, 31877, (neg.) var. 30594.

JUSTICHE.   n.f. jurisdiction, lordship. P 24578.

L

(LABORER).   v.intr. work. 24630.

LAIDURE, LEDURE.   n.f. 1. insult, injury, wrong. 25352, 28626; 2. shame. 25003, 28695.

(LAIER).   v.tr. 1. let, allow. 21775, 23869, 25686. *laier aler*. let go, allow to go. 10163, 23799; 2. leave, abandon, relinquish. 21799, 23097, 24201; 3. (+ dir. obj. + *a* + inf.) neglect, fail, omit (to do s.th.). 22897, 23940, 23949; 4. leave be, leave (s.th.) at that. 23511, 25412, cf. *laier ester*. leave be, put aside. T 21392, L 24209. Further, see *laissier*; the two verbs often share forms as well as meanings.

LAISSIER, LESSIER.   v.tr. 1. (+ *de*) cease to speak (of). 9457, 19607, 23121, cf. *laissier la querelle, la parole*. 27220, 29776; 2. (+ *ne* + subj.) omit, neglect (to do s.th.). 19625, 23087, 24415; 3. cease, stop (doing s.th.). 19988; 4. put down, lay aside, let go. 20050, T 20196; 5. leave, abandon, relinquish. 10031–20167, 20891, 21030. inf. as n.m. 28757. *laissier ester*. leave be. 20853, 21392, 24209, cf. *laissier am pes*. leave in peace. 30614; 6. let, allow. 21726, 22260, 23808. *laissier movoir, aler*. let go (dog), give (horse) its head. 20309, 21250, 23812. *laissier corre*. gallop, set one's horse to a gallop. 22024; 7. set aside, put aside, abandon. 22903, 23793, 26611; 8. neglect, omit (to do). a) (+ dir. obj.) T 20572, b) (+ *a* + inf.) S 22897. see also *coi*. v.refl. allow oneself. 23117. In general, we find only those forms of the fut. and cond. which correspond to those of *laier*, but there are long forms at 21030 and 24415, plus Q 22430, S 22897.

LAISUS, LAISUZ, LESUS.   adv. up there. 24324, 24420, 27631. (in heaven). 21798, 24026, 24123. At 25524, the MS reading is *de lesus*, not *le lesus*, while at 21798 we should read *laisus*, rather than *la sus*, although the distinction is somewhat artificial.

LAIT, LET.   n.m. insult, injury, wrong. 28332, 28510.

LAMBRE.   n.m. panelling, wainscoting. 10011–20143, 21108, 22788.

LAMBROISIEE, LENBRUISIE.   adj.f. (p.p.). panelled, wainscoted. 10006, 21928, 22455.

LAMBRUNS.   n.m. panelling, wainscoting. L 10005. This form, with final *n*, is not common.

LANCIERS.   n.m.pl. 9991. lance-holders. The reading of L, *lances en lanciers*, is perfectly satisfactory; the *lances et lanciers* of the other MSS is less so, though possible. cf. *hantiers*.

LARDEZ. n.m.pl. cuts of meat. 25308, 30296.

LARRIZ. n.m. hillside, uncultivated ground. 19648. The *larri* of P 23167 is almost certainly an error.

LARS. adj. P 20011. The comparatively rare (nom.) form of *large*, 'broad'.

LASCHIER. v.tr. let go, release. 26073, 26143. v.intr. let up, tire. 23299 (ELM).

LATIN. n.m. 1. latin. 22096, 31616; 2. speech, language (of birds). 29265.

LAZ. n.m.pl. laces (attaching helm to hauberk). 23288.

LÉ. adj. (also n.m.). wide, broad. 9801, 21803, 24741. see also *ancoste*, *lonc*.

(LEDANGIER). v.tr. insult, maltreat. 23987, 28678. In each case, the sense is probably one of verbal, rather than physical, mistreatment, but it is impossible to be sure.

(LEDIR). v.tr. insult. 31941.

LEECE, LEESCE. n.f. joy, happiness. 9507, 21469, 22731.

LEGIER. adj. 1. active, in good health. 9817; 2. lively, loose (tongue). 23505; 3. agile, adroit, quick. 29797, 30199, var. 26255; 4. lithe, supple. K 25204. *de legier.* easily. 24672.

LERMER. v.intr. weep. 23623.

LETRE. n.f. 1. (pl.) letters (of the alphabet), writing. 22093, 25259, Q 31614; 2. writing, inscription. 22101, 22153, LPTV 31614; 3. written source, or author's account? 29206; 4. letter, missive. 29653; 5. latin. 31614 (EU).

LEU, LIEU. n.m. 1. spot, place. 9545–19672, 22491, 27432; 2. direction? P 22535, cf. 9648 *de plusors leus* — in many places (= by many people). *de leus an leus.* here and there, at intervals. 19689. *(an) nul leu.* 1. nowhere, never. 19714, 19970, 25199; 2. anywhere. 20568. *par leus.* here and there, at intervals. 20201, 27954. *an leu de.* instead of. 23026. Note the composite forms *nuliu*, *nuleu* in L 20568, M 25199, and Roach's note to 20568.

LEZ. n.m. side. 24711, 30118, 30147. *lez a lez.* side by side. 9805–19905. *de toz lez.* from all sides, on all sides. 22982, 23018, 23459. prep. beside, by. 9594, 20228, 20380.

LÏART. adj. grey. 21458.

LIE. n.f. lees. Wine *norri seur lie* (23722) or *sus lie* (30299 (ES), where the var. have the more usual *nori sor lie*) was strong, good quality wine.

LIGE. adj. denotes a feudal bond, between overlord and vassal, or vice versa. The use in 10174 is slightly fig. (a typical use of feudal terminology for a love-relationship), as is that in *ligemant* adv. 28291, where there is probably no suggestion of a strictly feudal bond, and we might translate 'devotedly, faithfully'.

LINTEL. n.m. door-post (rather than the actual lintel). S 21102. This is, however, a somewhat unsatisfactory reading.

LIOIS. n.m. (hard) limestone. 26309.

LIOIT. see *joïr*.

LISTE. n.f. band, border. 31615.

LISTEE. adj.f. (p.p.). striped, decorated in stripes. var. 24506, S 25232.

LIUEE. n.f. league's distance. 20621, 21300, 23149.

LIVROISON. n.f. *de livroison.* abundantly, freely. 26921.

LOBE. n.f. empty talk, lies. 20785.

LOBERIE. n.f. trickery, lies, duplicity. App. VIII S 12, 32. *sanz loberie.* truly. S 23528.

LÖER. v.tr. 1. praise, esteem. 22223, 24582, 27213. cf. *fere*; 2. counsel, advise. 25170, 27325, 29666. v.refl. (+ *de*) be pleased (by). 29901, P 27348. *löé.* p.p. (adj.) renowned. 30331.

LOI.   n.f. 1. nature. 29708; 2. custom. 29892; 3. fashion. P 23173. *a loi de*. like. 31560.

LOIEMIERS.   n.m.pl. lime-hounds. P 20122.

LOIGE, LOGES, LOJES.   n.f.(pl.). 1. hall, entrance hall. 21085, 23406, 24384; 2. gallery. 28781, 28941, 29731; 3. tent. 30034, 30238, 30284. *loges galesches*. shelters made from leaves and branches. 24763. It is not always possible clearly to distinguish between 1. and 2.

LOIGIER.   v.refl. encamp, lodge (in the open, i.e. in tents). 30014, 30022, 30057.

(LOISIR).   v.intr. (impers.) permit (to do s.th.). With person as ind. obj., gives a sense of 'be able to'. *loira* fut. 3., 21834 (the emendation of E's *laira* is not strictly necessary), *lut* pret. 3., KMQ 9926.

LONC.   n.m. length. 30586. *an lonc et an lé*. in both directions, all over. 24296. also *de lonc et de lé*, Q 24295, S 24296. *(aler) de lonc, au lonc une liuee*. (go) along a league, (go) a league's distance. KLPT 20621. adv. *(longue)*. a long time? 26059. prep. beside, alongside. Q 22821.

LORAIN.   n.m. head-gear, head-harness (horse). 25487, 29346, 29459.

LUÉS.   adv. immediately, forthwith. 19759, 9919, KL 9757. (+ *que*) as soon as. 32209.

LUS, LUZ.   n.m.pl. luce, pike. 22582, 24146, 24576.

LUT.   see *loisir*.

M

MAAILLE.   n.f. farthing, half a denier. 20787.

(MACHONER).   v.tr. create. T 24742.

(MAILLIER).   v.intr. strike, hammer. 25007.

MAIN.   n.m. morning. 19885, var. 20652, P 20763. adv. early. 29980.

MAINIS, MAISNIS, MASIS.   n.m. building. 20042, L 9898–PT 20041. Probably a var. form of *maisnil*, with the final *l* falling, although the rhyme-word in L and T, *messeris/maisereïs*, would also normally have a final *l*.

MAINTENANT.   adv. *tot maintenant*. immediately, forthwith. 9830, 10025, 20308. *de maintenant* has the same meaning 20423, 22168, 25644. It is possible, however, that *(ferir) de maintenant* means 'with one's hands, with the sword, at close quarters', cf. *demanois*, in T 20548, P 20838.

MAIS, MES.   adv. 1. but. 19635, 19643, 19661; 2. (neg.) a) no longer, henceforth. 19619, 22754, 25388; (= (no) further) 31021, b) never (before). 22563, 32050; 3. (neg.) with *onques, ainz*. never (before). 9553–19675, 9700–19818, 10030–20166; 4. (neg.) never (again). 20347, 20406, 22783. (also with *jor*); 5. ever, at all. 21677, 24848, 27439; 6. still. 23612. *annuit mes*. tonight. 21672, 25342, 25584. *hui mes*. a) (for) today, now. 21832, 25353, 27591, b) (neg.) the same, but with the sense '(not) any more'. 24464, 24929. 28589 *je n'am puis mes* — I cannot help it. conj. (+ *que*). 1. (+ subj.) except (that), providing. (refers to an eventuality). 20611; 2. (+ indic.) except (that), but. (refers to an actual fact). 24789, 24891, 25079. 27404 *N'i a plus, mes que vos copez* — all you have to do is cut; 3. 29173 *Mais que leur destrier ont beü* — once their horses had drunk. The *mais que* of L 10032 is an editorial error; the MS reads *puis que*. In general, the adversative form of this word is spelt *mais*, the temp. form *mes*.

MAISEREÏS, MAISERIUS.   see *meseriz*.

MAISNERES.   see *masneres*.

MAISNIS.   see *mainis*.

MAÏSTÉ.   n.f. majesty. 21520, 23603, 26483.

MAL, MAU.   n.m. 1. harm, ill, suffering. 20020, 20083, 23916. *metre a mal*. harm, injure. 9495. *mal traire*. experience hardship, suffer. 31040, KLPU 24995; 2. wrong, evil, misdeed. 25808, 26732, 28089. *tenir (q.ch.) a mal*. think, consider (s.th.) to be wrong. 23709, 30651. also *noter (q.ch.) a mal* K 23709. adj. bad, unpleasant. 20435. *mau pas*. difficult passage. 19641, 26525, 31326. In 19641, the sense is 'difficulty, danger'. *ariver a mau port*. get, walk into trouble. 30783. 20081 *Trop mal i serïez antrez* — it would have gone ill with you if you had entered (the boat). MU 10246, U 22123, cf. *mar*. *mal fere*. behave badly. 20629.

MALAIGE, MALAGE.   n.m. sickness, illness. Q 29035. This is probably the sense of P 29811 also, given the idea that love is a sickness.

MALAIRE, MALLAIRE.   see *aire*.

MALEÏ.   adj. (p.p.). accursed. S 31540.

MALEÜREZ.   n.m. (adj.). unfortunate, wretch. 27395. cf. *eür*.

MALICES.   n.f.pl. evil, wickedness. 9952.

MAMBRER.   see *manbrer*.

MAMELOT.   adj. 28549, 28557. untried. The sense of this term is given in lines 28557–75. I do not feel, though, that it is 'weichlich' (T-L V 1004, 23), or 'effeminé' (God. V 131b), but rather 'baby, suckling'. L has *maminot*, M *mamelin*. see also *masneres*.

MANANTIE.   n.f. domain, possessions. 30641, App. II L 9.

(MANBRER, MAMBRER).   v.intr. (impers.). (+ ind.obj. of person, + *de*) gives a sense of 'remember'. 9869, 27970.

MANIER.   adj. *arc manier* longbow (as opposed to a crossbow). App. VII TV 244.

MANÏER, MENOIER.   v.tr. 1. touch, handle. 10027–20163, 27952; 2. smooth, stroke? S 29304.

MANIERE, MENIERE.   n.f. 1. (way, manner) *an quel maniere?* in what way? 10112–20248. *de grant maniere*. greatly. 20688, 21986, 26119. *an, de, par tel maniere*. in such a way, thus. 9934–20066, 24003, 24416. *an nule maniere*. a) in any way. 9874, b) (+ *ne*) in no wise, (not) at all. 27470, 28157, 31209. The sense of *an mainte maniere* (24930) seems to be almost 'often'; 2. sort, kind, nature. 22595, 24516, 24622. *de manieres*. various, of different sorts, diverse. 24575, 27033, 30137. also *de maniere*. 26188 (EPS).

MANOIR, (MENOIR).   v.intr. 1. live, reside. 20420, 21798, 23673; 2. stay, remain. rej.r. 25198 (inf. as n.m.) This is an acceptable reading, but isolated. In MS 31905 we find the alternative inf. *maindre*.

MANOIS, MENOIS.   adv. immediately. 25364, 28109, 30441. In 22047, the meaning may be 'with his sword', with the idea of hand-to-hand combat, cf. *demenois*, *maintenant*.

(MANOVRER).   v.tr. 1. make, construct, create. 24742, 26134, 29369; 2. work? Q 24506.

MANUEL.   n.m. horn. Q 26642. T-L, God. list only forms with *e* in the initial syllable, cf. *menuier, moienel*.

MAR.   adv. 1. (+ past tense) a) 19792 *tant mar fu!* — unhappy man!, b) 10246–20452 *mar le pansastes* — you will regret the idea (= the action), cf. 22123. *mal* is sometimes substituted for *mar* in these expressions; 2. (+ fut.) 28198 *Ja mar vos douterez de rien* — do not fear anything, there is no reason to fear anything, cf. 32538. On *mar* and its meaning(s), see the excellent study by B. Cerquiglini 'La Parole médiévale' (Paris, 1981) pp. 128–245.

MARESCHAUCIES.   n.f.pl. stables. Q 21363.

MARRISSON. n.f. grief, lamentation. S 31163.

(MARVOIER). v.intr. go out of one's mind. App. VII TV 1249.

MASIS. see *mainis*.

MASNERES, MAISNERES. adj. household. TV 28557. That this word (introduced for *mamelot*) means 'of the household' is clearly indicated by TV 28549, where *mamelot* is replaced by *de maisnie*; it is probably a form of *maisnier*.

MATIRE. n.f. 1. work, subject (-matter). 20002; 2. sort, kind. var. 24576. *d'une matire*. the same, evenly matched. Q 28831.

MAU. see *mal*.

MAUFÉ. n.m. devil. 23432.

MAUFETE. adj.f. deformed, misshapen. 23196.

MAUMETRE. v.tr. harm, injure. 19854. p.p. 1. hurt. 20500, 24962; 2. damaged. 25377.

MAUPARTIE. adj.f. (p.p.). Q 29050. ill-proportioned, badly-made? Not in T-L, cf. God. V 126b.

MAUTAILLIE. adj.f. (p.p.). ill-fitting. 26848, 29050.

MAUVÉS. adj. Normally 'cowardly'. 24172, and (as n.m.) 20592, 24794, (also 23328, etc. as proper noun), but we also find the weaker sense, 'bad'. 27474. Q 24962 might mean 'in a bad way'.

MAUVESTIEZ. n.f. villainy, disgrace. 21766.

MEDECINE. n.f. magic. 29503.

(MEHAIGNIER). v.refl. (mutual refl.). injure, hurt one another. 26911.

MEÏSMEMANT, MEESMEMANT. adv. 1. particularly. 22906; 2. likewise, and. 26962, 27332, 28984; 3. 28095 *A ses deus mains meïsmemant* — with his (very) own two hands.

MELODIE. n.f. 1. music, sound. 26645; 2. (source of ?) delight, rapture. U 32060.

MEMOIRE, MIMOIRE. n.f. (or n.m.). 1. memory, reason. 19618; 2. recollection. (with approximately the sense 'story'?) 23021 (E), Q 24298. *tenir an memoire*. 29356. The sense of ES is hardly clear; that of the other MSS must be 'remember, cherish'. *metre (avant) an memoire*. tell. 31422. *fere memoire (de)*. mention. P 23022.

MENÇONGIER. v.intr. lie. S 23023.

MENER. v.tr. 1. lead, guide. 9967–20097, 23748, 23926; 2. lead, take. 10138–20272, 21363, 23751. — with a sense of 'take with one, keep company with'. 23222, 23336, 23354. *mener an destre*. lead (horse). 23831, 25978. *an mener* frequently means 'lead, take away', but the addition of *an* does not always correspond to the idea of 'away'. 22456, 22461, 22677; 3. lead (life). 20392, 23843, 25805; 4. press, oppress. 22049, 26009. p.p. hard-pressed. 24847; 5. show, manifest (emotion). 22739, 22793, 29532, cf. *demener*; 6. *mener noise*. make a noise. 26655. *mener une parole*. speak of s.th. 30364, cf. rej.r. 20392, where the sense might simply be 'do'. see also *glas*.

MENIERE. see *maniere*.

MENOIER. see *manïer*.

MENOIR. see *manoir*.

MENOIS. see *manois*.

(MENTEVOIR). v.tr. mention. M 31784. cf. *amantevoir*.

MENU. adj. 1. small. 22509; 2. thick. 25206, 31656. close together, in *les menuz sauz*, *les saus menuz* — rapidly. 26877, 30153, App. VII TV 1080. adv. finely, thickly. 22360, 23251, 26890, see also *saffré*, *tresgiter*. *menu et sovant*. frequently, (with blows) in rapid succession. 9733, 9763, 10259.

MENUEMANT.   adv. frequently. 20521, 26909.

MENUIERE.   adj.f. sharp (tongue). 23506, cf. *cor menuier*. a high-pitched, sharp-toned horn. S 26642. also *menuier* n.m. with the same sense. MQS 24843, MQS 24867, M 26642.

MERC.   n.m. mark, imprint. 21316.

MERCI.   n.f. 1. mercy. 19879, 22055. *Deu merci*. Lord have mercy (on us). 9615–19737. *an la merci (de)*. at the mercy (of). 21893. *proier, crïer merci*. ask for mercy. 9788, 20885, 20889. *fere merci (a)*. have mercy (on). 23568; 2. pardon. I beg your pardon. 20858. *soue merci*. begging his pardon. 28727; 3. thanks. *(la) vostre (grant) merci*. thank you. 19887, 23238, 28343. *randre merci*. thank. 26043. *savoir merci (a)*. be grateful (to). 20999.

MERCÏER.   v.tr. 1. ask pardon. 19995; 2. be grateful. 20655, 28970; 3. thank. 20749, 21568, 21943.

MERIR.   v.tr. repay. (s.o. — ind.obj., for s.th. — dir.obj.). 21271, 23482, 30823.

MERITE.   n.f. (just) desserts. 31976.

MERVEILLIER.   v.refl. 1. be surprised, marvel. 9590–19712, 10002–20134, 20752; 2. wonder. 22560, 23564, 25216. The first meaning is much the more common. Note the tetrasyllabic inf. *merevoilier* in Q 23637, cf. C1, Q 14124.

MERVOILLE.   n.f.(pl.). amazing, surprising thing. 9616–19738, 9917, 9955–20085. *Ce n'estoit se mervoille non* (etc.). it was amazing. 9982–20112, 24573, 24721. *a (grant) mervoille(s)*. greatly. 10050, 20447, 20917. (also *mervelle*, S 10050). In 23216, might *a grant mervoille* mean 'in great wonderment'? 22576 *Ne lou tenez mie a mervoille* — do not be surprised (by it). 26178 *mervoille est* — it is surprising; cf. 30555, 31203.

MESAIGE.   n.f. Q 22916. This is undoubtedly an error, cf. the rhyme with *plaise*; Q's model probably had *mesaie* (for *mesaise*), cf. *Fergus* 3565(A). Nevertheless, such a word might exist.

(MESAVENIR).   v.intr. turn out badly (for), go ill (with). 25396 (E).

MESCHEANCE.   n.f. mishap, mischance. 26029, 26765, 27733.

(MESCHEOIR).   v.intr. turn out badly (for), go ill (with). 24935, 27434, 30086.

MESCOINTE.   adj. App. VII TV 528. Possibly 'at a loss', or should we read *mes cointe*, 'still courageous' or something similar?

MESCROIRE.   v.tr. doubt. 24056, 31907, var. 23022. *sans mescroire*. without doubt, certainly. var. 24578.

MESERIZ.   n.m.pl. building(s). 9923, L 9898–T 20042. *maiserius* (L 9923) reflects the acc. form in *-il*, but *maisereïs* (T 20042) is unusual.

MESESE, MESAISE.   n.f. 1. discomfort, displeasure. 22916, 24316, 24538; 2. (pl.) torments. P 24118.

MESESTANCE.   n.f. trouble, discomfort. PTV 29530. (pl. in T).

MESIERE.   n.f. wall. 27671, 28072, 32096.

MESIRE.   n.f.? P 32065. This word is not in the dictionaries. It might be for *mestire* (= *maiestire*) or *mestrie*, cf. CM S 37643 *mestrie: cimetire*, and mean 'authority, mastery'.

MESON.   n.f. room. 24385.

(MESPRANDRE).   v.intr. 1. do wrong. 10195–20333, Q 22013; 2. (+ *vers qn.*) wrong (s.o.). 20930.

MESPRENANCE.   n.f. *par mesprenance*. wrongly, criminally. Q 26766.

MESPRISON.   n.f. wrong, misdeed. 22922, 23310, 24402.

MESTIER.   n.m. 1. need, use. *estre mestier(s)*. be useful, needful. 19930, 25040, 28175. *avoir mestier(s) (de)*. need. 20413, 21206, 22254. *avoir mestier (a)*. be useful. 21151, 28049, 31834. 22745 *Tuit cil qui mestier n'i avoient.* — all those who had no business there. *avoir mestier.* a) be useful, avail. 22516, 23660. (EP) 25018 *n'i a mestier confort* — there is no help for it, b) be needful, necessary. 22765, 25340, 31391; 2. a) business. 26423, b) profession (ironic). 28736. *servir d'un mestier.* perform a function, carry out work. 9951–20080.

MESTRE, MAISTRE.   adj. 1. main, chief. 9965, 26837, 28524; 2. (+ *de*) capable, able (to). 25827, 26552, 31466; 3. in charge. 28334, 29941.

MESTRIE.   n.f. 1. mastery, dominion. 26240; 2. skill (of reading the stars). 27914.

(MESTROIER).   v.tr. govern, rule (over). 25145 (ES), 27241 (ESTV).

MESURE.   n.f. *a sa mesure.* of the right size, made to measure. 22309, 29791, 29881. *par mesure.* of the right size, well-proportioned. S 23927.

METRE.   v.tr. 1. put, place. 10086–20220, 10094, 10180. *metre jus.* a) put down. 10208–20350, P 10250, b) help down (from horse). 21516, 23465, 23867. *metre (qn.) a reson.* address, speak to (s.o.). 21563, 24543. *metre (q.ch.) devant (a qn.).* place (s.th.) before (s.o.), serve (s.o. with s.th.) 24047. *metre longuemant (a).* take a long time (over). 24158, 27278, 28972. *metre la, les main(s) a.* work on, touch, put one's hand to. 24629, 32544. *metre an male voie.* lead into bad ways. 25800, cf. *metre a (droite) voie.* put on the right track, direct, help. 26214, 27604, but *metre a la voie.* put to flight. 30279, see also *frapier. metre an conte.* relate, include in the story. 26083. *metre avant.* a) put forward, present, relate. 26101, 31422 (cf. *memoire*), b) persist in. 28753. *metre son cuer an amor.* devote o.s. to, take an interest in, love. 26430. *le metre an soufrir, sofrance.* give up, leave aside (issue, idea). 27212, 29596. *metre (q.ch.) seure, sus (qn.).* lay (s.th.) at the door of (s.o.). 28747, 28763. 28904 *Que vos sus moi le champ metez* — that you leave me the responsibility of the dispute. *metre el retor.* start back, turn back (horse). 28848. *metre an rime.* rhyme, put into verse. 29205. *metre an obli.* forget. 30896. *metre non (+ a).* name. 31072. see also *covant, covenant; delaie, respit; cure, force; abandon; mal*; 2. set up (table). 21374, 21378; 3. add. 26530; 4. 26886 *Kex sa lance mit an deus tronçons* — Kay broke his lance in two. v.refl. 1. (with a variety of adv., *fors, aprés, outre, anz*, etc.) go, come. 21052, 22102. *se metre au retor, ou retorner, el repere.* (also *se metre a son retor*). return, start back. 20706, 25553, 26493. *se metre am prison.* give o.s. up as a prisoner, place o.s. in captivity. 21336, 21526, 25030. *se metre a la voie, ou chemin.* set off. 21443, 28447, 30954. *se metre an poine.* take trouble, make an effort. 28230; 2. (+ *a, an*) arrive (in), enter. 23576, 27510; 3. (+ *a* + inf.) start. 27859; 4. (+ *an qn.*) place o.s. in the hands of s.o. 28926; 5. (+ *an*) involve o.s. (in). 30764.

MIAUDRES.   comp.adj. (nom.). 1. better. 27485, 29207; 2. *li miaudres.* best. 9617–19739, 9776–19874, 9827. as n.m. 27172, 28321, 28556; (= the best part?) 29206.

MIAUZ.   n.m. *au miauz que* (+ *pooir*). as best one can. 20754, 23253, 23276. also *miauz que* (+ *pooir*). 23893. adv. 1. better, rather, more, etc. 19847, 21621, 22536. 21202 *Vos porrïez assez miauz dire* — you could be more polite, more reasonable. *miauz me vient, vandroit.* it would be better for me. 20594, 24320, 29596. see also *covenir*; 2. best. 21697, 22619.

MIER.   see *or.*

MIMOIRE.   see *memoire.*

MIPARTIE.   adj.f. (p.p.). made, divided in(to) two parts, of two colours. 24777, U 26848.

MIRER.   v.tr. look at. 29547.

MISERICORS.   adj. merciful. 24087.

MISODOR.   n.m.pl. (good quality) horses. 30788, App. VII TV 620 (sing.).

MOIEN.   adj. middle (finger). 26042.

MOIENEL.   n.m. horn. 24843, 24867, 26642.

MOILON.   n.m. middle. LP 29125.

MOLUZ.   adj.pl. (p.p.). sharp. 20508 (a borrowing from C1), M 23250.

MONDES.   adj. clean (in a moral sense). QS 24052. It is possible that this actually represents the *mondez* (p.p.). of M, meaning 'cleansed'.

MONTER.   v.intr. 1. amount to. 26092 *Ne sevent que bons conte montent* —(they) cannot tell a good story (from a bad one); 2. *am pris monter.* win renown. 29012.

MOT.   n.m. 1. word. *a un mot.* in a word, briefly. 21390. *mot a mot.* word by word, word for word. 22096, 23970, 25283. *mot parler, dire, soner, respondre* (+ neg.). say, answer a single word. 22697, 23063, 23071; 2. note, blast (on horn). 26643, 32171, 32176; 3. bark. 27638; 4. (pl.) conversation. 27990.

MOVOIR.   v.tr. 1. move. 21144; 2. *movoir guerre (a).* wage war (on), attack. 31097. see also *estal.* v.intr. 1. set out, go. 19986, 19997, 20309; 2. S 24381 *ce dont le cuers li movoit* — that which preoccupied him. v.refl. 1. move, leave, go. 20401, 24430, 25701; 2. move, start to move. 27464, var. 26032, M 9673.

MU.   adj. silent. 28047, 30594 (ES), var. 23697.

MUEBLE.   n.m. rej.r. 22583. The apparent meaning here is 'riches, possessions'. The line is hypermetric, as well as the reading being isolated.

MÜER.   v.tr. *müer la color.* change colour (person). 28872. see also *estal.* v.intr. 1. change. 10107–20243, 22693, 23680. 23635 *Ne me puet li cuers . . . müer que ne* (+ subj.) — I cannot help but, cf. *changier.* P 27706 *Et se li sens ne li müa* — and if he is still in his right mind; 2. moult? (p.p.). KU 22239. p.p. troubled (weather). 27918.

MUGUETES.   adj.f.pl. *noiz muguetes.* nutmegs. 23026.

MUSART.   n.m. fool. 20847, MQ 28746. adj. foolish. 30852.

MUSER.   v.intr. 1. (+ *seur*) contemplate. 22757; 2. idle, waste time. 24436.

MUSIE.   see *or*.

N

NA.   enclitic form. = *ne la*. see *tronçoner*.

NAGE, NAIGE.   n.f. *sanz nage, a naige*. without a boat; in, with a boat. 9862–20012. see Roach, note to 20012.

NAGIER.   v.intr. sail, travel in a boat. P 20012, P 22440. In 20012, the sense is rather simply 'cross the water'.

NAIE.   part. of negation. no, not I. 23982, 25059, 25760.

NAÏS.   adj. native (of), born (in). MS 31406.

NASAL.   n.m. nose-piece (helmet). 24984.

NEANT, NOIENT, NOIANT.   (neg. part.) n.m. 1. nothing. 23423, 28052, 31456; 2. (as part. of negation). no, not at all. P 20606. *de neant.* a) at all. 21884, P 22906, b) (+ neg.) not at all, in no wise. 28677, 28895, 29376. *neant plus.* no more. 23285. adv. (+ neg.) not at all, in no wise. 22032, LT 21115, KL 21161.

NEELÉ.   adj. (p.p.). inlaid with (black) enamel, nielloed. 9559, 23017, S 9823.

NELUI, NULUI, NULLUI.   pron. (acc. case of *nul*). 1. (+ neg.) no-one, (not) anyone. 20022, 21881, 24275; 2. anyone, someone. 21133, 25271, 29179.

NES, NESUNE, NISUNE.   adv.; pron.f. 1. Although the editor separates *nes* (= (not) even) from the following *une*, in 10102, 10205, 28325, this is really an artificial distinction, since *nesune* (*nisune*) means '(not) any, not one'. *Nesune* also occurs at var. 26617, where U has the disyllabic *neïs* + *une*, which of course can be distinguished from *nes(une)*, L 25119; 2. *Nes* in P 30595 means 'no more than'. *nes + un* occurs in App. IV M 164.

NIULE.   n.f. clouds, mist, darkness. L 25659. cf. *nublece, nuilee*.

NOBLOI.   n.m. nobility, distinction. App. VII TV 118.

NOËR.   v.intr. swim. 26408.

NOIANT, NOIENT.   see *neant*.

NOITONIERS.   n.m. boatman. (Q 9942–) 20077, (Q 9965–) 20095.

NON.   n.m. renown. 21349, 29825, LQ 28406.

NONE.   n.f. hour of nones, sometime in the early afternoon (12.00–3.00 p.m.). 23735, 24242, 25166. *basse none*. just before, shortly before nones. 21961.

NORROIS, NORROIZ.   adj. of Norse stock (horse). 22401, 27821, 31532. Unusually, occurs as n.m. (= Norway) in (AL) 9646–19778.

NOTER.   see *mal*.

NOVELIERE.   adj.f. loose, given to chattering (tongue). P 23506.

NUBLECE.   n.f. clouds, mist, darkness. 25659, 29253. The *niulece* of L 29253 is not found in T-L, but God. has *nulece* (V 541c). cf. *niule, nuilee*.

NUILEE.   n.f. clouds, mist, darkness. TV 29253. cf. *nublece, niule*.

NUL.   (pron.) n.m. (nom. *nus*.) no-one, nobody. 9526, 19831, 19912. pron. (not) one. 9554–19676, 28316. adj. 1. (+ neg.) no, not any. 9536, 19661, 19714; 2. any. 9666, 19971, 20072. see also *faille, jor, leu, maniere, peine, respit, rien, trestot*; see also *nelui*.

NULLUI, NULUI.   see *nelui*.

O

OANZ, OUAN.   adv. this year. 21345, 25350. The reading in 21345 is not entirely satisfactory; the var. are better.

OCOISON.   see *achoison*.

OEVRE.   see *uevre*.

OÏE.   n.f. sound. 24395, 32178, Q 24870.

OIR.   n.m. heir. 26562.

OÏR.   v.tr. hear, listen to. 19638, 9581–19703, 9591–19713. 9764 *oiant tote sa gent*— before all his retainers, cf. PS 31895; 2. heed. 24114, 26217, 30502. v.intr. 9583– 19705, 23977, 26069. *tot an oient*. out loud, clearly. 23492 (E), see Roach, note to this line.

OIRRE, OIRE.   n.m. journey. 24059, 26189. *grant oirre*. rapidly, hastily. 20618, U 29570. *an oirre*. quickly, forthwith. 21923, 25981, 26122.

(OISELER).   v.intr. hunt birds (falcon). 28413.

OISEUSE.   n.f. waste of time, pointless activity. 20429.

OR.   n.m. gold. 10017–20151, 10066–20200, 10067–20201. 21172 *a or batue* —decorated with gold leaf? also 22970, cf. *batre. or musie* (also *musi, musique* in var.). golden mosaic work. 10005, var. 24506. *ormier* (or more correctly *or mier*). pure gold. var. 27610, M 27996. M 30704 *a or frasez* — decorated with gold embroidery, cf. *orfresez, orfrois*, and also *vermoil*.

ORAILLE.   n.f. edge. 19645 (E), KMQU 21268. cf. *eur, eure* (2), *oriere, orle*.

ORE.   see *eure* (1).

ORER.   v.tr. *orer dahé (a)*. curse, wish evil on. 9489, 30212. v.intr. pray. 23845.

ORFANTEZ.   n.f. *cheoir an orfantez*. become an orphan, be left helpless. 24200.

ORFRESEZ.   adj. (p.p.). decorated with gold embroidery. S 30704. cf. *or, orfrois*.

ORFROIS, ORFROIZ.   n.m. gold brocade, gold-embroidered cloth. 9564–19687, 10158–20292, 28097. cf. *or, orfresez*.

ORÏANT. adj. (pres.p.). shining like gold. S 22293. from the rare verb *oriier*, cf. T-L VI 1278, 31.

ORIERE. n.f. edge (wood). T 19645, TV 30935. cf. *eur, eure* (2), *oraille, orle*.

ORLE. n.m. edge. 21268, KQ 31819. In K 20545, *orle* seems to mean the whole shield; *pars pro toto*, or an error? cf. *eur, eure* (2), *oraille, oriere*.

OSTEL. n.m. lodging. *avoir l'ostel Saint Julien*. be well-lodged, well-received. 26946. This example has been put forward in support of the idea that this expression means 'sleep in the open', but clearly this is not the case, although it is possible, as G. Ebeling suggested (*Auberee* p. 139), that the speaker is being ironic in this instance. see also *prandre, tenir*.

OSTELER. v.tr. lodge. 25544. v.refl. lodge, spend the night. 23538.

(OSTER). v.tr. 1. take off. 20877, 25692, 25875; 2. take away. 22804, 23029, 28115; 3. raise (siege). var. 22856. v.intr. come off, be detached. M 9740. In 19869, the sense of the imper. *ostez* seems to be more or less 'stop!', cf. App. IV MQU 136, where it is 'no, no!', or 'certainly not!'. In 10038–20174, it is merely an exclamation of surprise.

OSTERINS. n.m.pl. fine (silk) cloths. 30145.

OUAN. see *oanz*.

(OUBLÏER, OBLÏER). v.tr. 1. forget, neglect. 20416, 25681, 25806; 2. leave, pass by. 21064. v.refl. (always + neg.) 1. (+ *de* + inf.) fail to do what one should? 9960, 26150; 2. waste time, hesitate. 21258, 21860, 22814. *estre oublïez du sens*. be bewildered, lose one's reason? rej.r. and P 26180. (Although the reading of E is defective here, it is surprising that the editor adopted the reading of S, rather than that of P; the other MSS omit.)

OUSTRER, (OUTRER). v.tr. 1. defeat. 19883, 21331, 25090; 2. surpass. 27488; 3. bring to an end (siege). M 22856.

OUTRECUIDERIE. n.f. 1. presumptuous, arrogant action or speech. 27814 (P has *outrequidie*), TV 27824; 2. presumption, arrogance. 30777.

OUTREEMANT. adv. entirely, completely. 22052.

OUTREQUIDIE. see *outrecuiderie*.

OUTRER. see *oustrer*.

OVRAIGNE. n.f. work, decoration. 9555.

OVRE. see *uevre*.

P

(PAIER). v.tr. (and mutual refl.) *paier un cop*. strike, give a blow. 21174, 22353, 22357.

PALETÉ. adj. gold-spangled. App. VII TV 248.

PALEZ. T 23192. Error? There are three words which might be possible in the context: a) *palé* (p.p.), striped, or set with stakes; b) *palet* (adj.), somewhat pale; c) *palé(s)* (n.m.), palate. However, none of them is altogether satisfactory.

PANDANT. n.m. slope. 9883–20031, 9896, 20377.

PANE. n.f. 1. border or lining of fur. 22165, 22661, 27765; 2. (coll.) feathers. 23179; 3. upper edge (of shield). LTV 30206.

PANSER, (PENSER). v.tr. think (with an extended sense, 'do'). 10246–20452, M 21198. v.intr. (+ *de*). 20297 *Or pant Diex de son retor* — may God bring him safely back again; for the form *pant*, see Roach, note to this line. 27624 *si panse d'esperoner* — put your mind to hurrying. v.refl. think to o.s. 20629, 21290, 22003.

PAON, PAONCEL, PAONNET.   see *poon.*

PAR.   prep. as part. of reinforcement, with the approximate meaning of 'much'. 19677, 9771, 19964. *par si que.* on condition that. 19891, 20667, 23523. also *par ainsi que.* 28022. *de par.* from, on behalf of. 19892, 19958, 19965. 27392 *estes vos de par De?* — are you a christian? *de par Dieu.* in God's name. Q 21505. *par sus.* over. 20496 (E). *par trois fois.* three times. 20574.

PARAIGE.   n.m. noble birth, social standing. 24621, TV 24622.

PARANOIT.   P 27590. *par anoit* (= *par anuit*)? As it is introduced by the scribe, one might expect this to mean something, yet it seems simply to be an error.

PARCLOSE.   n.f. end. 31824 (EKQ). One would prefer *Qu'i* or *Qu'ele* in the following line, rather than the *Si* of S. Then *a la parclose* would mean 'finally, in the end'.

PARCREÜZ.   adj. (p.p.). 1. big. 21129, 23207; 2. long (grass). var. 32161.

PARFERE.   v.tr. finish, complete. 26772, LPTV 31123.

PARFIN.   n.f. *a la parfin.* finally, at last. var. 31956.

PART.   n.f. 1. side, direction. *d(e l)'autre part (de).* a) on the other side, the far side (of). 9876–20026, 9890, 9943, b) on the other hand, for his, her part. 21261, 21457, 26478, c) in the other, the opposite, direction, towards the other side. 21831, 21978, 26805. *celle part.* there, in that direction. 20697, 20781, 21106. also *de celle part,* with the same sense, 21074 (EP). *de totes parz.* on all sides, all around. 22556, 32039. *de quele part.* a) wherever, whichever way. 24650, b) from where. 27791. *quel part.* a) where. 25095, b) wherever. 27337. *a une part.* on, to one side. 27788 (ES). *d'ambes parz.* on both sides. 30283. *a la senestre part.* on the left. 30516; 2. *la meillor part.* the best part. 27740. The sense of *a soue part* (25809) is probably 'with him (God), with the chosen'.

PARTIE.   n.f. 1. side. 22629, 26807; 2. direction. 25669.

PARTIR.   v.tr. 1. scatter, separate. 27180; 2. split. M 21274. see also *geu.* v.intr. 1. (+ *de*) leave, go away from (person, place, thing). 22226, 25632, 25774; 2. go (away), leave. 25659, 27195; 3. split asunder. 31135; 4. split. rej.r. 19668. v.refl. 1. (*s'an partir*). go (away), leave. 9523, 21001, 21659; 2. (+ *de*) leave, go away from (person, place, thing). 9569–19693, 20681, 21008. In 26947, we find *s'am partir de*; 3. (+ *de*) avoid? Q 9526. inf. as n.m. separation. 9744, 25921 (or = outset?), 27159.

PAS.   see *mal.*

PASSAGIER.   n.m. ferryman. S 9942, S 9945, S 9965.

PASSER.   v.tr. 1. cross, pass through or over. 9862–20012, 9873–20023, 20035; 2. get through, survive (day). 24801; 3. pass (through), thrust. K 23992. *passer sa fience.* break one's promise, go back on one's word. LPS 27346. v.intr. 1. cross, pass through or over. 9925–20057, 9963–20093, 24247. (also, + *a*, 26727); 2. pass, go (through). 23992, 32276, 32401; 3. (often impers.) pass (of time). 20405 *Passé a bien cinc ans* — at least five years have passed, cf. 20938, 22073. 25708 *Dou matin estoit ja passé Tant que.* — the morning was far advanced, so that, cf. 28424. 26738 *Molt lonc tans avoit ja passé* — a long time ago. 30394 *ainçois deus jors passez entiers* — within two days. 31015 *ancor n'a pas tier jor passé* — not three days ago. cf. 31261, 31767. 31079 *li quinze jors Seront . . . demain passé* — two weeks ago tomorrow; 4. pass by. 20406, 20731, 25183; 5. pass, go away. 25654; 6. go, travel? 26517 (E). *passer outre.* a) cross. 9879, 9891, 25987, b) pass through. 20485, c) go on, go (on) one's way. 20833, 22129, 30585, also *passer avant* Q 9864, go (any) further.

PAUMELLES. n.f. straps (of strap-hinges). 19679 (ET). This appears to be the earliest attestation of this meaning of the word.

PAUMOIER. v.tr. brandish (lance). P 22002, Q 22019. The first of these references is curious, and suggests an error for *pomier*.

(PECHIER). v.intr. (impers.) 22836 *Mes s'am Perceval ne pecha* — but if Perceval was not found wanting.

PEINE, PAINE, PEIGNE, POINE. n.f. 1. effort, discomfort, pain (physical or mental). 20524, 20958, 23296; 2. sorrow, distress. 21652, 22930, 24787; 3. trouble, difficulty. 31288. *por nule peine.* (not) at any price, (not) for anything. 19971, 20072. *a (molt)(grant) peine.* a) hurriedly? 21320, b) in (great) distress. 22050, c) reluctantly. 22940, d) with (great) difficulty. 24847, 26154, 28870. *fere peine (a).* cause trouble (to). 21006. *estre an peine.* a) endure hardship. 22670, b) take trouble, make an effort. 26396, c) (+ *de*) have trouble, difficulty (in). 26896, d) wonder, wish to know. 32060. *se metre an peine (por).* try, strive (to). 28230. 22082 *ne vos soit peine* — it it is no trouble, cf. 31788, also *s'il ne vos iert peine.* 32378, 32432. 29378 *Ne ne li fu . . . peine Que* (+ *ne* + subj.) — and it was no trouble to him to. cf. 32172 *ne li fu peine* — he was pleased.

PENER. v.tr. 1. torment, torture. 23117, 30443; 2. punish, drive hard. 27326. v.refl. strive, make an effort, take trouble. 9736–19852, 21066, 21364. (= ride hard) 26103, 27376, 28492. p.p. tired, (physically) distressed. 21284, 22810, 24684.

PENIS, PENIX. adj. enduring, hardy. App. VII TV 937.

PENSER. see *panser*.

PER. n.m. adversary. 22365.

PERCHE. n.f. peg, hook (for clothes). 21723.

PERCHEOIR. v.intr. (inf. as n.m.). M 26892 *au percheoir* might mean at the moment of falling (from a horse), although this would be curious in the context, and suggests an error.

PERRELE. n.f. L 30639. Probably 'sand, gravel', although *parele* 'sorrel, dock' might be as appropriate.

PERRIERE. n.f. S 26019. Although such a meaning is not attested, this must mean 'precious stone(s)', cf. *perrerie*, etc.

PERRUCHAI. n.m. 31247 (EMS). (S has *perrochoi*, but retains the rhyme with *merveillai*). Formerly considered a *hapax*, this word also occurs (*perruchois* n.m.pl.) in the prose *Lancelot*, (Micha) IV p. 9, l. 18, and, as *perruchoi*, in Johannes' *Pseudo-Turpin* (ed. Walpole, XV l. 11). God.'s definition, 'terrain pierreux' fits all three examples, and is probably correct, but Micha's 'chemin pierreux' is also possible.

PESANCE. n.f. distress, unhappiness. 27734, TV 27441. *fere pesance (a).* distress, put out. 24908.

(PESER). v.tr. 1. distress, displease. 20947, 22265, 25590; 2. weigh. 29770. v.intr. (impers.) (+ *a*) distress, displease. 9759, 20867, 20888. *ne vos poist mie.* if you please. 20714, 30678, cf. 31853. Note v.impers. + dir. obj., 27728. *pesant* (pres.p.) 1. heavy. 20512, 26921, 27416; 2. hard, fierce (combat, adventure). 21976, 32541, L 9708.

PIECE. n.f. 1. (for a) long while, (a) long time. 27433. usually *grant piece.* 9611–19733, 22493, 23691. *(de)(grant) pieç'a.* some time ago, for some time (past). 19993, 21719, 23575, cf. S 9586 *il i a piece que* (+*ne* + indic.) — it has been some time since; 2. (for) some distance, a long way. 27928, L 9969. 21059 *Desi qu'a grant piece de voie* — until he had gone some distance; 3. (pl.) pieces, fragments.

26162, 32550. 27063 *am piece de terre* — in one place? 30085 *Tant con ansamble an tanra piece* — as long as one piece remains?

PIRE.   n.m. paved road. P 20727. cf. T-L VII 924, 22.

PIZ (1).   n.m. (comp.adv.) *avoir lou piz*. have the worst (of a combat), be defeated. 21292.

PIZ (2).   n.m.(pl.). chest. 9669, 9681, 28850. *de pis a pis*. chest to chest. TV 24965.

PLAIDEÏCE.   see *aplaideïce*.

PLAIN (1).   n.m.(pl.). open fields, open countryside. S 22240. *au plain*. in the open. 25876. adj. 1. smooth. (L 10097–P 10100–) 20236, 20380, 22304. *de terre plaine*. from level ground, straight from the ground. 25535. *a terre plaine*. on solid ground. 26153; 2. open. *plaine(s) terre(s)*. open fields, open country(side). 23576, var. 22232. (adv.) *a plain, de plain*. a) freely. 26074, 26144, b) forthwith, rapidly. 31579. Because of the undifferentiated spelling, it is not always easy to distinguish this word (Lat. PLANUS) from *plain* (2) (Lat. PLENUS).

PLAIN (2).   adj. 1. complete. *ne pas avoir plain pié (de)*. not have the smallest quantity (of). 20797, 26584. (adv.) *de plain*. a) full(y), properly, squarely. 20545, 21266, 24980, b) fully, completely. 27118, 30837. *au plain*. with all one's strength. 20798 (E) (strictly, n.m., but probably a var. of *a plain*). *a plain*. a) full(y), properly, squarely. 30814, Q 21266, b) completely. T 24130. Cf. *plain* (1).

PLAISEÏZ.   n.m. 1. copse, thicket. 26603; 2. hedge. Q 9898. cf. *plessiez, ploieïs*.

PLAISIER.   see *pleissier*.

(PLANOIER).   v.tr. stroke, caress. M 25441. cf. *aplanoier*.

(PLASTRER).   v.tr. coat, cover. KTV 32290. This may well be the earliest attestation of this word. L has the more usual *plastrir*.

PLATES.   n.f.pl. plates, strips (gold). SU 32291.

(PLEISSIER).   v.intr. give ground, give way. Q 27177 (spelt *plaisier*, cf. L 9898). In LMU 9898, the *haies plaisies* are hedges which have been reinforced, probably by being properly cut and 'laid' or 'layered'. (Lay(er)ing consists of cutting half through the bulk of the stems of the bushes, bending them over, and weaving them in and out of the remaining stems, which are left vertical, cut down to the required height.) This technique could correspond to either the original sense ascribed to this word by G. Tilander (*ZfrPh* 47 (1927), 523 ff.), 'battre, abattre', or to the evolved sense, 'plier, courber'. The *voies pleissiees* of 9898 (A) could be 'hedged', or perhaps 'beaten'. see also *plaiseïz, plessiez*. cf. note, below.

PLENDISSOURS.   n.m.(pl.?). P 30800. While the reading of P appears to be corrupt here, it is possible that this word, unattested elsewhere, is genuine. Besides *resplendissor*, both *esplendissor* and *splendissor* are attested (T-L III 1218, 52) and also *plendor* as well as *(e)splendor* (T-L VII 1134, 24). Note that God. quotes this line, but under the form *splendissours*, in which he follows Potvin.

PLESSIEZ.   n.m. copse, thicket. 28204, K 26603. cf. *plaiseïz, ploieïs*.

PLET, PLAIT, PLEST.   n.m. 1. affair. 20598; 2. discussion, conversation. *tenir plet (de)*. discuss, argue, speak (about). 21400, 27578, 31986. *sanz plus de plait, sans autre plet*. without further ado. 22184, 22482. *por nul plait*. (not) for anything, in spite of all entreaty. 30449. *fere plet (a)*. (ill-)treat, (mis-)handle. Q 9717, but 25884 *Que vos feroie plus lonc plet?* — need I tell you any more?

PLEVIR.   v.tr. 1. *plevir sa foi*. pledge o.s., give one's word. 21333, 21338, 24628; 2. (*q.ch. a qn.*, but often with understood obj.) promise, assure (s.o. of s.th.). 24917, 27876, 30864; 3. (*q.ch. a qn.*) promise (to s.o. to do, undertake, s.th.). 29626.

PLOIEÏS.   n.m. V 26603. The normal meaning of this word (as n.m.) is 'enclosure, fence', cf. *plaiseïz, plessiez*. In this instance, it may be a mechanical substitution of one word for another similar word, and it might be unwise to assume that this word can also correspond to 'copse, thicket', the most probable meaning of *plaiseïz* in the context.

(PLOIER). v.tr. KS 9898 *haies ploies* are probably the same as *haies plaisies*. see *pleissier*.

(PLONCIER). v.intr. P 28868. A form of *plongier*, here (fig.) 'plunge, rush'.

PLUIOUSE. adj.f. rainy, wet. 31134 (EMS). L has *pluviouse*, P *plouinouse*, or *plovinouse*. cf. T-L VII 2001, 15; God. VI 232a.

PLUS. comp. n.m. *ne plus ne mains, ne mains ne plus*. nothing (else). 27422, 27493, 31416. *n'i a plus*. there is no more to be said (or done), there is no alternative. 22935, 23377, 24195. *n'i ot plus*. no more was said or done, there was no further ado. 23059, 26876, 27017. *sans plus et sans mains*. exactly. 29425. 20253 *Et feïst dou plus* — and he would have done more. 29204 *Assez i avroit plus que tant* — there would be more than enough. see also *fere*. (adv.) *plus que*. besides. 23640. *De ce n'i a, ot ne plus ne mains* (+ *que ne* + subj.). there is no more to be said. 27768, 29956. 9672 *plus tres grant*. This is simply a reinforcement, meaning 'greatest'; the order *tres plus grant* would be more usual, but cf. T-L X 598, 23.

PO, POI, POU. n.m., or neutr. 1. (a) little. (also + *de*). 9713, 21500, 23220, see also *eure* (1); 2. a little way. 9864, 23765. 26587 *Si ne l'an iert se molt po non* — and he was scarcely troubled (by it). *a po*. a) +*que* + *ne* + subj., b) + *ne* + indic. — gives a sense of 'almost' (plus positive phrase). 9752, 20578, 24966. The sense of S 22324 *a poi se tient que* is the same. also *par (un) po* (and *por po*, in var.) with the same sense and the same constructions. 20653, 21275, 21652.

POËSTÉ. n.f. 1. force, strength, power. 24069, 24082, TV 31795; 2. power, authority, control. 25391, KMQU 22869.

POËSTRE. n.f. force, strength. K 27186. The form *poëstre*, as opposed to *poëste*, is attested by the rhyme in one or two of the examples given by T-L.

POI. see *po*.

POIGNAL. adj.f. handy, wieldy. S 23815, S 25948.

POIGNANT. (etc.) see *poindre*.

(POINDRE). v.tr. spur. 28866. v.intr. 1. gallop, rush, charge. 19795, 9797, 10251; 2. run, hurry (on foot). 21161, see Roach, note; 3. sprout, spring up (grass). 27030. inf. as n.m. charge, gallop. K 9672. pres.p. as adj. sharp, pointed. S 22338.

POINE. see *peine*.

POINGNEOR. adj.(pl.). warlike, brave. (possibly n.m.pl. 'warriors'). MS 31851.

POINT. n.m. square (of chessboard or checked cloth). 20170 (E), 30705 (E), L 10017. see Roach, notes to 20170, 30705.

POINTAL. n.m. point. 25948.

POINTET. n.m. (+ neg.) (not) at all, (not) in the slightest. 25532 (E).

POIOR. comp.adj. worse, less able. 31851.

POIS. n.m. *sor mon pois*. against my will, to my displeasure. T 25595.

POMEL. see *poncel*.

PONCEL. n.m. small bridge. 24249. It seems likely that the *pomel* of the var. is the original reading, meaning 'small dome'.

PONTENIER. n.m. ferryman. 9942, 9965, L 9969.

POOIR. v.intr. be able (to). sometimes more or less translates 'succeed (in)', and sometimes gives a sense of 'may, might'. 19613, 19614, 9526. 20559 *plus tost qu'il pot* — as quickly as he could, cf. 23070, 23768. inf. as n.m. 1. capability, capacity, ability. 20503. *a son pooir*. (etc.) to the best of his (etc.) ability, as much as he can (could), etc. 9946, 22059, 25023; 2. strength, force, power. 26561, 26586, 27462. see also *aiesier, ainçois, ainz, mais, miauz, quanque.*

POON, PAON.   n.m. pawn. 10033–20169, 27700. Note also the *paonnet, paoncel* of P, T in 20169.

POPRE.   adj. actual. 29299 (EQ). A form of *propre*, as in the var.

POR.   prep. The normal sense of this word is 'because of, for'. 19764, 10103–20239, 26607. *por que.* why. 20434. *por ce que.* because. 20746, 20952. *por lui.* for his sake. 21561. *por errer.* for a journey, for travelling. 22519. *por vostre amor.* because of (my) love for you. 22824. *por morir.* even if it were to kill him, cause his death. 23689. see also *huchier. por que* (+ subj.). a) so that, is such a way that. 26008, b) provided that. 27978, 30051. see also *tant.*

(PORCHACIER).   v.tr., intr. 1. do, achieve. 26582, 31925, MU 25549; 2. make, create M 32298.

PORCHAT.   n.m. business, task. Q 25548.

PORCHAUCIEES.   adj.f.pl. (p.p.). 20040 (E). The most probable meaning of this would seem to be 'beaten' (track), cf. various derivatives of CALCARE, FEW II/1 63b, although then we would expect a form *porchauchiees.*

PORGARDER.   v.intr. look, observe. App. VII T 306.

PORPANS, PORPENS.   n.m. 1. care, attention. 9644. *am porpens.* troubled, worried. 31411; 2. preoccupation, intention. 28500, 30276.

PORPANSER.   v.tr. think up, imagine. var. 24118. v.refl. 1. think (to o.s.), reflect. 9713, 23555, 24091; 2. think, decide. 21674, 27590.

PORPOINT (1).   adj. (p.p.). 20151 (EP). This must be the p.p. of *porpeindre* (cf. *point* 25256), 'painted all over', cf. the *hapax* recorded by God. VI 298b.

PORPOINT (2).   adj. (p.p.). quilted. var. 21548. We should probably read *un auqueton Porpoint, d'un vermeil siglaton*, the latter being the material of which the quilted *auqueton* is made.

(PORPRANDRE).   v.tr. 9718 *il porprant terre desor lui* — he (the knight) forces him (Perceval) to give ground. The addition of *desor* modifies the usual sense of *porprandre terre*, cf. T-L VII 1549, 25.

PORPRE.   n.f. fine quality cloth (usually purple or crimson). 22308, 24752, 24776.

PORPRIS.   n.m. fortified enclosure. QS 9534–PT 19658. cf. *porprise.*

PORPRISE.   n.f. fortified enclosure. 9534–19658. cf. *porpris.*

PORQUERRE.   v.tr., intr. do, achieve. 25549, K 26582.

PORRIERE.   n.f. dust-cloud. App. VII TV 401.

PORT.   n.m. 1. port. (used fig.) 21238, 30766; 2. (pl.) passes. KMQU 23445.

(PORTRAIRE).   v.tr. 1. write, paint (letters). 21990, MQ 25259; 2. draw, paint. 24262, KMQU 25256. p.p. painted, decorated with painting(s). 24298, 32280, MQ 9598.

PORTRAITURE.   n.f. painting, decoration. 24303.

PORVEÏR.   v.intr. look. App. VII TV 307.

POSE.   n.f. period of time. *grant pose.* (for) a long time. 25160, 26470, 31472. also *longue pose* 28046, *en pose* M 23726, with the same sense. *al, a chief de pose.* eventually, finally. var. 31824.

POSNEE.   n.f. presumptuous, arrogant action. 21196, 30604, 31304.

POU.   see *po.*

POZ.   n.m. pulse. T 21651. It is curious to find this word used with *issir*, although *pous* and *alaine* are frequently linked, cf. T-L VII 1670, 9.

PRAEL, PRAIEL, PREEL.   n.m. (small) meadow. 10250, 20985, 27835.

PRANDRE, PANRE, PRANRE, (PRENDRE). v.tr. 1. take. 9574, 9694, 10033–20169; 2. cut off. 19816, 10170–20316, 21846; 3. catch, capture, take (incl. chess move.) 10042–20178, 24880, 25091; 4. (cf. 1.) accept. 23740, 31380. *prandre conroi (de)*. take care (of), look after. 20744, 20759. *prandre compeignie (avec)*. go (with). 20750. *prandre ostel*. take lodging, lodge. 22159. *prandre sa voie*. set off. PS 21040, cf. *prandre un chemin*. take a road. 20770. see also *cuer, estal, garde, respit, tor*. v.intr. (+ *a* + inf.) begin, start (to). 20563, 20692, 21098. *prandre ansamble*. join together. 32552. 23570 *pitié li prant* — he is filled with pity, compassion, cf. 25028. *pris*. (p.p.). a) captured, prisoner. 22874. *se randre pris*. yield o.s. as a prisoner. 21341, 25056, b) trapped, caught (out), undone. 22234, 32136, c) distressed, distraught, put out. 23695, 25398, d) (physically) distressed, tired. M 29138.

PREU. n.m. advantage. 25406, 30854.

PRIME. n.f. (hour of) primes, 6 a.m. 21483, 21581, 26117. *primes* adv. (at) first, for the first time. 26237, 28252, 29751. *a prime(s)*. first, for the first time. 24713, 25711. *or primes*. now. 26452.

PRINCIPAL. adj. excellent, superior. 24080.

PRISON. n.f. 32138. While this must be fig., the exact meaning is unclear; 'distressing circumstances, danger'?

PROPRE. see *popre*.

PROPREMANT. adv. 32395 *An s'escuielle propremant* — from his (the king's) own dish.

(PROVER). v.tr. try (out), test, prove. 28715. 32564. L 9620–P 19742. p.p. proven. 19992. v.refl. 27357 *qui am bien se prueve* — who exercises, practices goodness, valour.

PRUEC. conj. (+ *que* + subj.) if, provided that. P 27978, P 30051, P 30484. cf. *por*.

(PUIER). v.intr. (+ *amont, anson, sor*). go up, climb. 29882, var. 31494, M 23164.

PUISCEDI. adv. since (then), afterwards, after that. 27328 (LPS) since you began? 27735 (KLPTV), L 30090 (error?). The two latter instances have *p. que*. The amount of variation in the readings shows that this word troubled many of the scribes, cf. Roach, note to 27328.

PULLENT. adj. stinking, loathsome, horrible. 24115.

PURE. adj.f. (as n.f.). *la pure*. the whole truth, the absolute truth. S 21683. cf. Foulet C1, 245, *pur*.

Q

QUANQUE, QANQUE. (neutr.) whatever, everything (that). 19881, 19930, 20517. 21887 *de quanque set* — as far as she knows how. adv. 1. (+ *pooir*) in every way (possible), as much (fast, loud, etc.) as possible, as much (etc.) as one can. 19903, 21252, 21937; 2. while. 20317, 20437, 21741. E only, see Roach, note to 20317.

QUARRÉ, CARRÉ. adj. (p.p.). square, four-cornered. 21827, 21864, 22344. In some cases, the sense might simply be 'strong', but there is no way to be sure; a lance-head may have been four-cornered in longitudinal section. T 23150 is either an error, or an unusually extended sense, 'big'.

QUARREL, CARREL. n.m.(pl.). large flat stone, used in building walls. 21120, QS 22632. While this may also be the meaning in 22568, 24258, 31152, the context inclines me to think that the sense might rather be 'square tower'. This precise sense is not positively attested, but cf. T-L II 52, 20 'viereckige Bau?'.

QUARTIER, CARTIER. n.m. quarter. 24754. *de quartier* (shield). divided into four fields, or quarters. 23100, 24913. also K 20545, where *orle* seems to mean the whole shield, cf. *orle*. The meaning of *de quartier* when applied to a lance is less clear, 22002 (ES).

QUASSEMENT. adv. quietly. P 22700. cf. T-L II 63, 23.

QUE QUE. pron. (rel.) whatever, no matter what. 25640, 26732. conj. while. 10175, 10263, 21185. cf. *quanque*.

QUERELLE. n.f. affair, business. 21003, 27866, 29540. combat. 20990. 27220 *D'eus vos voil laissier la querelle* — I want to stop talking of them.

QUITE. adj. 1. free, freed (of, from), relieved (of), excused (duty, obligation, etc.). 20951, 22875, 24050; 2. unhindered, unharmed. 21784, 23230, 23770. used adverbially: freely, without hindrance. 23808, 26011, 30674. see also *clamer*.

(QUITER). v.tr. (*q.ch. a qn.*) free (o.s. from, of s.th). 31457.

QUOI. see *coi*.

R

(RAASTIR). v.refl. 25404. We appear to have here *se raastir de bataille a qn.* attack s.o. again, cf. *re-* 1., *aastir*. The *se* is lacking in KMU 25403, cf. God. VI 526b.

(RABANDONER). v.refl. charge, rush forward. 26879 cf. *re-* 2.

(RACHEMINER). v.refl. set off again. 20909, 24231, 25715. cf. *re-* 1.

RACOINTIER. v.tr. relate, tell. 28696 (P). cf. *re-* 4.

(RACOISIER). v.intr. quieten, calm down (again). TV 25660. cf. *re-* 3., *acoisier*.

RADE. adj. swift-running, rushing (river). 20010, 21665, 25984.

RAFREMER. v.tr. P 22869. This must mean 'bring to an end' (T-L VIII 168, 5.) cf. *re-4*.

RAFRENER. see *refrener*.

RAIER. v.intr. 1. shine (sun, moon). 23545, 24229, 30375; 2. run, flow (blood). 25009. (The *roier* of E 23545 might have been retained.)

RAIES. n.f.pl. M 25349. I can see no reason for the editor's exclamation mark here; the word is well attested with the sense 'sunbeam', as here.

RAIN. n.m. 1. branch. 20792 (where E has *rant*, no doubt with silent *t*.); 2. (pl.) points (of stag's antlers). 24781; 3. QS 24171. The rhymes here (*fains, vilains*) attest the form, but do not entirely preclude the possibility that this is an error. While it is possible to imagine this word being used to indicate a sunbeam, there does not seem to be any such attestation; however, cf. FEW X 39b.

RAINER. adj.? S 20966. Is this a var. of *ramier*, 'wild' or related to *rain*, 'antlered', or is it a verb?

(RALUMER). v.intr. regain one's sight. App. XI K 10. cf. *re-* 3.

RAMANTEVOIR. v.tr. mention, bring into conversation. (sometimes with a nuance of 'recall'). 26401, 26720, 28733. cf. *re-* 1., 4.

RAMÉ. adj. 1. spreading, branching (mainly applied to *forest*). 21583, 21955, 24832; 2. antlered (stag's head). 25900, KSU 26292. cf. *ramu*.

RAMPANT. adj. (pres.p.). rampant (heraldic term). (LS 9598-) 19720, 21643, 29281. P 19720 *rampoit* is the same sense of *ramper*.

RAMPONES. n.f.pl. mockery, jibes, derision. 28505 (E).

RAMPOSNEMENT. n.m. mockery, derision. S 23480.

RAMPOSNER, (RAMPONER). v.tr. mock, deride. 20663, 24999, 28877.

RAMU. adj. 1. antlered (stag). 22239, 24781, 25439; 2. spreading, branching (forest, tree). 23162, 28254 (ES), 32072. cf. *ramé*.

RANDIR. v.intr. gallop. LU 30794. cf. *randoner*.

RANDON. n.m. *de randon*. The essential idea contained in this expression seems to be one of speed, sometimes with a nuance of impetuosity, also. 23783, 28211, cf. 28804, 28853, 26608. The idea of force or violence is present in MQ 24394, and possibly in 9730, 24393 and var. 21871, but in each of these latter instances the sense might be that of *an un randon* 22235 (S -*d'un randon*), var. 9730, 'in succession, one after another'. cf. *randonee*.

RANDONEE. n.f. *an une randonee*. in succession. 22832. *de randonee*. rapidly? 26620. cf. *randon*.

RANDONER. v.intr. gallop. 23243. cf. *randir*.

RANDRE. v.tr. 1. give (up), surrender. 9779, PT 19886; 2. give back, return. also with the sense 'get (s.th.) back (from s.o.)'. 10194–20332, 10197–20335, 22314; 3. give (off) (light, heat, etc.). 22528, 24342, 24745; 4. give (greeting). 23468, 26482, 28100. *randre prison*. give o.s. up as a prisoner. 30865. see also *gré, merci, reson*. v.refl. 1. surrender, yield. 9785, 19960, 19965; 2. go. 9851.

RANLUMINER. v.tr. 1. decorate, brighten. 27955 (EKLP); 2. illuminate, brighten. 32295 (ELTV) (K has *reluminer*.). cf. *re-* 4.

RANT. see *rain*.

(RAPAIER). v.tr. calm, choke back (anger). 25409 (EKU). cf. *re-* 3.

RASEOIR. v.tr. 1. besiege. 31347, cf. *re-* 2; 2. put back. L 10089, cf. *re-* 3. v.intr. 1. sit down again. 27947; 2. put o.s. back, replace o.s. (chess-pieces). 27986, L 10052. At 27986 P has the comparatively rare inf. *rassir*. cf. *re-* 3.

(RASTANDRE). v.intr. wait. 31492. cf. *re-* 2. Only E has the form with -*st*-.

RASTIZ. adj. rej.r. 31585. Presumably an error.

(RATAINDRE). v.tr. catch up (with). 20633, P 20611. cf. *re-* 1., *ataindre*.

(RATIRER). v.tr. prepare, make ready (again). P 22938. cf. *re-* 1., *atirier*.

RAÜSER. see *reüser*.

RAVALER. v.intr. go back down, fall back. 27426. cf. *re-* 3.

RAVERTIR. v.refl. remember. 25668. cf. *re-* 4., *avertir*.

(RAVESTIR). v.tr. restore, re-furnish (room). TV 24614. cf. *re-* 3.

RAVINE. n.f. (headlong) charge, gallop, etc. 9672, 20482, 28819.

RAVINOSE. adj.f. steep? (road). K 27512.

(RAVISER). v.tr. 1. In 23594 and var. 23695, this word could mean either 'examine, look closely at', or 'recognize'. I would incline towards the latter sense, but the meaning could be different in the two instances, cf. *re-* 1. or 4.; 2. see. 26878. cf. *re-* 2. Here, also, the sense might rather be 'recognize'. v.refl. pay attention. U 23695.

(RAVOIER). v.tr. redirect, set (back) on the right road. S 20747. cf. *re-* 1., *avoier*.

RÉ. n.m. P 27613 *Tout contre tout a mis el ré*. I am unable to make any sense of this, whether it be *ré* 'fire, furnace', *ré, reus* (cf. T-L VIII 368, 15), or something else.

RE-. (also R-). prefix. The principal functions of this prefix can, broadly speaking, be divided into four main categories.

1. reiterative. Expresses the idea of 'again', in the sense of a repetition of a previous action. see *raastir, racheminer, ramantevoir, rataindre, recorre*.

2. adversative. Expresses the idea of opposition contained in such phrases as 'for his part', 'in (his) turn', etc., and also the mild opposition of 'also, too'. 26879 *Qui contre lui se rabandone* — who in turn charges towards him. 31347 *La lou rasist li rois Artus* — and there (in turn) King Arthur besieged him. 31492 *An celle gaires ne rastant* — nor does he stay long on that one, either. S 24009 *Et qui touz nos*

redeffera — and who will also make an end of us. see also *raviser*, *rehater*, *relessier*.

3. opposite. Expresses an action performed in the opposite direction (or manner) to a previous action, *rapaier*, *raseoir*, *ravaler*, *recliner* — or simply a return to a previous state, *racoisier*, *ralumer*, *ravestir*. This sense is frequently conveyed in Eng. by 'again', or 'back'.

4. neutral. Here the prefix has little or no real, or discernible, function, at least in relation to the basic verb, but has become an integral part of the word, *racointier* (although this might contain a nuance of 'repeat'), *ranluminer*, *ravertir* (essentially = *avertir*), *refrener*. *ramantevoir* might be thought to come into this category, or, in its sense of 'remind, recall', into that of 1.

(REBIFER).   v.intr. turn up (nose). 23185 (ES). cf. *reborsser*, *rebricier*, *remuser*.

REBONDIE.   n.f. reverberation. U 24344. cf. *bondie*, *rebondir*.

(REBONDIR).   v.intr. reverberate, echo. MSU 29420. cf. *rebondie*.

REBORS.   adj. *fere rebors*. mix up, tell in disorder, the wrong order (stories). 26088.

(REBORSSER, REBOURSER).   v.intr. turn up (nose). MQU 23185. cf. *rebifer*, *rebricier*, *remuser*.

(REBRICIER).   v.intr. turn up (nose). LP 23185. A *hapax* as far as this meaning is concerned, perhaps an error for *rebracier*, yet in *Partonopeus de Blois* 9316, we find *rebriquer* and *rebifer* as alternatives, with the sense 'rebuke', so it is possible this identity was extended to other meanings. cf. *rebifer*, *reborsser*, *remuser*.

RECELEE.   n.f. secret. 26296. *sanz recelee*. openly. 28641. *a recelee*. quietly. P 22455 (applies to 22456), K 22664.

RECERCELEZ.   adj.pl. (p.p.). curling, ringleted (hair). 29365.

RECET.   n.m. dwelling (-place), (place of) shelter, refuge. 20707, 23537, 24556. cf. *reçoit*.

(RECHOSIER).   v.refl. T 22949. This is presumably for *rechocier*, a picard form of *reco(u)chier*, 'go back to bed'. cf. *re-* 3.

(RECLINER).   v.tr. bow, bend (again) (head). 30619. cf. *re-* 3., *cliner*.

RECLUS.   n.m. cell, hermitage. 10230–20384 (KLPT have *renclus*).

(RECOILLIR).   v.tr. App. VII TV 275 (*requeut*). receive (an enemy, an attack), i.e. deal with, treat. cf. *re-* 4.

REÇOIT.   n.m. 31031, 31034. (E only?). In printing *reçoit*, the editor clearly identifies this word with *recet*, which is the reading of P at least. I am inclined to think (with A. W. Thompson, see *Speculum* 49 (1974), 145) that it rather corresponds to *recoi*, cf. T-L VIII 435, 50, where the form *recoit* is attested, as well as *requeit*), although the meaning is still similar '(secluded) dwelling, refuge'. That this is not *recet* is made more plausible by the fact that elsewhere the scribe of E uses the form *recet*; cf. *recet*, and C1 (E) 2101, 3053; CM 34815, 40450.

RECONDER.   see *conder*.

(RECORRE).   v.refl. (mutual refl.) (+ *sus*) attack one another again. 23286. cf. *re-* 1.

RECOVREES.   adj.f.pl. (p.p.). (+ *de*) in possession (of), endowed (with). App. VII TV 128.

RECREANZ.   adj. (pres.p.) as n.m. coward, good-for-nothing. 10216–20358. In Q 22052, while the v.tr. meaning 'conquer, defeat' is not unusual, *recreant* appears to have the function of a p.p., unless we are to assume a severe ellipsis.

(REDEFFERE).   v.tr. bring to an end. S 24009. see *re-* 2., *desfaire*.

REFERMER, REFREMER.   v.tr. strengthen again, restore. KMQU 22869. cf. *re-* 3.

(REFLAMBOIER).   v.intr. shine, gleam. 24761, 26634, KPT 26870. cf. *re-* 4.

REFRAINDRE.   v.intr. *sanz refraindre.* without restraint, unceasingly. App. VII
TV 999. cf. *re-* 4.
REFREMER.   see *refermer.*
REFRENER.   v.tr. curb, restrain, control. 22869 (E). L has *rafrener.* cf. *re-* 4.
(REGANCHIR).   v.intr. duck back, withdraw. 9634. cf. *re-* 3., *ganchir.*
REGARDE.   n.m.? Q 22638. This might convey the act of looking, although we
   should expect it to be n.f., and it is probably an error for *regarder.* L 22696 might
   be the same, but it is more probable that *El regarde* means 'she sees (that)'.
REGARDER.   v.tr. 1. look at. 9573, 21597, 22694; 2. heed, pay heed to? 24649,
   25531. v.intr. look. 21742, 22566, 23773, see also *regarde.* v.refl. look around.
   10183–20323, 10236. inf. as n.m. looking. 22638, 22696, 26080. cf. *re-* 4, *garder.*
REGART.   n.m. 1. (cause for) concern, worry. 9889; 2. *au, ou regart.* looking,
   watching? MQ 27792.
REGORT.   n.m. stream, channel. 27653.
(REHATER).   v.tr. 1. prepare quickly (food). 27277, cf. *re-* 2., *haster*; 2. press
   (again). var. 23302. cf. *re-* 1., *haster.*
REHUICHIER.   v.tr. call back. 32258. cf. *re-* 3.
RELAIER.   see *relessier.*
(RELEECIER).   v.intr. become joyful (again), regain one's spirits. 24381. v.refl.
   U 31187 has the same meaning, but is probably an error. cf. *re-* 3 and *esleecier,
   resleecier.*
(RELESSIER).   v.tr. *relessier aler.* let go, give (horse) its head. 22342. (MS have
   relest = relaier). cf. *re-* 2., *laissier.* v.refl. (+ *de*) excuse o.s., be dispensed (from).
   P 31187, where L has *relaier,* v.tr. 'excuse (from)'. cf. *re-* 4., *laier, laissier.*
RELEZ.   n.m. remission. T 24102.
RELUMINER.   see *ranluminer.*
(REMAILLIER).   v.intr. strike, hammer again. 25007. cf. *re-* 1., *maillier.*
REMENOIR, REMANOIR.   v.intr. 1. stop, stay, remain, be left. *remés* p.p. 9654, 21431,
   remés pret. 1. 22860. 21547 *Si remest an un auqueton* — and he was left wearing
   an *auqueton.* 32046 *La nuiz remest.* — the night became; 2. (impers.) 22837 *Am
   Blancheflor ne remest mie* — Blancheflor made no objection, provided no
   obstacle; cf. 28137, 32267; 3. (impers.) 26783 *Einsint remest* — that is how things
   stayed. pres.p. *estre remenant (de).* remain (as a part of). 23524, 29647. *a
   remenant.* permanently, on a permanent basis? L 27162. *de remenans.* remaining. var. 31410. cf. *re-* 4., *manoir.*
REMERIR.   v.tr. repay. 31005. cf. *re-* 4., *merir.*
REMÉS.   see *remenoir.*
(REMETRE).   v.tr. put back. L 10086. cf. *re-* 3., *metre.* v.refl. 1. go back. 25092. cf.
   re- 3., *metre*; 2. *se remetre a la voie.* set off again. 21661, 30009. cf. *re-* 1., *metre*; 3.
   S 20706 *Et se remetoit el retor* — and he was returning. The *re-* is unnecessary
   here, cf. *metre,* and is probably due to the analogy of *re-tor.*
REMOVOIR.   v.tr. move, cause to move. var. 31947. v.intr. move. 27461, 31947
   (EMP). v.refl. move. 27457, KMQU 27464.
(REMUCHIER).   v.refl. go back, thrust o.s. back. There is no idea of hiding, here.
   App. VII TV 863. cf. *re-* 3.
(REMUSER).   v.intr. turn up (nose). K 23185. It would be possible to see this as
   remusé, rather than *remuse,* with an elliptical construction (cf. God. VI 587a);
   there seems to be no attestation of a verb *remuser.* cf. *rebifer, reborsser, rebricier.*
RENCLUS.   see *reclus.*
(RENVOLEPER).   v.tr. wrap up again. L 32592. cf. *re-* 3.

REONDE. n.f. *a la reonde*. (all) around, round about. 22100, 25136, 26052.

REPAIREZ. adj. (p.p.). 22300. The exact sense of this word is uncertain; T-L's definition, 'in gutem Zustand', is clearly correct in essence, but also vague.

(REPASSER). v.refl. S 25409. Possibly 'feed (on)', cf. God. VII 50b, but an error for *se repaisier* 'calm down' (cf. T-L VIII 874, 49) seems more likely.

REPERE, REPAIRE. n.m. 1. residence, dwelling. 24060, 31806, where the MS reading is of course 'a *un* suen repere'; 2. return. *estre el, au repere.* return, be back. var. 22898. see also *metre.*

REPERIR. v.intr.? (inf. as n.m.) M 21199. Probably for *resperir*, with a sense of 'recover' or 'recovery'.

REPLANEZ. adj.pl. (p.p.). planed, smooth. KMT 22300. cf. *re-* 4.

REPLANI. adj. (p.p.). full, filled, (well-) endowed, furnished. 22565 (ES), 24614 (EQS, L has *rapleni*), 28619 (ES). There may be a nuance of 'again' in 24614.

(REPONDRE). v.refl. hide. App. VII T 873 (V has *reporre*, either an error, or a denasalized picard form). p.p. *repuz.* hidden. 20568, 30238.

REPUZ. see *repondre.*

REQUERRE. v.tr. 1. attack. 9706–19824, 9715, 21288; 2. ask (for), seek. 22113, 25149, 25155. 10123–20261 *ainz mes d'amer ne fui requise* — no-one has ever sought my love (before), cf. 29815; 3. visit in pilgrimage (saint). 21555; 4. seek, look for. 27859.

RESBAUDIR. v.tr. increase, enhance, brighten. 23036, 28906. cf. *re-* 4.

RESCLAIRIER. v.tr., intr. see *re-* 3., *esclairier.* L 25601, LU 30688.

RESCLARCIR. v.intr. 1. brighten, become clear again (night). 25660; 2. start to shine (again). LT 24228, L 29084. cf. *re-* 1., 3., *esclarcir.*

RESLEECIER. v.tr. cheer up, make happy (again). 28231, LP 29259. cf. *re-* 3. v.intr. be glad, rejoice. var. 26822. cf. *re-* 4., *esleecier.*

(RESNIER). v.intr. talk, speak. 24729, var. 30328, P 23697.

(RESOIGNIER). v.tr. fear. MS 31057. p.p. (as adj.) feared. 25768. cf. *re-* 4.

RESON (1). n.m. echo, reverberation. 9578 (–PT 19700). *jeter reson.* obtain a response? K 20576.

RESON (2), RAISON. n.f. 1. words, speech. 20576, 21522, 22921. 31759 *a petit de raison.* briefly. *metre a reson.* speak to, address. 21563, 24401, 24543. *randre reson.* give an account of o.s., answer. 26701, P 23421; 2. right, fairness, reasonableness, etc. 22065, 23233, 28584. *par reson.* rightly, properly. 27699, 31473, M 22304. *avoir raison.* be right. 22003; 3. reason, cause. 22083, 22105, 26012. *dire, conter la reson (de).* explain (about). 31787, 32241, 32519; 4. truth? cf. 3. 23959, 24796, var. 26548; 5. business, affair. 25299, 31102?; 6. sense, significance. 27919. *par tel raison.* in this way, in such a way. 25043, 25244, 28959.

RESONER. v.intr. echo, reverberate. var. 24341.

(RESORDER). v.refl. E 26806 (rej.r.). For *resorter*, meaning approximately 'turn back'?

(RESORTIR). v.tr. push back, oblige to retreat. (fig.) 30354. cf. *re-* 3.

(RESPASSER). v.intr. get well, be healed. (L 9792–) 19895, 28705.

(RESPISSIER, RESPESCHIER). see *espessier.* cf. *re-* 4.

RESPIT. n.m. 1. delay. 10149–20283, 22385, 22888. (*sanz nul respit*). *prandre respit (de).* put off. 23048. *metre an respit* means the same. 28268; 2. postponement, period of grace. 31868, 31870. cf. *respoitier.*

(RESPOITIER). v.tr. 1. put off, delay. 27824; 2. spare. Q 28684. cf. *respit.*

RESTER.   v.tr. (*qn. de q.ch.*, or *q.ch. a qn.*). accuse (s.o. of s.th.). 28370, P 28568, S 28733. Probably also Q 28677, where the idea is that Bagomédes was attacked without accusation, i.e. without justification.

(RESTRAINDRE).   v.tr. screw up (eyes). MQ 22699.

(RESTRE).   v.intr. be again. 28881. *restre au cos ferir* corresponds to *estre au cos referir*, with the prefix *re-* transferred. cf. *re-* 1.

(RESVANOÏR).   v.refl. disappear again. 29132. cf. *re-* 3., *esvanoïr*.

(RETERDRE).   v.tr. dry (eyes). U 22699. cf. *re-* 3.? 4.?, *terdre*.

(RETIRER).   v.tr. (ELST) 22698 *retire Ses iauz a soi* — he lowers his eyes. The sense of P — *retire Son cuer* — is less clear. cf. *re-* 3.

(RETOMBIR).   v.intr. echo, reverberate. var. 29420. cf. *re-* 4., *tombir*.

RETOR.   n.m. 1. return. 20297. *sans (nul) retor.* a) certainly, definitely. 26451 (where I would read *trestor*), b) straight, directly. 31952, var. 27810, U 9967, cf. *trestor. fere son retor.* return. 21685. see also *metre* (tr. and refl.); 2. bend, elbow (river). TV 27653.

RETRAIT.   n.m. utterance, aphorism. App. VII TV 885.

RETRAITE, RETRETES.   n.f.(pl.). 1. *a la retraite.* a particular way of delivering a blow in sword-fighting (backhand?). 23255; 2. (pl.) verbal attacks, slander. 28939.

RETRAITIER.   v.tr. relate, recall. KQTV 28696.

RETRERE, RETRAIRE.   v.tr. 1. move (chess), cf. *re-* 2. (var. 10036–) 20172, (MQ 10039–) 20175, 10041–20177; 2. relate, recount, tell, say. 20230, 20776, 23939; 3. withdraw, pull out. 23826. v.intr. say, tell. 23947, 24166, 27068.

RETRONCHIER.   v.intr. L 32164.? It seems unlikely that this is *retrouchier* for *retorchier*, with an intr. sense.

REÜSER.   v.tr. drive back(wards). V 26878 which is in fact an error. v.intr. retreat, give ground. 9761–19867, App. IV MQU 21, and this may have been the original reading in App. IV MQU 25. v.refl. refrain, keep (from). Q 28735.

REVEL.   n.m. arrogance, pride? 25295.

(REVERTIR).   v.intr. return. M 29082. cf. *re-* 4.

RIBAUT.   n.m.pl. rabble, common soldiery. M 31332.

RIFLEÏS.   n.m. wasteland. Pot. 21931–T 19647.

RIFLOIS.   n.m.pl. thickets, brushwood. LS 9471.

RIGOLAGE.   n.m. pleasantry, trifling, trifle. MQ 29811.

RÏOTE.   n.f. U 31360. Probably means 'anxiety, trouble', and applies here to King Carras.

ROBEORS.   adj.pl. Q 26088. A loose sense, meaning 'villainous'? more probably, simply an error for *rebors*.

ROC.   n.m. rook, castle (chess). 27952.

RÖÉ.   adj. (p.p.). decorated with a pattern of circles (cloth). 22678, MQ 27262, where the *roié* of K rather = *raié*.

RÖEUSE.   adj.f. L 23151. For *ronceuse* 'brambly'? Or might *ja ro(u)euse* stand for *jaroneuse*, and mean 'strewn with branches'? Or could this represent 'rough' (from Lat. RUGA)? Of these three, *jaroneuse* seems the most probable, as it eliminates the need to explain the curious *ja*.

ROICHEZ.   n.m.pl. Q 23650. Although this might simply mean '(blunted) lance' (the usual sense), I suspect it is an extended meaning, 'javelin, dart', cf. Eng. "rocket".

RONÇOIZ.   n.m.pl. bramble bushes. 9471 (A).

RONIAX.   adj.pl. Q 30297. Unless this is a form *ronel* for *roné* (cf. T-L VIII 1365, 48), we should probably read *roviax*, see *rovel*.

ROTE.   n.f. 1. troop(s), entourage. 27144; 2. (disorganized) crowd. P 30268.

ROUËL.   see *rovel*.

(ROUSILLIER).   v.intr. S 29247 *Et ot rousillié a plantez* — and there had been a heavy dew.

ROVEL.   adj. red. K 23172. We should also read *rovel*, not *rouël*, at M 30032. The sense is rather 'reddish, tawny', as probably in Q 30297, where we might read *roviax* for *roniax*. Note that in M 30032 the word is used as n.m. '(reddish) horse', or even as a name, cf. T-L VIII 1516, 48; God. VII 254a.

(ROVER).   v.tr., intr. ask. 21328, 27409, 27817. v.intr. seek, wish (to). P 22154, Q 28430, P 31471. all these latter have *ruis* — pres. indic. 1.

RU.   n.m. stream. 31819.

RUIS.   see *rover*.

RUISTECE.   n.f. strength, force, valour. P 29402, P 31053.

RUITE.   adj. 1. strong, hardy (person). 25117; 2. fierce, weighty (blow). 27176, 27189; 3. bleak, rough, wild (mountain). var. 23155.

RUSER.   see *reüser*.

S

SA.   enclitic form. (*si la*). see *covescler*.

SABLONNOIE.   n.f. sandy piece of ground, terrain. S 26239.

SACHIER (1), (SAICHIER).   v.tr. 1. pull, tear, wrench (at). 9735, 23294, 30602; 2. draw (sword). 21212.

SACHIER (2).   v.tr. U 29704. At first sight, the reading of U *Car on ne set a pou sachier Cuer de fame* makes little sense. However, I think we have here a variant spelling of *sasier* (Lat. SATIARE), meaning 'satisfy' (cf. *sacïer* as a variant of *sasiier*). The sense is then clear 'one cannot easily satisfy a woman's heart with a little'.

SAFFRÉ.   adj. (p.p.). *menu saffré.* a standard epithet for a hauberk, whose exact meaning is uncertain; the basic sense is 'fine'. var. 23759. cf. *dessasfrer*.

SAICHIER.   see *sachier* (1).

SAIGNIÉ.   adj. (p.p.). marked, decorated. 24982 (ELV), KM 27953.

SAINGNORIZ.   adj. (pl.). noble, fine, distinguished. Q 22202, Q 24694.

SAINT.   n.m.pl. 1. bells. 22733, K 22958; 2. decoration in the form of bells? K 22658.

SAISON.   n.f. *de saison.* (fig.) (of) good quality, delicious (kisses). 27883.

SAMBLANCE.   n.f. 1. appearance, fashion. 22302. *par samblance.* in appearance. var. 32077; 2. (EPU) 32077 *an sa samblance* — to his mind, in his opinion. S 32362 *Si com il m'estoit en samblance* — as it seemed to me, apparently; 3. vision? MS 32077. *fere samblance a.* be comparable to? U 22302.

SAMBLANT.   n.m. appearance. 25813. *fere samblant.* pretend. 26712. *fere mauvés samblant.* show bad feeling. 27474. cf. *chiere*.

SAMPRES.   adv. directly, straightaway, (very) soon. 27573, S 27159.

SAMTE.   Q 23108. Error. (= *s'amte*, i.e. his aunt?).

SANC.   see *berserez*.

(SANER).   v.intr. be healed, get well. S 27545.

SANS.   see *sens*.

SANSMELLEE.   adj.f. (p.p.). ill, prostrate(d), as a result of a strong emotion. 29937.

SARCU.   n.m. tomb. 31917.

SARMON.   n.m. sermon. *faire lonc sarmon.* beat about the bush. 22702. V 25290 *sanc (= sans) lonc sermon.* briefly.

SAUVAIGINE.   n.f. wild animals, game. 22238.

SAVEUR.   n.f. seasoning, sauce? S 27288.

SAVOIR.   v.tr. 1. know, be familiar with, be aware of, etc. 9466, 9528, 9619; 2. discover, learn, see. 21018, 21133, 21794. see also *gré*. v. intr. 1. (+ inf., also + *a* + inf., in var.) know how, be able (to do s.th.) 19678, 20342, 20807. 25778 *Ainz ne me soi aparcevoir* — I never noticed. also with a sense of doing s.th. enough to achieve a required result: 25096, 27005, 27801. In 24939 the sense might be 'have to', or 'learn how to'; 2. know. 19774, 9773, 9838–19928; 3. realise, be aware. 19846, 9892. *savoir avant*. learn more. 23452.

SECORCIÉ.   adj. (p.p.). with one's garment(s) kilted up. 25491 (ES), MSU 26204. cf. *escorciez*.

(SEELER).   v.tr. 1. attach, fasten? 9823; 2. enclose. Q 22628, App. IV MQU 90.

SEIGNORAIGE.   n.m. force, power. 30644.

SEIGNORIE.   n.f. 1. power, force, strength. 32151, LPTV 31115, App. VII KTV 73; 2. mastery, lordship. App. VII TV 196.

SEJOR.   n.m. respite. 22868.

(SEMONDRE).   v.tr. (*qn. de* + inf.) invite, urge (s.o. to do s.th.). 20073 (E), 32421, 32504.

SEN.   n.m. 1. direction. 24554, 25669, 27586; 2. way. *en nul sen*. somehow, in any way. 28570. *par tel sen*. in such a way. 28959; 3. sense, cleverness. 29402. cf. *sens*.

SENEFÏENCE.   n.f. sign. 32233, 32479.

SENEZ.   adj. clever, sensible. 23864, 26332, 29818.

SENORÉS.   adj. P 31586. Probably an error for *sororé*, but cf. God. VII 360b, *seignoré*, where this instance is quoted, under the meaning 'seigneurial, princier'.

SENS, SANS.   n.m. 1. skill, cleverness. (S 10018–) 20152, 27684, KMQU 9643, magic art? 26758, 27913, 31881; 2. senses, mind. 23072. *issir fors dou, de son sens*. go mad. 25816, 31557. *estre hors, fors dou, de son sens*. be mad. 28310, 28499, 30822. see also *giter, oublïer, tresaler, tresmüer*; 3. (good) sense, wisdom. 23373, 26425, 29479; 4. direction? 31558 (EPQ). The *sens* of 30985 is probably pl. of *sen*. *de toz sans*. on all sides. 9643 (ALS); 5. way. *an nul sens*. in no wise. 20840 (ES). *par tel sans*. in such a way. 25244. *an quel sens*. how, in what way. 26590. *an toz sens*. in every way. 27924. P 20840 *en mau sens Avés faite ceste estoutie* — you should not have committed this arrogant act.

SEOIR, SEÏR.   v.intr. 1. sit, be sitting. 19754, 19949, 9913–20047; 2. be situated. 9890, 22533, 22605; 3. (+ *a*) be agreeable (to), please. 21732, 22839, 29867. v.refl. 1. sit down. 10003, 10025, 27696; 2. sit, be sitting. 26371, 28547, 29445. *seant*. pres.p. (as adj.) 1. situated. 9884–20032, 28416, Q 21707; 2. agreeable, pleasing. Q 22299.

SERAINE, SERAINNE.   n.f. siren. 25451, 26365.

SERI.   adj. 1. calm, clear. 22741, 22954, 25781; 2. bright, light. var. 22741. adv. clearly, loudly. Q 29262. In spite of the form, P 23064 *siereement* may be the adv. from this adj., meaning 'quietly, gently'. It is conceivable, however, that it is *serreement*, with much the same sense; God. has one example (from the *Mort de Garin*) which could mean 'quietly, secretly'.

SERMONIAUS.   n.m.pl. sermons. App. VI P 16. A form *sermonel* does not appear in the dictionaries, although this is in Potvin.

SESIR, (SAISIR).   v.tr. grasp, seize. 29520, 30793. p.p. *saisies (de)*. in possession (of), endowed (with). TV 29508.

SEUR, SOR (2).   prep. 1. on (top of). 9479, 9626–19754, 9641 (–T 19773); 2. above, over. 9539 (–PT 19662), 23119, 31022; 3. before, beyond. 9828, L 10070. *seur tote(s) rien(s)*. above all things, extremely. 9810–19910, 27356, 28386; 4. beyond, beside. 9883 (–PT 20031), 9890 (–PT 20034), 21123; 5. because of. 22912 *seur ce* — because of that, on that basis; 6. during, over (meal). 23724, 30328. see also *muser*.

SEURE, SORE.   adv. *monter seure*. mount. L 9929. see also *corre*.

SEURFEZ.   n.m. lack of moderation, overweening. 30849. cf. *sorfaites*.

(SEURNOMER).   v.tr. call, give an epithet. 29066 (EQU). cf. *seurnon*.

SEURNON.   n.m. surname, epithet. 21658 (ES), S 29066. cf. *seurnomer*.

SEURPLUS.   n.m. the rest, what happened next. 22835.

SEURPRANDRE.   see *sorprandre*.

SEURVEOIR.   v.tr. survey, look down on. 28783, T 20206.

SEVIAU.   adv. (+ *non*) at least. 31011. cf. *viax*.

SIAUT.   see *soloir*.

SIEREEMENT.   see *seri*.

SIFAITEMANT.   adv. 1. thus. 24028 *Estre l'estuet si faitemant* — it must be so, this is how it must be; 2. (+ *con*) as, in the way that. 28339, 28978, 29249. The editor prints this as two words.

SIGLATON.   n.m. silk cloth. 21548, 27259, 30145.

SIMPLE.   adj. 1. demure. 27270, 31215 (EMPS); 2. pleasant, friendly? L 10097.

SIMPLEMANT.   adv. simply, humbly. 30907, T 30908.

SINOPLE, XINOPLE.   n.m. red (or green). 27037 (possibly green), 30141, 32289.

SIRE.   adj. in control, well-established. 20676, 22750. This appears to be an adj. use of *sire, seignor*, cf. *mestre*, also T-L II 1178, 11, where *dame* is treated as adj., and glossed 'souverän, obenauf, herrlich und in Freuden', etc.

SOFRANCE.   see *metre*.

SOHAIDIER, SOUHAIDIER.   v.tr. absol. 1. wish for, desire. P 24660, S 23024; 2. 29368 *ausint con souhaidiez Eüst esté* — as though she had been created by wishing, cf. *de sohaidier*. by wishing. 24660 (E); 3. wish (= have what one wishes for). 29515. 23024 *Autant con fust a souhaidier* — as much as they could wish for; cf. 27289, var. 25887.

SOHAUCIER.   v.tr. lift up. 27400. cf. *soufauchier*.

SOIF.   n.f. hedge, fence. 21669.

SOLIER.   n.m. upstairs room. 24384, MQ 24383.

(SOLOIR).   v.intr. be (or have been) wont, used (to). 21639, 23650, 24892.

SOMELLOS.   adj. sleepy. K 9473.

SOR (1).   adj. 1. pale chestnut, (golden) brown (horse). 9479, 27071, 29095; 2. blond, golden (hair). 24519, rej.r. 20236.

SOR (2).   see *seur*.

SORARGENTEES.   adj.f.pl. (p.p.). decorated with silver. App. VII KTV 51.

SORE.   see *seure*.

SORFAITES.   n.f. presumption, arrogance. P 30849. This appears to be a *hapax*. T-L refers to God., who has this one example; FEW gives no references. cf. *seurfez*.

SOROREZ.   adj. (p.p.). gilded, plated. 31586. (P has *senorés*.)

(SORPRANDRE), (SEURPRANDRE).   v.tr. 1. overwhelm, subdue. 25144, 25156 (ELMV); 2. surprise. 25775.

SOU.   enclitic form. a) for *si le*. 19837, 20453, 23585, b) for *se le*. 20277. cf. Roach, note to 20273.

SOUFAUCHIER.   v.tr. raise, lift. M 27400. There is no need for the editor's exclamation mark, see God. VII 548b, T-L IX 712, 22. cf. *sohaucier*.

SOUFRIR.   v.tr. *armes soufrir*. bear arms. 25113. see also *metre*.

SOUHAIDIER.   see *sohaidier*.

SOURDOIS.   comp.adj. the worse (for it?). 29870 (S) see Roach, note to this line. U 26907 *Au relever fu li sordois* — when he got up, he was the worse for it? probably an error.

SOURQUETOUT.   adv. above all, what is more. S 27480. cf. *anseurquetot*.

SOUSTIMANT.   adv. 1. finely, cleverly. 24284. (P has *soutiuement*; read *soutivement*?); 2. discreetly, stealthily. 31166.

SOUTE.   n.f. fear, anxiety. var. 21155. T-L has only 2 examples of this word, both from Benoit's *Chronique des Ducs de Normandie*.

SOUTEINE.   adj.f. desolate, deserted. 31575.

SOUTILLIER.   v.tr. fashion, create (cleverly, with skill). S 32298.

SOVIN.   adj. supine, (lying) on one's back. P 28863.

SULLANT.   adj. sweating, in a sweat. 20522 (E), 31526.

T

TABLE.   n.f. 1. sheet, plate (metal). 32291. cf. also 24287, 24296, etc., where the sense is between this and 'table'. The *talle* of E 24296 is probably a simple error, not picard *ta(u)le*; 2. var. 21707. *table dormant*. A fixed table of some sort, as opposed to the more usual tables which consisted of boards on trestles. cf. *Le Bel Inconnu* 3095 and 2920–21, which suggest that the board part of the table may have been removable, as usual, while the *dormans* were fixed supports. Note also God.'s erroneous interpretation of *table dormante*, under *ormante*. This word seems to appear in texts *c.* 1200, and may be assumed to have come into use shortly before that.

TAION.   n.m. grandfather. 28012.

TAIZ.   adj. rej.r. 31585. Probably an error.

TALENTIS.   adj. desirous (of), keen (to). P 22681.

TAMAINTE.   adj.f. so many. K 32106. (= *tant mainte*, cf. L).

TAMPORAL.   n.m. (period of) time. 25274.

TANCIER.   v.intr. quarrel, fight. 28728, M 28749. cf. *tençon*.

TANT.   n.m. (also pron.) 1. this (much). 10080–20214, 20231, 10122–20258; 2. so many, so much. 19630, 25709, 26582. *plus que tant*. more than enough, too much? 29204. adj. (declined or invariable). so much, so many. 9460, 9461, 9495. adv. 1. (+ *que*, + *de*) a) as much, so much, so many (that). (also temp.). 19612, 9468, 9518, b) (always + *que*). often adds the sense of 'until'. 9465, 9474, 19647, c) a lot? 20587, P 20173, d) enough. 21047, 24646, 24661; 2. (qualifying adj.) so, such. 21617, 23008, 24610; 3. (qualifying adv.) so. 21269, 21620, 24284. *tant que*. i) see b), *supra*, ii) as far as, up to. 20063, 20872, 21086. 24470 *Tant qu'a Perceval ne fina* — she did not stop until she reached P., iii) to such an extent (that), so that. 22049, 22749, 23300, iv) (+ *subj.*) however much. 24110, 25124, 29487. (also *ja tant* + *ne* + subj., 29518), v) until, before (with past or future tenses). 9570, 9834, 23128. *tant qu'atant que*. until. 23142. *tant com.* a) as long as. 19990, 23126, 23133, b) as much as. 10116–20252, 21732, 22100 (= as far as). *an tant comme*. while. 25242. *(ne) tant ne quant*. not at all. 20954, 23595, 30735. *por tant*. for this reason. 9719. *tant come*. what, that which. Q 9774. cf. *entretandis*, *tamainte*.

TANVEMANT. adv. finely. 24289.

TASSIEL. n.m.pl. 1. decoration (door)? P 19681; 2. Probably *cassiaus*, M 29460, is an error for *tassiaus*, here 'clasps'.

TECHES. n.f.pl. qualities. 29495.

TEMPRE. adv. early. L 30954; (= soon) L 27573. *tempre et tart.* (both) early and late, all the time. App. VIII S 22.

TEMPREE. see *trampee.*

TENANT. n.m. *an un tenant.* without interruption, without pause. 22075, 22711. adj. strong, resistant. 30802. cf. *tenir* tr. 8.

TENÇON. n.m. argument. *sans tençon.* freely. S 25290. cf. *tancier.*

TENDRIERE. adj.f. (+ *de* + inf.) keen (on), given (to). M 23505.

TENIR. v.tr. 1. hold back, prevent. 9526, 31268; 2. hold, have in one's possession. 9606–19728, 9762, 10205–20347; 3. (+ *a, por*). consider (to be). 9664, 20592, 20785, acknowledge as 22722, 22892, cf. *mal.*; 4. give (shade). 9983–20113; 5. keep (by force, against s.o's will). 21770, 25032, 30754; 6. (*q.ch. de qn.*) a) accuse (s.o. of s.th.)? 28662, b) owe (s.th. to s.o.), hold (s.th. from s.o.). 31456, 31457; 7. continue (with). 28757; 8. resist, withstand. 28817. *tenir chemin, voie,* etc. follow, go along (road, etc.) 9476, 9512, 21027. *tenir ostel.* keep house, entertain. 9809–19909. cf. *tenir d'ostel.* keep in one's household, entourage. 26567 (EPS). *tenir prison (a).* go as a prisoner, give o.s. up as a captive (to). 22057, 23421. *tenir (la) compeignie (de).* keep company (with). 25749, 26277. *tenir cort (1), feste* etc. hold court, etc. 28486, 28551, 28587. *tenir conte de.* take account of, heed. 28504. *tenir parole.* speak. var. 27250. *tenir cort (2).* a) keep on a short rein (horse). P 23554, b) harrass. P 24873. *tenir (de haut).* stretch, be tall. Q 31588, cf. *bracie.* see also *coi, covenance, cuer, droiture, plet.* v.intr. (+ *a*) adjoin, be beside. 27647. v.refl. 1. (+ *de* + inf.) refrain (from). 9621, 23374, 23478; 2. stop, stay, wait. 9635, 29149, S 9487; 3. be? 20387; 4. (+ *a*) keep up (with). 20473, 28805; 5. hold one's own (in battle). 27194; 6. (+ *a, por*) consider o.s. (to be). 29522, 31707; 7. go. 30989; 8. be silent. U 20642; 9. *se tenir ansamble.* join. 23182. see also *coi, piece, po.* Note the inf. *tenoir* in LTV 29604; the variants suggest this may have been the original reading.

TENSER. v.tr. protect, keep (from). L 10079.

(TERDRE). v.refl. rub one's eyes. App. XI K 10.

TERME. n.m. 1. time, deadline. 31890. *au plus cort terme qu'il porroit.* as soon as he could. 28159, 29080. Q 22902 *mes se vos dessirez le terme* — but if you are impatient (to return); 2. (period of) time. M 26738. cf. *termines.*

TERMINES. n.m. 1. end, deadline. 24800 *venuz est vostre termines* — your time has come; 2. (period of) time. var. 26738. cf. *terme.*

TIERCE. n.f. (hour of) tierce, 9 a.m. 19653, 21584, 23547. also *tierce de jor.*

TINTER. v.intr. sound. M 31320.

TIRE. n.f. 1. *a tire.* without (a) pause, without a break. 22186, 23032, 27658; 2. *d'une tire.* of one sort, the same (= evenly matched?). 28831.

TOMBIR. v.intr. shake, reverberate. P 27428.

TOR (1). n.m. 1. circuit. 21079; 2. turn, wheeling about. a) 28244 *An autre voie prist son tor* — he turned off a different way, b) joust, charge. 30262, 30808; 3. somersault. *fere le tor de Mez.* be unhorsed. 28935. This is doubtless the sense of *tornel* also, U 28950; 4. (pl.) times. P 22048. see also *chief.*

TOR (2). n.m. hand's breadth, small quantity. 32354 (EMPU). This word is more usually spelt *dor*, see Roach, note to this line.

TORBLECE.   n.f. cloud, gloom, bad weather. P 25659. This appears to be a *hapax*; it could of course be an error for *torblence*.

TORMANTER.   v.tr. agitate (violently). 32031.

TORMENTE.   n.f. storm. 25779.

TORNEBOËLLE.   n.f. somersault. 30174 (ES).

TORNEL.   see *tor (1)*.

TORNER.   v.tr. 1. turn, direct. 20680, 24773, 24905, see also *chantel. torner a (au) desbarat*. defeat. (KL 10044–) 20180, cf. *desbarat. torner a la chace*. put to flight; 30254; 2. (+ *a*) interpret (as), consider (to be). 30344. v.intr. 1. go, turn away. 9513, 31352; 2. (+ *a*) turn out. 9631 *Tort a gaaing ou tort a perte* — whether it turn out well or badly, for good or ill. see also *declin*; 3. come, go, (re-)turn. 19969, 23574, 25443. *torner arier(e)*. return, turn back. 10155, 21677, var. 21136; 4. turn (aside), be deflected (sword). 21844, 24983; 5. leave = escape, get away (fig.). 28642; 6. 21134 *ce lui torne a grant annui* — it is irritating (troublesome) to him, cf. 22266, 23541. v.refl. go (away), leave, set off. (generally *s'an torner*.) 9522, 19934, 20302. with the same sense as intr. 5., 31308.

TORSSIS.   see *tortis*.

TORT.   n.m. wrong. 9660, 27478. *avoir tort*. be (in the) wrong, make a mistake. 28913. adj. *son tort chemin*. the wrong road, way (because not straight). 21056.

TORTIS.   n.m.pl. torches. 26683. S has *torssis*, cf. God. VIII 749c, *torcheis*.

(TOUSER).   v.tr. cut, trim (hair). var. 23198.

TRAIRE.   see *declin, mal*.

TRAITIE, TRAITIEE.   n.f. bowshot (distance). 24749, 26541, 31588. One wonders if this is meant literally in the latter two instances. The *treciee* of M 24749 and the *traitee* of U 26541 would seem to be errors.

TRAITIS, TRAITIZ, TRESTIZ.   adj. (pl.). 1. long and slim. 20236 (T), 22295; 2. long drawn-out (blast on horn). 26643.

TRAIZ, TREZ.   n.m.pl. moves (chess). 10046–20182.

(TRAMETRE).   v.tr. send. 22972, 23471, 23972.

TRAMPEE.   adj.f. (p.p.). tempered (steel). 29790, var. 23262, Q 26131. cf. *atramper*.

TRECIEE.   Error, see *traitie*.

(TRESALER).   v.intr. fail. KLTV 27706 *se li sens ne li (me) tresva* — if he is (I am) still in his (my) right mind. cf. *sens, tresmüer*.

(TRESGITER).   v.tr. 1. create, construct. 20126 (EPT), KMU 22628; 2. 22035 *Onques bataille a champions Ne fu plus menuz tresgitee* — never was (even) a combat between (picked) champions more fiercely contested.

TRESLIZ.   adj. with triple linking (hauberk). 9682. The meaning of *treliz* in S 26532, applied to a bridge, might be similar, but makes poor sense.

(TRESMÜER).   v.intr. change. U 27706 *Et se li sens ne tresmüa* — and if he? had not lost his mind. cf. *tresaler, sens*.

TRESPANSEZ.   adj. (p.p.). pensive, sunk in thought, worried. 30626, 32576.

TRESPASSER.   v.tr. 1. cross, go through, over. 9858–20008, 21981, 22523; 2. pass by. 20626, 30034, 31606; 3. pass (time). 27011; 4. pass, go along (road). 26070, 31966; 5. (*foi*) go against, betray (duty, obligation). 30628. v.intr. 1. pass (through, by). 20409, 20843, 20987. pres.p. a) *en trespassant*. as they passed one another. 20492, b) as n.m.pl. passers-by. 20390; 2. (temp.) pass, come to an end. 32513; 3. (+ *de*) leave. Q 28706. cf. P 22525 = go?

(TRESSAILLIR).   v.intr. shiver, quiver. 29854. cf. *entresalir*.

TRESSEIGNIÉ. adj. (p.p.). decorated. M 27954. This word appears to be unattested elsewhere. cf. *anseignier, antresaignier, saignié*.

(TRESSÜER). v.intr. break out in a sweat. 28874, S 25847.

TRESTIZ. see *traitis*.

TRESTOR. n.m. detour. *sanz (nul) trestor*. 1. without doubt, certainly. 9868–20016, 26233, 26451, see *retor*; 2. straight, directly. 9967–20097, 27810 (or = 3.?), 28201; 3. (temp.) without delay, directly. 27573. cf. *retor*.

(TRESTORNER). v.intr. change. 10108–20244. v.refl. (+ *de*) turn off, turn aside (from). 9969 (AS). pres.p. as adj. changeable, fickle. 23506.

TRIFOIRE. adj. (n.f.) *uevre trifoire*. 26198. A form of open-work, incrusted (usually) with gold.

(TRIPER). v.intr. jump about, gambol. 27717.

TRISTOIRE. adj. rej.r. 26198. Probably an error.

TRONÇONER. v.tr. App. IX Q 55 *Onques tant na poi tronçoner Que la poïsse resouder*. The normal meaning of *tronçoner* 'break in pieces' would make little sense here, but the dictionaries offer no example of a sense 'put together, place together', or anything similar, which is what we would expect here. This may therefore be an error (replacing *ajoster*, for example) but what is interesting is the enclitic form *na = ne la*, cf. C1 Roach, note to E 5668, and *covescler*.

TRONE, TROSNE. n.m. sky. 25575, 32052.

TROS. n.m.pl. *les tros*. at a trot. P 27643.

U

UEVRE, OVRE, EUVRE, OEVRE. n.f. 1. affair, business. 22081, 27935, 30476; 2. situation. 23233, 24488?; 3. (artistic) work, decoration, etc. 24509, 27651, 28003; (pl.) = embroidery. 24521, cf. 27680? see also *trifoire*; 4. written work (author's source?). Q 29344, M 31595.

US. n.m. fashion, custom. 23173 *a l'us de Cornuaille* — in the Cornish style.

USAIGES. n.m.pl. custom, habits. 32460.

USEZ. adj. (p.p.). accustomed, used (to). 30476.

V

VA. see *voie*.

VAIR. n.m. vair, fur of grey and white squirrel. 22588. adv. 1. blue-grey, clear (eyes). var. 22296, L 10097; 2. dapple-grey? (horse). L 22401. The form *vers* may also correspond to this word in 22296 (E), 27271 (EKS), while the *vert* of 30807, 30815, applied to arms and armour, is probably due to confusion of *vair* (or *ver*) 'shining, polished', with *vert* 'green'. On this point, see A. J. Holden's note to *Ipomedon* 6034, in his edition.

VALOR, VALLOR. n.f. 1. merit, good quality or qualities (person or thing). 9540, 9980, 23373, and, by extension; 2. courage, valour. 9585?, 25001, 31799. These meanings are not always easy to distinguish.

VANTAILLE. n.f. Originally a flap of chain-mail, attached to the hauberk, covering the lower part of the face. Later, the lower portion of the helm (possibly attached separately), perforated to allow respiration. It is impossible to be certain which is intended in this text, cf. 9742, 25008, but the former is perhaps more likely.

VAVASOR. n.m. minor nobleman. 21019, 22458, 22514.

VENIR.   v.intr. 1. come, arrive. (also *an venir*, v.refl. *s'an venir*, with no change in sense.) 19938, 20092, 10010. *bien veigniez.* welcome. 29886; 2. (temp.) 20911 *Tant que ce vint androit midi* — until noon. cf. 22248, 26412, cf. 21069 *tant . . . Que li vespres vint aproichant* — unti it drew near to vespers. 27159 *Qant vandra ancui au partir* might be a similar (impers.) usage; 3. happen. 25212. *venir sus (a).* attack. 19848. *venir au desus (de).* defeat, get the better of. 20882, 30656. *venir au repantir de.* come to regret. 21199, 25597. *venir a mervoille (a qn.).* amaze, surprise. 22812, cf. Q 9664 *il li vint a grant ennui* — it vexed him greatly, cf. *torner.* see also *chief, gré, miauz.*

VENT.   see *voie.*

VENTELER.   v.intr. float in the wind (banners). App. VII KTV 7, KTV 24, KTV 53.

VENTREILLIER.   v.intr. roll about, lie. App. VII TV 914. A borrowing from C1, see Roach, note to 27055, cf. C1 E 9338.

VEOIR, VEÏR.   v.tr. see. 9501, 9592, 19714. imper. *vez, veez . . . ci.* see (here), here is (etc.). 9516, 10193, 22717. (= Mod.Fr. *voici*). also *veez . . . la.* 25252. 31009 *je ne voie l'eure Que . . . soie* — I do not see when I shall be, I do not envisage (ever) being. p.p. *veüe.* visible. 23147. pres.p. 24898 *voient ses iauz* — before his (very) eyes, cf. 26979, 31895. v.intr. *veoir a qn. fere q.ch.* see s.o. do s.th. 23221 (ES). *veoir de qn. que* (+ v.) see that s.o. is . . . 23298.

VEREL, VERROIL, VERROILL.   n.m. lock. bolt. var. 9558.

VERGONDER.   v.refl. be put to shame. 24802.

VERMEILLON.   n.m. vermilion. 32288.

VERMOIL.   adj. (subject case, pl., *vermaux, vermauz*) also as n.m. red, vermilion. While it is natural enough to find this word applied to blood, 20826, 22362, the face, 22297, 23491, and even flame, 25621, 25739, as well as a host of other objects (cloths, armour, buildings, crosses), it is more surprising to find it qualifying the sun, 25416, P 27014, and gold, 9556–19682, 9565, 24759; cf. however, Eng. 'red gold'. The use of *fin* or *esmeré* (or both) with every one of the examples of *or vermoil* effectively rules out the possibility that this corresponds to Mod.F. *vermeil* 'silver-gilt'.

VERS.   see *vair.*

VERTU.   n.f. 1. force, strength, power. 26218, 26719, 27136. *a, par vertu.* forcefully, with force. 20312 (E), 21806. also *de grant vertuz,* with the same sense, 23246, but this is the reading of E only. *de tel vertu.* with such force. 23990, 24339, 24416, cf. 31936; 2. 27612 (E) — the sense of the var. here is 'quality, property' (of precious stones); the sense of E is less certain, perhaps 'relics'.

VERTUAL.   adj. powerful, efficacious. 31211 (EPS). The reading of M, where *vertual* is n.m., (= 'qualities, properties, efficacity'?), may well be an error. It is not supported by P, as it would appear from God., who quotes both; the reading of P given by Potvin (33543), recorded by God., seems to be an invention of the editor, probably influenced by M.

VERVIELES.   n.f.pl. staples or loops (into which door-bolt slides). P 19679.

VESPRE.   n.m. (hour of) vespers, 6 p.m., used loosely for 'evening, dusk'. 21069, 24433, 26402. n.f.pl. vespers, bell(s) for vespers. 26930.

VESPREE.   n.f. late afternoon, evening, dusk, nightfall. 21282, 22288, 23536.

VESTIR.   n.m. garment. rej.r. 29437.

VÏAIRE.   n.m. face. 21325, 32464.

VIAX.   adv. at least. TV 24322. cf. *seviau.*

(VILENER).   v.tr. insult, illtreat. S 28678. v.intr. behave basely, badly. 22013.

VILONS.   n.m.pl. Q 31314. villages? Perhaps for *vilo(i)rs,* cf. God. VIII 244c.

VIONOIZ. n.m.pl. 9472 (A). Doubtless a derivative of Lat. VIBURNUM (as A. W. Thompson suggested, see *Speculum* 49 (1974), 145), with the sense '(land covered in) clumps of guelder-rose or wayfaring-tree'.

VIS. n.m. *ce li est vis, ce m'est vis*, etc. (as) it seems to him (etc.), in his (etc.) opinion, etc. 9467, 9474, 19653. also *vis li estoit*. 25619, cf. 26159. see *avis*.

VOIDIER, (VUIDIER). v.tr. empty. 22742, 22797, var. 28484. *voidier le champ*. leave the field (of battle). 27098 (E), cf. *vuidier (la) place*. retreat, give ground. KQU 9760.

VOIE. n.f. 1. road, track, way. 19894, 9898–20040, 10227. *an la voie*. on the way. 21033. *la droite voie*. the right way (the shortest way). 25972, 26071, 26281, cf. *tort*. also *a droite voie*, 26214, *leur droite voie*, 28008. see also *changier, haster, metre, piece, prandre, tenir*; 2. (fig.) a) course of action. 22895, b) *an male voie*. on the path of evil. 25800; 3. travelling, journey. 23049, 27365, 30940. *estre a la voie*. be on one's way, set off. 24061. *tote(s) voie(s)*. anyway, in any case, all the same. 26730, 27590, 30774. *(ne savoir) ne va ne voie, ne vent ne voie (de)*. (know) nothing at all (of). App. VII TV 1250.

VOISIEE. adj.f. S 9959. clever, subtle? Perhaps p.p. meaning 'tricked'. Neither meaning makes much sense in the context.

VOLOIR, VOLLOIR. v.intr. (sometimes + inf.; + *que* + subj.) wish, want (to). 19631, 20602, 21432. *volsist ou non*. whether he like it or not, willy-nilly. 9685, cf. *volent ou non* 30278. 10193–20331 *que me volez?* — what do you want of me? 28717 *Voudra a pié ou a cheval* — as he wishes, on horseback or on foot, cf. MQ *voille a p. ou voille a c.*. inf. as n.m. (also pl.). desire, will, wishes. 21892, 22751, 22918. *a son voloir*. to one's heart's content, to one's liking, as one pleases, etc. 21291, 27695, 29334.

VOLU. adj. vaulted. 22454, S 31918.

VOSTE, VOTE. n.f. vault, vaulted building. 20379, 20382, 20386. *a voste*. vaulted. 21156.

VOSTEZ. adj. (p.p.). vaulted. 20144.

VOSTIZ. adj.pl. vaulted. 10012, 22625.

VUIDIER. see *voidier*.

W

WIDIER. see *voidier*.

X

XINOPLE. see *sinople*.

Y

YDE. n.f. (or m.). terror, fear. 31149 (ELP).

YNDE. adj. indigo-blue. 22990, 24484, 32203.

Note on (a)arbrer

This family of words is very sparsely attested. For *arbrer* (v.intr.) T-L quotes one example from the *Vie de S. Gregoire* (ed. P. Meyer in *Romania* 12 (1883), 145 ff.) 2478. God. quotes one example, from *Partenopeus de Blois* 3065. FEW notes instances in the Continuations (presumably TV 13127, cf. Foulet's glossary) and *Foulque de Candie* 5377. AND notes *Ipomedon* 5059 (= Holden 5061).

For *aarbrer* (v.intr.) God. quotes one example, with the definition 'grimper dans des arbres', in which he is followed by FEW. In the context given, this example could easily mean 'se cabrer', but I have been unable to trace God.'s reference to verify this. *aarbrer* (as v.refl.) occurs in *Troie*, var. 23635, but is not noted by the dictionaries. One surmises that this was the example G. Paris had in mind when he said (a propos of *enarbrar*, *Romania* 7 (1878), 467) '. . . il s'agit d'un cheval qui s'aarbre, comme on disait en ancien français'; but he may have known of other examples, variants in other texts.

For *enarbrer* (v.refl.), FEW notes *Troie* (23635, no doubt) and three examples in *Li Fet des Romains* (p. 490 l. 27, 661 12, 696 4), printed as *s'en arbrer*.

For *arbri(i)er*, *arbroier*, T-L attests v.intr. and refl. ('sich bäumen'), with examples from *Fergus*, *Doon de Maience* and Thomas's *Tristan*, while God. has v.refl. ('se cabrer') from the *Roman de Jules César* and ('se plier, se tordre') *Doon*. AND (under *arbrer*) notes the forms *arbreier*, *arbroier* (intr.), and lists *Le Sermon de Guischart de Beauliu* 1318 ('rise up (in anger)'). FEW (*arbroier*) mentions only Thomas's *Tristan* (Turin[1] 207) ('se cabrer'). There is an interesting occurrence in *Fergus* (MS P, var. to 5904), where the context *Li chevaliers son cop arbrie* suggests the verb is tr., meaning 'raise, prepare to strike', though cf. T-L.

Note on foillolé

The dictionaries are rather vague about the exact meaning of this word, when it is applied to horse-trappings, etc. The passage in *Durmart* 9999–10008 suggests that one colour (here, green) is *foillolé* on another (here, silver). That is, it would seem to be cut and sewn on in small pieces (*fuelletes*), so that the silver is hidden, but with the stitching only on one side, like a hinge, so that the silver shows through the green when the pieces move in the wind, as here. I find Brault expresses much the same view in *Early Blazon*, concluding that *fallolé* is probably synonymous with *papeloné*, 'scaly'.

Note on pleissier

I find my supposition is confirmed by Eng. 'plash', 'pleach'.

APPENDIX I

CORRECTIONS TO THE TEXT

The following list of *corrigenda* is mainly based on a close examination of the base manuscript, E. Most of the errors in the text are clearly attributable to slips at the printing stage, or to minor alterations which have crept in between the original transcription and the final version, to omissions of variants, etc. In the very rare instances where the editor has clearly misread the text, this can be directly attributed to the disadvantages of being able to work only from photographs, and these corrections are only possible after a close inspection of the actual manuscript, usually with the aid of a magnifying glass.

I have divided these *corrigenda* into four types: 1. (a) corrections to E which affect the actual reading of the text. (b) corrections to E which affect only the presentation of the text. This includes changed spellings, and also several instances of a letter or letters which were not legible in the editor's copy, or when that copy was made, but which can now be read. 2. corrections to E which affect only the variants, that is to say words affecting the reading of E, but where that reading should be, or has already been, rejected. 3. corrections to other MSS, which, naturally, affect only the variants. Some of these corrections are conjectural, i.e. not verified, and are marked as such by an asterisk. Excluded are a certain number of remarks on the readings of E, which can not be called corrections as such, cf. Chapter 3, note 22. Each correction will be given in the form of a line-reference, followed by the correct reading, with the corrected word(s) or letter(s) underlined, then by any remarks or explanations.

1.(a)

19881. Ma <u>terre</u> est vostre et quanque j'ai.   The word <u>terre</u> is written very small, with the letters very close together, whence the editor's reading <u>mie</u>.

20792. Si con li rain i <u>acroichoient</u>.   A very close scrutiny reveals that this is indeed the reading, in spite of the note to this line.

23431. Puet estre el l'a <u>ansorceré</u>.   It is impossible to justify the editor's decision to read <u>ansorceté</u>, both when comparing the relevant letter to other examples of <u>r</u> and <u>t</u>, and in the light of his choice in other, similar cases, see <u>infra</u>.

23648. An <u>celle</u> grant forest dela.   The scribe may have intended to write <u>-st</u>, and indeed the letters incline towards one another in a way which might suggest this; however, the <u>t</u> has no cross-stroke, and I feel <u>celle</u> is the only possible reading, as well as coinciding with the other MSS. In 26232, <u>celle</u> is written in a very similar manner; indeed, one might even think the second l̲ was crossed like a t̲, but I would print celle in both cases.

25524. Celle jure Dieu de̲ lesus.

26451. Je voldroie sanz nul trestor.   There is a certain amount of confusion possible when deciding if a particular letter is a c̲ or a t̲, in MS E. In this case I would give the scribe the benefit of the doubt, and read trestor, which I would print, cf. the reading of U, and 26237 etc.

26580. Litorés de Baraguidan.   In spite of my remark concerning the previous correction, I am certain that in this case we have a t̲ and not a c̲. One wonders if this character is not actually Li tousés de Baradigan (or Garadigan), i.e. Li vallés de Baladingan in Le Bel Inconnu, cf. the readings of L and TV 26580, and LMQTUV at 29054.

28140. Tant que̲ li jors esclarciz fu.

28672. Si jugiez se j'é tort ou non.   This is a similar case to 19881, and no doubt is possible on close scrutiny; it is necessary to read j'é̲ rather than je̲, cf. MS S.

30704. De dras de soie eschequetez. This is the counterpart of 23431; there is absolutely no doubt in my mind that we have a t̲ in this case, cf. MS U.

31806. Un jor fu a un̲ suen repere. MS a .i. s. r.

1.(b)

21756. Belle fait il et je de cui.   In this instance the MS has been repaired, the wrinkle mentioned by Roach presumably having cracked; as a result, many letters which were not visible before can now be read, most of them clearly. At the same time, some letters which Roach was able to read are now illegible, but I have taken no account of this. With the exception of 21798 and 21820, Roach's conjectures are confirmed in every case, and each of these corrections, up to 21833, affects only the presentation of words or letters bracketed by the editor.

21757. Me doi esmaier ne (dout)er̲.

21758. Certes sire nou quier cel̲er.

21759. Fait elle si li prant a dire̲.

21772. Dont j'e formant lou cuer marri.

21796. Isnellemant son̲ haubert vest.

21797. L'iaume lace l'espee̲ çaint.

21798. Et jure Dieu qui l(a)isus maint.   An i̲ is clearly visible beside the end of what must be the a̲; the spelling laisus is common in E, cf. 24026, etc.

21799. Que son ostel ne la(i̲)ra mie.

21800. Por nule cho(s̲)e qu'an li die.

21807. Vasal qu(i̲) vos̲ a ci conduit.

21808. Bien seroiz herbergiez annuit.

21812. Lou che(v̲)al voit si s'an aïre.

21813. Por ce que̲ sus l'erbe pessoit.

21814. D'une maçue̲ qu'il tenoit.

21815. Li done̲ un cop deresoné.

21817. Lors n'ot (q̲)u'irier am Perceval.

21818. Son escu̲ prant et vient aval.

21820. Som̲ bon cheval voudra vangier.   There is no doubt that the letter is m̲, not n̲.

21824. Li jeanz̲ le tient molt por fol.

21825. De ce̲ que einsint vers lui vient.

21826. Sa maçue̲ ampoigniee tient.

21828. Si l'a̲ tout contremont levee.

21830. <u>Mais</u> il l'a fait a lui faillir.

21831. Que <u>ganchiz</u> est de l'autre part.

21833. Car <u>s'il</u> li puet un cop ataindre.

22474. Or me devez <u>lo</u> vostre dire.

22790. An la salle ot grant <u>bastestal</u>.

23135. Dou Saint Graal la <u>verit(é)</u>.   This is surprising; although there is a trace of an <u>e</u> at the end of the line, it is the merest scratching, hardly in ink at all, and certainly not the work of the scribe, nor a proper correction.

23224. Et <u>li</u> chevalier li escrie.   This is visible through a film of some sort of deposit.

23473. <u>Pe(r)cevaux</u> qui ne vos het mie.   The scribe has omitted the <u>r</u> in his abbreviation: <u>Pec'</u>.

23686. Fait Percevaux <u>Je</u> ne savroie.

23774. De <u>loint</u> choisist an une angarde.   cf. my remark on 26580.

23830. Sa <u>soreur</u> baille lou destrier.

25357. <u>S'i(l)</u> vos plait annuit remanez.

25732. <u>Pe(r)cevaux</u> molt tost descendi.   cf. 23473.

25840. Qui d'autrui chose n'ait <u>anvie</u>.

26193. <u>Out regardé</u> si s'an torna.   Although Roach has accurately reproduced E's reading, I would maintain it, and print as indicated.

26941. Fait Percevaux <u>mes</u> pansez d'el.

27057. Jostes ancontres <u>et</u> mellees.   The abbreviation <u>7</u> is now visible, probably after a MS repair.

27097. Tenoit ou poing <u>le</u> branc d'acier.   cf. 27057.

27531. Fu ainsint quant le vos <u>baillai</u>.   cf. 23224.

27795. Endemantiers que g'iere <u>ainsin</u>.   The <u>a</u> is written so close to the preceding <u>e</u> as to appear to be a single stroke, and so with the following <u>i</u> looks like <u>u</u>; one should print <u>ainsi</u> or <u>ainsin</u>, of which I would favour the latter.

27839. Et la teste si l'<u>am</u> porta.

28101. Et <u>il lor</u> respont gentemant.   cf. 23224.

28668. <u>Bag(o)medés</u> sanz nul desroi.   cf. 23473.

28807. Proie qu'il a de <u>loint</u> veüe.   cf. 23774.

29015. Et de toz biens bien <u>anteichiez</u>.

29728. Qui molt est <u>coriageus</u> et fiers.   cf. note to this line. It would appear that the scribe wrote <u>coriajeus</u>, and that he, or someone else, then wrote a g over the <u>j</u>, and almost on top of the <u>a</u>, giving a reading <u>corigeus</u> or <u>coriageus</u>, of which I would print the latter, although it is not an orthodox spelling.

29782. Mais que li <u>Ch(evalie)rs</u> Petiz.   The scribe omitted the tilde after the <u>ch</u>.

30190. Li ranc <u>asamblent</u> tot a fet.   cf. 23224.

30540. <u>Enmi</u> lou chemin aresté.

31054. Gauvains lo voit vers lui <u>s'adresce</u>.

31776. Et bien quarante <u>ch(evalie)rs</u>.   cf. 29782.

2.

Variants only.

21697. E. iert <u>deseus</u> g. (or <u>de sens</u>?)

22352. E. L'<u>un</u> a l'a.

22643. E. <u>Que</u> n. i.   Some editors might leave <u>que</u> for <u>qui</u>, but for simplicity and conformity I have included this and similar examples as var.

22695. E. <u>Que</u> m. a.

23318. E. <u>et</u> ie uaurai.   and not <u>Et</u> ie.

23490. E. Li rois <u>rist</u> s'an fu.
23880. E. d. parut li <u>jors</u>.
24293. E. <u>.I.</u> pandoit. The I·is clearly flanked by the full stops used to denote numerals.
24639. E. no variant. Given the above-mentioned difficulty there can be in distinguishing <u>c</u> and <u>t</u>, I would give the benefit of the doubt to the scribe in this case.
24832. E. no variant. The word is clearly <u>arbre</u>, although the scribe's habit of often crossing his <u>b</u>'s explains the editor's error.
25043. E. Par t. r. <u>et</u> par t. m.
25137. E. l'ot <u>fermee</u>.
25429. E. <u>Que</u> m. an.
25436. E. <u>Que</u> sus e.
25848. E. de la <u>puor</u>.
25883. E. <u>Que</u> m. b.
26587. E. iert <u>cei</u> m. There is an extra stroke here.
26606. E. <u>d</u>. ciel ne.
26788. E. <u>Ce</u> v.
26957. E. <u>Ainz</u> s. The <u>i</u> is even dotted.
27145. E. j. <u>anssamble</u> o. This original <u>ansansamble</u> was corrected by an erasure, but the second <u>s</u> was inadvertently left; one could, of course, print this form.
27369. E. est <u>garees</u> d.
27421. E. Qui <u>anorte</u> an avoit m.
27739. E. le b. <u>cers</u> anz.
28131. E. <u>Que</u> de b.
28270. E. ne li <u>portoit</u>. This is clearly a <u>t</u>; if we print <u>r</u>, how are we to justify printing <u>ansorceté</u> in 23431?
28761. E. <u>Que</u> de ce.
28981. E. <u>A celle</u> ce s.
29325. E. le vos <u>queer</u> c.
29338. E. no variant. See note to this line. We can clearly read <u>Ne d( )ule riens</u>; what we find between the <u>d</u> and the <u>u</u> looks like an <u>a</u> corrected to <u>en</u>, and we should print de nule.
29423. E. Si <u>clerc</u> s. This is clear, although trivial.
29471. E. h. <u>m</u>. dou d.
29695. E. Un p. <u>porroie</u> f. While the scribe may have intended to write <u>por joie</u>, he clearly wrote a double <u>r</u>.
29702. E. <u>Que tot</u>.
29858. E. <u>si</u> sera. There is some doubt possible here, but the relevant letter appears to be an <u>l</u> corrected to an <u>s</u>.
29961. E. C. <u>ieestuz</u> et. The scribe certainly appears to have written <u>i</u> (not dotted), then <u>e</u>, rather than <u>v</u>.
30247. E. <u>Des</u> trestout.
30275. E. Et <u>abatre</u> am. It would be possible to read <u>abarré</u>. The editor is mistaken in suggesting that E's reading is hypometric.
30830. E. Le c. de son <u>de son</u> d.
31112. E. <u>Que</u> t.
31305. E. li r. <u>ealarras</u>? This certainly appears to be the MS reading; the first <u>a</u> and the <u>l</u> are very close together, but the initial letter is <u>e</u>, not <u>c</u>.
32512. E. li <u>mangieris</u>. This is the theoretical reading, since the MS reads <u>mang'is</u>.

3.

9486.   K. Li chevaliers q.*   I assume this is actually the variant of K; it is not the reading of L, see Appendix II *infra*, and cf. MQ.

9764.   MQSU. cil (Q il) <u>o</u>. t. la g.*

9948.   <u>L</u>. Fuiés quele vos.*   Or perhaps KL? This is the reading of L, certainly, but I have been unable to check K.

20012.   P. <u>ni</u> peust nagier sans nages.*

21397.   U. sont <u>tuit</u> ensemble.

21631.   KLMPQST. <u>resgardee</u>?*   E certainly has <u>esgardee</u>, but so does P, according to Potvin.

23210.   for P, read Q.

23231.   KMU. Por co que v. en a. <u>ris</u>.*

23912.   read (P <u>Quant</u>, and U <u>Bien sai</u> at end of lines.

24524.   KLMQTUV add Trestotes le <u>claiment</u> (MQ etc.   This is the spelling of U; I have been unable to check K.

25555.   K. <u>Ne</u> destre en.*

30018.   MQ: <u>Sa idier</u> le f. nu (Q nut) i.   The reading of MQ should be understood, not as <u>S'aidier</u> (so Roach), which leaves a hypometric line, but as <u>S'a Idier</u>.

For further corrections to the variants of L, up to A 10268, see Appendix II.

It should perhaps be pointed out that, in general, the 1530 prose version is of little assistance for resolving textual or manuscript difficulties. However, it does confirm the reading 'acroichoient' in 20792 (1530: accrochoient).

APPENDIX II

TRANSCRIPTION OF C2ɪ IN MS L

This transcription is included for several reasons. Given that I believe C1ii/C2i is a unit, and that the break comes at A 10268, it seems logical to extend the dual L/A presentation of Roach's C1 SRed. up to that point. L has a fairly independent version of C2i, and no full transcription exists. It is an important piece of text in that, as stated above, L may well give the most primitive version of C1ii: if this is the case, it may also be true for C2i. Finally, the transcription allows easy reference for the evidence quoted in Chapter 2 concerning the C1/C2 division.

It is a straightforward transcription of the manuscript, with the usual resolution of abbreviations, etc. No corrections have been made whatsoever; few would be necessary, and they have been left to the discretion of the reader. The punctuation broadly follows that of Roach. The line-numbering is continued from Roach's edition of C1 (L); the numbers in brackets refer to his edition of C2 (A), for convenient cross-reference. Underlining indicates a difference between this transcription and the readings of L indicated by Roach's variants and App. II. It should be noted that the new foliation of L has been used, so that Roach's 161 now = 164, 162 = 165, etc. Notes will be found at the end of the transcription.

D'iaus deus le conte ci vos lais,	
Si rediromes ci aprés	
De Perceval la verité,	
Qui ot en tante terre esté	9512 (9460)
Et trovee ot tante aventure	
Et fait mainte bataille dure	
Dont il avoit l'oneur eüe.	
Un jor ot sa voie tenue	9516
Tant qu'en une forest entra,	
Mais saciés bien c'ain n'esgarda,	
Ce li est vis, jor de sa vie,	
Forest qui tant fust effreïe.	9520 (9468)
Ensint le covint cevaucier	
.ii. jors sans boivre et sans mengier	
Par bois, par landes, par riflois,	
Par bruieres, par jenestois,	9524
Enclins, famellos et pensis,	

Tant c'au tier jor, ce m'est avis,
Entra en un cemin ferré
Et l'a tenu et tant erré   9528 (9476)
166c   Que il vint en .i. quarefor.
Iluec trova .i. veneor
Seur .i. caceor bauçant sor;
A son col ot .i. rice cor   9532
De fin ivoire, gros et blanc;
.I. berserez tot baut au sanc
Seur le ceval triers soi portoit;
Coples de ciens que il menoit   9536 (9484)
Ot devant lui bien jusc'a vint.
Le chevalier qui vers lui vint
Choisi, s'estut por lui atendre
Et por les noveles aprendre   9540
Des dehés qu'il ooit orer,
Ses savoit il sans demander.
Percevaus vint vers lui arrant,
Sel salua tot maintenant.   9544 (9492)
Cil dist: 'Je ne vos salu mie,
Chaitis! qui par vostre folie
Avés mis tantes gens a mal.
Jamais en nule cort roial   9548
N'avrois en vostre vie honeur,
Qu'a la cort le Roi Pesceur
Fustes, et n'enquesistes mie
Les secrés: ce fu grans folie,   9552 (9500)
Que la lance sainier veïstes
Devant vos, et si n'enquesistes
Por quel aquoison el sainoit,
Ne del Graal o il aloit.   9556
Se vos l'eüsiés demandé,
Cest regne eüsiés restoré,
166d   Et mis en joie et en leece
Ciaus qui or sont en grant tristece.   9560 (9508)
Peciés vos i a fait faillir,
Molt par vos en devés haïr.
Fuiés vos de ma compagnie,
Dolereus, et ne tenés mie   9564
Ceste voie: tornés alleurs,
Car ce seroit vostre doleurs;
Alés ariere maintenant.
Veés les esclos ci devant   9568 (9516)
D'un ceval a envers ferré.
S'il vos avoient tant mené
Que trovisiés le cor pendu
Au portal, s'averiés perdu   9572
Vostre pris, et sans nule faille
N'en torneriiés sans bataille.'
Atant s'en part delivrement;

Et Percevaus plus n'i atent,   9576 (9524)
Ains dist: 'La u je cuit morir
Iroi, ne m'en puet nus tenir,
Quant teus honte m'est avenue
Qui par tot le mont est seüe.'   9580
Ainsi cevauce molt iriés.
Ne s'estoit gaires eslongiés
Quant devant lui voit .i. castel
Enmi la lande, fort et bel,   9584 (9532)
Et n'i vit borde ne maison
Fors la porprise d'environ.
Les murs voit blans et nués et haus,
Ne leur pooit mal faire assaus;   9588

167a Et si n'avoit entor fosé,
Fors plaine terre et molt biau pre.
Sor le portal ot une tor
Qui estoit de molt grant valor,   9592 (9540)
N'i ot tor ne torete plus;
Porte i ot d'un fust d'ibenus.
Si tos com Percevaus le vit,
A soi meïsme pense et dit   9596
Que molt est en gast leu assis
Li castiaus, ce li est avis.
Tant erra que il vient devant,
N'i trova nule rien vivant;   9600 (9548)
Entor ala tot maintenant
Tant c'au portal revint errant,
Si vit la porte bien fremee.
Molt longement l'a esgardee,   9604
C'ainc mais nul jor de son aé
Ne vit nule de tel biauté,
N'ovree de si ciere ovrengne;
Car de fin or vermel d'Espagne   9608 (9556)
Fu trestote la ferreüre,
Li corueil et l'enclaveüre.
.I. gros anel d'or nöelé
Enmi la porte avoit fremé.   9612
Signeur, a cel anel pendoit
.I. cors d'ivoire, blans estoit
Plus que n'est fleurs de lis ne nois,
Par la guige d'uns ciers orfrois.   9616 (9564)
De fin or vermel ert bendés
Et trop ricement atornés.

167b Quant Percevaus le voit, si dist
Que ja puis Dex ne li aït   9620
Que il d'iluec se partira
Tant que le cor soné avra.
Son hiaume a maintenant osté,
Et quant son vis a desarmé,   9624 (9572)
Le cor commence a regarder,

Sel prent tantos sans demorer
Et le sona si durement
Et si cler et si hautement 9628
Que la contree d'environ
Dona par le cor grant reson.
N'a mie longement esté,
Puis que il ot le cor soné, 9632 (9580)
Qu'il oï el castel aler
Gent, ce li fu vis, et parler,
Et que uns dist: 'Avés oï?
Ainc mais cis cors ne sona ci! 9636
Cil est plains de molt grant valor
Qui l'a soné par tel vigor.'
Puis dist: 'Faites tost aporter
Mes armes a mon cors armer.' 9640 (9588)
Et Percevaus, qui l'escouta
Estrangement se mervella
De la parole qu'ot oïe,
Car de celui ne veoit mie. 9644
Lors garda par une overture,
Qui fu les une desmointure
De la porte, si vit passer
.I. vaslet, et li vit porter 9648 (9596)
167c Un rice escu de geules fines,
A un lion ranpant d'ermines;
La guige en fu tote d'orfrois.
D'un molt rice paile grigois 9652
Estoit li escus enarmés
Molt cointement, et atornés.
En une sale s'en entra
Li vaslés ki l'escu porta. 9656 (9604)
Bien vos puis dire sans mentir
Que Percevaus vausist tenir
Defors a la porte l'escu,
Car de grant biauté l'ot veü. 9660
A la porte fu longement
Et sans compagnie de gent.
Et quant il ot grant piece esté,
Si prist le cor et ra soné 9664 (9612)
Plus cler et plus haut que devant.
Adonc oï tot maintenant
.I. home qui dist: 'Dex, merci!
Certes, mervelles ai oï. 9668
Li miudres chevaliers del monde,
En cui gregneur proëce abonde,
A soné le cor, bien le sai:
Encor ancui le proverai.' 9672 (9620)
Atant se tint de plus parler.
Et cil s'esforce de soner
La tierce fois pas grant aïr.

175

A itant a veü issir	9676
Hors de la sale .i. chevalier	
Armé sor .i. molt grant destrier,	
167d Tot covert d'un vermel samit;	
Onques nus hom mellor ne vit.	9680 (9628)
Molt vint aprés lui chevaliers,	
Vaslés, serjans et escuiers.	
Tot a gaaing u tot a perte,	
Lors fu molt tost la porte overte.	9684
Quant Percevaus les a coisis,	
El pre ariere s'est guencis	
Et se tint sos .i. olivier;	
Iluec atent le chevalier.	9688 (9636)
Et cil s'en ist molt abrievés	
De la porte, trop bel armés,	
Qar mervelles li avenoit	
Une corone qu'il avoit	9692
Sor son hiaume molt bien asise.	
Pieres i ot de mainte guise	
En la corone de tos sens;	
Au faire estut molt grant porpens.	9696 (9644)
C'estoit signes qu'il estoit rois,	
Sires d'Irlande et de Norois.	
Si tos com il en fu issus,	
De pluisors gens fu coneüs	9700
Li escus que Percevaus ot,	
Et le destrier qu'il cevaucot.	
Molt en ot el cuer grant dor	
Li rois, et dist par grant amor:	9704 (9652)
'Biaus sire Dex, li miens amis	
Ou est remés, n'en quel païs?	
Puis que l'envoiai en Bretagne,	
N'oï de lui veraie ensagne.	9708
168a Mais a ses armes que voi la	
(Ne sai qui est cil qui les a)	
Sai or bien qu'il est pris u mors;	
Se jo ai duel, n'est mie tors.'	9712 (9660)
A ces paroles vint el pre,	
Le chevalier a desf'ié;	
Et li chevaliers lui ausi,	
Qui or le tient a anemi.	9716
Atant fierent des esperons;	
Plus joins que .i. esmerellons	
S'entrevient lances baisies	
Et les enarmes enpognies,	9720 (9668)
Les escus joins devant as pis.	
Li pres fu biaus, vers et floris,	
Et li ceval fort et corant.	
En leur ravine plus tres grant	9724
S'encontrerent li chevalier,	

Qui molt erent hardi et fier;
Si jostent vigerosement
Par vertu et bien vistement.   9728 (9676)
Li chevaliers del cor brisa
Jusqu'es poins sa lance et froissa;
Et Percevaus l'a si feru
Que il li a percié l'escu   9732
Bien haut endroit le gros del pis.
Seur le hauberc qui ert treslis
Si roidement asist la lance
Que maintenant sans demorance,   9736 (9684)
Vausist u non, l'a jus porté
Trestot envers enmi le pre.
168b Si com il dut otre passer,
Si li estut a encontrer.   9740
Li ceval vont de tel aïr
Qu'a la terre le fist caïr
Otot le sien destrier ensamble.
Tele ire en a que tos an tranble,   9744 (9692)
Si resaut sus molt vistement,
De son arçon l'espee prent;
N'a pas traite la rice espee
Qui li avoit esté donee.   9748
Tant fu iriés vers son destrier
Que la teste li vint trencier,
Et li dist: 'Bien m'avés honi,
C'onques mais mes cors ne caï;   9752 (9700)
Non feïst il mie sans vos,
Dans ceval mal aventuros,'
Fait se il. En meïsme l'eure
Li corut li chevaliers seure,   9756
Et il l'atent et cil le fiert,
Qui par grant ire se requiert.
Molt l'asaut vigerosement,
Et Percevaus bien redesfent   9760 (9708)
Son cors a l'espee d'acier.
Lors veïsiés hiaumes trencier,
Et comencier si fort bataille
Que je vos di de voir sans faille   9764
C'on ne vit mais si grant estor
De deus chevaliers a nul jor,
Ne si grans caus, ne si morteus,
Ne si pesans, ne si crüeus.   9768
168c Quant Percevaus conoist et voit
Celui qui si se conbatoit,
Et qu'il est si bons chevaliers,
Si preus et si fors et si fiers,   9772
Si le dota molt durement.
Lors se desfendi sagement,
Et se porpense que peu vaut

Envers celui qui si l'asaut   9776
Et requiert par si grant vigor
Qu'a fine force et par estor   (9716)
Li tost place, et fait tel anui
Qu'il porprent terre deseur lui,   9780
Et le demaine laidement
Quel part qu'il viut a son talent.
Por tant assés plus l'en dotoit
A ce que il li redonoit   9784
Grans cols par la u l'atagnoit.
Tant qu'en son cuer bien s'aparçoit
Qu'il est mors s'il ne se desfent,
Si prent et cuer et hardement;   9788 (9724)
Seure li cort otot l'espee,
Si l'en dona si grant colee
Amont el hiaume reluisant
Que cil en vait tot cancelant;   9792
Adonc la requeut a ferir.
Par hardement et par aïr
Li a l'escu tot detrencié
Que il avoit tant covoitié;   9796
Mais cil l'en rent le gerredon,
Car bien .vii. cols en .i. randon
168d De l'espee li done tex,
Li mains caisans est molt crüeus.   9800 (9732)
Menu se fierent et sovent;
La les veïsiés durement
Sacier et boter et enpaindre;
Molt se paine cascuns sans faindre   9804
De son compagnon damagier.
Les hiaumes font fondre et ploier
Et les cercles d'or jus voler,
Les mailles des coifes entrer   9808 (9740)
Es frons, qu'il sainent durement
Par les ventailles, car sovent
S'entrebleçoient au hurter,
Au partir et a l'asambler.   9812
Tant dura la bataille issi,
Signeur, que por verté vos di
Que trestuit cil qui esgardoient
Por la pitié d'iaus .ii. ploroient   9816 (9748)
Et sont angoisseus sans mentir
Que il nes osent departir.
Por le peril u il les voient,
A poi que d'ire ne desvoient.   9820
Tant a duré des deus vasaus
Li dure estors que Percevaus
Senti bien de son chevalier
Qu'il le faisoit afoibloiier.   9824 (9756)
Lués maintenant si le hasta

Et si durement le grava,
Que bien li poist u mal li face,
Li tost tot a force la place, 9828
169a Sel fait ariere raüser.
Del brant qu'il tint trencant et cler
Le fiert si menu et sovent
Que cil, oiant tote sa gent, 9832 (9764)
Li dist: 'Biau sire chevaliers,
Ne soiés si crüeus ne fiers.
Estés! ge vuel a vos parler
Por de vostre estre demander. 9836
Molt vos voi jovne, ce m'est vis,
Si n'ai pas vostre non enquis;
Molt par le vauroie savoir.'
Et cil li respondi le voir: 9840 (9772)
'Sire, nel sai, se Dex m'aït,
Fors si come la gent me dit,
Que mes drois nons est Percevaus.'
'Vos serois li miudres vasaus, 9844
Fait cil, et li plus renomés
Qui onques fust de mere nes.
Biaus sire, je vos rent m'espee:
Nostre bataille avés finee, 9848 (9780)
Tot a force m'avés conquis.
Ne cuidoie pas que fust vis
Chevaliers qui me conquesist.'
Lors se vaist vers lui et li dist: 9852
'Biaus sire ciers, a vos me rent
Tot a vostre comandement.'
Quant Percevaus voit k'il li prie
Merci, et que il s'umelie, 9856 (9788)
Quite li claime bonement
La bataille, par tel covent
169b C'au roi Artu tantos ira
Com il respassés essera, 9860
Et se metra sans autre esgart
Cn sa prison de soie part.
Cil l'a volentiers creanté;
Ainsi sont andui acordé. 9864 (9796)
Atant vinrent es pres pognant
Chevalier, vaslet et serjant,
Qui maintenant les desarmerent,
Laiens el castel les menerent. 9868
En une cambre grant et lee,
De dras de soie encortinee,
Molt soavet les despoillierent
Et en aprés si les coucierent 9872 (9804)
En deus rices lis les a les.
Ainc ne fu hom si honorés
Come fu la nuit Percevaus.

Molt par fu rices li ostaus 9876
Que li chevaliers fist tenir.
Seur tote rien faisoit servir
Et honorer et festoier
Perceval, le bon cevalier. 9880 (9812)
Ne vos porroie pas conter
La grant honeur ne deviser
Que il li fist a ce sejor.
Ensi furent jusc'a un jor 9884
Qu'il erent tuit sain et legier.
Icel jor oïrent noncier
C'au haut pui del Mont Dolereus
Avoit .i. piler mervelleus. 9888 (9820)
169c Par tel devise fais estoit
Que trestot environ avoit
Cros de fin or, bien seelés.
Mais il n'ert hom de mere nes 9892
Qui i poïst pas aresnier,
Por rien qu'il feïst, son destrier,
Se li miudres n'estoit del mont
D'armes seur trestos ciaus qui sont 9896 (9828)
Au jor qu'il aloit essaier.
Tot maintenant, sans delaier,
Que Percevaus conter l'oï,
A dit: 'Vrais Dex, que fa ge ci? 9900
Jamais, certes, repos n'avrai
Tant que la verité savrai,
Se je sui prosdom u mauvais:
Et nuit et jor irai adés, 9904 (9836)
Tant c'au piler puise venir;
Car lors savrai bien sans mentir
Se je serai bons chevaliers.'
Armes et cevaus et deniers 9908
Li fist li chevaliers venir;
Et cil tantost, a son plaisir,
Que il les voit, les mellors prant,
Si s'en arma molt vistement. 9912 (9844)
Puis est seur .i. destrier montés
Qui devant lui fu amenés;
Grans ert et fors et molt isniaus,
Hardis et aisiés et biaus. 9916
Et cil del cor sans targier plus
Dist qu'il iroit au roi Artus
169d Et qu'il se rendroit en sa cort
Ançois que il plus se sejort. 9920 (9852)
A ces paroles desevrerent
Li dui chevalier, puis errerent
Et tint cascuns son droit cemin.
Tant erra ce promier matin 9924
Li bons Percevaus et ala,

Les landes del Cor trespassa,
Tant qu'il vint en une riviere
Qui molt ert grans et roide et fiere.   9928 (9860)
Molt estoient haut li rivage,
Nus n'i poïst paser sans nage.
Jusc'a l'iaue vint cevaucant,
Si s'arestut .i. poi devant.   9932
Par uns entresains qu'il i vit
Conut certainement et dist
Qu'il trova le Roi Pesceor
En cele eve sans nul trestor.   9936 (9868)
Lors li menbra del bel ostal
Et de la lance et del Graal,
Dont rien n'enquist ne demanda;
Grant ire et grant angoisse en a.   9940
Volentiers pasast la riviere,
S'il poïst en nule maniere,
Car molt vit bele la contree
De l'autre part et bien puplee.   9944 (9876)
Lors prie a Diu que il li doist
Trover passage u gé u pont
Par u il puist otre passer.
Atant recomence a errer,   9948
170a Tot le jor cevauca issi
Tant que ce vint aprés midi.
Lors vit sor l'eve en .i. pendant
Un castelet trop bien seant.   9952 (9884)
Ne sai por quoi le vos devis,
C'ainc n'en vi nul si bel asis.
Molt par i avoit noble tor
Et rices bailles tot entor,   9956
Si fort que de rien n'ot regart;
Sor l'iaue sist de l'autre part.
Quant il otre passer ne puet,
Bien set que faire li estuet   9960 (9892)
Avant l'ostel s'avoir le <u>ve(u)t</u>
Adonc a ceminer aqeut
Et si a puis chevaucié tant
Qu'il est venus a un pendant;   9964
Iluec trova unes trencies
Entre deus grans haies plaisies.
La voie n'estoit gaires lee
Et si estoit molt poi antee.   9968
Outre se met vers .i. maisnis,
Et trova uns viés messeris,
Un fondeïs d'un castelers.
Rices ymages, ciers pilers,   9972
De mabre fin trestos entiers,
I avoit plus de .iii. milliers;   (9900)
Si ert encore li portaus

Entiers, qui molt ert fors et haus;	9976
N'i avoit plus sale ne tor.	
Percevaus ala tot entor	
170b Et dist: 'Ci fait mal sejorner	
Quant l'en n'i puet arme trover.'	9980 (9908)
Et que vos iroie acontant?	
Tant vait et ariere et avant	
C'au portal vint, dedens entra.	
D'une pucele qu'il trova	9984
Seant desos .i. olivier,	
Ou il li vit son cief pignier,	
Ne vos vuel conter ses biautés,	
Car trop i demoroie assés,	9988 (9916)
Ne les mer<u>ves</u> qu'il veïst,[1]	
Mais la pucele qui la sist	
Li toli lués tot a veoir,	
Car encontre sailli por voir	9992
Et li dist: 'Or ça, biaus amis,	
Passage avrés, molt l'avés quis.'	
Hors des maiserius le mena,	
Et Percevaus tant l'esgarda	9996 (9924)
Et desirra tant a passer	
C'ainc rien ne li pot demander.	
Devant le portal ont trovee	
Une mule bien afeutree.	10000
Seure monta la damoisele,	
Qui tant ert avenans et bele;	
Jusc'a la rive le mena,	
Un petit calan desferma.	10004 (9932)
La mule, qu'i fu costumiere,	
Sailli dedens par tel maniere	
Que tos li calans est branlés.	
Puis li a dit: 'Biaus sire, entrés.'	10008
170c Mais Percevaux pas n'i entra,	
Car ses cevaus lués s'aarbra	
Et sali ariere d'aïr	
Ne vos vuel pas tot faire oïr,	10012 (9940)
Coment ele le dut noier,	
Se ne fusent li pontenier:	
De l'autre part de la riviere	
Avoit une molt grant cariere;	10016
Gens avoit dedenz qui crioient	
A haute vois, et si disoient	
Par verité au chevalier:	
'<u>Fuiés, qu'</u>ele vos viut noier.	10020 (9948)
Mors estes se vos i entrés.'	
Ne vos seroit hui racontés	
Li mestiers dont cele servoit,	
Ne la malise qu'ele avoit.	10024
En la nef ne puet nus entrer	

Qu'en l'iaue ne face verser;
Et les ravisoit, ce dist l'en,
A la cort le roi Brandisen.   10028
Onques nus hom vivans n'oï;
Puis icele eure qu'il nasqui,   (9956)
Nule rien tant autre angoisier
Com cele fait le chevalier   10032
D'entrer ens, et quant ele nel pot
Engignier, molt grant ire en ot,
Si s'est tantos esvanuïe.
Et cil ne s'oblioient mie,   10036
Qui venoient o la carriere,
De crïer qu'il alast ariere;
170d Tant qu'a la rive sont venu,
Si l'ont en leur nef receü;   10040
Ensamble o eus otre passa.
Grans mervelles li reconta,   (9964)
Signeur, li maistres ponteniers,
Puis li mostre .i. cemin pleniers   10044
Qui le menront sans nul trestor
A la cort le Roi Pesceor.
S'il les set droitement tenir
En mains d'un jor i puet venir.   10048
Atant les lait, et si s'en torne,
De la nef ist, plus n'i sejorne;
Molt comence tost a errer
Et entra lués en un penser   10052
De la cort que il quere vait.
Par ce pensé le cemin lait
Que li ponteniers li mostra:
Amont la riviere torna,   10056
Et quant il ot grant piece alé,
Si a le bel castel trové
Que orains el conte vos dis,
Qui deseur l'iaue estoit asis.   10060 (9972)
Tant erra qu'il vient a l'entree,
Si voit la porte desfermee;
Lors dist que dedens enterra
Por la grant biauté que il a.   10064
A la promiere porte vint,
Parmi le boile entra et tint
Sa voie tot droit a la tor
Qui molt estoit de grant valor.   10068 (9980)
171a Ne par ert se mervelle non
Des herbergemens d'environ,
Ne del onbrage que tenoient
Dui pin qui en la place estoient;   10072
A ce voër molt entendi
Lors fu conté qu'il descendi[2]
De son son ceval, puis l'aresna.

Au pié de la tor apuia   10076 (9988)
Son escu, et est sus montés
En la sale par uns degrés.
Laiens vit lances en lanciers,
Coples a ciens et colers ciers,   10080
Et clers espius, trencans, burnis,
En roides hantes, bien forbis.
La sale fu de grant biauté
N'onques en nule roiauté   10084 (9896)
N'esgarda hom si tres cier lit
Com il trova enmi et vit,
Covert d'un fres paile grigois
Ainc si rice n'ot quens ne rois.   10088
Lors cuida il molt bien trover
Gent o cui il poïst parler,
Mais n'i vit nule rien vivant.
Au lit s'adrece maintenant,   10092
Desus s'asist et si pensa;
Son cief et ses mains desarma.   (10004)
Puis a la sale regardee
Qui a fin or ert tote ovree,   10096
Tot environ et par desus,
Et li lanbruns d'or musi tos,
171b Onques ne rois ne enperere
N'ot si tres bele ne si clere.   10100
Lors dist: 'Molt par fait ci bel estre.'
Atant voit .i. huis devers destre.
Quant il le vit, si se leva
Et vint la droit, si s'apuia,   10104
Si voit unes loges trop beles;
D'erbe fresque et de fleurs noveles
Erent joncies lués tot droit;
Si bone odor laiens avoit   10108
Qu'il n'est espice de valeur
Dont cil n'i sente la flaireur.
Signeur, ja celer nel vos quier,
En mileu ot un escequier   10112
A poins d'azur et de fin or;
Par molt grant savoir furent Mor
Les rices escés d'or polis
D'esmeraudes et de rubis.   10116 (10020)
Ne vos puis dire leur biauté;
Molt par rendoient grant clarté,
Car vos savés bien que ce sont
Les plus cieres pieres del mont.   10120
Li geu furent trestuit assis.
Seur .i. feutre de paile bis
Vait Percevaus laiens seoir
Por les escés qu'il viut veoir,   10124
Et comença a manoier

Les geus qu'il vit seur l'escequier.   (10028)
A soi meïsme pense et dit
C'ainc mais si rices geus ne vit,   10128
171c Ne jamais jor <u>ces</u> ne verra
<u>Puis</u> que d'iluec departira.
Lors prent .i. des paons atant
Et dit que il le trait avant.   10132
Autresi tos, sans plus d'esgart,
Traistent li giu de l'autre part;   (10036)
Et Percevaus quant veü l'a,
A dit: "Ostés! ce que sera?"   10136
Puis traist encontre vistement.
Tot autresi isnelement
Retraist li geus. Et cil que fist?
Par foi, j'ai reconté qu'il prist   10140
Et il lui, ce dist <u>por</u> verté.
Lors fu a desbarat torné.   (10044)
Et que vos iroie alognant,
Ne trestos lor trais acontant?   10144
C'au daesrain en fu matés
Li bons Percevaus, c'est vertés;
Estrangement en fu maris.
Mais assés plus fu esbahis   10148
De ço qu'il vit tantos par eus
Les geus raseoir en lor leus.   (10052)
Lors joa tant que mas refu
Trois fois. Tel duel en a eü   10152
Que par ire les escés prist,
El pan de son hauberc les mist
Et dist: 'Jamais ne materois
Nul chevalier, car n'est pas drois.'   10156
Puis vint molt tost droit as fenestres,
La grant iaue vit sor les estres,   (10060)
171d El plus parfont les veut geter.
N'i avoit mais que del rüer,   10160
Quant une damoisele vint
As fenestres, qui le retint.
Un samit vermel ot vestu,
Brodé de fin or et tisu,   10164
Et ele fu a desmesure
Bele sor tote creature.
De l'iaue s'en issi tant hors
Que par desus paru li cors   10168
Tos, des la çainture en amont.
Lors dist: 'Sire, li escec sont
En ma garde; nes getés mie.
Car vos feriiés vilonie,   10172 (10076)
Qu'el monde ne puet on trover
Si biaus, si les doit on garder.'
'Pucele, fait il, ge sui ci

Tos seus, et por verté vos di 10176
Que vos pöés molt bien tenser
Les rices escés de geteter.
Del tot ferai vostre plaisir,
S'o moi volés caiens venir; 10180
Molt par ferois grant cortoisie
Car tos sui seus sans compagnie.' (10084)
'Sire, fait el, je vos requier
C'ains remetois sor l'escequier 10184
Les escés, puis irai a vos,
Car n'est pas drois que soiés sos.'
A itan tos rasis les a
Seur l'escequier, si retorna 10188
172a Com il ains pot a la pucele,
Si li a dit: 'Amie bele,
S'il vos plaist, or venés amont,
Car li escec asis resont.' 10192
Et cele en vient lués droit a lui;
Par grant amor l'asist les lui:
Entre ses bras laiens as estres
La mist par une des fenestres. 10196
Dejoste l'escequier s'asisent,
Mainte parole s'entredisent
Et mainte bele envoiseüre,
Et conterent mainte aventure. 10200
Percevaus la voit si tres bele
C'ainc mais dame ne damoisele
Ne vit a nul jor qu'il fust vis
De sa biauté, ce li est vis; 10204 (10100)
Car ele fu et gente et grans,
Simple vis ot, ex vairs rïans,
Biau cors, biaus bras, et beles mains;
Et biaus dois graisles, lons et plains 10208
Avoit, et biau contenement,
S'ert trop de bon afaitement.
Por son estre, por sa biauté,
Vint une si grant volenté 10212
Au chevalier tantos d'amer
Qu'il comença a sospirer,
Et dist: 'Dex! com est tos müés
Mes corages et trestornés.' 10216 (10108)
'Sire, fait ele, c'avés vos?'
'Quoi? fait il, trop sui angoisos,
172b Damoisele, de vostre amor,
Si ne vos vi ainc mais nul jor; 10220
Qui n'a nule rien en cest mont,
De totes les coses qui sont,
Ne sai por coi vos en mentise,
Que tant amase ne vausise 10224
Avoir plus que vostre cors,

Qu'el mont n'est nus plus biaus tresors.
Trop avroie grant manantie,
Se je vos avoie a amie.'   10228
Et cele li respont: 'Biau sire,
Je ne sai que vos volés dire;
C'ainc mais ne fui d'amer requise
Ne tant ne quant en nule guise.'   10232
Quant cil l'oï, sa l'acola,
Vers li se traist, si la baisa
Et dist: 'Doce dame, merci!
Car faites de moi vostre ami.'   10236
'Sire, dist cele, or est assés.
Quant tele est vostre volentés
Que a force m'avés baisie,
G'en sui et dolente et irie,   10240
Mais or le soferrai issi.
Bien vos creant por voir et di,
Se jamais l'aviiés pensé,
Molt esseroit cier comperé.'   10244
'Pucele, fait il, trop seroie
Mors et honis, se gerpisoie
La plus bele rien c'ains fust nee,
Que Dex m'a ci seule amenee.'   10248
172c Lors la traist vers soi et feïst
Plus s'ele nel contredesist.
Et li a dit: 'Biau sire, estés!
Se vostre vie point amés.   10252
Mors seriiés ja et occis,
Se vos plus m'aviiés requis
Que seulement ma volenté.
Je vos otroi que de bon gre   10256
Vos amerai; mais vos ferois
Mon comandement, qu'il est drois.'
'Pucele, fait it, molt seroie
Orgellos, se je nel faisoie.'   10260
'Sire, or m'atendés .i. poi ci;
Ja revenrai, je le vos di.'
En une cambre s'en entra,
Un blanc bracet li amena,   10264
Et dist: 'Joste ceste ceste riviere,
Qui parfonde est et rade et fiere,
Fist .i. parc mesire mes pere.
Amis, foi que je doi Saint Pere,   10268
.I. cerf i a, blanc come nois;
Ainc nel pot prendre quens ne rois.
Ne ja a nul jor nel prendra
Nus hom que cil qui m'amera.   10272
Ves le bracet au cerf cacier.
Or si pensés de l'esploitier,
Car bien vos vuel dire et mostrer,

Se vos m'en pöés aporter	10276
La teste, si devés savoir	
Que je vos amerai por voir.	
172d Vos armes porterois o vos,	
Car li pars est aventuros.	10280
Molt seriiés avilonis	
Se vos estiiés desgarnis,	
Sans armes seur vostre destrier,	
Quar tost sordent grant destorbier.'	10284
'Dame, fait il, ge m'armerai	
Mon cief et mon cors. Puis ferai	
Del tot a vostre volenté.'	
Lors a son cief tantos armé,	10288
Et descent jus par les degrés;	
Puis est sor son ceval montés,	
Son escu et sa lance prist,	
Et la damoisele li dist:	10292
'A cele bretesque est l'entree	
Del parc. La porte est desfurmee.	
Ves le braqet, gardés le bien,	
Quar il ne cangeroit por rien	10296
Le blanc cerf.' Aprés li mostra	
Le bracet, et cil l'apela.	
El parc entra, le cerf trova,[3]	10298a
Et il lait le brachet aler;	
Au cerf comença a hüer.	10300 (10164)
Et li brachés a tant tracié	
Et tant suï et tant chacié	
K'a un haut rochier l'a ataint.	
Perchevaus d'aler ne se faint,	10304
Qui est a joie et a grant feste;	
Del cerf a prise tost la teste.	
Et si est tos entalentés.	
173a Qu'il or avra ses volentés	10308 (10172)
De la pucele qu'il tant ainme	
Ki ja tot sien lige se claime.	
Que qu'il entent au cerf desfaire,	
Une pucele de malaire	10312
Vint chevalcant parmi le lande.	
Vit le brachet, plus ne demande,	
Par le coler d'orfrois l'a pris,	
Devant li sor son arçon mis;	10316 (10180)
Atant s'en torne vistement.	
Et Percevaus isnelement	
Se regarde, son braket voit	
Que cele devant li tenoit,	10320
Si s'en aloit grant aleüre.	
De nule rien ne s'aseüre,	
La test prent, puis est montés	
Et vait aprés molt abrievés.	10324 (10188)

'Bele, fait il, atendés moi.'
Cele dist: 'Non ferai, par foi.
Et se ge bien vos atendoie,
Dites que g'i gaaigneroie.   10328
Veés moi ci, que demandés?'
'Bele, mon braket me rendés;
Et sachiés molt avés mespris
Qui sans mon congié l'avés pris.   10332 (10196)
Rendés le moi, si ferés bien.'
Cele dist: 'Je n'en ferai rien.
Mon cerf avés pris sans congié,
Si en ai mout mon cuer irié.   10336
173b Cele qui ça vos envoia,
Onques, certes, ne vos ama;
En autre guise avrés s'amor.
C'est li brakés qui jamais jor   10340 (10204)
Ne tenrés nis une seule eure.'
'Si ferai, se Dex me secheure,
Fait Percevaus, jel vuel avoir.
Metés le jus par estavoir,   10344
Car quant je plus vos prïeroie,
Bien sai que mains esploiteroie.'
Cele respont: 'Si m'aït fois,
Force faire n'est mie drois.   10348 (10212)
Et force me pöés vos faire,
Mais molt en avrés grant contraire,
Si serés a tos jors honis
Et vis recreans et fallis.   10352
Mais s'alés la a cel arcel,
La troverés vos un tonbel
U il a paint un chevalier.
Tant li dites sans atargier: 10356 (10220)
'Vassal, que faites vos ici?'
Le brachet avrés, je vos di.'
Et Percevaus li respondit:
'Nel perdrai pas por si petit.'   10360
Lors prent le braket, si s'en torne;
Desi k'a l'arcel ne sejorne,
Car la voie molt bien savoit.
La tombe et une crois i voit,   10364 (10228)
Et si avoit .iiii. pertrus,
Tot aussi come a un enclus.
173c Et Percevaus a dit en haut:
'Dans chevaliers, se Dex me saut,   10368
De nïent faire s'entremist
Qui ci en cest tombel vos mist.
Levés sus, trop avés geü.'
Dont se regarde, s'a veü   10372 (10236)
Deriere soi un chevalier
Trestot armé sor son destrier;

Mais molt fu noire s'armeüre,
Plus que nule meure meüre.   10376
Et que vos porroie conter?
Cil li a dit sans arester:
'Sire vassal, que volés vos?
Trop estes fiers et orgellous.   10380 (10244)
Par molt grant orgoil m'apelastes,
Mais sachiés que mar le pensastes.'
Fors s'eslonge, sel vait ferir.
Qant Percevaus le vit venir,   10384
Son braket et la teste a prise,
Sor un molt bel prael l'a mise.
Vers celui point isnelement,
Si s'entrefierent vivement   10388 (10252)
Et des lances tels cols se donent
Que eles ploient et arçonent,
Et enmi le pre s'abatirent
Et li cheval sor els kaïrent.   10392
Cil metent les mains as espees
Si s'entredonent grans colees;
Menu et sovent s'entrefierent,
Des espees bien se requierent;   10396 (10260)

174a Onques mais si dure mellee
Ne fu veüe n'esgardee.
Et que que cil se combatoient
Et a eus ocire entendoient,   10400
Uns chevaliers trestos armés
Revint vers aus tos abrievés;
Le teste et le braket en porte.
Et Percevaus se desconforte   10404 (10268)

Molt durement, cui pas n'agree.   (E20531)
En sa main destre tint l'espee

Notes

1.   In some ways the reading of L is superior here, suggesting that Perceval
     would have seen great wonders, but that the maiden's beauty monopolized
     his attention.
2.   The manuscript is hard to decipher here; the reading looks more like *faconte*
     than anything else, but I would read *fuconte* rather than Roach's *raconte*.
3.   The last nine and a half lines of this column were erased, and the text given
     here was written over the erasure. As a result, a tercet was left at 10297, and
     the distribution of rhymes was upset, which the scribe corrected in the next
     column, by writing the last line of 173a on two lines. The importance of this
     point, which Roach does not mention, is that the somewhat independent
     version given by L throughout C2, up to this point, clearly continued beyond
     A 10162, and at least up to A 10170, or the equivalent. Of course, we cannot
     say how much further, if at all, it extended after that. From what we can see
     of the original reading, which is not much more than some of the initial
     letters, the text erased bore no resemblance to the text replacing it.

APPENDIX III

SELECT BIBLIOGRAPHY

TEXTS

1. *Perceval* and Continuations

Perceval le Gallois, edited by Ch. Potvin, 6 vols (Mons, 1865–71, reprint, Slatkine, Geneva, 1979).

Der Percevalroman von Christian von Troyes, edited by A. Hilka (Halle, 1932).

Le Roman de Perceval ou le Conte du Graal, edited by W. Roach, second edition (Geneva, Paris, 1959).

Le Conte du Graal, edited by F. Lecoy, CFMA, 2 vols (Paris, 1973–75).

The Continuations of the Old French Perceval of Chrétien de Troyes, edited by W. Roach, 5 vols (Philadelphia, 1949–83).

La Continuation de Perceval de Gerbert de Montreuil, edited by M. Williams and M. Oswald, CFMA, 3 vols (Paris, 1922, 1925, 1975).

Perceval le Gallois. The prose version printed for Galiot du Pré, Paris, 1530.

2. Others

Beroul, *The Romance of Tristan*, edited by A. Ewert, 2 vols (Oxford, 1939, 1970).

Bliocadran: A prologue to the Perceval of Chrétien de Troyes, edited by L. Wolfgang (Tübingen, 1976).

Li Chevaliers as deus espees, edited by W. Foerster, (Halle, 1877, reprint, Rodopi, Amsterdam, 1966).

Chevalier see *Two Old French Gauvain Romances*.

Chrétien de Troyes, *Erec und Enide*, edited by W. Foerster (Halle, 1890, second ed., 1909).

—— *Erec et Enide*, edited by M. Roques, CFMA (Paris, 1979).

—— *Cligés*, edited by W. Foerster (Halle, 1884).

—— *Cligés*, edited by A. Micha, CFMA (Paris, 1978).

—— *Der Löwenritter: Yvain*, edited by W. Foerster (Halle, 1887).

—— *Le chevalier au Lion: Yvain*, edited by M. Roques, CFMA (Paris, 1975).

—— *Der Karrenritter: Lancelot*, edited by W. Foerster (Halle, 1899).

—— *Le chevalier de la Charrette: Lancelot*, edited by M. Roques, CFMA (Paris, 1965).

—— *Guillaume d'Angleterre*, edited by M. Wilmotte, CFMA (Paris, 1971).

La Cote Mal Taillie, edited by G. Paris, *Romania*, 26 (1897), 276 ff.

The Didot-Perceval, edited by W. Roach (Philadelphia, 1941).

Durmart le Galois, edited by J. Gildea, 2 vols (Pennsylvania, 1965–66).

The Elucidation: a Prologue to the Conte del Graal, edited by A. W. Thompson (New York, 1931).

Eneas, edited by J-J. Salverda de Grave, CFMA, 2 vols (Paris, 1925, 1931).

Les Enfances Gauvain (fragments), edited by P. Meyer, *Romania* 39 (1910), 1 ff.

Fergus, edited by W. Frescoln (Philadelphia, 1983).

Gautier d'Arras, *Eracle*, edited by G. Raynaud de Lage, CFMA (Paris, 1976).

—— *Ille et Galeron*, edited by F. A. G. Cowper, SATF (Paris, 1956).

—— *Ille et Galeron*, edited by E. Löseth (Paris, 1890).

Golagros and Gawayne, in *Syr Gawayne*, edited by Sir F. Madden (London, 1839).

Hue de Rotelande, *Ipomedon*, edited by A. J. Holden (Paris, 1979).

—— *Protheselaus*, edited by F. Kluckow (Göttingen, 1924).

Hunbaut, edited by H. Breuer (Dresden, 1914).

Inconnu see Renaut de Beaujeu.

Joseph see Robert de Boron.

Lancelot (en prose), edited by A. Micha, TLF, 9 vols (Paris, Geneva, 1978–83).

The Mabinogion, translated by G. Jones and T. Jones (London, New York, 1974).

Marie de France, *Les Lais*, edited by J. Rychner, CFMA (Paris, 1973).

Meriadeuc see *Li Chevaliers as deus espees*.

La Mort le Roi Artu, edited by J. Frappier, TLF (Paris, Geneva, 1964).

Mule see *Two Old French Gauvain Romances*.

Partonopeu de Blois, edited by J. Gildea, 2 vols (Pennsylvania, 1967–70).

Percyvelle see *Syr Percyvelle*.

Perlesvaus: Le Haut Livre du Graal, edited by W. A. Nitze and T. A. Jenkins, 2 vols (Chicago, 1932, 1937).

La Queste del Saint Graal, edited by A. Pauphilet, CFMA (Paris, 1967).

Raoul de Houdenc, *Meraugis von Portlesguez*, edited by M. Friedwagner (Halle, 1897, reprint, Slatkine, Geneva, 1975).

—— *La Vengeance de Raguidel*, edited by M. Friedwagner (Halle, 1909, reprint, Slatkine, Geneva, 1975).

Renaut de Beaujeu, *Le Bel Inconnu*, edited by G. Perrie Williams, CFMA (Paris, 1978).

Robert de Boron, *Le Roman de l'Estoire dou Graal*, edited by W. A. Nitze, CFMA (Paris, 1971).

Syr Percyvelle in *The Thornton Romances*, edited by J. O. Halliwell (London, 1844).

Le Roman de Thèbes, edited by G. Raynaud de Lage, CFMA, 2 vols (Paris, 1966, 1968).

Thomas, *Les Fragments du roman de Tristan*, edited by B. H. Wind, TLF (Paris, Geneva, 1960).

Thompson, A. W., 'The text of the Bliocadran', *Romance Philology*, 9 (1955–56), 205–09.

Le Roman de Troie, edited by L. Constans, SATF, 6 vols (Paris, 1904).

Two Old French Gauvain Romances: Le Chevalier à l'épée, La Mule sans frein, edited by R. C. Johnston and D. D. R. Owen (Edinburgh, London, 1972).

Wace, *Le Brut de Wace*, edited by I. Arnold, SATF, 2 vols (Paris, 1938, 1940).

—— *Le Roman de Rou*, edited by A. J. Holden, SATF, 3 vols (Paris, 1970–73).

Der altfranzösische Yderroman, edited by H. Gelzer (Dresden, 1913).

also

Brayer E. and Lecoy F., 'Fragment d'un nouveau manuscrit de la première continuation du Perceval de Chrétien de Troyes', *Romania*, 83 (1962), 400–07.

ARTICLES, CRITICAL WORKS, ETC.

Brown, A. C. L., 'The Grail and the English Perceval', *Modern Philology*, 16 (1919), 553 ff.; 17 (1919/20), 361 ff.; 18 (1920/21), 201 ff., 661 ff.; 22 (1924/25), 79 ff., 113 ff.

Bruce, J. D., *The Evolution of Arthurian Romance*, second edition, 2 vols (Göttingen, 1928).

Brugger, E., 'Bliocadrans, the father of Perceval', in *Mediaeval Studies . . . G. S. Loomis* (Paris, New York, 1927), 147–74.

—— *The Illuminated Tree in two Arthurian romances* (New York, 1929).

—— 'Der sog. *Didot-Perceval*', *Zeitschrift fur französische Sprache und Literatur*, 53 (1930), 389–459.

—— review of J. L. Weston's 'The legend of Sir Perceval', *ZfSL*, 31 (1907), 122–62.

Busby, K., '*Syr Perceval of Galles, Le Conte du Graal*, and *La Continuation-Gauvain*: the methods of an English adaptor', *Etudes Anglaises*, 31 (1978), 198–202.

Delbouille, M., 'A propos des rimes familières à Chrétien de Troyes et à Gautier d'Arras', in *Mélanges . . . Lecoy* (Paris, 1973), 55–65.

François, Ch., *Etude sur le style de la continuation du Perceval par Gerbert et du Roman de la Violette par Gerbert de Montreuil*, fasc. L. Bul. (Liège, Paris, 1932).

Frappier, J., *Autour du Graal* (Geneva, 1977).

Gallais, P., 'Formules de conteur et interventions d'auteur dans les manuscrits de la Continuation-Gauvain', *Romania*, 85 (1964), 181–229.

—— 'Gauvain et la Pucelle de Lis', in *Mélanges . . . Delbouille* ii, 1964, 207–29.

Heinzel, R., *Ueber die französischen Gralromane* (Vienna, 1891).

Hoffmann, W., *Die Quellen des Didot-Perceval* (Halle, 1905).

Ivy, R. H., *The manuscript relations of Manessier's continuation of the Old French Perceval* (Philadelphia, 1951).

Lomis, R. S., *Arthurian Tradition and Chrétien de Troyes* (New York, 1949).

—— ed., *Arthurian Literature in the Middle Ages* (Oxford, 1959).

Lot, F., *Etude sur le Lancelot en prose*, second edition (Paris, 1954).

—— 'Encore Bleheri-Breri', *Romania*, 51 (1925), 397–408.

—— 'Les auteurs du Conte du Graal', *Romania*, 57 (1931), 117–36.

Marx, J., *La légende arthurienne et le Graal* (Paris, 1952).

—— 'Etude sur les rapports entre la continuation de Manessier et le cycle de Lancelot en prose . . .', *Romania*, 84 (1963), 451–77.

—— *Nouvelles recherches sur la littérature arthurienne* (Paris, 1965).

Meyer, P., 'Wauchier de Denain', *Romania*, 32 (1903), 583–86.

—— 'Versions en prose des *Vies des Pères*', in *Hist. Litt. de la France*, 33 (1906), 258–92.

Micha, A., *La tradition manuscrite de Chrétien de Troyes* (Geneva, 1966).

Newell, W. W., 'Legend of the Holy Grail III: The continuations of Chrestien', *Journal of American Folklore*, 10 (1897), 299–312.

Nitze, W. A., *On the chronology of the Grail Romances*, Manly Anniversary Studies (Chicago, 1923), 300–14.

Paris, G., *Perceval*, in *Hist. Litt. de la France*, 30 (1888), 27–29.

Payen, J.-Ch., in *Grundriss der romanischen Literaturen des Mittelalters*, vol. 4/i *Le Roman jusqu'à la fin du xiiie siècle* (Heidelberg, 1978), 354–61.

Roach, W., 'The conclusion of the Perceval Continuation in Bern MS 113', in *Studies in honour of Albert C. Baugh* (Philadephia, 1961), 245–54.

—— 'Transformations of the Grail theme in the first two continuations of the Old French *Perceval*', *Proc. Am. Phil. Soc.*, 110 (1966), 160–64.

Les Romans du Graal aux XIIe et XIIIe siècles (Paris, 1956).

Roques, M., 'Le manuscrit fr. 794 de la Bibliothèque Nationale et le scribe Guiot', *Romania*, 73 (1952), 177–99.

Vial, G., 'L'auteur de la deuxième continuation du *Conte du Graal*', *Trav. Ling. Litt.*, 16, Strasbourg, 1978, 519–30.

Weinberg, B., 'The magic chessboard in the *Perlesvaus*: an example of mediaeval literary borrowing', *Pub. Mod. Lang. Assoc. America*, 50 (1935), 25–35.

West, G. D., *An Index of proper names in French Arthurian Verse Romances 1150–1300* (Toronto, 1969).

—— *An Index of proper names in French Arthurian Prose Romances* (Toronto, 1978).

—— 'Grail Problems I: Silimac the Stranger', *Romance Philology*, 24 (1970/71), 599–611.

—— 'Grail Problems II: The Grail Family in the Old French verse romances', *Romance Philology*, 25 (1971/72), 53–73.

Weston, J. L., *The Legend of Sir Perceval*, 2 vols (London, 1906, 1909).

—— 'Wauchier de Denain . . . and the Prologue of the Mons MS', *Romania*, 33 (1904), 333–43.

—— 'Wauchier de Denain and Bleheris', *Romania*, 34 (1905), 100–05.

Wilmotte, M., *Le Poème du Gral et ses auteurs* (Paris, 1930).

—— 'Gerbert de Montreuil et les écrits qui lui sont attribués', *Bull. Acad. Roy. de la Belgique*, 3 (1900), 166–89.

Wrede, H., *Die Fortsetzer des Gralromans Chrestiens von Troyes* (Göttingen, 1952).